W. E. B. DU BOIS
and American Political Thought

W. E. B. DU BOIS
and American Political Thought

FABIANISM AND THE COLOR LINE

Adolph L. Reed Jr.

New York   Oxford   Oxford University Press   1997

Oxford University Press

Oxford   New York

Athens   Auckland   Bangkok   Bogota   Bombay   Buenos Aires
Calcutta   Cape Town   Dar es Salaam   Delhi
Florence   Hong Kong   Istanbul   Karachi
Kuala Lumpur   Madras   Madrid   Melbourne
Mexico City   Nairobi   Paris   Singapore
Taipei   Tokyo   Toronto   Warsaw

and associated companies in
Berlin   Ibadan

Copyright © 1997 by Oxford University Press, Inc.

Published by Oxford University Press, Inc.,
198 Madison Avenue, New York, New York 10016

Library of Congress Cataloging-in-Publication Data

Reed, Adolph L., 1947–
W. E. B. Du Bois and American political thought : fabianism and the
color line / Adolph L. Reed, Jr.
p.   cm.
Includes bibliographical references and index.
ISBN 0-19-505174-2
1. Du Bois, W. E. B. (William Edward Burghardt), 1868–1963—
Philosophy.   2. Afro-Americans—Intellectual life.   3. United
States—Intellectual life—1865–1918.   4. United States—
Intellectual life—20th century.   I. Title.
E185.97.D73R44   1997
305.896'073'092—DC20   96-847

1 3 5 7 9 8 6 4 2

Printed in the United States of America
on acid-free paper

To the memory of Earl E. Thorpe (1924–1989)

—neighbor, benefactor, friend, colleague, and, most of all, trailblazer in the critical study of Afro-American intellectual history and historiography.

Acknowledgments

This book is first of all, obviously, an explication of Du Bois's political thought as it evolved over the course of his life. As such, however, it grows from three broader, overlapping concerns. First, the study emerges from an effort to locate the ideological premises and presumptions that have undergirded black politics and political thought in the twentieth century. Most specifically, the impetus derived from my attempt to make sense of the decline of radicalism's constituency and persuasive capacities in black politics during the 1970s and 1980s by examining ways that the theoretical and ideological underpinnings of black protest thought have converged on the imperatives of conventionalist American liberal politics. A second, related objective is exploring how the dominant patterns of black American political debate historically have connected with the premises, frames, and issues contemporaneously shaping American political discourse more generally. Finally, this book is bound up with my concern to develop a clear and practically grounded, nonidealist perspective on the history of political thought. I have sought an approach that does not reduce to an ahistorical, teleological account of Great Men, Great Books, and Great Ideas extracted from the purposive contexts within which their meanings were shaped—the pragmatic politics and political debates of their specific times. For many reasons Du Bois seemed an ideal template for pursuing these objectives simultaneously.

The motives impelling this study, to that extent, are political as well as intellectual. It should not be surprising, therefore, that on occasion the press of current events took me away from the book altogether for lengthy stretches—for instance, to write a short article on the 1984 Jesse Jackson campaign that turned into another book—even in the midst of what I imagined to be final revisions. I've revised, reshaped, and rethought the manuscript several times, often in small but consequential ways, in response to developments in my own understanding, as likely as not brought about through interaction with the evolving political situation. All this has been to the good, I believe. The text and arguments have become clearer for the effort, partly as I've worked out conceptual issues more firmly, partly because the continuing elaboration of dynamic historical processes exposes more of their embedded tendencies and possibilities.

Along the way, many people have read all or parts of the study that became this book and have provided useful comments, suggestions, sources, and perspectives. Among those who stand out are: Bruce Ackerman, Jean-Christophe Agnew, Claude W. Barnes, John Blassingame, John Bracey, William Boone, Timothy Breen, Michael K. Brown, James T. Campbell, John Brown Childs, Michael Dawson, Michael Ford, Victoria Hattam, Rickey Hill, David Hollinger, Gerald Horne, M. Njeri Jackson, Gerald Jaynes, Mack H. Jones, Jennifer Jordan, Ivan Karp, Martin Kilson, Corinne Kratz, Jim Lee, Willie Legette, Chris Lowe, Charles Mills, James Morone, William Munro, Earl Picard, David Plotke, Adolph Reed Sr., Clarita M. Reed, Dorothy Ross, James Scott, Stephen Skowronek, the late Earl E. Thorpe, Robert Wiebe, Brett Williams, Hoda M. Zaki, and Patricia Zavella.

James Oakes and Judith Stein have read the manuscript with great seriousness and care. The quality of their suggestions is matched by the quality of their friendship and support. They exemplify the clearest and most honest possibilities of engaged historical thinking, and they live as they work.

Gerard Fergerson's work on Du Bois and race and medicine at the turn of the century ran in some ways parallel to and has helped to sharpen my own. Stuart Clarke hectored me into confronting the literary-theoretical turn in the writing of Afro-American intellectual history. Mary L. Dudziak was among the first to be subjected to reading revisions of the manuscript, and her comments were as useful as her own work on the Cold War's impact on the civil rights movement. Kathryn Oberdeck and the mentally indefatigable Jacquelyn Dirks, fellow diggers in fin de siécle American intellectual history, have contributed much to this project in a conversation that we have shared for well over a decade. In addition to specific insights and other suggestions, I have gained substantially from the intellectual breadth and critical depth with which they approach American Studies and their emphasis on the field's openness to social scientific sensibilities, not to mention their friendship and comradeship.

Jonathan Scott Holloway, Michele Mitchell, and Dean Robinson have been important sounding boards and careful, critical readers. More than that, both individually and as a group they have been an inspiration, and not only for their enthusiasm for the project. Their scholarly work promises to make major contributions to establishing the study of the history of Afro-American thought on the theoretically and contextually textured, tough-mindedly engaged foundation for which critics have called for more than half a century. I feel especially fortunate to have been able to participate in an intellectual community with them and to count them as friends. The same is true of Nikol Alexander, Michelle Boyd, Claire Jean Kim, Steven A. Light, Desiree Pedescleaux, Francesca Polletta, and Drew Smith. They also have been careful, enthusiastic, and helpful readers, and their work, though not in the history of thought, similarly promises to broaden and deepen the conceptual and theoretical base of Afro-Americanist scholarship. Gordon Lafer and Eve Weinbaum, Americanists of yet another sort, also have inspired me both in their important scholarship and their theoretically sophisticated insistence on approaching political science as an instrument of political action.

Linda Seidman at the University of Massachusetts-Amherst provided invaluable assistance, with good cheer and impressive acumen, in the Du Bois Papers. Phil and Sharon McBlain, of McBlain's Books in Hamden, Connecticut, have been bibliographers and supportive friends as much as booksellers. David Roll was a wonderfully sympathetic and encouraging editor, even as one more immediately pressing commitment after another delayed the last chapter. I wish him the best in his new career and hope this book repays his confidence.

I am uniquely indebted to Timuel Black, Ishmael Flory, Vernon Jarrett, Tony Mazzocchi, Frank Rosen, and the late Lois Ann Rosen, as well as to my father—all of whom connected with Du Bois's life through the postwar political involvements they shared with him. Not only do their reflections and perspectives, indeed their lives, link Du Bois's time concretely to ours; they also underscore the practical significance of his political development, notwithstanding its theoretical inner tensions and incompleteness, and the deeper continuity of his courage and commitment to the ideal of a just society.

I have learned much more than I can indicate here from Micaela di Leonardo, whose contributions run throughout this book and extend far beyond it. Mary Summers has been a dear friend, colleague, useful critic, and comrade, but more; she has been and is family, and a model of human decency.

Touré F. Reed disengaged from his own dissertation prospectus to throw himself into constructing this book's index. I appreciate and cherish his efforts as I do every breath he has taken in his life.

This leaves a special group of individuals, best described by saying that I imagine them as readers for everything I write because they are the audience closest to home. Preston Smith has been a friend, confidant, and intellectual compatriot for more than two decades; much of this book's shaping and reshaping over the years shows the traces of our interaction around the larger intellectual project we share. I couldn't wish for a better friend, collaborator, and critic than Kenneth Warren, whose work realizes the greatest possibilities of politically engaged Americanist and Afro-Americanist scholarship; his presence nearly compensates for the Chicago winters. Joe Wood is a similarly kindred spirit who has helped me especially to think through the historical and contemporary nexus of cultural ideology and politics. None are more closely implicated in this book than Ian Shapiro, Rogers M. Smith, and Alex Willingham. My work is saturated with the effects of an interaction with Rogers and Ian that has nurtured and helped me since we all came together in New Haven in the early 1980s. In a way, we grew up together intellectually, and our lives have been entwined accordingly. In particular, Rogers and I, as Americanists who wander around the nineteenth century a lot, discovered early on that we shared a common intellectual and political agenda, though we came at it from rather different directions. That turned out to be just the tip of the iceberg, as we grew from junior colleagues to pals to trusted friends to family; he'll blush and deny it, but he's simply one of the very best, most consistently principled, and decent people I've ever known. Alex's relation to this book goes longest and deepest. My first exposure to the problem of Afro-Americanist intellectual historiography came in his graduate seminar (after he helped to recruit me to graduate school), as did my initial encounter with the systematic, grounded study of Afro-American or any other political thought, and he directed the dissertation in which this book originated. Over thirty years he has been my hanging partner, fellow activist, professor, advisor, and oldest friend, the one who can always be counted on and whose judgment always counts.

Finally, I want to note the contribution of someone who has no idea that he has made it—Johnny Adams, New Orleans's famous "Tan Canary," from my own Holly Grove neighborhood. The beauty of his incomparable warblings has been solace and splendor for me for decades and a powerful link to home and ground; his combination of brilliant artistry, personal warmth, and insistent dignity embody the best of the sensibility of the era that spawned us both.

Contents

All social life is essentially *practical*. All mysteries which lead theory to mysticism find their rational solution in human practice and in the comprehension of this practice.

—Marx, *Theses on Feuerbach*

One final word about giving instruction as to what the world ought to be. Philosophy in any case always comes on the scene too late to give it. As the thought of the world, it appears only when actuality is already there cut and dried after its process of formation has been completed. The teaching of the concept, which is also history's inescapable lesson, is that it is only when actuality is mature that the ideal first appears over against the real and that the ideal apprehends this same world in its substance and builds it up for itself into the shape of an intellectual realm. When philosophy paints its grey in grey, then has a shape of life grown old. By philosophy's grey in grey it cannot be rejuvenated but only understood. The owl of Minerva spreads its wings only with the falling of the dusk.

—Hegel, *Philosophy of Right*

W. E. B. DU BOIS
and American Political Thought

Introduction

Du Bois—Afro-American and American Political Thought

WILLIAM EDWARD BURGHARDT DU BOIS is generally recognized as a central figure in the history of Afro-American politics, a major contributor to more than a half-century's debate over the condition of and proper goals and strategies for blacks in the United States and, more broadly, peoples of African descent, worldwide. He enjoyed an unusually long and prominent career as a scholar, essayist, and activist. He was a pioneer in the formation of sociology as an academic discipline in the United States, author of one of the first revisionist histories of Reconstruction, a founder of the National Association for the Advancement of Colored People (NAACP), shaper—along with first Booker T. Washington and then Marcus Garvey—of two pivotal controversies over racial strategy, elder statesman of the Harlem Renaissance, hero of Nkrumahite Pan-Africanism, militant foe and victim of McCarthyism. Moreover, among prominent Afro-American political actors in this century Du Bois is perhaps the most systematic thinker (at least insofar as coherent writing is the expression of systematic thought). No other black intellectual or activist has written so much or so widely, and few have been so insistent on grounding strategic thinking on clear normative and theoretical principles.

It is, therefore, something of an anomaly that Du Bois, more than others, has been claimed by advocates of many different, often diametrically opposed, ideological positions. Sometimes he is linked simultaneously with apparently

3

contradictory stances. Against Washington, he has been understood as a defender of radical activism *and* as a pristine idealist. Against Garvey, he has been cast as an elitist integrationist; yet he was to leave the NAACP a few years later in part because the organization rejected his proposals for strengthening institutions within the black community even in the context imposed by segregation. Communists have claimed him, his elitism notwithstanding, as have anticommunist Pan-African nationalists.

This anomalous legacy, which makes the intellectually rigorous Du Bois appear as a champion who can be appropriated on an equal basis by any and all political tendencies, becomes less puzzling with the recognition that (even though he has been the object of a considerable secondary literature) little book-length scholarly work has concentrated on the theoretical dimension of Du Bois's political thought. Those who do attend to his political ideas typically either consider Du Bois's thought in an ancillary way, restrict themselves to cataloging his various positions on racial strategy, or are flatly hagiographical.

Only two major studies of Du Bois have attempted—though not with equal success—to develop interpretations that account carefully for his theoretical and philosophical commitments and their relation to his strategic positions. Arnold Rampersad's *The Art and Imagination of W. E. B. Du Bois* is an exemplary work in that regard; Joseph P. DeMarco's *The Social Thought of W. E. B. Du Bois* is noteworthy more for its attempt than its execution.[1] Rampersad's study may perhaps best be described as a critical intellectual biography; he wants to unravel the antinomies of Du Bois's consciousness, the existential tensions that defined his individuality and expressed themselves throughout his intellectual activity, particularly in his creative work. *The Art and Imagination of W. E. B. Du Bois* certainly informs the study of Du Bois's political thought, but it is not primarily a study of his political ideas; its interpretive thrust is more broadly cultural and philosophical, although Rampersad is obviously alive to the political-theoretical implications of Du Bois's artistic and philosophical dispositions. By contrast, DeMarco is more directly concerned with political ideas, but his account tends to sanitize Du Bois's thought to conform with more contemporary liberal, social democratic sensibilities. DeMarco's volume is weakened also by an often superficial and sometimes questionable approach to the philosophical tendencies to which it relates Du Bois, but the deeper problem is his impulse to represent Du Bois, without tension and irony, as a hero for our time.[2]

The Dangers of Racial Vindicationism

The hagiographical, sanitizing impulse is all too common in the study of Afro-American thought and especially prevails in Du Bois scholarship, in part because Du Bois's prominence overloads the ideological significance of characterizing him and defining his legacy. Examination of the historically conditioned foundations of his thinking, therefore, has taken a backseat to establishing or reaffirming his position in history. Despite its manifest focus on setting straight the historical record, that orientation—which I have associated elsewhere with a principle of racial vindication[3]—is acutely vulnerable to and virtually defenseless against producing anachronistic interpretations. Those who use it tend to seek "anticipations" of later (usually current) ideas in the thinking of those to be elevated, and tend to exaggerate their uniqueness as thinkers or political agents. The former tendency reinforces the natural temptation to impose contemporary or otherwise congenial meanings on the utterances of past agents; the latter, in diminishing the need to consider agents as participants in historically specific modes of political discourse, removes an important source of interpretive discipline.[4] So Manning Marable, for example, claims Du Bois, who was conscientiously agnostic in his public life, for a putative tradition of "prophetic Christianity" in Afro-American politics, on the basis of his occasional use of biblical metaphor[5] and defends a contention that he was most of all a "radical democrat" by arguing that the "Talented Tenth was a strategy to win democracy for all black Americans."[6]

There is, of course, a clear, objective basis for this vindicationist orientation. Not only has there been a real need to restore awareness of Du Bois's place in American history after his vilification and persecution in the last years of his life, but the Afro-Americanist tendency to affirm the significance of blacks' contributions to history is also a deeply embedded and organic legacy of generations of trivialization, denial, and disparagement by intellectual convention. Moreover, the vindicationist temper has produced useful and important biographical scholarship. Francis L. Broderick and Elliott M. Rudwick in separate but closely related biographies provided what has been perhaps the standard view of Du Bois as race leader or black activist spokesman.[7] R. Charles Key[8] and Dan S. Green and Edwin D. Driver[9] focus on reconstructing his role in the development of academic sociology in the United States. Arthur L. Johnson has attempted to situate him in the canon of sociological theory.[10] Charles H. Wesley and Jessie P. Guzman have emphasized his contributions as an academic historian.[11]

Some of this scholarship clearly succumbs to excessive claims, as with Eugene C. Holmes's presentation of Du Bois as a notable figure in the development of American positivist philosophy,[12] but the most serious limitation of the vindicationist literature is that, in giving priority to affirming blacks' rightful claim to historical contribution, it accepts a propagandistic imperative that hinders critical reflection on its subject matter. As early as the 1940s, William T. Fontaine examined implications of this racial "defense psychology," noting that it often leads to a conceptual narrowness and atheoreticism.[13] Since that time the study of Afro-American thought has congealed as an academic endeavor largely circumscribed by the intellectual constraints that Fontaine described. Unhappily, the vindicationist orientation has been institutionalized, solidifying its ideological attractiveness with the force of disciplinary orthodoxy.

Scholars' confusions and disagreements in categorizing Du Bois are evidence of the inadequacy of vindicationism. Moreover, the Du Bois anomaly arises as much from his being ignored by Americanists as from his being attended to hagiographically by Afro-Americanists. Thus, Du Bois illuminates the persistence among Americanists of a scandalous disposition to construe blacks (if including them at all) simply as objects of American civic discourse—to define the American "we" as inherently white. This orientation produces a fundamentally impoverished understanding of the evolution of American political life and debate, and two of its forms in particular have reinforced intellectual narrowness among Afro-Americanists. First, there is the propensity to define the history of American political thought as a narrative that marginalizes or excludes both race as an issue and nonwhites as participants. Second, there is the subordination of research and commentary concerning black Americans to an extrinsic objective of race relations management, that is, constraint by the imperatives of the "Negro Problem" framework. These two tendencies—as well as the broader orientation they embody—have taken different substantive forms, and even the new revisionist intellectual historiography has reproduced the equation of "American" and "white" (and all too often "male").[14] Specifically, however, when the study of Afro-American thought began to develop as an academic specialty, its received bias toward atheoretical, racial vindication was buttressed in different ways by the consensualist framework overtaking American intellectual historiography and a distinctive, new scholarly approach to race relations.

Consensualism in Cold War Intellectual Historiography

The study of Afro-American thought began to form a body of significant literature and a broadly cohesive *problematique* in the 1950s and early 1960s, during a period when the larger study of American political thought—reflecting the Cold War cultural milieu—centered on the idea of a transhistorical normative (or spiritual) consensus: an overarching American national character.[15] That representation of an essentially noncontroversial foundation of shared values and ideals had limiting consequences for Afro-Americanists. Locating this consensus demanded definition of the essential American character on a level so abstract that all areas of structurally grounded conflict receded from view. This meant, among other such devices, construing "American" to mean white (perhaps even "native" white) and thereby reducing the messy race issue to epiphenomenal status—an ultimately exogenous problem to be noted parenthetically, if at all.[16] Of course, the normative consensus merely reasserted the long-standing exclusion of blacks from the main narrative of American history, but it also formalized the intellectual and institutional barriers separating the two areas of inquiry and restricted Afro-Americanists to the study of strategies for (what had been called in the early twentieth century) "race adjustment."

The consensual frame imposed a static backdrop to examine Afro-American thought against, helping further to restrict the scope of Afro-Americanist inquiry. Holding "American ideals" or "American society" constant analytically obscures the extent to which blacks have participated in an evolving national grammar of political debate and thereby reinforces the vindicationist disposition to ignore the historical specificity and contextuality of black political discourse. Moreover, reifying the idea of a normative consensus exclusive of blacks fuels the tendency to conceptualize black thinking narrowly as a set of debates over strategies for reacting to the alien consensus. This view has authorized the familiar approach of categorizing black thought into sets of strategic or tactical dualisms (militance/moderation, protest/accommodation, integrationism/nationalism), and it has meshed especially well with the other intellectual development that influenced the formation of the Afro-Americanist field.

The "American Dilemma" as Heuristic and Ideology

The study of Afro-American thought took shape also in the context of a general expansion of scholarly interest in the Afro-American experience beginning in the decade or so following World War II. That broader expansion cohered around a reformulation — most cogently articulated by Gunnar Myrdal [17] — of the "Negro Problem" as both a matter for national moral (and pragmatic) concern and an appropriate object for enlightened social engineering at the hands of national policy elites. Two elements of the postwar climate helped this new focus take root. First, the changing geographic distribution of the black population destabilized the view that the status of blacks was a peculiarly southern problem. [18] Second, concern with resolving the race problem converged with and received a boost from the Cold War imperative. Existence of a formalized racial hierarchy in the United States was an embarrassing contradiction of the new national image as leader of the "Free World." America's new role as principal exemplar of the virtues of capitalist democracy in a global ideological struggle required greater sensitivity to the ways in which "world opinion" viewed domestic caste arrangements. [19]

Underlying both those practical sources of interest, however, was the familiar perception of the black population as an exogenous appendage to American society. The Cold War perspective and the impetus to recast the Negro Problem in national terms equally approach black Americans primarily as objects of administration; in each case the purposive stimulus instrumentalizes the Afro-American condition and experience to the goal of race relations management. Cold War–inspired interest has been more likely cynical, and its objectives have been more likely cosmetic. But even well-intentioned racial liberalism has been predisposed toward an ethnocentric purblindness to the relatively autonomous dimensions of black thought and action. The initial formulation that "America" has a "Negro Problem" not only reproduces the principle of black marginalization in the national experience; it also implies that the black experience exists only insofar as it intersects white American concerns or responds to white initiatives. Ralph Ellison identified the latter implication in Myrdal's unquestionably sympathetic study as an instance of a general tendency to view blacks "simply as the creation of white men." [20]

I cannot here undertake systematic discussion of the various ways in which this outlook imprinted itself on postwar scholarship about blacks, although that

is an important line of inquiry to pursue.[21] A general effect of the "Negro Problem" focus on the study of Afro-American thought, however, has been to lend
privilege to an approach that conceptualizes black political discourse only in its
tactical dimension, as a debate over alternative styles of response to white
agendas. Like the exclusionist consensualism, the Negro Problem viewpoint limits Afro-Americanists to charting a terrain of recurring, typically bipolar debates
over racial program or political style.[22] While a few scholars have pointedly
noted the intellectual inadequacies of this approach,[23] it has nonetheless dominated discourse about Afro-American political thought. Even self-conscious attempts to transcend it have not been able to break entirely with its narrow focus
on racial tactics and its penchant for ahistorical dualism.[24]

However, attributing this problem solely to white racism or ethnocentrism
or even to Cold War anti-intellectualism does not adequately account for it.
There is, after all, a concrete basis for reading the terms of Afro-American political debate as a pragmatic, reactive discourse. Even when Myrdal observed that
"Negro thinking in social and political terms is thus exclusively a thinking about
the Negro problem,"[25] he was not so much empirically wrong as analytically
incomplete. The same is true of his following elaboration:

> Negro thinking is almost completely determined by white opinions—negatively
> and positively. It develops as an answer to the popular theories prevalent among
> whites by which they rationalize their upholding of caste. In this sense it is a
> derivative, or secondary, thinking. The Negroes do not formulate the issues to
> be debated; these are set for them by the dominant group. Negro thinking
> develops upon the presuppositions of white thinking.[26]

The Unheard Internal Critique

Nearly a decade before Myrdal, black historian L. D. Reddick issued a call for
the study of Afro-American history to "escape the provincial nature of its first
phases . . . [and to] *re-define the area of subject matter in terms of a larger focus;*
[to] *re-cast its catalog of the determinative influences affecting Negro life and re-
examine the social philosophy implicit throughout the work*" (emphasis in original).[27] I have already mentioned Fontaine's critiques, and E. Franklin Frazier
was perhaps the most trenchant critic with this contention:

> Most Negro intellectuals simply repeat the propaganda which is put out by
> people who have large economic and political interests to protect. . . . We
> have no philosophers or thinkers who command the respect of the intellectual
> community at large . . . men who have reflected upon the fundamental prob-
> lems which have always concerned philosophers such as the nature of human
> knowledge and the meaning or lack of meaning of human existence.[28]

Earl E. Thorpe, author of the first—and still unequaled—general Afro-
American intellectual history has maintained that the black intellectual typically
has suffered from "restriction of his *Weltanschauung* to the narrow confines of

race, hypersensitivity, and an inferiority complex which displays itself in a thousand and one ways."[29] He went on to proclaim, echoing Reddick from a generation earlier, that as of 1960 "the time had probably come when Negro History should be subjected to more comparative studies and to broader interpretive emphases."[30] Afro-Americanists' tendency toward interpretive narrowness, Thorpe acknowledged, is in part a direct function of their subject matter in that much of Afro-American thought is "basically accommodation and attack thought."[31] (In another volume he examined the debilitating implications of that bias for Afro-American historiography in particular.)[32] At the same time he—like Myrdal, Reddick, Fontaine, and Frazier—found this discourse of "accommodation and attack" to be a natural, predictable consequence of racial exclusion and denigration both in the society at large and in the study of American life.

Myrdal's depiction is eloquent, if rather paternalistic:

> The Negroes are so destitute of power in American society that it would, indeed, be unrealistic for them to try a flight into a wider range of problems. It seems functional and rational that they restrict their efforts to what is nearest home. They are not expected to have a worth-while judgment on national and international affairs, except in so far as Negro interests are concerned. To most groups of white Americans it would be preposterous and impudent, or at least peculiar, if Negroes started to discuss general problems as ordinary Americans and human beings. They are allowed—in various degrees—to protest; or it is, at any rate, taken for granted that they should protest. But they are neither expected nor allowed to participate. So the Negro protest and the white expectation harmonize and accumulate in their effects to narrow the range of Negro thinking.[33]

He then recalled the "queerness . . . felt by the foreign observer when he turns over the leaves of the hundreds of recent books and articles by white Americans on American democracy and its implications . . . [to find that] the subject of the Negro is a void or is taken care of by some awkward, mostly uninformed and helpless, excuses."[34]

In those observations Myrdal, like Thorpe and the other black critics, identified the practical historical bases for the circumscription of both black discourse about politics and the study of Afro-American thought within a tactical, racial frame. Unfortunately—and ironically, given his intentions—in construing the question of the status of blacks in the United States as the "Negro Problem," he inadvertently committed precisely the transgression he lamented. Positing an abstracted "American Creed," in relation to which the treatment of blacks is held to be anomalous, already separates the Afro-American population in principle from the notion of "American society." Thereby, in representing them as outside—indeed as objects of—the only pertinent normative discourse, the Myrdalian view deprives blacks of any basis for autonomous agency.[35] That is what Ellison detected and recoiled from as a profound and dangerous flaw in Myrdal's work. Where Myrdal differed from Reddick, Fontaine, and the others was not so much in what he saw in black thought but in how he responded to it. Because he was not particularly concerned with the state of black social or political agency, let alone with advancing it, he could take the apparent absence of normative autonomy in black political discourse simply as given. For Myrdal that lack of autonomy was a fact of life, an inexorable, though deplorable, consequence of racial subordination; moreover, for him the alternatives were only assimilation or continued "racial provincialism."[36] To the others it was, while historically and sociologically understandable, a problem to be confronted and overcome, hence their various calls for self-conscious reflection on the theoretical commitments underpinning black intellectual activity.[37]

It is natural enough—given the primacy of racial subordination and oppression—that Afro-American thinking has been so thoroughly dominated by issues of racial strategy. What Myrdal overlooked, however, is that even the narrowest, most "provincial" lines of debate derive from and are structured by a normatively significant language of politics, a discourse bound by shared "values, beliefs, perceptions, and concepts."[38] In their various critiques Fontaine, Reddick, Thorpe, and Frazier in effect were calling for black intellectuals to adopt a more critically reflective stance vis-à-vis the foundations of prevailing patterns of black social and political discourse.

Those critiques might usefully have informed the *problematique* of Afro-American intellectual history, but they were overwhelmed by a combination of the cultural force of the Myrdalian view and the endemic racial vindicationism that was the critics' main target. Those two outlooks, strengthened by association with postwar successes in the civil rights struggle, undercut reflection on embedded norms by devaluing, in slightly different ways, the historical contextuality of political debate. The consensual American Creed view, because of its own ahistoricism, uncoupled scholarship from the need to ground interpretations in historical specificity. The predictable result has been a tendency toward interpretive presentism.[39] Vindicationism is almost by definition a form of presentism; in seeking to elevate black thought by showing its elegance or pertinence to skeptics in the here and now, the vindicationist orientation is intrinsically susceptible to viewing the past "in abstracted relationship to analogues in the present."[40]

Under these influences, Afro-Americanist scholarship congealed around an intellectual core characterized by naïveté concerning both the historical autonomy of political thought and the theoretical and epistemic foundations of its own enterprise. As a consequence, research has been largely blind to the regions of deeper normative meanings that are tacit within expressly pragmatic black political debates; for penetrating those regions requires reconstructing the historically specific intellectual conventions that set the terms of episodic controversy. Not having access to the conventional groundings of black discourse, furthermore, undermines the project of commenting other than trivially on the durable features and self-driving characteristics of Afro-American thought. Instead, such commentary has tended to depict either a perennial chase after platitudinous symbols—"freedom," "equality," even "struggle"—or a Whiggish saga of the linear unfolding of a grand idea.[41]

Poverty of Interpretation in Contemporary Afro-American Thought

For students of Afro-American thought the call for critical reflectiveness is therefore most importantly a call for making the normative underpinnings of black thought accessible. Thus we must examine texts as historical artifacts of specific discursive communities. This in turn entails a need for greater theoretical self-consciousness about two discrete aspects of our approach to our subject matter; one bearing on the relation between the Afro-Americanist and Americanist fields, and the other more generally on the history of ideas. First, to the extent that black thought takes shape within a broader American language of politics, credible recovery of the normative principles tacit in black discourse requires accounting for that constitutive grammar of political debate. Eric Foner, for example, has suggested a new angle on black strategic thinking during Reconstruction by noting its relation to contemporaneous republican strains in American thought.[42] The study of Afro-American thought can be enriched by rigorous study of American thought and should be so informed.

Second, we should be more attentive to the ways in which interpretation is itself a normatively pregnant activity. Thus far the field's methodological innocence has foreclosed that issue and in the process has hampered development of coherence. This methodological innocence—a function of the prevailing naïveté about historical contextuality—has left Afro-Americanists without a basis for discussing either interpretive standards or purposive orientations to research. This point should not be taken to suggest a call for a research "paradigm." Such an effort hints of solipsism and would deploy scholarly resources most inefficiently. Besides, exercises in paradigm building very likely invert their Kuhnian inspiration anyway. By forgetting that paradigms—when and where they exist— are born, not made, efforts to call them into existence commit a version of the well-known error of confounding the history of science and its summary reconstruction as a sequential logic in the philosophy of science. In this area Hegel's dictum holds: "The way is the long way around"; one might add, "if there is any way at all." Rather, what I am suggesting is simply that we inform our work with the insights—and the ambiguities—generated by hermeneutical and otherwise procedural discussions throughout the broader history of ideas (and, for that matter, literary criticism).

Proper attentiveness to historical contextuality requires breaking the thrall of presentism and similar forms of interpretive naïveté, which in turn requires cultivating an attitude of humility and cautious self-doubt in approaching texts. These qualities can be enhanced by making the field's reigning assumptions and procedures objects of scrutiny and by considering Afro-American thought to be a "relatively autonomous" subset of American thought in general and the history of ideas writ large. This is the path, consonant with the critiques articulated by Thorpe, Fontaine, Reddick, and Frazier, to locating the distinctive foundations of Afro-American discourse.

There are in fact signs of growing scholarly concern to relate Afro-American thought to broader intellectual currents. Although that concern seems keenest in works on Du Bois, who was among the most intellectually cosmopolitan black political actors, scholarship throughout the field has become more likely in recent years to express an interest in connecting black thought to European and white American theories and theorists. In addition to the studies by Rampersad and DeMarco, Wilson J. Moses and William S. Toll also have sought with very productive results to provide intellectually contextualized accounts of episodes of black thought. Cornel West's and Marable's efforts are somewhat less successful. Both volumes are oriented more toward demonstrating that their black subjects were intellectually comparable to and/or conversant with the work of prominent European and white American theorists than toward situating those subjects within some constraining pattern of discourse.[43]

s latter approach, which is only an elevated vindicationism, opens to two related interpretive failings. First, making the link rests on extracting the principal subject matter from its immediately constitutive discourse. No matter what might plausibly be said about the putative links, therefore, this interpretive style actually impedes recovery of the autonomous bases of black thought. Second, the vindicationist concern with asserting an intellectual tie between black and white "greats" leads to seeking links between agents operating within quite different *problematiques*. The issues most meaningful to Hegel, for example, were not of the same sort as those of greatest priority to Du Bois.[44] To the extent that the agents being linked respond to different questions, comparison must focus on their answers, that is, on their positions on reified issues such as "the state," "justice," "democracy." While this approach may inform our understanding of the vectors of influence running between individuals joined through texts,[45] it does not convey much sense of the discursive communities in which those texts are embedded, the concrete issues they seek to resolve. David A. Hollinger describes this problem clearly:

> Questions are the points of contact between minds, where agreements are consolidated and where differences are acknowledged and dealt with; questions are the dynamisms whereby membership in a community of discourse is established, renewed, and sometimes terminated. To focus instead on a belief or value attributable to an individual or to a collectivity of individuals is at once to move back from those authentic, contingent relationships; when historical subjects are said to hold a belief or value, those subjects are endowed with merely abstract, static characteristics (for example, a belief in "progress" or in "republicanism") that may or may not be shared by a virtual infinity of other subjects who may or may not interact with each other. Yet when these same ideas are viewed in their capacity as answers to questions shared with other persons (for example, "What is the national destiny of America?" or "What kinds of political conduct are virtuous?"), they become contributions to discourse.[46]

The search for explicit links to Euroamerican philosophical luminaries originates, obviously, in a desire to exalt black thought, to demonstrate the existence of a complex Afro-American intellectual tradition that is worthy of scholarly estimation. Ironically, the means undermines the end in part because it rests on counterproductive premises concerning "greatness" and intellectual tradition. What greatness is, how it is determined, or how far it exists beyond the ideological dispositions of those who proclaim it are very much unsettled issues about which, for present purposes at least, I shall take refuge in agnosticism. However, seeking to compare or to find signs of "influence" across discursive contexts forces argument by analogy; that is, this search consists in finding positions or stances—"answers"—that appear similar in the texts of the respective agents. This sort of interpretation readily lends itself to the "reification of doctrines." The latter can ensue in a variety of anachronisms,[47] to which studies of Afro-American thought hardly have been immune. Yet its most damaging implication for the field is that it confounds the philosophical and historical dimensions of the history of ideas[48] and thereby substitutes arguments concerning the internal consistency of texts for confrontation of Afro-American discourse squarely in its own context. Frank examination of and critical reflection on the black experience are foiled, once again, by the impulse to vindicate it.

Although it is important to draw attention to these interpretive problems as methodological issues, the fundamental challenge is actually to reconstruct contextually grounded currents of Afro-American discourse. Debates about substantive interpretations are in the long run more invigorating and rewarding than debates about how to interpret, and accounts of the specifically political elements of black intellectual history, now that the major framework for debate for two-thirds of the present century—the struggle against formal racial segregation—has lost its strategic foundation, may be especially important. Because the antisegregationist imperative no longer imposes a reasonable semblance of strategic unity, inquiry into the normative presuppositions of Afro-American discourse may indeed produce arguments that have value not only for scholars but also for citizens. At any rate, that hope is one vanity that students of Afro-American thought might in this context forgivably indulge.

Du Bois is, for reasons that I indicated above, ideally suited as a focal point for such a study. Because he was a central participant in and commentator on debates over most of that two-thirds of a century, unraveling the foundations of his thought may contribute significantly to critical reconstruction of the normatively structured discourse about politics shared by black intellectuals during the segregation era. Moreover, because Du Bois was more attentive than most agents to theoretical debates and *problematiques* outside the black community over that period, his thought reflects with particular clarity and immediacy the embeddedness of the categories of black debate in broader patterns of American political discourse. Those at least are premises on which this study rests.

Corporate Industrialization, Collectivism, and the New Intellectuals

Historical Context in the Formation of Du Bois's Thought

Corporate Hegemony

THE EARLY YEARS of Du Bois's life were also the early years of the development of industrial capitalism as the dominant cultural force in the United States and in much of Europe. Those were the years of European colonial expansion into Africa and Asia and of American experimentation with and uncertainty about resolution of the "Negro Problem." Du Bois was born in 1868, the year of the Fourteenth Amendment's ratification. He began his studies at Fisk University in 1885, the year of the Berlin conference that divided Africa into spheres of influence for the European colonial powers, and he married and undertook his Philadelphia study in 1896, the year of the *Plessy* decision. He joined the faculty at Atlanta University at the crest of popularity of the ideology of the New South, of which Atlanta was considered the capital, and he joined the debate with Booker T. Washington over industrial education at the high point of the corporate merger movement.[1] Perhaps most important for Du Bois's development, though, was his matriculation at college just as the social role and focus of the university were being redefined. He matured, moreover, in a critical intellectual environment dominated by three ideological responses to the consolidation of corporate industrialism: collectivism, the cooperative commonwealth (the font of a homegrown American socialism), and antimodernism.

Carol S. Gruber has noted that in the decades following the Civil War, the structure of higher education in America underwent a major reorganization. The related dynamics of urbanization and industrialization increased the social need for scientific and technical knowledge; simultaneously, original and experimental work in science and engineering increasingly commanded more respect from students and others than the classical curriculum.[2] At the same time growing economic concentration increased the demand for mechanization in industry, and the status of technical and scientific education rose with rising demand. Those factors combined to create a perceived need among practitioners to professionalize the technical fields, especially engineering. The desire to regulate entry to the field and further to enhance status led to establishment of licensing requirements and of intensification of university courses of study.[3] However, the guild activities of the nascent technical professions were not alone sufficient to reshape higher education. Professionalism was one of several currents in the society that happened to flow together into a tide of higher education reform.

The last quarter of the nineteenth century was a period in which American culture began to show signs of an erosion of religious influence, and the university community was greatly affected. University professors and independent intellectuals were in the forefront of what Gruber calls the "advancing secularism" of the era.[4] Evolutionism's influence was felt widely in the culture, as the spread of Social Darwinist ideology attests,[5] and religiosity suffered accordingly. However, secularization was spurred even within theology itself. "Like the doctrine of natural selection, textual criticism of the Bible also called into question the infallibility of the Scriptures. Imported from German university centers, the higher criticism, as it was known, subjected Holy Writ to rigorous historical analysis."[6] Both faculty and administration—a distinction that became increasingly meaningful as the university rationalized itself—were imbued with the new optimistic, secular orientation. In fact, a marked secularization could be seen over the late 1800s in the composition of college trustee boards, which traditionally had been dominated by clergy.[7]

The university was affected not only by the changing cultural climate and the increasing importance of technical knowledge in the burgeoning industrial economy. A third development also fed change more directly. Growing government interest in education as a social utility—an interest that was demonstrated as well in the public education movement—led to increases in funds available for support of initiatives in higher education. At the same time, the coffers of universities were blessed by the caprice, "pecuniary emulation," and bad conscience of the Gilded Age's robber barons, as well as the latter's interests in social and economic rationalization. Gruber suggests in this regard that "accumulation of great fortunes made private capital available just at the time that the business community was beginning to identify education with material success."[8]

As a consequence of those developments a climate came into existence that favored the extension of two related processes of professionalization in the university. Originating in the natural sciences and reflecting the impact of science on American thought, a pattern formed in the latter years of the nineteenth century for "the professionalization of knowledge characterized by the emergence of discrete scholarly disciplines."[9] Psychology was reconstituted on an experimental basis during this period, and moral philosophy yielded the social sciences and history.[10] At the same time, the academic vocation both reflected the curricular division of labor and congealed as a profession whose identity was secured by "definition of standards of preparation, performance, protection and rewards."[11] The German experience exerted a major influence on the professionalization and scientization of American higher education through the Gilded Age, and during those years as well came the signs among intellectuals of a developing ideology of social intervention based on expertise.[12] If American academics came to an *an sich* consciousness as a professional group in the post–Civil War era, by the First World War the institutional apparatus—complete with specialized disciplines, guild associations, and trade journals—had been generated to mediate passage to the *fur sich* of a social stratum joined by certain common premises about themselves and the world.

The changing shape and thrust of the university was in fact an element of a more profound sociological phenomenon involving redefinition of the roles and self-perceptions of intellectuals in response to the industrial reorganization of American society. The functional basis for this redefinition lay in the steady growth of the corporation as the pivotal economic form and its impact on the social division of labor. Large-scale corporate production not only precipitated increasing demand for technical labor; but the impetus to rationalization of production and distribution processes, which ensued in separation of mental and manual tasks, generated increasing demand for purely administrative, managerial, and language-manipulating labor.[13] At the same time, proceeding industrial concentration and urbanization were accompanied by growth in the social-administrative apparatus. The administrative responsibilities of the state became more important at national and local levels, and rationalization of social life in general became an issue for conscious social policy.[14] Intellectuals' place in the society grew accordingly as the demand for functionaries grew.[15] These historical circumstances accommodated proliferation of the distinctive type of intellectual associated with the new university and professional subcultures. In articulating various theoretical and administrative responses to large scale industrial capitalism, this new intellectual type became a driving force in constitution of the distinctive ideological baseline of the twentieth century. Not only did they share a common functional location in the social division of labor, but the new intellectuals congealed around certain shared attitudinal characteristics. Among those characteristics are (1) a disposition toward puzzle solving as an orientation to purposeful activity; (2) an inclination to think in terms of systems and wholes and parts; and (3) a commitment—at least in principle—to self-correcting, reflexive language which delegitimizes claims to validity based on references to ascriptive authority and grounds validation on a relatively impersonal standard of truth.[16]

Those shared dispositions and attitudes about the proper conduct of social discourse were enforced institutionally by means of credentializing and licensing requirements to generate what Gouldner has referred to as the "public ideologies"[17] of the intellectuals. Professionalism and related therapeutic, technocratic, and meritocratic postures are grounded in a common outlook that acknowledges the social and ethical propriety of a hierarchy of knowledge and expertise. The fact that talent or knowledge appears as an intrinsically rational, and therefore unquestioned, "natural" basis for stratification discloses an aspect of the ideological self-interestedness of the new intellectuals; for, under critical scrutiny, hierarchy of knowledge is no more a manifestation of immanent social rationality than is any other hierarchical scheme.[18] Indeed, the fundamental views of the proper organization of human society around which intellectuals tend to converge emphasize the importance of precisely those activities that are characteristic to intellectuals.

The positive valuation of consciously *organized* society is a distinctive outlook of corporate-era intellectuals.[19] Planning and systematically rational organization as ideological commitments stress the importance of anticipation, prediction, and control as orienting principles of social organization. Planning, the application of formalistic rationality as a model for social life, technicization of experience, and assertion of administration as the proper mode for maintenance of the social fabric do not merely stress the importance of the activities engaged in by intellectuals. By their intrinsic appeal to supranormative, allegedly objective or scientific standards of efficacy, these value premises remove the structuring of human institutions from the realm of political discussion. Because the notion of an objectively rational social organization denies the appropriateness of interest-groundedness for decision making, it thereby disallows consideration of the relation of those very premises to the pursuit of intellectuals'—or any other group's—stratum interests.[20] Consequently, even when intellectuals have participated in broad social reform movements and have deployed their skills to service in the generation of ideologies for those movements, their participation has been conditioned, overtly or not, by the particular interests of their stratum. It is in that sense that James Gilbert writes, discussing the period in question,

> Often the reform role of the intellectual was quite distinct and self-consciously different from the interests of the rank-and-file of reform movements. The intellectual's assumptions and the implications of his actions were sometimes special for the very reason that they expressed the interests of a developing intellectual elite as well as allegiance to a set of reform ideas.[21]

Collectivism

Gilbert proposes "collectivism" as a common rubric that "signifies the general area of agreement among those intellectuals who committed their careers and hopes to such different movements as socialism, progressivism and managerialism."[22] The collectivist outlook entails typically an emphasis on expertise as a legitimate, decisive social force, notions of the impartiality and neutrality of the state and resonant assumptions of the neutral, guiding role of technology. In the collectivist outlook realization of social justice depends on neutrality and scientific impersonality as major weapons.[23] Additionally, collectivism advances modern secularism by its commitment to a view of the centrality of the economy in society. *Pace* Gilbert:

> Collectivism, then, emerged as a general theory of society in which economic institutions were the key element. Possibilities for social interaction and political reform derived from the mass nature of these economic institutions. Although many collectivists wished to preserve such older values as individualism, they were nonetheless forced by their understanding of the scale of social problems to consider as a solution pitting social organization against injustice, or translating such older economic ideas as laissez-faire into theories of competing groups. Pluralism, a variant of collectivist thought, is an example of one direction which these assumptions often took. But other concrete theories also expressed the same central assumptions about social organization; only the details varied.[24]

Viewed thus, the collectivist rubric subsumes theoretical continuities that unite the various social programs—socialism, progressivism, managerialism, and social engineering in general—advocated by the new intellectual stratum. The essence of the industrial democracy and rationality around which many of those intellectuals converged tends toward a technicization of social life that amounts to extension of the civil service model to the private sector.[25] This view entails not only a commitment to a certain notion of equality but it also authorizes the principle of meritocracy on which intellectuals typically base their claims to special status. In fact, Gilbert observes, "even those intellectuals who seemed willing to sacrifice the rights of private property for the sake of social control over production were unwilling to surrender their belief in a hierarchical society. Many wished only a more truly meritocratic class system."[26]

In both progressivism and the mercurial and eclectic phenomenon that was American socialism, similar technicist and hierarchical moments were prominent. At a theoretical level, in fact, the socialist and progressivist visions often are difficult to distinguish. Gilbert observes that "[s]ocialism, to many radical intellectuals, was merely a set of demands completely divorced from a specific system of empiricism. The ideological distinction between a Progressive and a socialist intellectual could often be eliminated by juggling their demands."[27]

For Gilbert, however, socialism provides a central theme around which other collectivist ideologies oscillated. He differentiates "two broad strains of socialist thought [that] were distinguishable in the writings of Americans," one of which came directly from Marx and the other of which "more closely resembled liberal reformism."[28] He notes:

> Evolutionary socialism and reform capitalism shared a common theory of a vanguard, whether of experts or political leaders, who would lead the way to-

ward a radical alteration of American society. Both movements relied upon
Darwinian metaphors and the predictions of modern social science. Both defined the trust or corporation as the central problem and the primary force of
progress. And both, feeling that modern society's problems were universal, appealed to an international reform community. . . .

   In practice, however, the intellectuals saw *themselves* at the leading edge
of civilization.[29]

Gilbert does not, however, confront a deeper sense in which Marxist and
non-Marxist stances converged. A clear attraction of the collectivist outlook—
socialist or otherwise—lay in its validation of that perception of the intellectuals'
importance. Having observed that the collectivist intellectuals tended to believe
that progress "would inevitably rest . . . upon the emergence of an intellectual
vanguard which could articulate the half-hidden laws of social development,"[30]
Gilbert avers:

> Their writings often reflected a familiarity with the past and the future, as if
> both were familiar terrain. This sense of predicting the future course of society
> fed an almost irresistible urge toward utopianism. The "discovery" of sociologi-
> cal laws, the belief in rapid change, the interchangeability of knowledge from
> one broad field to another, suggest a carelessness which is often the mark of
> excessive enthusiasm. However sure or unsure intellectuals were about where
> society was going, they felt certain that it was on the verge of immense change
> which they could influence.[31]

It is understandable in this regard that Gilbert asserts that the collectivism
he describes should be juxtaposed conceptually to Marxism; the tendency was
elaborated specifically as an alternative to the Marxist critique's radicalism and
embrace of class conflict. Yet, Gilbert's own investigation uncovers threads connecting the Fabianism that he discusses even with Bolshevism. The "inter-
changeability of knowledge" finds its apotheosis in the dialectics of nature and
Lysenkan biology.[32] The special relationship to history and the transcendent
vanguard speak as clearly of Lenin, Trotsky, Bukharin, and Stalin as of Charles
Steinmetz and Edmund Kelley. Beneath their certainly quite significant differences over the question of violent seizure of power and class struggle, revolutionary Marxism and Fabianism in some ways are strikingly similar in outlook. Both
exalt science and scientificity; both advocate rationalistic organization led by an
intellectual vanguard, and both display elements of inevitability and utopianism.

   Karl Korsch proffered one of the earliest and most coherent critiques of
Bolshevism from a radical Marxist perspective. Writing in the early 1920s,
Korsch detected the fundamental theoretical similarities undergirding Leninism
and Kautskyan social democracy, and among those similarities he included their
common deprecation of the subjective, volitional realm of human experience.[33]
By 1930 Korsch had concluded that Bolshevism was separated from evolutionary
social democracy mainly by the peculiarities surrounding Russian society and
the decomposition of its ancien regime. Revolutionary Marxism, Korsch argued,
in grounding its critical vision in a scientistic automatism, had opted to swim

along with the philosophical and ideological mainstream of twentieth-century bourgeois society.

While Korsch focused his critique on Lenin and Plekhanov, Albrecht Wellmer has gone on to identify tendencies in Marx's own work that resonate with the positivist assumptions lying at the base of other collectivist ideologies.[34] Moreover, Alvin W. Gouldner has presented a view of the Marxist heritage that emphasizes an ambivalence at its core. He finds a coherent, fully developed tendency in Marxism toward a positivist scientism and deterministic objectivism that characterize other, nonrevolutionary industrial-era ideologies; on the other hand, Gouldner also identifies a "critical Marxism" which, in addition to emphasizing historicized critique and the relative autonomy of subjectivity, tends toward a secularized, apocalyptic, and egalitarian utopianism. The former tendency, which Gouldner calls "scientific Marxism," shares with antirevolutionary collectivism and social management ideology biases toward evolutionism, automatism, and the reduction of social life to the object of administration. According to Gouldner's view, both tendencies are distinctly present in Marx, and for that matter Hegel, and their dialectical interaction has constituted the liberatory and sometimes repressive legacy of Marxism.[35]

Nor is Bolshevism's continuity with evolutionary socialism and other collectivist variants visible only in the philosophical realm. Lenin and his cohorts' fascination with scientific management indicates that even a newly triumphant and enthusiastic revolutionary Marxism might well be considered in one sense simply a more politically aggressive and successful version of Gilbert's collectivism.[36] The commonalities were observable from 1917 and before. Formalization of social development in the centralized plan; homogenization of human interests before the requirements of administration; enforcement in the party, factory, state, and society at large of a hierarchical organization that allocates privileged positions to intellectuals and intelligentsia—all are characteristics of a Bolshevism that does not fully transcend but apotheosizes the collectivist rhythm of the twentieth century. Lenin himself already in 1902 had identified revolutionary socialism and its consciousness as the original property of intellectuals; Bolshevism became a radical program for molding society to their vision.[37] The Hungarian sociologists George Konrad and Ivan Szelenyi contend that, in part through its professionalization of revolution,

> Bolshevism enabled the intellectuals to rid themselves of the ideological ballast which they had been obliged to carry as representatives of the working class. For in treating the proletarian state as the *sine qua non* of socialism the Bolsheviks made an end of socialism as a political, economic, and social problem, simplifying it to a mere matter of organizing state and economy. The Bolshevik intellectuals did not ask in what sort of institutional order the associated producers would find maximum political and economic freedom, but only: How can state and economy be organized so that every decision-making position will be monopolized by the party's trained cadres, and in such a way that those power positions cannot be limited in scope by other kinds of legitimation (be it tradition, capital ownership, or political representation)?[38]

After noting the brevity of the period of democratic experimentation and workers' control that followed the seizure of power in Russia, the authors conclude:

> Bolshevism, then, offered the intellectuals a program for freeing themselves of the duty of representing particular interests once power had been secured, and it used particular interests simply as a means of acquiring power. With the expropriation of the expropriators—that is, with the transfer of the right to dispose over the surplus product from landlords and capitalists to intellectuals in power, or to worker cadres whose political positions and functions made intellectuals of them—and with the destruction of the immediate producers' organs of management and control, the Bolsheviks traced the outlines of a new rational redistributive system and, within it, indicated the position of the teleological redistributors, called to represent the interests of all society expertly and professionally.[39]

It is noteworthy in this context that Lenin defined the revolutionary Social-Democrat as a "Jacobin who totally identifies himself with the *organization* of the proletariat, a proletariat *conscious* of its class interests."[40] Bolshevism, as a model of revolutionary Marxism in the period of industrial social reorganization, is distinguishable from other collectivist ideologies principally in its Jacobinist radicalism, its political aggressiveness and willingness to force its program of rationalist homogenization on society through rupture. In its fundamental intellectual impulse, Bolshevism joins other collectivist stances as a realization under contemporary historical circumstances of a central strain of the *telos* of the bourgeois Enlightenment, the domination of the concept over its object.[41]

Thus Gilbert's contraposition of Marxism and collectivism overstates the differences in their philosophical and epistemic foundations. While other collectivists stood apart from and reacted against revolutionary Marxism as a social and political program, what separated many Marxists from other collectivist intellectuals was less their visions for the ultimate organization of society than disagreement over appropriate means and agencies for realizing that vision. A strain of Marxism, therefore, is revolutionary more for its Jacobinism than its goals; it represents, rather than a critical alternative to the social order of mass industrialization, the "unhappy consciousness" of its managers.

This clarification is important with respect to Du Bois because in diminishing the difference between Marxism and "collectivism" it also diminishes the significance of the issue of when or whether he actually became a revolutionary Marxist. Insofar as collectivism can be seen as an intellectual orientation encompassing at least some variants of revolutionary Marxism, the issue loses its relevance for interpretation of the organizing principles of Du Bois's thought. In fact, in the remainder of this study, I shall demonstrate that throughout his career Du Bois's writings rested on a conceptual foundation that is compatible with the collectivist outlook and that this orientation is evident in his attitudes about the importance of science in social affairs and the proper organization of the Afro-American population as well as in his specific concerns with political positions, such as Pan-Africanism and socialism.

The developing tendency to cast the world in collectivist terms was more than an ideological expression of the self-perception and guild interests of the new stratum of intellectuals. Its origins lay more broadly in an attempt to respond to the sense of cultural dislocation attendant to the processes of institutional reorganization taking hold in American society at the end of the nineteenth century. In that context of passage from a familiar mode of national existence to one that was not only quite new and different but also did not seem to develop organically from its predecessor, the canon of values that had constituted the legitimating framework for bourgeois social relations was destabilized, if not rendered flatly inappropriate. This phenomenon, which T. J. Jackson Lears has summarized as a "crisis of cultural authority,"[42] provoked searches in a variety of venues for paths to restoration or reconstitution of a national normative order. The collectivist outlook was attractive in this regard because it promised to resolve the problem of teleological drift and to do so, moreover, in a manner that both emphasized order as inherently virtuous and accepted the new structural arrangements more or less happily on their own terms.

The cultural crisis derived most directly from displacement of the immediate community as primary context for defining and comprehending one's place in the world and relation to others. The development of a national market system, carried by the railroads, not only brought communities closer together; it also redefined relationships within and between communities in a variety of ways, including "incorporation of space and time as factors among the elements of production," overrode the autonomousness of the idiosyncratic patterns of community life and subordinated them to the imperatives of homogenizing logic.[43] This logic destroyed the dual bases on which rested the local community's authority as a source of social order: "its ability to manage the lives of its members, and the belief among its members that the community had such powers."[44] Already by the 1870s and '80s the "island community" was no longer an adequate ground on which to orient social and political—let alone economic—life, and the concerns of businessmen and public figures reflected this decline through a recurring emphasis on the problems of splintering and fragmentation.[45]

As the community lost its power to provide cultural self-definition for the stratum of respectable burghers, that function came to be performed for a steadily growing body of Americans by impersonal affiliations and attachments. Over the 1880s and '90s, for example, a truly national, sociologically cohesive upper class congealed, largely by means of elite intermarriage across cities. Identification of suitable partners and associates in this far-flung network was made possible by the development of a set of shared symbols and criteria that denoted propriety and signified membership in the group.[46]

At the same time that the upper class was rationalizing itself on a national basis, a new middle class was forming, mainly in the growing cities. This new middle class included professionals and specialists in business, labor, and agriculture who were "awakening both to their distinctiveness and to their ties with similar people in the same occupation . . . [developing] . . . consciousness of unique skills and functions, an awareness that came to mold much of their lives."[47] The members of this middle class "found their rewards more and more in the uniqueness of an occupation and in its importance to a rising scientific-industrial society."[48] Their ability to see their functions in the new system led them to look toward the future with optimism, to see progress, which indeed they often sought to hasten by an "earnest desire to remake the world upon their private models," as Robert H. Wiebe describes the reform impulse among them.[49] It was that reform-oriented element of this new middle class that nurtured the various expressions of the collectivist outlook generated among its intellectuals, in part as a project of "building a new structure of loyalties to replace the decaying system of the nineteenth century communities."[50]

Of course attraction to a collectivist *weltanschauung* was not the only prominent ideological response to the cultural crisis wrought by capitalist industrialization. Wiebe indicates that in the 1880s the "most significant characteristic shared by [the] many anxieties was the desire for community self-determination, and anti-monopoly was its most common means of expression."[51] In that context, a considerable strain of reform thinking over the 1880s and '90s contained a protest against what was perceived to be a closing off—or even a hijacking—of the social "commons" by large private interests, against the corporation's preemption of values of community and on behalf of a call "for the community to reabsorb the corporation."[52] Populism, and still later, an element of the home-grown variety of American socialism were to grow out of this strain of thought, which was structured largely around the image of the "cooperative commonwealth." This image, which received perhaps its most systematic expression in the writings of Laurence Gronlund, Edward Bellamy, and Henry Demarest Lloyd, was both a widely propagated social-organizational ideal and an emblem of the community's reassertion of its control over industrialization.[53]

Yet, as Gilbert observes, the image of the cooperative commonwealth was not intrinsically incompatible with the collectivist outlook; Bellamy's *Looking Backward* in particular, he notes, "appears again and again as a kind of unconscious archetype in writings about the solution to industrial problems" among later collectivist ideologues—both socialist and not.[54] Certainly, Bellamy's utopia indicated that the commonwealth could be constituted in an enlightened, corporatist despotism, and for him as well as for Gronlund the path to resolution of cultural crisis lay in vesting the national state with a more highly rationalized, administrative version of the cultural and normative responsibilities that had been sundered from the community by the development of private power in the large corporation. The state, in other words, was to become the community, substituting the precision of self-regulating—and thus totalitarian—rational administration for the more personal and relational basis of legitimacy that had been abolished by large-scale industrialization.[55] In this regard, even though these critics were more attentive than others to the cultural disruption and other evils spawned by the new institutional arrangements and were therefore less likely to champion industrialism as pure progress, the heart of their critiques—as expressed in their reconstructive vision—affirmed the functionalist rationality that drove the corporate-industrial juggernaut. They were, therefore, predisposed to an authoritarian-bureaucratic resolution by both the centralizing logic of their presumptions concerning rationality and the conformism inherent to the communitarian ideal. The small town, after all, is saved from a frightful totalitarianism only because its face-to-face framework provides some space for negotiation of tolerance for idiosyncrasy, but even that applies only for those judged to be insiders.

Another tendency among intellectuals disclosed quite a different reaction to the late nineteenth century's cultural crisis. For those associated with this tendency, as for the advocates of cooperative commonwealth, the new industrial culture developing around them could not be seen as unmitigated progress. However, their response differed inasmuch as they rejected—at least rhetorically—the entire normative apparatus of industrialism. These antimodernists' critiques "stemmed from revulsion against the process of rationalization first described by Max Weber—the systematic organization of economic life for maximum productivity and of individual life for maximum personal achievement; the drive for efficient control of nature under the banner of improving human welfare; the reduction of the world to a disenchanted object to be manipulated by rational technique."[56] That is, they reacted against the core principles of the new industrialism.

Strategically, this reaction entailed embracing "premodern symbols as alternatives to the vagueness of liberal Protestantism or the sterility of nineteenth-century positivism" and adapting those symbols to modern ends.[57] Antimodernists typically understood the cultural crisis as a problem of overcivilization for which the quest for authenticity of experience was held out as an antidote. Pursuit of arts and crafts, the cult of the strenuous life and the martial ideal, and exaltation of the "primitive" were among the more common avenues through which the antimodernist impulse was realized. However, without rehearsing the complexity of the antimodernist epicycle that Lears describes so provocatively, the most important aspect of the antimodernist critique is its ambivalence. Lears notes:

> [A] drive toward autonomous action coexisted with a longing for dependent passivity. Alongside pastoral poetry, magazines printed hymns to material progress. Maples and ferns acquired greater romantic appeal as more were uprooted by enterprising frontiersmen. . . . By remaining linked to activism, oceanic feelings helped to generate the pastoral haze which obscured the rise of industrial capitalism; they also incorporated temporary, revitalizing respites from achievement. They reinforced accommodation as well as protest.[58]

Collectivism, the "cooperative commonwealth," and antimodernism were not only the three major types of intellectual response to industrialism. Each has a direct bearing on Du Bois's political thought. His views on black culture certainly reflected the tracings of an antimodernist tension, and his substantive view of socialism was very much influenced by the cooperative commonwealth. Most of all, Du Bois's thought was formed in the great cauldron of collectivist ideas in the last two decades of the nineteenth century and the first decade or two of the twentieth. He was very much a man of his time; as I shall show in the remainder of this study, he approached all his intellectual and practical activity throughout the course of his career from a vantage point heavily conditioned by a distinctive commitment to collectivist and related assumptions.

The Philadelphia Negro and the Consolidation of a Worldview

The Philadelphia Negro and the Social-Scientific Ideal

THE PHILADELPHIA STUDY demands the attention of those concerned with Du Bois's political thought for several reasons. It is practically a commonplace at this point to refer to the place of Du Bois's study in the history of American sociology.[1] In that sense *The Philadelphia Negro* is important because it helps to disclose aspects of Du Bois's early attitudes about sociological knowledge, its nature and purposes, and the relation between knowledge and action. His work in Philadelphia also, since it represents his first systematic confrontation of the structures of Afro-American existence, is significant as an indicator of his early thinking about Afro-American life. Consideration of the assumptions that he brought to the investigation and the findings that he constructed helps locate Du Bois's thinking in relation to that of his contemporaries and suggests themes and attitudes that recur or are elaborated in his later work. The Philadelphia study in fact lays out core themes and perspectives that persisted through the remainder of his life. Finally, the idea that such a study should be commissioned in the first place originated from the social ideology prominent among liberal-progressivist reformers of the time. The fact, therefore, that Du Bois was selected to conduct the research is significant; *The Philadelphia Negro* is the major artifact of Du Bois's dialogue with both social-scientific and reform ideas and movements at the turn of the century.

Philadelphia in the 1890s was held widely to be a political-machine town of first-order disrepute in which the bugbears of graft and corruption that so disturbed the sensibilities of middle-class citizens abounded. In a fit of reform the University of Pennsylvania and Professor Samuel McCune Lindsay were charged with documenting the extent to which "the corrupt, semi-criminal vote of the Negro Seventh Ward" was the engine that propelled the machine.[2] Du Bois, who says that he was unaware of and uninterested in "the theory back of the plan of this study of Negroes,"[3] leaped at the opportunity to engage in the meat of scientific sociological research.

The Philadelphia study provided Du Bois with an opportunity to follow his heartfelt desire "to put science into sociology"[4] by generating factual data to discipline discussion within the field, and, moreover, he shared with the reformers a concern with what both he and they perceived to be a certain moral laxity and softness of character that existed within the black community. The "Creed" of the American Negro Academy, in whose organization Du Bois was involved during the time he worked on the Philadelphia study, maintained that the first and greatest step toward settlement of black-white friction lay in "correction of the immorality, crime and laziness among the Negroes themselves."[5] The young sociologist would agree with reformers that undesirable traits existed within elements of Philadelphia's black population. Unlike impatient liberals, however, he would go on to seek to identify the "removable causes" of those traits and to demonstrate that they were characteristic only to a certain segment of the population and by no means were endemic to Philadelphia blacks as a whole.[6]

Thus Du Bois's intellectual orientation made him an attractive candidate to direct the study in the eyes not only of McCune Lindsay but also of Susan P. Wharton, a prominent member of the Executive Committee of the Philadelphia College Settlement. Wharton in fact played a major role in bringing Du Bois to Philadelphia.[7] The Wharton connection underscores the sense in which *The Philadelphia Negro* is an example of the union of social science and reform ideology.

The Philadelphia Negro proceeds from a definite view of proper urban social organization. This view suffuses the study and serves as a model according to which the black Philadelphia population is analyzed. The model, not unexpectedly, reflects the norms of turn-of-the-century middle-class propriety. The strengths of Philadelphia's black community are seen as those of its characteristics that most approximate the model of bourgeois convention; the weaknesses that Du Bois identifies are those characteristics that most flaunt the conventional model. Broadly speaking, this model emphasizes, among other things: (1) monogamous nuclear family organization; (2) temperance and orderliness as behavioral principles, including thrift and internalization of disciplined work habits; (3) favorable disposition toward formal education and training in the ways of urban civilization; and (4) legitimation of class hierarchy within the racial community. These elementary values are stated explicitly or are strongly implied in Du Bois's text, and his analysis of black Philadelphians in their light provides insights to his view of the world at the time.

Family organization figures prominently in Du Bois's concern, which is that of the scholar as social activist, and his approach typifies the "social problems" research orientation that has organized a strain of sociological inquiry throughout the history of American sociology.[8] Moreover, the family specifically was becoming a matter of growing interest among progressive reformers, largely because of their concern with Americanization of immigrant populations; social science was mobilized to assist in the noble cause, and the family appeared as weak link and unavoidable obstacle in the chain of socialization which had to be adjusted to modern American conditions.[9] Du Bois shared his contemporaries' concern with the family as the hub of social life and sought in his study to identify "weaknesses" in black family structure and to suggest appropriate remedial action. His commitment to demonstrating the Negro's equality also impelled him to laud the black family's strengths when appropriate.

Having identified a "low condition of morals" which had persisted as a serious problem—although one that was only to have been expected in its origins among a "barbarous people forced to labor in a strange land"—within certain strata of the black population in Philadelphia, Du Bois then set out to locate the sources of that problem.[10] One that he identified lay in the disproportion of women to men in black Philadelphia. This disproportion, he contended, led to illegitimate birth—a condition whose stigma he presumed—and "an unhealthy tone in much of the social intercourse among the middle class of the Negro population."[11] He noted a tendency toward casual sexual involvement and was disturbed that the "lax moral habits of the slave regime still show themselves in a large amount of cohabitation without marriage."[12]

The immediate socioeconomic basis for this phenomenon did not escape Du Bois; for he cited the dislocation accompanying the migration experience and black males' chronic inability to earn enough money to support a family as pressures that disposed toward the unstable coupling and uncoupling patterns that he observed. On the one side, urban loneliness could prompt youths to "thoughtlessly marry"; on the other hand, once marriage proved not to allow the wife's withdrawal from the labor force, pressures toward dissolution of the union were likely to mount. These circumstances, combined with the migrants' lingering orientation to a casual morality, made desertion, separation, and divorce all too common, as was indicated by the proportion of all charity aimed at blacks that was requested to alleviate the conditions spawned by broken households.[13]

Although he observed that this moral easiness tainted the entire community in some degree, he made it clear that the problem did not permeate the population at all levels. Principally affected were the "masses" of working people, whom he characterized as "willing, honest and good-natured; but . . . careless, unreliable and unsteady,"[14] and the "lowest class of recent migrants and other unfortunates" who were "absolutely without social standing" among the vast majority.[15] For this underclass of loafers Du Bois had little sympathy; he saw them as the "dregs which indicate the former history and dangerous tendencies of the masses."[16] While he strove to identify structural bases for loose family bonding and cohabitation among the masses of working blacks and suggested possibilities for remediation, of the loafers he noted only that they are "absolutely without home life" and implied that their promiscuity was intrinsic to their class and irremediable.[17] He found their easy lifestyle so repugnant as simply to wish it swept away, and he indicated thereby the breadth and depth—at least in his estimation—of stratification in the black community. He not only showed the "aristocratic" and middle working strata to have different, more appropriate family structures; he also perceived the former strata to have certain exemplary responsibilities toward the rest of the community, excluding the dregs, of course.

He identified the "widespread custom of seeking amusement outside the home" as a threat to the development of stable family and community life.[18] This custom he felt to be "of no particular moment" when practiced by "the richer and more ostentatious," but he was troubled that the tendency toward partaking of public entertainments would "set an example to the masses which may be misleading."[19] Du Bois's reasons are made clear in a statement that equally illustrates the relation that he believed should pertain between the different strata of the black community: "The mass of the Negro people must be taught sacredly to guard the home to make it the centre of social life and moral guardianship. Thus it is largely among the best class of Negroes, but it might be made even more conspicuously so than it is."[20]

Du Bois's views on the family reflect the peculiar situation of a black progressive intellectual in turn-of-the-century American culture. On the one hand, the desire to safeguard the family by eschewing external entertainments can be seen as—and indeed Du Bois argued for it in these terms—an attempt to stabilize community life to provide a rudder for an increasing urban population. In this context the family was to Du Bois a more effective institutional foundation for the community than the church, which he saw as the family's principal rival for associational commitment. The church ultimately was linked to residues of the "tribal system" and therefore was inappropriate for satisfaction of the organizational requirements of a modern urban community. Therefore, Du Bois maintained that the increased emphasis on family life that he recommended "undoubtedly means the decreased influence of the Negro church, and that is a desirable thing."[21] The exhortation to shore up family life, then, is in this sense an expression of Du Bois's commitment to cultural evolution and progress.[22] On the other hand, Du Bois was defending the family—it should be understood that he meant specifically the family in its monogamous, nuclear form—in part against the centrifugal pressures associated with urban life. It was not only the church that drew people away from the home, but the family suffered also in the face of "hall concerts" and "elaborate parties" in addition to saloons and other haunts.[23] Moreover, it was not merely the nuclear family that suffered. The lure of outside entertainments weakened the organic community in which the nuclear family remained encompassed once it has been cut away from its extended bondings; for, as Du Bois pointed out, "simple neighborhood gatherings and visits" also diminished in significance.[24] The family was to be protected against the atomizing depredations and excesses of urban civilization.

There is a troubling ambivalence here. Du Bois posited the family as a requirement for development of the stable organization of social life needed to permit the Negro to ascend the "scale of civilization." However, this family form had to be instituted, as a matter of conscious social action, at a time when the nuclear model, as well as the "homely virtues of honesty, truth and chastity"[25] with which the Victorian bourgeois model had made its mark, were losing their historical foundation and legitimacy—even among Du Bois's progressive contemporaries.[26] Du Bois appears to have been aware that the family form that he recommended for black progress was elsewhere a drag on progress; he was a consistent supporter of the principle of gender equality. His ambivalence, however, mirrors the position of the Afro-American population at the time. As the era of corporate consolidation opened, blacks had not yet begun to participate in small-scale capitalist accumulation and the elaboration of classically bourgeois institutions. Du Bois, unlike spokesmen who ignored the historical thrust, observed that the economic foundations of the entrepreneurial social order had been superseded by large-scale capitalism.[27] Nevertheless, without an effective critique of industrial capitalism's organization of life or an alternative vision of social relations, Du Bois was forced to uphold the orthodox institutional model characteristic to the entrepreneurial order as the base from which to develop a productive, stable community infrastructure among Afro-Americans.[28] Moreover, like many of his contemporaries he identified corporate collectivization with Progress while at the same time rejecting the social ills with which this collectivization was organically connected. A consequence was that he often tended to oscillate between romanticization of folklife and exaltation of the ideologies of social rationalization, including social engineering. This tension can be seen in the essays comprising *The Souls of Black Folk*, and Du Bois reveals it perhaps most clearly during the prewar era in the ambivalent reaction of Blessed, the largely autobiographical hero of his first melodramatic novel, to the gradual civilization of Zora, the "heathen hoyden" folk girl with whom Blessed is involved in the rural South.[29]

Notwithstanding his wistfulness about folk culture, Du Bois considered the Negro character generally to be in need of substantial "uplift," to use the term of the day. This need was demonstrated in various facets of black life besides the problem of weak family structure. Du Bois observed, for example, that poor—as distinct from "very poor"—black families tended to be "inefficient, unfortunate, and improvident."[30] More than efficiency had, in his view, to be taught, however; he noted that "in habits of personal cleanliness and taking proper food and exercise, the colored people are woefully deficient."[31] Eating habits could stand improvement, as well as could general household organization benefit from training in efficiency. Nor were these undesirable traits entirely restricted to the poor; they even fettered and distorted blacks' attempts to lift themselves from an undesirable condition. He noted that "[t]he tendency of the classes who are just struggling out of extreme poverty is to stint themselves for food in order to have better looking homes; thus the rent in too many cases eats up physical nourishment."[32]

Nevertheless, despite the persistence of these traits Du Bois did not see them as intrinsic to the race, a view which was one of the "misconceptions" that his study intended to correct. Instead he was careful to identify the historical and environmental origins of the undesirable characteristics:

> Here then we have two great causes for the present condition of the Negro: Slavery and emancipation with their attendant phenomena of ignorance, lack of discipline, and moral weakness; immigration with its increased competition and moral influence. To this must be added a third as great—possibly even greater in influence than the other two, namely the environment in which a Negro finds himself—the world of custom and thought in which he must live and work, the physical surrounding of house and home and yard, the moral encouragements and discouragements which he encounters.[33]

The combination of the slave experience, the cavalier way in which emancipation had been conducted and the pressures of the urban environment gave vent to the various weaknesses among Du Bois's black Philadelphians. These weaknesses, at the same time, were symptoms of the ultimate failing in the black community. This failing, that area in which "the Negro shows his greatest deficiency" and which was "the one hardest for the freedman to learn" was in the "art of organization."[34] Organization, which Sheldon Wolin considers a key theme in contemporary western political thought,[35] figures prominently in Du Bois's assessment not only of the black condition but also of social life in general. For the Afro-American to be deficient in organization was a serious matter because "[t]he real test . . . of the advance of any group of people in civilization is the extent to which they are able to organize and systematize their efforts for the common weal; and the highest expression of organized life is the organization for purely benevolent and reformatory purpose."[36]

The weakness in organization was evident in a number of instances of Afro-American group life, and the signs among the general population of "lack of discipline"[37] or of "parents untrained for their responsibilities"[38] or of lack in "foresight and forehandedness, and in 'push' "[39] indicated a need for conscious organization and guidance of the community so as to counteract the ultimate consequences of poor organization—crime and general corruption. Crime, to Du Bois, constituted "the open rebellion of an individual against his social environment."[40] Indeed, he traced criminal activity to "lack of harmony with social surroundings."[41] The unsettling influence of the migration experience, unfair limitations on opportunities for social and economic advancement, crowded and otherwise undesirable living conditions—all combined with the historical tendencies toward disorganization and improbity to form an environment in which criminal activity was a predictable occurrence.

Du Bois took care, naturally enough, to distinguish his point about pressures toward black criminality from currently popular interpretations that linked criminality to biological characteristics.[42] For the apostle of scientific sociology and committed racial advocate, environmental and historical factors lay at the source of the embarrassing fact of a black crime rate that was significantly higher than the general population's. However, notwithstanding blacks' greater likelihood to be arrested when innocent of any crime or when having committed minor offenses for which whites might not be arrested, Du Bois underscored the personal dimension of criminal behavior and tied the latter to his perception of historically ingrained characterological weakness. Emphasizing personal responsibility also helped Du Bois to avoid the pitfalls of a facile social determinism that was in later years to become the bane of black intellectuals.[43] In this regard he maintained that education, or the elimination of illiteracy, by itself would not solve the problem of black crime, an assertion that was backed by what appeared to be the increasing intelligence of black criminals.[44] However, the responsibility was not only individual; the race, even though "consciously and intentionally wronged," had an obligation to reform itself as a group to act in accord with demands made upon it by "members of a civilized community." Meeting this racial obligation for group rehabilitation—and this is in part what distinguished Du Bois from Booker T. Washington—also required demanding the institutional wherewithal to effect self-development, but organization for reform was nonetheless a critical vehicle for improvement of the black condition.[45] Not only formal education and training were required to better the black Philadelphian, but considerable doses of character instruction were needed as well. Without this tutelage even political participation—the remedy with which Du Bois's name is so often identified—would turn sour and reinforce the group's negative qualities.

Du Bois observed that suffrage had produced mixed indications of black Philadelphians' capacity to employ the tools of popular government. Vote selling, patronage, and blind allegiance to party label—the cardinal electoral vices in the eyes of progressive reformers—abounded among blacks in Philadelphia, to Du Bois's dismay.[46] Added to these problems was a brazen assumption among many at all levels of the community that the purpose of political activity should be to generate or secure a job for oneself.[47] However, the black experience with the franchise hardly was to be seen as a failure; for he noted in a statement that also indicates his substantive political preferences:

> At the same time the Negro has never sought to use his ballot to menace civilization or even the established principles of this government. . . . Instead of being radical light-headed followers of every new political panacea the freedmen of Philadelphia and of the nation have always formed the most conservative element in our political life and have steadfastly opposed the schemes of inflationists, socialists and dreamers.[48]

The lack of discipline and temperateness which were manifest to Du Bois indicated that the group needed to be organized to overcome its bad traits, those residues of bucolic life and by-products of oppression that adversely affected black integration into urban civilization. However, organization for its own sake was no panacea for the race's problems; the group was to be organized to be led down the correct path for its future. That path did not, as Du Bois's statement about "inflationists, socialists and dreamers" made clear, enter the terrain of general social reorganization; nor did it make any demands upon the social context in which the Philadelphia black community found itself other than that specifically racial barriers to opportunity be removed. Rather, the purpose of organization in Du Bois's eyes was to assist in effecting the adjustment of the race to a social environment from whose hegemony he was not exempt. He quickly decided that the group as a whole needed tutelage and preparation for modern civilization, and nearly as quickly he decided upon the "better classes" of the Negro community as the historical agency responsible for carrying out the mission of organization and tutelage.

Despite occasional utterances that acknowledged exploitative behavior on the part of the wealthy and powerful, Du Bois accepted the capitalist division of labor and its accompanying system of social hierarchy as given. He talked of the dignity and necessity of domestic service,[49] and with a condescension that carries tones of the feudum he assured that "even a Negro bootblack could black boots better if he knew he was a menial not because he was a Negro but because he was best fitted for that work."[50] Similarly, he proclaimed that the American employing class of his day, although "not . . . wholly philanthropic" possessed "the best average intelligence and morality of the community."[51] In this observation Du Bois only stated an assumption that was held by progressives generally—even, sometimes ambivalently, by the radical dreamers. At any rate, acceptance of the prevailing dynamic of capitalist organization left him little better equipped than his contemporaries to perceive its dependence on tragic human consequences.

A clear demonstration of this problem is provided by his comments on the Midvale Steel Works in a section that was then outside Philadelphia.[52] He abstracts management's comparatively enlightened racial policies from the overall work context in this plant which was the site of Frederick Winslow Taylor's highly publicized initial experiments at industrial engineering and "scientific management." Those experiments figured prominently in the regimentation and standardization of the American labor force and the consolidation of management control over the production process.[53] Still, the point is not so much that Du Bois's automatic commitment to the current social order prevented him from developing a critique of scientific management; few if any of his intellectual contemporaries maintained such a critique, and overwhelmingly they were enthusiastic supporters—Du Bois among them—of what purported to be the application of scientific principles to work organization. What distinguishes Du Bois's discussion of Midvale is that he gives no indication of being aware that Taylor's experiments had gone on there only a few years earlier and with a good deal of publicity. His restricted focus on adjustment of the black community to its institutional surroundings may have led Du Bois to overlook completely this interesting coincidence of racial liberalism and Taylorization. However, it is in his proposals for the training and guidance of the black population—including explicit and implicit identification of who should be responsible for that training and guidance—that Du Bois most exemplifies his adherence to progressivist intellectual conventions.

Though he was emphatic that the race's future lay in education and training for growth in addition to unity and organization, in his Philadelphia study Du Bois did not provide a detailed view of the focus that he would give that training. Bemoaning the circumstance that "no benevolent despot, no philanthropist, no far-seeing captain of industry" had been available to provide or was interested in providing industrial training to compensate for competition from whites in masonry and related trades, Du Bois recounted the loss of blacks' position in Philadelphia's artisanry market.[54] He noted as well that discrimination forced into domestic service numbers of blacks who had no facility for those professions, but who either were failures or looking for something better to come along. He pointed out that if discrimination were overcome, "there would have been room for a second movement, namely, for training schools which would fit the mass of Negro and white domestic servants for their complicated and important duties."[55] Training should be geared to employment, the inadequacies of opportunities for which Du Bois saw at the root of many other black problems; therefore, as a matter of priority, "the object of social reform should be so to diversify Negro employment as to afford proper escape from menial employment for the talented few, and so as to allow the mass some choice in their lifework."[56] Beyond these comments, which provide more a sense of general orientation and tone than substance, Du Bois said little in *The Philadelphia Negro* about the specifics of the training that he recommended. However, in an essay published some four years after the Philadelphia study he made more explicit remarks.[57]

Training the people, Du Bois indicated, must begin with training those who will train them. "The very first step toward the settlement of the Negro problem," he declared, "is the spread of intelligence," which in turn required the spread of free public schools and, by extension, colleges.[58] He did not hold general intelligence, though, to constitute a sufficient definition of the training mission. Specific skills for employment also needed to be taught, and of course, those values in which the black masses had been found to be deficient also needed shoring up by the racial training program.[59] Indeed, intelligence and skill were not enough to uplift the black population; also required was instruction in that "combination of homely habits and virtues which we may loosely call thrift."[60]

So far as the method for advancement of the race was concerned, therefore, Du Bois presented the following brushstroke: "What is the remedy? Intelligence—not simply the ability to read and write or sew—but the intelligence of a society permeated by that larger vision of life and broader tolerance which are fostered by the college and university. Not all men must be college-bred, but some men, black and white, must be, to leaven the ideals of the lump."[61] Therein is embedded the agency appropriate to undertake this program of training for transformation. Du Bois's faith in education and training necessarily implied faith in the educated and trained, and the latter, the Talented Tenth with whom Du Bois so often is identified, occupied a more significant place in his early work than is apparent in what has become by now a banal identification. From the outset Du Bois was motivated by a desire to distinguish conceptually and ideologically an elite stratum within the black community and to articulate a social agenda for that elite. At the very beginning of the study Du Bois cautions that "every group has its upper class, it may be numerically small and socially of little weight, and yet its study is necessary to the comprehension of the whole—it forms the realized ideal of the group, and as it is true that a nation must to some extent be measured by its slums, it is also true that it can only be understood and finally judged by its upper class."[62]

One of the tasks that Du Bois set for himself was to document the existence of this "best class of Philadelphia Negroes . . . who constitute the aristocracy of the race" and who were often "forgotten or ignored" when considering the black population of Philadelphia.[63] Much later in the exposition he again deplored the general tendency in the community to see the black population as "one practically homogeneous mass," and, while allowing that some broad cultural and historical justification might exist for this blurring of social vision, he felt obliged to note that "wide variations in antecedents, wealth, intelligence and general efficiency have already been differentiated within this group."[64] Moreover, it was not only he, the social scientist, who was displeased with the popular failure to discern the variegations of the black community. "Nothing more exasperates the better class of Negroes," Du Bois confided, "than this tendency to ignore utterly their existence."[65] To rectify the oversight and to assuage the sensibilities of the overlooked, he then proceeded to define the four classes or "Grades" that he perceived to populate black Philadelphia:

> Grade 1. Families of undoubted respectability earning sufficient income to live well; not engaged in menial service of any kind; the wife engaged in no occupation save that of house-wife, except in a few cases where she had special employment at home. The children not compelled to be bread-winners, but found in school; the family living in a well-kept home.
>
> Grade 2. The respectable working-class; in comfortable circumstances, with a good home, and having steady remunerative work. The younger children in school.
>
> Grade 3. The poor; persons not earning enough to keep them at all times above want; honest, although not always energetic or thrifty, and with no touch of gross immorality or crime. Including the very poor, and the poor.
>
> Grade 4. The lowest class of criminals, prostitutes and loafers; the "submerged tenth."[66]

The distinction of these strata was not to be taken lightly. For the lowest stratum Du Bois had no sympathy and was disturbed that segregated housing patterns too often made it impossible for the "better classes" to escape proximity to this "criminal class." To relieve the upright community of the burden of that lowest class, he advocated slum clearance, a project that he likened to cleaning a cesspool; he did intimate, however, that one first should know "where the refuse can be disposed of without general harm."[67] Indeed, he did not seek democratic social intercourse for the black community across class lines; one of his concerns about what he perceived to be the surplus of women in the black population was that, in addition to the strains it forced onto general morality, that situation led to "lowering the standard of admission to certain circles, and often gives one the impression that the social level of the women is higher than the level of the men."[68]

When Du Bois spoke of class, he referred not so much to groups defined on the basis of their relation to the process of social production. Nor did he have in mind groups aggregated principally on the basis of income or any other readily identifiable characteristics. Rather, his view of class was an amalgam of behavioral criteria and morals, beliefs, and sentiments. What separated the classes in the black community was more than anything else the variation in their behavioral and attitudinal responses to the social order of urban capitalism. That a behavioral criterion was primary for Du Bois's categorization, however, reflects the structure of the community as well as the Victorian ideal of gentility. Income variation by and large was not that great, as employment opportunities were restricted. Therefore, the distinctions among the population tended to be most pronounced in such spheres as "push," "drive," constancy, and refinement. Education, of course, was another yardstick, but even here the differences could not be very great because higher education was uncommon even for the higher status families. Nevertheless, this is not to suggest that these distinctions were either artificial or without meaning. The type of differentiation proposed by Du Bois indicates the priorities and self-perceptions of the developing elite within the black community as well as Du Bois's commitment to that elite as the natural leadership and highest expression of the aspirations of the race. Like Frazier over twenty years later,[69] Du Bois determined that the "best Negro families,"[70] which together constituted what he perceived to be the "germ of the great middle class,"[71] should be responsible for providing instruction, models of behavior, and a social agenda for the rest of the population. He decided that this stratum was that by which the race should be judged because the elite represented the possibilities of the Negro, the attributes and station to which others in the group should aspire.[72]

Du Bois understood that the members of the turn-of-the-century urban black elite were "not to be sure people of wide culture and [that] their mental horizon is as limited as that of the first families in a country town."[73] He determined that they nevertheless constituted an "aristocracy" of the race and as such should not only enjoy their status but also, like any aristocracy, had obligations to their people. A problem, however, was that the elite forgot that "the first duty of an upper class is to serve the lower classes."[74] In part this problem ensued, so Du Bois felt, from the circumstance that the Negro's development had not been autonomous. The appropriate patterns of interaction and mutual obligation had not taken hold among the various black strata because of the way in which the Afro-American social structure was mediated by the larger society. Therefore, even though the elite formed an "aristocracy of their own people with all the responsibilities of an aristocracy, . . . they, on the one hand, are not prepared for this role, and their own masses are not used to looking to them for leadership."[75] In an extraordinarily revealing passage Du Bois linked the retardation of development of institutionalized role relationships among the race's strata to the inappropriateness of democracy as a social form at that stage of Afro-American development: "If the Negroes were by themselves either a strong aristocratic system or a dictatorship would for the present prevail. With, however, democracy thus prematurely thrust upon them, the first impulse of the best, the wisest and richest is to segregate themselves from the mass."[76] Just as he saw this impulse to intraracial segregation as natural enough, Du Bois maintained that whites' tendency to lump all blacks together produced an unhealthy reaction among aristocratic blacks who felt the need to distinguish themselves from the mass. The black upper class, therefore, in order to avoid the indignity of being mistaken for servants refused to take leadership of the race and even shrank "from the free and easy worship of most of the Negro churches . . . and . . . from all such display of publicity as [would] expose them to the veiled insult and depreciation which the masses [suffered]."[77]

That Du Bois construed this particular circumstance to be a major problem of black life is instructive and portentous of his subsequent development. His perception that "premature" participation in certain aspects of American society was dysfunctional opened the possibility of a call to close ranks within the race and to insulate it institutionally from the dominant society, if only in a limited way for the purposes of survival and incubation of institutional structures vital for the race's development. Repeatedly over the following years, most dramatically during the Depression, when his advocacy of racial-group economic co-operativism contributed to his demise at the NAACP, Du Bois would advocate precisely such a position. Already at the turn of the century he had decided that black advancement would be enhanced by a period that combined insulation of the community from aspects of the society as a whole with institutionalization of a regime of preparatory tutelage, organized and administered by the race's aristocracy and aimed at inculcating in the masses the values and techniques appropriate for urban industrial civilization. Throughout Du Bois's career the related principles of insulation and tutelage recur even as the specific purposes for them vary. His commitment to these two principles indicates his fundamental adherence to a view of the Afro-American population as a more or less backward mass which had to be molded organizationally for modern life.

Running through both his advocacy of insulation and tutelage of the race and his concern that whites acknowledge the differentiation of the black community is his commitment to what he perceived to be the elite among the black population. The community needed to be insulated to some extent so that the elite's program of uplift could take shape and be implemented. White acknowledgement of the existence of stratification was important not only because white legitimation would encourage the black aristocracy to perform its historical mission but also because the aristocracy deserved special acknowledgement on the basis of talents, accomplishments, and character. This commitment to a view of social organization built upon elite-orchestrated movement toward progress also remained constant through Du Bois's life, in both the national and international spheres. This is hardly a startling observation, since elitism is associated with Du Bois's name as frequently as are Pan-Africanism and protest, if not more so. What is important here, though, is that the characteristics of his elitist commitment be made concrete and grounded conceptually and historically.

One of the interesting aspects of Du Bois's early intellectual work, in fact, is the manner in which his evolutionism and his adherence to prevailing notions of racial group ideals combined to lay the basis for, or to reinforce, his commitment to consolidation of a historical agenda for the nascent black elite.

Du Bois's early notions of race suggest echoes of Herbert Spencer's pacific evolutionism and bear a family resemblance to Lester F. Ward's "social karyokinesis"—the process of nationbuilding through a cycle of conquest, subjugation, caste, noncaste inequality, replacement of military subjugation with a system of law and right, state formation, forging of the population into a coherent people, and the rise of patriotism and appearance of a nation.[78] Du Bois defined a race as "[a] vast family of human beings, generally of common blood and language, always of common history, traditions and impulses, who are both voluntarily and involuntarily striving together for the accomplishment of certain more or less vividly conceived ideals of life."[79] Although he shared with Ward's reform-Darwinist teleology the view that racial evolution was progressing toward a united world, for him the end often seemed to be more pluralist than assimilationist. Du Bois, like most of his contemporaries, at that point saw race as a central and unalterable force in human society. There was no doubt, he maintained, as to the "universal prevalence of the race idea, the race spirit, the race ideal, and as to its efficiency as the vastest and most ingenious invention for human progress."[80] The united world, while bound by the universalization of civilization, would be more harmonic than homogeneous.

Presaging the "cultural nationalism" with which he later was to be identified,[81] he emphasized cultural and historical factors over biological and phenotypic ones in accounting for racial differences and continuities. "The deeper differences," he averred, "are spiritual, psychical differences—undoubtedly based on the physical but infinitely transcending them."[82] He then elaborated a notion of "national character" by articulating what he contended were pivotal elements of the racial/national character of various groups, each of which in its own way strives to develop "for civilization its particular message, its particular ideal, which shall help to guide the world nearer and nearer that perfection of human life for which we all long."[83]

Within this scenario of racial-group idealism, blacks had not yet given their full message, and, moreover, if that message were to be given, a precondition would have to be that the race unite. For development of higher culture and refinement of spirit, Du Bois maintained, "only Negroes bound and welded together, Negroes inspired by one vast ideal, can work out in its fullness the great message we have for humanity."[84] Of course, such unity could not exist without organization, and to that end he proposed a recomposition of the black community under the leadership of an elite of social engineers. Among other organizations required to express the race's message, the Negro needed, according to Du Bois, an "intellectual clearinghouse, for all those products of the Negro mind, which we may call a Negro Academy."[85] The purposes envisaged for this academy were to unite and lead blacks, for the academy "aims at once to be the epitome and expression of the intellect of the black-blooded people of America, the exponent of the race ideals of one of the world's great races."[86] In spite of the fact, though, that the Academy was to be "(a) Representative in character, (b) Impartial in conduct, (c) Firm in Leadership," it was to represent not "all interests or all factions . . . but the best thought, the most unselfish striving and the highest ideals."[87]

This recommendation, that intellectuals take over stewardship of the race, suggests a link between the reform-Darwinist fascination with expertise and the developing collectivist focus on social engineering. The outcome in either case was legitimation of an expanded, managerial role for intellectuals in American society, and Du Bois was equally at home with either vantage point, as well as their shared implication. Du Bois's scientific interests led him just as naturally to the need to consolidate the influence of intellectuals and other members of the germinal elite. In an article published shortly before *The Philadelphia Negro* he threw down the gantlet to the ministerial spokesmen whom he perceived to be carryovers from an earlier, less sophisticated day. Du Bois expected that they should yield their privileged place in group affairs to trained, secular intellectuals: "I now wish to insist that the time has come when the activities of the Negro church must become differentiated and when it must surrender to the school and the home, and social organizations, those functions in a day of organic poverty it so heroically sought to bear. . . . Upon the school and the home must rest the burden for furnishing amusements for Negro youth."[88]

So Du Bois stood at the turn of the twentieth century, with a commitment to social-scientific progressivism and on the verge of being caught in the tug-of-war between the poles of his own epistemological orientation, the tension between the competing practical imperatives implied in his call for systematic study of the Afro-American community: advancement of "scientific knowledge and social reform."[89] In chapter 4 I shall examine the eruption and resolution of this tension as an intellectual and ideological phenomenon. However, his various oscillations and manifold interests notwithstanding, certain core principles of Du Bois's thought—the faith in science, reason and expertise, and a corollary, fundamental assumption of the efficacy and propriety of an elite-driven model of social life—were set. In this respect the remainder of his career can be seen as modifying and elaborating these principles through changing historical circumstances. Nor does that appear an unseemly corralling of intellectual growth; after all, *The Philadelphia Negro* appeared when its author was thirty-one years old. His association with a variant of socialism, his move into political activism and opposition to imperialism all, as I shall argue in subsequent chapters, retain the premises of the liberal collectivist paradigm, adjusting and extending them through personal intellectual maturation and confrontation of particular historical conditions.

Science and Progress

The Unity of Scholarship and Activism

Du Bois's CAREER can be read from one vantage point as a series of oscilla-tions between scholarly pursuit and social activism. Such a reading would be suggested by reflection on his movement, after thirteen years on the Atlanta University faculty, to the NAACP for nearly two and one-half decades, then back to Atlanta University for ten years and then back to the NAACP. Furthermore, within his writings scholarly detachment and a hortatory posture often coexist even in a single text.[1] His simultaneous commitments to scholarship and activ-ism might appear unusual or even contradictory in an era when ideological conventions and a de facto division of intellectual labor assign the two categories to quite distinct spheres and agencies. However, in the cultural and intellectual milieux in which Du Bois undertook his career, a different set of conventions governed the relationship between academic and temporal activity. Scholars showed little reluctance to intervene in practical affairs, and professionalistic ideologies had not yet hardened the boundaries separating proper academic en-deavor and social or political engagement.

For Du Bois the bases of that orientation are visible in his views on science and the purpose of knowledge; in this chapter I shall demonstrate how those views led him to a normative presumption of the unity of scholarship and activ-ism. Moreover, not only was that presumption immanent in Du Bois's work from the beginning of his career, but it also illuminates a link between his attitudes on science and knowledge and his well-known conceptions of the nature and functions of race leadership.

On completion of his work at the University of Pennsylvania, Du Bois took what was to become a fateful step by moving in 1897 to Atlanta, where he had been hired by Atlanta University to "take charge of the work in sociology, and of the new conferences which they were inaugurating on the Negro problem."[2] Still imbued with his sense of a mission to rectify racial misconceptions by means of enlightenment, he saw an excellent opportunity to take off full tilt on his chosen course. Moreover, going back to his days at Fisk University in Nashville, when he had taught in rural Tennessee during the summer, Du Bois felt a call to participate in the education of those black young people who were fit by their talents for academic pursuits.[3] The thirteen years that he spent at Atlanta constituted perhaps his most fertile period as an empirical social scientist, and the series of monographs published under his direction there were the first attempts at comprehensive study of Afro-American life.[4]

Du Bois assumed his faculty position at Atlanta University with three objectives that were, characteristically, not altogether modest.[5] His expectation was that his work would be able (1) to expand the boundaries of sociological inquiry, (2) to document the Negro, and (3) to assist in training the black intellectual elite, which he felt to be the necessary motor for advancement of the race. These objectives were mutually reinforcing. The study of the black community was to provide, in Du Bois's view, a basis for expanding the boundaries of the field;[6] scientific knowledge stood as an aid to blacks as a tool of social reform and enlightenment,[7] and what became the "Talented Tenth," if it were to lead properly, would have to be trained in the laws and principles of social organization and would need to be equipped with scientific information about the black community and the world at large.[8] The undergirding principle of his work at Atlanta University, though, was his high valuation of science, as he demonstrated in his wholeheartedly positivistic approach to sociology.[9]

For Du Bois sociology was exclusively a positivist discipline. He characterized the field as the "science that studies the actions of human beings and seeks laws and regularities among those actions"[10] and as "the science that seeks to measure the limits of chance in human action."[11] His concern, furthermore, was with unification of "theory and practice," both within the sociological field—for which he defined this unification as the crucial task of the first half of the twentieth century[12]—and between the findings of social science research and social decision making. His reflections, as contained in his 1940 volume *Dusk of Dawn*, on the intellectual milieu that prevailed in the social sciences when he undertook the Atlanta enterprise are instructive in this regard. After noting the then greatly constraining "difficulties of applying scientific law and discovering cause and effect in the social world,"[13] he observed:

> Social thinkers were engaged in vague statements and were seeking to lay down the methods by which in some not too distant future, social law analogous to physical law would be discovered. Herbert Spencer finished his ten volumes of

Synthetic Philosophy in 1896. The biological analogy, the vast generalizations, were striking, but actual scientific accomplishment lagged. For me an opportunity seemed to present itself. I could not lull my mind to hypnosis by regarding a phrase like "consciousness of kind" as a scientific law. By turning my gaze from fruitless word-twisting and facing the facts of my own social situation and racial world, I determined to put science into sociology through a study of the conditions and problems of my own group.[14]

He continued:

I was going to study the facts, any and all facts, concerning the American Negro and his plight, and by measurement and comparison and research, work up to any valid generalizations which I could. primarily with the utilization object of reform and uplift; but nevertheless, I wanted to do the work with scientific accuracy. Thus, in my own sociology, because of firm belief in a changing racial group, I easily grasped the idea of a changing developing society rather than a fixed social structure.[15]

These comments indicate that Du Bois was not—at least by his later years—insensitive to some concerns of the sociology of knowledge, but they also affirm Arthur L. Johnson's claim that Du Bois at the turn of the century was "in complete agreement with the new trend of sociological thinking at that time . . . which emphasized . . . change and process as characterizing the nature of society."[16] A problem, though, is that a disjunction exists between what Du Bois held to be the focus of scientific activity and his stated commitment to a model of a "changing developing society." The search for laws and regularities closes off the ends of inquiry in a way that implies an epistemic bias against social dynamism.[17] For Du Bois, however, as for many of his contemporaries, this tension was bridged by a call to activism, by definition of the teleological purposes of scientific inquiry so as to include explicitly its mobilization in service to the universal social goals of progress and reform.

Elliott M. Rudwick notes that Du Bois, especially early in his career, shared the "faith of an important segment of America's social scientists that knowledge would lead to the solution of social problems."[18] Indeed, four broad intellectual "schools" or approaches organized patterns of discourse within the nascent social sciences during those years, and beneath each lay a pair of related "background assumptions"—that certainty is both realizable and desirable as a goal around which to organize the pursuit of knowledge, and that attainment of such certain knowledge provides a necessary basis for ensuring social progress.[19] On the one hand, Social Darwinism—at least in its "reform" version—and German rationalist historicism beckoned with their neat, elegantly global interpretations. These approaches not only promised certitude by virtue of their pretensions toward nomological coherence; as unabashed teleologies they incorporated the principle of progress into the texture of the social laws they discovered and charted. On the other hand, positivist scientism promised a more detailed and precise model of certitude, even though it sacrificed the macroscopic coherence of the rationalist and Darwinist orientation. While that sacrifice tended to require collateral scaling down of the notion of progress to "the bloodless entelechy of a society-centered dynamic equilibrium,"[20] pragmatism compensated the loss, not so much by restoring a macroscopic dimension as by emphasizing the necessity for human agency and the possibility of "intelligently guided melioristic social reform."[21] Although pragmatism originated in a critique of positivism's mechanistic excesses, in at least one important sense it constituted a literal "fleshing out" of the positivist framework rather than an alternative to it. As R. Jeffrey Lustig notes, positivists and pragmatists shared a "central commitment to method . . . preoccupation with one step in the process of inquiry and confusion of it with the whole." This shared commitment "revealed itself in the assumption—sometimes explicit, sometimes hinted, but always there—that the important questions of life were really questions of technique and method."[22] Thus, pragmatism can be construed as a "humanized" positivism that invigorated the latter's notion of progress by emphasizing the importance of human action—an emphasis which, more likely than not, was rendered in practical terms to mean social engineering.

Du Bois was amply exposed to each of those four orientations, and his writings reflect their influence on his thinking as it matured. In chapter 3 I noted tracings of reform-Darwinist and other evolutionist influences on his outlook; about this view there is a general consensus among scholars. Arnold Rampersad even contends that it was the influence of Spencerian ideas that led Du Bois through his fifteen-year concentrated focus on empirical sociology.[23] (In that respect his intellectual trajectory would have been representative of those of many of his contemporaries in the social sciences.) His German experience built on a rationalist foundation that had been laid several years earlier in his Victorian-inspired education at Fisk. His senior paper there had been on Otto von Bismarck, and in that essay he disclosed the depth of his rationalist bent as well as an emphatically Prussophile tendency that must have been reinforced at Harvard and no doubt induced him to look favorably on German intellectual styles.[24] Joseph DeMarco finds evidence of Ludwig Gumplowicz's influence in *The Conservation of Races,* and Du Bois's connections with and favorable impressions of Gustav von Schmoller and Heinrich von Treitschke are well known.[25] By 1897 all four strains were visible in Du Bois's texts; while *The Conservation of Races* displayed rationalist and reform-Darwinist tendencies, his "Program for a Sociological Society" proclaimed an unambiguously positivistic model of social science and a pragmatist-like commitment to the wedding of knowledge and action.[26] Dan S. Green and Edwin D. Driver argue convincingly for a view of Du Bois's scholarly commitment that identifies social reform as an ultimate end of intellectual pursuit. However, those authors, perhaps as a by-product of their concern to categorize him among the precursors of contemporary scientific sociology, on the one hand tend overly to emphasize the extent of his partisanship on the "fact" side of the fact/value dichotomy and his commitment to "pure" research; on the other hand, they read into his thinking a too early and sweeping rejection of the "philosophical speculations and armchair theorizing of sociologists like Herbert Spencer."[27] Despite the statements quoted above from 1940, at the time of his direction of the Atlanta University series Du Bois did not show such signs of "impatience." In fact in one of the publications of that series he praised the work of both Spencer and Franklin Giddings specifically and recommended them for study.[28] Du Bois's view was that one should not engage scientific inquiry specifically in service to reform purposes but should conduct "objective" research and then employ the findings to inform reform efforts. Nevertheless, science and reform were linked in his thinking; he saw the former as giving direction to the latter. In this respect science was not simply a method for making sense out of natural and social phenomena; it functioned also as an ideology, an element of an agenda for realization of the interests of a particular stratum of the American social order.

Du Bois's early views on the need to define the role of and cultivate the cultured and educated elite within the Afro-American community demonstrate the ideological character of his view of science. He stated clearly—and in a way that reflected the unabashedly optimistic scientism of the day—what he believed to be the importance of scientific knowledge for social uplift. "Since now scientists have begun to study men and conditions of group life so carefully, persons who would better the world in any way must study and learn from the material collected here, just as in other lines we use the wisdom of the geologist or psychologist."[29]

Alluding to the requirements of "modern methods of reform" he pointed out that to have any likelihood of success a reform agenda must include three sequential elements: (1) study, (2) knowledge of work of others, and only then (3) actual effort.[30] This view warrants a privileged role for intellectuals, particularly social scientists, in formulation and direction of reform activities and implies the inefficacy of spontaneous, popularly based or self-organized political activity. Du Bois shared the perspective of his progressive peers for whom popular activism was marked with the stamp of dangerous irrationality.[31] Both mainstream corporate liberalism and much of what understood itself as socialism were predicated upon models of orderly, technicistically rational societal development—without the disruptive participation of the rank-and-file citizenry.[32]

James Gilbert's observations on the social role of collectivist intellectuals like Du Bois and their appropriation of science for their own purposes illuminate ideological ramifications of such an outlook:

> Occupying a position above the dialectic of social struggle, they felt able to judge the aspirations of the other classes. To support this position they invoked social science and the assumed objectivity of scientific observation. This became a common ideal which ran through much reform and socialist thought, and which developed as a guiding assumption of the academic world, of much modern legal theory, of research organizations and foundations, and of civil service and government bureaucracies. In effect, this emphasis upon expertise was a reverberation from similar theories which claimed that the state could be impartial toward competing social classes; or that technology had a neutral, guiding function in the development of industry; or even, that behind the process of evolution was a benign, directing nature. Neutrality and scientific imper-

sonality were decisive weapons in the struggle to achieve social justice in a world of bias and corruption.[33]

Du Bois's view of the special, guiding role of science, and corollarily of intellectuals, persisted over his lengthy career. At eighty-two years of age he was disturbed that "the scientific and ethical boundaries of our industrial activities are not in the hands of scientists, teachers, and thinkers."[34] However, consonant with his increased attention to perspectives resonant with concerns of the sociology of knowledge, his faith in science's capacity to realize rational social organization increasingly was mediated by his perception of the necessity of active intervention. Of his epistemological awakening, Du Bois recalled: "Gradually and with increasing clarity, my whole attitude toward the social sciences began to change: in the study of human beings and their actions, there could be no such rift between theory and practice, between pure and applied science as was possible in the study of sticks and stones."[35]

He intimated that this developing modification of his outlook exerted some influence on his decision to leave Atlanta University the first time. After having confronted the depths of racial oppression during his first appointment at Atlanta, he was moved to make the "great decision." "What with all my dreaming, studying, and teaching was I going to *do* in this fierce fight?"[36] He had been struck by the impossibility of being a "calm, cool, and detached scientist while Negroes were lynched, murdered, and starved."[37] From his earlier conviction that the social world could yield unambiguous truths he came to see the partiality and the limited rationality of truth. "Facts, in social science, I realized, were elusive things: emotions, loves, hates, were facts; and they were facts in the souls and minds of the scientific student, as well as in the persons studied."[38]

The injunction seemed clear—that is, from the perspective of subsequent reflection:

> I fell back upon my Royce and James and deserted Schmoller and Weber. I saw the action of physical law in the actions of men; but I saw more than that: I saw rhythms and tendencies; coincidences and probabilities; and I saw that, which for want of any other word, I must in accord with the strict tenet of Science, call Chance. I went forward to build a sociology, which I conceived of as the attempt to measure the element of Chance in human conduct. This was the Jamesian pragmatism, applied not simply to ethics, but to all human action, beyond what seemed to me, increasingly, the distinct limits of physical law.[39]

Francis L. Broderick discusses Du Bois's affinity for pragmatism as a means through which ethics could be freed from "scholastic dogma" and reconstituted on the basis of empirical observation and reason; pragmatism thus was attractive to Du Bois from this vantage point because it seemed to offer a way to save metaphysics in the modern age by making it a science.[40] Similarly, another student of Du Bois's thought finds that during the years before World War I he "participated in [the] intellectual tradition, emergent in the United States at the turn of the century, which was concerned to describe the relation between reliable investigation and ethically committed social practice."[41] However, his interest was not simply in description; he sought practical reconciliation—within both the world and himself—of the "dualism James saw as central to philosophy, and which he variously described as a conflict between empiricism and rationalism, positivism and religion, practicality and idealism, and the 'tough-minded and the tenderminded.' "[42] Pragmatism could give practical justification for pursuing the life of the mind, and furthermore it privileged intellectual activity above all other kinds of social practice because all human problems were to be understood as knowledge or information problems.

While this viewpoint elevates the sociological role of intellectuals as information verifiers, it also determines the value of knowledge ultimately by its utility. Thus Du Bois criticized the black "college man" for losing sight of the concrete social purpose of his education. It was necessary to recall that "[t]he object of the Negro college is to place in American life a trained black man who can do what the world wants done; who can help the world know what it ought to want done and thus by doing the world's work well may invent better work for a better world."[43]

Moreover, Du Bois often tended to see his scholarly work in a utilitarian vein as well. He declared the intention of *The World and Africa* to be a demonstration "that black Africans are men in the same sense as white Europeans and yellow Asiatics, and that history can easily prove this."[44] *The Gift of Black Folk,*[45] *Black Folk: Then and Now,* and *Black Reconstruction*[46] were to some degree similarly motivated. The point here is not that Du Bois's scholarship suffered from any lack of objectivity or impartiality; all ideas are partial. Rather, it is that for Du Bois scholarly pursuit always was linked directly and consciously with some purpose of social reform. Not so much a self-contained activity directed toward a community of scholars concerned first of all with the expansion of knowledge, research's fundamental purpose was to Du Bois the correction of popular misconceptions in the interest of social improvement. To that extent Du Bois shares a basic view of the role of scholarship—if explicitly political differences were held constant—with policy-oriented social scientists, the practical inheritors of the liberal tradition in the United States.[47]

At the same time, just as Du Bois defined the purposes of scholarly activity in relation to a notion of social intervention for realization of progress, the activism to which he adhered was more didactic than militant. Even after he became more trenchantly critical of capitalism, his strategy for opposition was ultimately the same—informing people of the facts. When considering major social issues confronting a war-torn world in the 1940s and opportunities for political improvement, he declared: "We must first, then, have wide dissemination of truth. But this is not all: we need deliberate and organized action on the front where race fiction is being used to prolong economic inequality and injustice in the world."[48]

Specifically, he emphasized the need for a type of reform education comparable to "missionary" work, whose purpose would be to educate the public to "facts of the distribution of property and income . . . accurate details of the sources of income and conditions of production and distribution of goods and use of human services in order that we know who profits by investment in Asia and Africa as well as in America and Europe, and why and how they profit."[49]

This stress on public education as a political weapon is not so simple as it may seem, however. Du Bois was sensitive to the propagandistic character of mass-information culture as well as the nonrational sources of popular attitudes, especially dangerous and retrograde attitudes like racism. The program of systematic popular education was one of two prongs of his strategy for eliminating racial antagonism, the one directed toward the white population. He maintained:

> White leaders and thinkers have a duty to perform in making known the conclusions of science on the subject of biological race. It takes science long to percolate to the mass unless definite effort is made. Public health is still handicapped by superstitions long disproved by science; and race fiction is still taught in schools, in newspapers, and in novels. This careless ignorance of the facts of race is precisely the refuge where antisocial economic reaction flourishes.[50]

For oppressed nonwhites his program differed. The exigencies of the situation of racial oppression required more active intervention on the part of the oppressed, Du Bois felt. For the latter therefore "we need organized effort to release the colored laborer from the domination of the investor." Even within the nonwhite group, however, education remained the ultimate lever of progress; for here also he stressed the tutelary function of leadership.[51] Du Bois's emphasis on education and information as the principal tools of social activism tied his views on science and progress to his ideas about leadership for uplift. The uplift mission was from the outset an integral element of his approach to knowledge and education. Preparation of a complement of race leaders was for Du Bois one of the principal purposes of the black college. The prospect of carrying out that mission was a source of great excitement for him early in his tenure at Atlanta University the first time. In one of the earliest studies he published under the university's auspices he declared that that institution "seeks, by maintaining a high standard of scholarship and comportment, to sift out and train thoroughly talented members of this race to be leaders of thought and missionaries of culture among the masses."[52]

In the modern world effective leaders must have, Du Bois argued, "knowledge of the forces of civilization that make for our survival, ability to organize and guide those forces, and realization of the true meaning of those broader ideals of human betterment."[53] The university, then, was charged with the responsibility to train these leaders. Moreover, as I shall demonstrate in chapter 5, when not primarily concerned with correcting misconceptions about the race in general, Du Bois's discrete research efforts were grounded in his desires to identify, describe, consolidate and orient a leadership elite in the Afro-American population. These desires suffused his research, coloring everything, from his choice of projects and problems for examination to his specific findings. Science and knowledge, then, were for Du Bois simultaneously above the fray of particular interestedness and beyond the confusions of everyday understanding; yet the value of knowledge was to be understood in relation to the requirements of social uplift and progress. He defined the dynamic of progress in interventionist terms as the extension of rational organization through society. Knowledge and progress were dialectically connected; intervention was the interest driving academic activity, and realization of the objectives of scientific activity by means of mass tutelage was the basis of activism. In this sense, for Du Bois academic and activist interests dovetailed. This was to some extent a function of his conceptions of and proposals concerning the social role of an intellectual elite in the black community and the latter's social-organizational needs.

Stratification, Leadership, and Organization

The Role of the Black Elite

IT IS GENERALLY KNOWN that Du Bois—at least in his early years—embraced an elitist program for Afro-American racial strategy. This aspect of his views may be, in fact, too well known. Because it has been so widely recognized, all too often his elitism is mentioned offhandedly, without critical examination or careful description of its substantive characteristics. As a consequence, especially among those who find it to be a blemish on an otherwise agreeable corpus of ideas, even scholars have tended to collapse that elitism into one of its historically specific artifacts—the famous "Talented Tenth" concept. That perspective is attractive because it helps to salvage a view of Du Bois that is neatly reconcilable with egalitarian values. Joseph DeMarco, for example, in striving to make Du Bois a consistent egalitarian, falls back on a claim that the "role of the Talented Tenth was dropped, by and large, from his writing" shortly after 1907.[1] Similarly, Gerald Horne sidesteps the elitism issue by contending that Du Bois "altered" his views on the Talented Tenth by the 1940s and by repeating the latter's claim that he had never advocated "building of an aristocracy with neglect of the masses."[2]

Despite these and other such no doubt well-intentioned circumventions, Du Bois's elitism does not appear only with the Talented Tenth, nor for that matter only with respect to his explicitly racial strategies. On the contrary, the elitist strain in his thought runs far deeper and is connected with his most basic views concerning proper social organization in general and organization of the Afro-American population in particular. He advocated a hierarchical model that accorded certain elements of the black population claims to special status and privilege; in his view the relation of this elite stratum to other Afro-Americans was mediated by a form of tutelary noblesse oblige. In this chapter I shall demonstrate that Du Bois remained committed throughout his life to the realization of a fundamentally elite-driven organizational model for the black population; that this model constituted the concrete link between his scholarly and activist pursuits; and that his interest in actualization of what he considered to be the mission of that elite was a core unifying principle of his thought, notwithstanding his various changes of political affiliation and program between 1900 and his death in 1963.

Du Bois went to Atlanta University already imbued, from his academic training, disposition, and work in Philadelphia, with ideas concerning the historical mission of the black elite. His social-scientific research program—indeed much of his entire academic project—was predicated upon a wish to cultivate that stratum and guide it toward realizing its mission. Three of the first four of the major publications of the Atlanta University series during the period of Du Bois's association were intended specifically to indicate the accomplishments of the achieving stratum of the black population (see chapter 4, note 4).

In his second study of the series, Du Bois investigated general community conditions in Petersburg, Virginia; Augusta, Georgia; Atlanta; Mobile, Alabama; Bowling Green, Kentucky; Clarksville and Fort Smith, Arkansas; Galveston, Texas; and the District of Columbia to find that race prejudice, by isolating blacks, threw upon the black community responsibility for "evolving its own methods and organs of civilization."[3] He found also that in those communities mechanisms of institutionalized benevolence were scarce among blacks and that instead a pattern of spontaneous, informal provision of welfare needs prevailed. These findings led Du Bois to conclude that the "problem of cooperation among members of the group becomes then the central serious problem."[4] Cooperation meant, however, the ability of the trained elite to generalize an agenda for the community, for Du Bois took the general situation of blacks in those cities as another indication of the necessity of the organizational role that he had advocated a year earlier for the American Negro Academy.[5] In the 1898 study he reiterated his earlier call for support and recognition of the Academy as an opinion-setting entity in the black community. Moreover, as a practical objective for the race and a goal of intraracial cooperation, Du Bois enthusiastically supported Alexander Crummell's call for black political participation and quoted approvingly the latter's assertion, endorsed by the Academy, that, "Our people can't be a people unless their leading men get positions and take part in government."[6] Significantly, the call to political participation was justified not by appeal to any specific social vision that could be realized but a claim that the Afro-American elite should have a share in governmental activity.

The next two studies in the series focused on business[7] and education[8] among blacks. Each sought to document characteristics of prominent and well-educated blacks and attempted to describe their significance among the black population as a whole. In addition to general documentation of black life, these studies were intended to provide a possible impetus to the Negro elite's development of self-consciousness as a stratum and to advocate to pertinent whites on behalf of the elite's claims to representation of black interests. These two hortatory objectives stand out when the studies—summary empirical monographs as they mainly are—are read through the filter of some of Du Bois's other work during this period. Most telling is his contention that one of the most important reasons for the study of Afro-American life is to aid social reform.[9]

Within three years after the study of "college-bred" blacks, Du Bois stated directly that one of the objectives of his work was to bring broader public attention to what blacks had done and were doing, and he proceeded to list black accomplishments in what he identified as the four chief fields of endeavor in the United States: "commerce and industry . . . ; . . . political life . . . ; the learned professions—law, medicine, preaching, and teaching; and . . . literature and art."[10] In that same year he published the article in which he argued most forcefully for his famous notion of the "Talented Tenth."

Actually, the views Du Bois expressed in his manifesto for the elite are only extensions and more explicitly argued affirmations of the outlook that had permeated *The Philadelphia Negro* several years earlier. However, in addition to being his most articulate call for elite primacy, the 1903 essay also reflects the growing readiness to adopt an activist posture and attitude that was visible in his writing during those years. He opened the essay with an assertion that the race was to be saved by its exceptional men,[11] and he declared a threefold task in his exposition: first, to show that the Talented Tenth was "worthy of leadership"; second, to show how this necessary elite might be educated and developed; and third, to show the elite's relation to the "Negro problem."[12]

He felt the issue of the elite's elevation to its rightful place at the head of the Afro-American community to be of critical import for two reasons at least. First of all, black Americans, because of their peculiar situation, were objectively more dependent than other peoples on organized guidance. He argued that "the Negro people need social leadership more than most groups; they have no traditions to fall back upon, no long established customs, no strong family ties, no well defined social classes. All these things must be slowly and painfully evolved."[13]

The reason for this unfortunate situation, of course, was the mediation of slavery as the fundamental constitutive element of the Afro-American experience. He averred: "[Slavery is] the legalized survival of the unfit and the nullification of the work of natural internal leadership[.] Negro leadership, therefore, sought from the first to rid the race of this awful incubus that it might make way for natural selection and the survival of the fittest."[14] So to all the other reasons that slavery was oppressive or irrational must be added its transgression of social-evolutionist rationality and unfair suppression of the aspirations of the most talented of the slaves. This perspective is interesting in two respects. It underscores the importance that Du Bois attached to the black elite's right to priority within the race and his general lack of sympathy for the rabble. Regarding the latter, he contended that they were to be "raised" by the "effort and example of this aristocracy of talent and character," and, noting that culture always filters down from the top, he argued for a relation in which the Talented Tenth "rises and pulls all that are worth saving up to their vantage ground."[15]

Du Bois's observation about slavery is noteworthy also because it led to an indirect identification of social activism as a vehicle for elite training. Discussing responses to slavery, he quotes Maria Weston Chapman on how the abolitionist movement trained "a throng of authors, editors, lawyers, orators and accomplished gentlemen of color."[16] He pointed out, however, that of the prominent black abolitionists some were self-trained and others had in fact received substantial formal education apart from the movement,[17] and that observation set the stage for a strong plea for university training for the Talented Tenth.[18]

In addition to his research program, during his years on the Atlanta University faculty, Du Bois made any number of attempts to generate vehicles around which the black elite could begin developing a program for the race. For instance, although the National Negro Business League came to be identified with Booker T. Washington, the idea originated with Du Bois. In fact, his early career is studded with a number of such efforts, ranging from his involvement with the American Negro Academy, to the various special committees for whose organization he called, to his efforts to organize journals targeted for elite consumption. These efforts culminated first in the predominantly black Niagara movement, then finally in the predominantly white-led NAACP. By the time *The Souls of Black Folk* appeared, Du Bois was clearly committed to identifying an appropriate vehicle through which to galvanize black protest of the sort he had been advocating.[19]

Protest, however, was not his exclusive goal. Equally important was creation of a sense of cohesion among the black elite. Since publishing his Philadelphia study, Du Bois had been disturbed at the Talented Tenth's reluctance to claim its rightful position of stewardship of Afro-American life. His first two magazines, the *Moon* and the *Horizon*, were aimed just as much at creating a sense of common identity and purpose among the black elite as at informing their readers and agitating against racial inequity. In each of these short-lived magazines he combined excerpts and summaries from foreign and domestic newspapers and journals, reading lists, editorials, and announcements in an attempt to mold and inculcate what might be termed a class outlook. The *Horizon* outlasted the *Moon*—which limped through a single volume—in part by becoming the official organ of the Niagara movement, which extended the publication's life to three years. Du Bois's real journalistic success awaited the *Crisis*, which he edited throughout his tenure with the NAACP. The *Crisis* also, despite its organizational affiliation, was under Du Bois a class/race magazine that followed the same basic formula as its predecessors, and his success is suggested by William Allison Davis's reminiscence; he recalls Du Bois's *Crisis* editorials as "the most powerful and terrifying experiences in the lives of middle class Negroes of both my father's and my own generation. The great majority of black children and adolescents who later became scholars, teachers, lawyers, and professional men during the second, third, and fourth decades of the twentieth century read The Crisis as a family magazine each month."[20]

The *Crisis* was very much geared toward black middle-class readership, and to that extent strove for general—not just political or educational—appeal, even to the point of running photographs of the "Crisis Maids."[21] And Du Bois included in his mission the propagation among his readership of positive images and its accomplishments. In this vein he declared, in a reversal of his contention of previous years, that the "American Negro does NOT stand in unusual need of moral training. It is the American white man who needs that."[22] This racial assertiveness did not end there.

Early in the magazine's history Du Bois asked his readers to take out enough subscriptions to guarantee "complete financial independence and the assurance of permanence" for the *Crisis*. He was concerned, as he saw it, not only for his own welfare but for the editorial integrity of the magazine.[23] Similarly, he called on his Talented Tenth readers to buy books so that black authors would acquire the latitude to break out of the straitjacketed molds imposed by a white clientele and become "privileged to follow the leadings of their own hearts and the laws which imperatively rule in the creation of literature." He continued in a passage that, while probably overstating the duress under which he previously had labored, nonetheless reflects the growth of his own convictions about addressing a black audience principally:

> One can see in almost every book written by a colored author that the work has been done under foreign dictation. The author has wished his book to be read and to be sold; he has written too much under this influence. The book has been planned for white readers. The transition from the custom of writing books of explanation and defense intended for white men to read to that of depicting our own experiences, giving our own interpretation of events transpiring or past, pouring out our own realities of feelings and longings, telling of God and his works as we see them has as yet hardly begun.[24]

Elsewhere he declared, "Instead of being led and defended by others . . . American Negroes are gaining their own leaders, their own voices, their own ideals."[25] Yet he was at that point the only black officer of the NAACP.

In this context Du Bois's association with the Harlem Renaissance is interesting, to the extent that that movement might be seen in part as an expression of the congealing consciousness of the elite. Alain Locke's manifesto for the period, the *New Negro: An Interpretation*, illustrates that aspect of what usually is thought to have been an aesthetic-folkloric movement.[26] Contributions by Charles S. Johnson,[27] Kelly Miller,[28] and R. R. Moton[29] proclaimed a new unity and commonality of purpose among blacks and officially buried the idea of "the two historic 'schools of thought' clashing ceaselessly and loud over the question of industrial and higher education for the Negro."[30] E. Franklin Frazier extolled the virtues of the new elite as a standard-bearer and force for the progress and uplift of the race as a whole.[31]

Besides his contribution to *The New Negro* Du Bois was quite visible in that celebration of a certain conception of Afro-American culture marketed by black intellectuals and white patrons during the 1920s. The pages of the *Crisis* regularly were turned over to the apostles of the "Negro Renaissance"; moreover, his volumes *The Gift of Black Folk* (1924) and *Darkwater* (1921) rank as major statements of the Renaissance cultural ideology.

For Du Bois the cultural celebration was tied up with both general race pride and a particular group sensibility. His references to black folklife, both in Africa and the United States, emphasized what he considered its primitive aspects. He lauded blacks' "sensuous, tropical love of life, in vivid contrast to the cool and cautious New England reason."[32] "The Negro," he proclaimed, "is primarily an artist."[33]

At the same time he was sensitive to the cultural responsibilities of the black middle class, deploring blacks' reluctance to buy books and art, even those blacks who enjoyed artistic consumption.[34] He also expatiated against the mammonism that he felt tended to accompany affluence among the new black middle class.[35] In a vein going back to *The Philadelphia Negro* he charged the New Negro exclusively with the cultural stewardship and civilizing mission that he originally had assigned them to share with the reigning white elites.

There appears to be a disparity between Du Bois's advocacy of the civilizing mission of the black middle class in relation to the rest of the black population and his exultation in the very "primitive," folkloric values that were the raw material of his Talented Tenth's civilizing mission. Several factors can be advanced to explain this anomaly. First, there is the racial defensiveness that takes the form of self-conscious exaltation of those values and behaviors that are generally considered by whites to be unacceptable.[36] Second, Du Bois retained into the 1920s at least vestiges of two Victorian commitments—a presumption of a nature/culture axis as a mechanism for characterizing human populations and a belief in the existence of inherent group temperaments or ideals.[37] In light of these views—and entirely consistent with the premises of the Renaissance—the civilizing mission lay not in extirpating the primitive, folkish qualities that marked the race's specific contribution to the world, but in refining and cultivating them. Finally, and in a similar vein, postulation of an exotic black particularity emphasizes a role for the black elite as keepers and translators of the culture. That role buttresses the latter's centrality within the black community; in that sense, then, the aesthetic-folkloric celebration was an ideology of the elite's spokespersons. It is likely that one or more of those factors had some role in generation of Du Bois's apparent ambivalence over exalting both the primitive and that which would transcend it. However, the Renaissance phenomenon indicates another ambivalence that Du Bois shared with his cohorts as proponents of black leadership.

For all its advocacy of black primacy over black affairs, the Negro Renaissance was dependent upon and reflected its clientage to white patronage.[38] Hence Du Bois often was ambivalent in identification of his audiences, alternately and sometimes in a given text simultaneously addressing the black elite, which he exhorted to be independent and to meet its historic duties, and liberal whites. In the Renaissance case the material condition underlying the ambivalence was ironic because of the assertiveness that characterized his praise of the racial spirit.

The pursuit of white patronage had been a central feature of Afro-American political and intellectual activity at least since the Age of Washington. Washington directed his appeal definitively to indigenous white advocates of the New South and their eastern capitalist affiliations,[39] and Du Bois's criticism seems largely directed at that same constituency—as, for example, when he exhorted the "Men of America" to make the Talented Tenth the leaders of the race.[40] Those "Men" were white elites—philanthropists and other opinion makers. Notwithstanding its literary merits and other substantive accomplishments, herein lies much of the historical significance of *The Souls of Black Folk*: in that volume Du Bois raised most coherently the demand for expanded access to the white elite agencies that were or could have been involved in disposition of the place of the Afro-American population in the developing order of corporate capitalism.[41] Moreover, despite its occasional stridency of tone, Du Bois's volume of essays was grounded in a perspective that was in some respects no less palatable than Washington's to the reform-oriented progressive intellectuals who were influential in the legitimation of black spokesmanship.

Du Bois expressed his sympathetic recognition of the dual losses of slave and master:

> Thus it is doubly difficult to write of this period calmly, so intense was the feeling, so mighty the human passions that swayed and blinded men. Amid it all, two figures ever stand to typify that day to coming ages,—the one, a gray-haired gentleman, whose fathers had quit themselves like men, whose sons lay in nameless graves; who bowed to the evil of slavery because its abolition threatened untold ill to all; who stood at last, in the evening of life, a blighted, ruined form, with hate in his eyes;—and the other, a form hovering dark and mother-like, her awful face black with the mists of centuries, had aforetime quailed at that white master's command, had bent in love over the cradles of his sons and daughters, and closed in death the sunken eyes of his wife,—aye, too, in his behest had laid herself low to his lust, and borne a tawny man-child to the world, only to see her dark boy's limbs scattered to the winds by midnight marauders riding after "damned Niggers." These were the saddest sights of that woful [*sic*] day.[42]

He pointed out as well that

> to no class is the indiscriminate endorsement of the recent course of the South toward Negroes more nauseating than to the best thought of the South . . . the ignorant Southerner hates the Negro, the workingmen fear his competition, the money-makers wish to use him as a laborer, some of the educated see a menace in his upward development, while others—usually the sons of the masters—wish to help him rise.[43]

This notion—that the "best" of the southern whites meant blacks well—recurred and may well have grown from, or at least reinforced, Du Bois's assumptions concerning reasonable men and civilized behavior. He reiterated from his undergraduate days at Fisk the call to build a university in the South so that the region could every year produce "a few white men and a few black men of broad culture, catholic tolerance, and trained ability, joining their hands, and giving to this squabble of the Races a decent and dignified peace."[44]

If broadly cultured black and white men were to be allies, however, their alliance could not be one of equals, since whites controlled the monetary and other resources necessary for social- or racial-uplift activities. Therefore, assertion of black aspirations was conditioned by the ironic circumstance that legitimation of those aspirations had to come from outside the Afro-American community in general and from upper-class whites in particular. Du Bois's conflict with Washington should be considered in the context of competition for access to that white patronage. The famous controversy derived largely from the fact that Washington had established monopoly over access to patronage sources. Although they clearly were in programmatic competition and articulated sharply different visions of blacks' place in American civic life, their conflict did not grow from deep philosophical differences about internal organization of the black population. After noting, on reflection in 1940, that their actual differences were more of emphasis than substance, Du Bois made clear the importance of Washington's monopolistic position as an issue:

> Contrary to most opinion the controversy as it developed was not entirely against Mr. Washington's ideas, but became the insistence upon the right of other Negroes to have and express their ideas. Things came to such a pass that when any Negro complained or advocated a course of action, he was silenced with the remark that Mr. Washington did not agree with this. Naturally the bumptious, irritated, young black intelligentsia of the day declared, "I don't care a damn what Booker Washington thinks! This is what I think, and I have a right to think."[45]

The conflict, therefore, was the culmination of a tension between the specific agendas and the legitimacy claims of different elements of the black elite and the various white support groups—New South ideologues, northern industrialists and reform intellectuals—to which those elements related for patronage and for other forms of validation. This view implies a necessary amendment of Mary Law Chaffee's contention that the industrial/classical education dichotomy originated in the respective interests of "Northerners" and white southerners.[46] That contention, while tending toward the right direction, is simplistic in three respects. First, it lumps together as "Northerners" both industrialists and reform intellectuals, who often saw the race issue rather differently. Second, that interpretation does not account for the mediation of intraelite conflict—generational or otherwise—among Afro-Americans. Finally, Chaffee's interpretation does not clearly conform to the facts; Robert L. Factor finds, for example, that northern industrialists as well as southerners favored industrial education.[47]

Of course, the differences between Washington and Du Bois were not entirely limited to the issue of the power of the Tuskegee Machine. The central fault line separating them and the political tendencies they represented was the demand for black civic equality and political participation. Du Bois and others unequivocally opposed Washington's acquiescence in the alliance of Redeemers and New South ideologues, an alliance predicated on expulsion of blacks from public life and codification of a regime explicitly based on white supremacy. The urgency of critics' objections to the Tuskegeean's stranglehold on black debate and access to support for uplift activity, in fact, derived principally from recognition that his machine's main function was to stifle challenges to the emerging Jim Crow social order. They understood that disfranchisement and loss of civil rights would ultimately destroy black aspirations. This fault line redefined the broad orientations toward racial strategy that had formed under the conditions of relative openness and expansive political mobilization that had flourished during the first two decades after Emancipation.

William S. Toll observes that by the end of Reconstruction three distinct views had emerged among black spokespersons with respect to the character and condition of the freedmen. From one perspective they were mainly seen as citizens seeking rights. From another they were ignorant peasants needing guidance, and in a third view they were "romantic evangels in search of a promised land."[48] These three views did not exhaust the articulated possibilities. The Colored Farmers Alliance represented an indigenous strain of black populism, and others emphasized blacks' status as laborers and workers. Yet by the 1880s the three perspectives Toll describes had converged around a general pattern of elite racial-strategy discourse premised on a nodal background assumption, namely, that the simultaneous and uneven development of slave and free strains in the black population decreed that the freedmen "needed a specially trained elite to help them replace the habits of slavery with the assertiveness of free men."[49] This elite black discourse became increasingly hegemonic as white supremacist victories narrowed the scope for more popular action. However, as Toll argues, two distinct approaches to the problem of racial agenda formation developed within that common rhetoric of elite tutelage.

On the one hand, Washington symbolized an approach that focused on "social rehabilitation," a concrete project of expunging the "social primitivism" that had taken root among blacks largely because of the slave experience. As Toll puts it succinctly: "While Yankee farmers and western yeomen had identified hard work as a means to freedom through the acquisition of a homestead, slaves had toiled through fear of the lash to enrich others. The problem for Washington lay in taking what Blacks had learned as southern workers and transforming it into an ideology that would enable them to benefit from the modernization of the region."[50] For Washington, therefore, the tutelary project was informed primarily by the earlier strain of thinking—most identified with Frederick Douglass—that emphasized the backwardness of the masses. Moreover, in Washington's view the road to progress was simple and direct; he accepted reflexively the Gospel of Wealth and had little sympathy for the ethical ambivalence with which more macroscopically inclined reformers assayed the dynamics of industrialization. His programmatic agenda settled happily on imparting a few rudimentary "skills," but most of all inculcating the social discipline required of good laborers and subordinate entrepreneurs. Thus the irony of this program that Du Bois pointed out becomes more sensible. The artisanal and yeoman skills on which the Tuskegee model rested rhetorically were indeed obsolescent, but they were not the ultimate point. The contradictory relation of industrial ideology and republican practicality probably reflected Washington's own confusions as a man caught between two eras. The ideology, however, was the real practicality; the substantive training was only a vehicle for effecting the characterological—and essentially ideological—project of rehabilitation.

On the other hand, Du Bois represented an approach to uplift that combined the three earlier perspectives to form a rhetoric and a programmatic orientation that emphasized "cultural revitalization," a focus that entailed combating the stigma attached to the race and building racial pride by taking note of black accomplishment.[51] Beneath this orientation lay a broader view than Washington's of the social dynamics to which the black population had to be adjusted and a more complex sense of the elite's mission, even though it shared some of Washington's enthusiasm about industrial progress and certainly shared the tutelary commitment. In a sense, the two approaches ran parallel. Du Bois never disputed, as his propositions in *The Philadelphia Negro* and later reflections in *Dusk of Dawn* and elsewhere attest, that vocational training and proletarianization were foremost objectives for the general black population. In fact as late as 1913 he held that it was still possible, though he lamented that the possibility was slipping away, "to make Negroes essentially Americans with American ideals and instincts."[52] However, in part because of his greater sensitivity to the teleological dimension of progress and his insistence that oversight of the acculturation project should be as much as possible in black hands, Du Bois stressed the need to prepare and strengthen the indigenous elite on which tutelary responsibilities rested. From that vantage point cultivation of a stratum of broadly trained, eminently civilized blacks who exercised full citizenship rights was a logical precondition for the commonly accepted task of racial uplift.

Intellectually, this perception probably derived from Du Bois's early notions concerning racial-group idealism. Politically, cultivation of such a stratum expressed the ideology most appropriate to the practical project that he and Washington shared, even though the latter, for biographical and other reasons, recoiled from the notion of an aristocracy of gentility. Sociologically (and this is perhaps one of the reasons that Washington—a thoroughgoing philistine—could not accept its ideological attributes), this focus carried the aspirations of a rising cohort of educated, comparatively urbane, reform-oriented black men and women[53] for whom the mission of race leadership was ultimately connected with individual and group status claims.

Despite their differences, though, the two black elite tendencies shared certain basic dispositions. Both Washington and Du Bois accepted the essential model of social hierarchy that prevailed in the society and maintained that "uplift" of the black population entailed an elite-driven accretion of the characteristics of "civilization."[54] This conception of uplift in turn implied an approach to social problems in general and to group organization in particular that connected with the general black population only as an object of social engineering. Therefore, the substantive alliances required to realize its programmatic agendas had to be sought outside the race. The common need for those alliances exerted pressure to harmonize the Afro-American elite's agendas and strategies—whether oriented toward "protest" or "accommodation"—with the main thrusts of corporate capitalism and therefore with each other as well.

In this regard August Meier notes that the gradualism of the "accommodationists" and their appeals to white morality were based on a perception of white loyalty to the Constitution, and he notes that the NAACP became the source of a lengthy legal struggle that also sought to capitalize on that perceived loyalty.[55] Elliott M. Rudwick notes that "Du Bois portrayed Washington's emphasis on industrial education as an essential link with the expansion of the Southern economy,"[56] and he points out that at a 1904 meeting representatives of the two camps agreed that "potential Negro leaders could profit from higher education, while the rest of the race should attend grammar schools and industrial schools."[57] The antagonists, moreover, were united in their programmatic advocacy of moral-institutional reorganization of the black population and in identification of upper-class whites as the appropriate element with which black leadership should be aligned.[58] This last commonality is of special moment for interpretation of Du Bois, as the relationship to white patronage figures prominently as a source of tension in the leadership competition within the black elite and at the same time suggests a practical confluence with the mainstream of the liberal collectivist social program. Since white support came by and large from corporate and other reformers who tended to move from the collectivist outlook, it is likely that black initiatives that were supported at all would at least be compatible with that outlook.

Du Bois had long sought to organize systematic research on Afro-American life, and he maintained a collateral interest in organizing the black intellectual elite for the purpose of establishing cultural and political hegemony within the race. Regarding the former concern, he called in 1900 for formation of a "Special Committee for the Study of the Negro Problems" that "should have general oversight of a series of social studies into the condition of the American Negro."[59] This initiative died for lack of funding support. Several years later he attempted to generate support for a "high class journal to circulate among the intelligent Negroes, tell them of the deeds of themselves and their neighbors, interpret the news of the world to them, and inspire them toward definite ideals."[60] Toward that end he wrote unsuccessfully to Jacob Schiff in 1905 for a financial contribution. Schiff was not moved by Du Bois's estimation of the need for the black intellectual elite to consolidate itself. In fact, the philanthropic community not surprisingly appears to have had little interest in independent black activity of any type. Rudwick indicates the operative sentiment; after identifying the Niagara movement as the congelation of black intellectual interests,[61] he then points out that an "essential failure" of that initiative was "its inability to attract the support of more than a handful of whites."[62] Thus the paradox: Du Bois found himself in the position of appealing for support of independent black political and academic initiatives to upper-class whites whose interests in black "uplift" activities were tied to criteria that were at best lukewarm to black self-organization.[63] So it was that after several years of attempting with not much success to compete for philanthropic support with Washington—who did not seem bound by any formal commitment to visions of independent initiative—Du Bois in his frustration castigated his opponent for having become so dependent on "the rich charitable public" that he was too compromised to powerful interests and therefore was unable to tell the truth about the needs of the race.[64] Yet the paradox was not transcended; indeed, it eventually would help force Du Bois out of the NAACP.

Du Bois, of course, as is attested to by his comments about the need for the black community to safeguard the autonomy of its intellectual workers, was never fully sanguine about this patronage relation. His insistence upon black support of black efforts doubtless was intensified by his conflicts with whites within the NAACP. All along, however, he had felt that white support should be oriented toward assisting in creation of an indigenous black leadership stratum and acknowledging the primacy of such modern black leadership as did exist. Apparently, during the period between the two world wars, he became unequivocally convinced that sufficient black leadership existed to assert its priority in Afro-American affairs.

One issue remains to be clarified concerning Du Bois's views on stratification of the black community. This issue relates to a subtle shift that occurred in his thinking during the years between *The Philadelphia Negro* and his approach to the Communist Party. In the early period Du Bois had taken the elite in its totality to constitute an aristocracy among the Afro-American population. He made no real normative or socially functional distinction among the different elements of the elite; the various segments—businessmen, teachers, professionals, functionaries—shared the common historical mission of uplift, and all enjoyed the same elevated status over the rest of the population. However, after he had been at Atlanta University for a few years he took greater note of the elite's internal differentiation and expressed disturbance over the appearance of a relatively philistine but well-off stratum of "farmers and gardeners, the well-paid porters and artisans, the businessmen"[65] that he felt lacked sufficient breadth of culture to act as true representatives of the race.

Several years later, after he had left Atlanta, Du Bois expressed concern that the intellectual elite had not received its proper recognition in relation to other strata. He reasoned that because black professionals had the vast majority of their interactions within the black community and workingmen had most of their daily interactions with whites, whites seeking to communicate with the black community did not even know the "natural leaders" and would wind up going to and forming opinions on the basis of intercourse with artisans.[66]

His commitment was to the "cultured classes," that is, not simply the black middle class writ large, but that complement that was trained in the techniques of modern civilization, the professional stratum that claimed knowledge and expertise as capital. It was this stratum that he saw leading his cooperative commonwealth in the 1930s and 1940s, and to whom he assigned a place atop the black population.

In 1940 he proposed a pyramidal view of the status hierarchy of the black community, in which "the poor, ignorant, sick and antisocial form a vast foundation" and whose "highest members, although few in number, reach above the average not only of the Negroes but of the whites, and may justly be compared to the better-class white culture."[67] He expressed a need for caution, however, in assessing this stratum's actual sociohistorical role, noting, for example, the group's propensities to "conspicuous consumption" and frivolousness. He observed that upper-class blacks felt isolated and alone as a result of segregation. They were often unable or unwilling to share in middle-class white society on the terms in which it was offered, and at the same time they tended to recoil from the vulgarity of their own lower classes.[68]

Nevertheless, he was optimistic in 1940 that blacks were building, as he felt they must, a class structure of their own. He felt that whether his "Talented Tenth" would be a "threat to the development of the whole race" or the vehicle "by which the level of culture in the whole group is going to be raised . . . depends upon the relations that develop between these masses and the cultural aims of the higher classes."[69] But on balance he was generally hopeful about the liberatory potential held out by the dynamic elite that he identified, even though after discussing the vector of its growth all he could fall back on for assurance was a call for unity across groups.[70] That is a point at which his consumer-cooperative strategy dovetails with the historical agenda that Du Bois imputed to the black elite.

One strength of the consumer organization was that its thrust could provide a means through which the elite could mobilize "training" of the masses.[71] In this way Du Bois allayed his fear that the elite's "leadership and authority within the group" would come to be constituted on the basis of wealth rather than talent. The consumer-cooperative strategy, then, was in this sense a mechanism for the germinal professional elite to consolidate and institutionalize its hegemony over other elements in the black community by virtue of claims to special expertise, appeals to unity and collectivity of interest (class invisibility), and an ideology of service.

Throughout the interwar years Du Bois was hardly a radical democrat although—partly in response to the growth of mass organization and protest—he showed signs of modifying his thinking with respect to intraracial stratification. As Arnold Rampersad points out, Du Bois disclosed in the novel *Dark Princess* (1928), that he "had nothing against kings and princesses, provided some were black. Indeed, he seemed to prefer royalty and saw no contradiction between it and his propaganda for the masses."[72] That observation recalls his alternation of extravagant pro-Bolshevik rhetoric and effusion over debutante balls in the pages of the *Crisis* a decade earlier. Indeed, Du Bois's commitments were not without apparent ambivalence.

Within four years after publication of *Dark Princess* he took refuge in the rationale of changing times to proffer a self-criticism, taking the NAACP as a vehicle for his partial retreat from the elitism with which he had been associated for nearly a third of a century. He maintained that the organization

> was formed at a time when the phrase, "the talented tenth," meant something for the advancement of men, when we were thinking along lines of that sort. We said "The people who are the exceptional people must of necessity be the ones who lead any group out of the wilderness. It is not a question of their advantages." And then we went further than that and quite naturally said, "This organization must also be for the advancement of the 'talented tenth.'" After all, if the talented tenth is the judge, the tool by which we are going to raise the Negro race, then the more we ourselves are raised, the more advantages we have, the more in the long run we are going to solve this problem.
>
> But there comes a question. "Are you thinking of the advancement of this tenth for your own sake or for the sake of the great mass of people? When it comes to the advancement of the great mass of people who is to be the judge as to what these people want and ought to have?" We are the ones who know what the masses ought to want, therefore, we are the ones who go ahead and lay down the program for these people, who manage; and while we have been going on with our program there has come actually a change in the thought of the world, a change . . . which says not only is the object of the organization advancement for the masses of people but that it must be dominated by the masses of people. That change is so fast that there are large numbers of people who have not heard it at all; large numbers who do not believe it. It is going to have a hard time making its way but it is going to make its way. The world more and more is going to be organized not simply for the masses of people but by the masses of people. They are going to be the ones who will dominate.[73]

He pointed out as well that the NAACP program was dominated by a negative eighteenth-century conception of freedom that not only did not address the populace's economic needs but also tacitly endorsed an agenda that would "build up inside of the Negro race an economic class, not quite clear as yet."[74]

Despite that self-criticism, Du Bois did not uncouple from his commitment to the black elite. His intimation that adherence to an agenda favoring the "Talented Tenth" had been historically appropriate at some earlier point may well have been sound, especially given disfranchisement and other conditions demobilizing the black population in the early 1900s. At that time, though, he had supported class-based suffrage restriction in principle for both whites and blacks, apart from the need to adjust to the practical realities of white supremacist exclusion. And the defense of historical appropriateness not only allows the critic to save face; it also, by interposing reified time between the agent and his ideas, prevents the critique from penetrating to the relational and ideological core of the discarded position.[75] Indeed, we already have seen that eight years after this self-criticism he proposed a pyramidal view of the Afro-American social structure that recycled almost identically the normative premises that had underlain his interpretation in *The Philadelphia Negro*. And his defense of his consumer-cooperative "Nation within a Nation" strategy against labor radical and former *Crisis* protégé George Streator's sharp criticism in 1935 indicates how much that strategy rested on the old Talented Tenth vision. In response to Streator's charge that he had too much faith in the black petite bourgeoisie's race leadership, Du Bois asserted that under current conditions he saw "but one path of salvation for American Negroes . . . and that is to get a growing group of young, trained, fearless and unselfish Negroes to guide the American Negro in this crisis, and guide him toward the coming of socialism throughout the world."[76]

Most instructively, in a 1948 address to the Boulé, a national organization explicitly for upper-status black men, Du Bois unveiled a fully reconstituted, "historically appropriate" version of the Talented Tenth, one that indicated that his view of the elite's mission (and, as I shall show in chapter 6, his conception of socialism) remained cast in essentially the same liberal collectivist mold as at the turn of the century, with only tactical modification induced by an admirable openness to empirical realities. Citing Marx as his influence, he commented that he had gradually come to see that the Tenth's "passport to leadership was not simply learning. Learning, knowledge, science carefully inculcated and deeply studied it must have; but fundamental would be its willingness to sacrifice and plan for such economic revolution in industry and just distribution of wealth as would make the rise of the group possible."[77]

He acknowledged that for quite some time he had answered class-based criticisms of his Talented Tenth strategy by arguing that class analysis did not apply to black Americans. He suggested however, that as time went on either he began to see more clearly or conditions changed, because he saw more class contradictions among blacks.[78] He noted as well that he had apprehended what was from his vantage point the paradox that "Negroes who had long trained themselves for personal success and individual freedom were coming to regard the end of segregation as an ideal and not as a means." To his dismay they were uncritical of what American society was in their insistence on being accepted in whatever it was.[79] He found it ironic, if not perfidious, that he and much of his cohort had developed the "idea of the Negro problem as being an evangel, a gospel where chosen men were trained and armed, and went out to take the leadership of the mass." Unlike the tendency he saw developing, his generation had not regarded themselves as "separate and superior to the masses, but rather as a part of the mass which was being equipted [*sic*] and armed for leadership and that leadership was of course for the benefit of the mass."[80]

As we have seen, this contrast nostalgically sanitizes his earlier views regarding intraracial differentiation. But we certainly cannot deny Du Bois the human prerogative of trying to assert a retroactive consistency over his life. Moreover, his observations demonstrate certain powerful insights. His critique of the new middle class's consumerism and facile acceptance of desegregation as an end rather than a means presaged the trenchant criticisms to be leveled by Frazier and Harold Cruse—who also felt that the black bourgeoisie had betrayed its historical mission—and the radical wing of the civil rights movement. And his criticism of the black church seems in retrospect to have anticipated Martin Luther King Jr., if it did not actually call him into existence. Du Bois declared: "Our religion with all its dogma, demagoguery, and showmanship can be a center to teach character, right conduct and sacrifice. There lies here a career for a Negro Gandhi and a host of earnest followers."[81]

When all was said and done, in the Boulé text Du Bois clearly established that he retained his commitment to the privileged role of the black elite; his practical response to the disturbing tendencies that he had identified was to raise the ante and exhort the Talented Tenth to adopt more concrete—and rather extreme—measures to live up to its mission. After identifying undergraduate fraternities (as he had done in his desperation toward the end of his first tenure at the NAACP) as providing a basis for a large race organization among the enlightened elite,[82] he strove to impress the emerging generation with the need to adopt an "ideal of plain living and high thinking."[83]

Because the ranks of the truly committed were small and, he feared, dwindling, he advocated solidifying and expanding them internally by several methods, including eugenics. He proposed child bearing and adoption as strategies to build the Talented Tenth,[84] as well as arranged marriages of children of Boulé archons.[85] The elite's newly specified mission mandated "the rehabilitation of the indispensable family group by deliberate planning of marriages with mates selected for heredity, physique, health and brains with less insistence on color comeliness or romantic sex lure miscalled love: youth should marry young and have a limited number of healthy children."[86] This, it turns out, was his substantive strategy for streamlining the Talented Tenth into the "Guiding Hundredth."[87]

In this respect, then, the change of position in Du Bois's thought that is most apparent in the post–World War II period turns out on examination not to constitute so much of a change at all. Such change as did occur in this regard reflects a reasonable adaptation of his basic premises to a new historical context and a desperate attempt to identify an appropriate historical lever, a critical agency to effect social reorganization. This change took two forms: (1) reformulation of his decades-long assertion of the Talented Tenth as bearers of the collective subjectivity of the Afro-American population, and (2) identification of the international proletariat as the embodiment of universal reason in the current period. The first position he saw as a response to changing historical conditions among black Americans. Central among those in his view was the progress of stratification within the black population:

> The outstanding fact about the Negro group in America, which has but lately gained notice, is that it is flying apart into opposition economic classes. This was to be expected. But most people, including myself, long assumed that the American Negro, forced into social unity by color caste, would achieve eco-

nomic unity as a result, and rise as a mass of laborers led by intelligent planning to a higher unity with the laboring classes of the world.

This has not happened. On the contrary, and quite logically, the American Negro is today developing a distinct bourgeoisie bound to and aping American acquisitive society and developing an employing and a laboring class. This division is only in embryo, but it can be sensed.[88]

Moreover, Du Bois already had been soured by having been ostracized by the black middle class when he was arrested as a Soviet agent in 1951. He recalled:

While, then, most of my educated and well-to-do friends . . . were scared by the war propaganda and went quickly to cover, an increasing mass of the Negro working class, especially the members of the so-called left-wing unions, rallied to my side with faith and money. This gave me a new outlook on social stratification within this group, which I once hoped would never develop. My faith hitherto had been in what I once denominated the "Talented Tenth." I now realize that the ability within a people does not automatically work for its highest salvation.[89]

However, Du Bois did not in his revision eliminate the black elite from its historic mission. Finally—after pointing out that black people on issues other than race are neither intrinsically radical nor intrinsically conservative[90]—he asserted that "the Negro intelligentsia must reassert its influence on the mass of Negro labor and wheel it into step with the world labor movement, especially in Asia and Africa."[91] Nor was this all; he went on once again to amend his Talented Tenth thesis, noting that in the present context "many educated and gifted young black folk will be as selfish and immoral as the whites who surround them and to whom the Negroes have been taught to look as ideals."[92] The historically responsible elite would be drawn and trained from the proletariat instead:

Naturally, out of the mass of the working classes, who know life and its bitter struggle, will continually rise the real, unselfish and clear-sighted leadership. This will not be automatic or continuous, but the hope of the future of the Negro race in America and the world lies far more among its workers than among its college graduates, until the time that our higher training is rescued from its sycophantic and cowardly leadership of today, almost wholly dependent as it is on Big Business either in politics or philanthropy.[93]

Not only the black working class was to march in the forefront of history. Du Bois noted that a "new era of power, held and exercised by the working classes the world over, is dawning and while its eventual form is not yet clear, its progress cannot be held back by any power of man."[94] So Du Bois, long-time proponent of a view of the inability of untrained workers to manage political affairs, in the postwar era seemed to assign to them a world-historical mission. However, there was an important though subtle wrinkle in his argument.

Regarding his revised perception of the role of the black elite, he made a tacit distinction in his text between intelligentsia and bourgeoisie. On the one hand, he disparaged the development of an acquisitive capitalist stratum in the black community; on the other, he identified with the "dream among the intelligentsia of an independent Negro vote devoted to Negro progress"[95] and exhorted the latter stratum to "reassert its influence" on the masses. The intellectuals and intelligentsia were, of course, the stratum for which Du Bois actually spoke all along. What is most likely the case is that he simply had attached the intelligentsia's agenda to that of the minuscule black bourgeoisie, who after all were status peers. Then, as the bourgeois stratum grew, elaborated itself, and declined as a source of critical politics, Du Bois was moved to focus his strategy for the intellectuals toward more direct stewardship over a mass, working-class-based—but intellectual-led—movement. Seen thus, this key reflex in Du Bois's class commitments and views of the proper organization of the Afro-American population for collective action remained fundamentally the same over his entire career.

Three Confusions about Du Bois

Interracialism, Pan-Africanism, Socialism

D U BOIS'S PROMINENCE in this century's Afro-American political life is widely
recognized. Yet attempts to categorize him with respect to the various strategic and ideological programs constitutive of black political debate have yielded
an uncommonly confusing picture. The confusion about locating Du Bois programmatically has two sources. The first is quite simple: Du Bois lived and
acted through several discrete social and political situations that seemed to him
to require different strategic responses for the race. Sometimes, especially when
sundered from the situations to which they were responses, the strategies that
he proposed appear to contradict one another. Analysts, then, have chosen and
defended one or another set of strategies or one or another period as authentically Du Boisian. This is a problem of temporal or contextual focus.

The other source of confusion has to do with conceptual focus. If examination is restricted to Du Bois's various racial strategies, which were usually the
central concerns of his writing, analysis will record a mélange of discrete political positions, but will gloss the normative and conceptual logic that organized
his worldview.

As I indicated in chapter 1, inattentiveness toward those social-theoretical
foundations of political discourse is a major problem in scholarship on Afro-
American thought in general.[1] Its role in generating confusion about Du Bois,
however, stands out for two key reasons. First, his prominence has increased the

likelihood that partisans of all sorts would want to claim him for their various agendas. Second, his unusually clear, self-reflexive intellectual approach makes confused and widely conflicting interpretations seem especially anomalous.

Through examination of Du Bois's utterances on three political programs with which he is typically associated, I shall argue in this chapter that his pronouncements cohere around certain core assumptions and values that he maintained over the course of his lengthy intellectual career. I examine Du Bois's views on (1) interracialism as an organizational principle for American society; (2) Pan-Africanism as an interest of the black world; and (3) socialism as a model for social organization in general. My concern here is to establish Du Bois's actual positions on those issues and to uncover the structuring logic of his thought by locating those positions in relation to one another as well as to the historical and discursive contexts within which they were developed.

Interracialism

Greater interpretive ambiguity surrounds the character of Du Bois's interracialism than other aspects of his thought. This is so in part because the status of interracialism as a political value was not controversial in the same way for Du Bois and his communicants as it has been among subsequent political theorists and intellectual historians.[2] The search for Du Bois's position requires extrapolation, often from incidental comments scattered over several decades and situations. When the broad range of possibly germane utterances is combined with the intentionality of the analysts, it is not surprising that conflicting, if not incompatible, interpretations occur.

Howard Brotz, for example, describes Du Bois as a "cultural nationalist."[3] Harold Cruse identifies him, although with qualifications, as a principal member of the integrationist tendency in the history of Afro-American thought.[4] Sterling Stuckey claims that Du Bois advocated nationalism even in the face of the latter's explicit disclaimer.[5] And Vincent Harding proposes that Du Bois should be seen as an anticipation of both radical nationalism and radical anticolonialism, as well as militant integrationism.[6] Moreover, each of these assessments is or could be derived directly from statements made by Du Bois. Yet consideration of certain contextual and intentional mediations on Du Bois's thinking allows an interpretation that integrates those discrete stances that have provided the basis for the varied and conflicting assessments of his position on this issue. These mediations are as follows: (1) his dual commitments to race pride and the heuristic of "racial group idealism" on the one side and the Victorian outlook that values "progress," defined as increasingly unitary, rational organization, on the other; (2) his commitment to the hegemony of the black elite within the Afro-American population; (3) his growing perception, influenced by the Depression and his reassessment of the sources of racism, of a need for the development of a self-help program within the race; and (4) his experiences within the NAACP.

Du Bois's pride in race coexisted with his enthusiasm at participating at the forefront of modern (European) culture and values; he could equally deprecate spontaneous Afro-American behavior and exalt black behavior and values and decry the bankruptcy of the European heritage. The dissonant ring to his ambivalent race pride to some extent is a function of his bombastic literary style; but the oft-mentioned phenomenon of his "two-ness" or "double consciousness," which I consider at greater length in chapter 7, is an expression of his antinomical commitment to what he perceived to be the Dionysian attractions of black culture and the Apollonian virtues of Euro-American civilization. Writing during the Harlem Renaissance, for example, his references to black folklife, both in Africa and in the United States, emphasized what he considered its primitive aspects. He lauded blacks' "sensuous, tropical love of life, in vivid contrast to the cool and cautious New England reason."[7] "The Negro," he proclaimed, "is primarily an artist."[8] However, this racial characteristic did not imply for Du Bois, as it did for many who extolled black spirituality, that the race required external tutelage to prepare it for modern civilization.

He asserted very early a conviction that Afro-Americans best handle Afro-American affairs. About this he was insistent, even in the early 1900s, as he advocated formation of a coalition of the best men of black and white races to attempt rationally to reorganize life in the South.[9] Du Bois's insistence on Afro-American primacy in determination and pursuit of Afro-American interests—regardless how elementally reasonable and appropriate that position was—also resonates with his intentions concerning the role of the elite within the Afro-American population. If the group is to speak for itself, still not everyone can speak at once—especially not if a single, collective agenda is to be fashioned. Cacophony could be avoided by allowing the race's "natural leaders" to rise. In an early call for unity and protest, Du Bois observed in 1903:

> Here is the path out of the economic situation and here is the imperative demand for trained Negro leaders of character and intelligence—men of skill, men of light and leading, college-bred men, black captains of industry, and missionaries of culture; men who thoroughly comprehend and know modern civilization, and can take hold of Negro communities and raise and train them by force of precept and example, deep sympathy, and the inspiration of common blood and ideals.[10]

As he noted in his Philadelphia study, blacks' developmental needs actually would have been best served in his view by a dictatorship of the elite; however, because the race had been thrust prematurely into interaction with the more advanced society and democratic institutions, the incubative stage of elite dictatorship was blocked.[11] Nevertheless, the historical mission of the elite stratum included demonstrating "the ability of the Negro to assimilate American culture."[12] In this sense, Du Bois's view of the collective racial interest in the black community's generation of its own spokesmen at least coincided with the hegemonic interest of the elite. However, although this position acknowledges a need for intraracial organization that at least in principle qualifies opposition to separation, it was not until the Depression that Du Bois sought to work out a program that accepted segregation as given. However, this program was not so much a radical departure from his previous views; his emphasis may only have stood out more because protest against Jim Crow had become overwhelmingly consensual as the organizing imperative of black politics.

He had begun developing his program of cultural-economic nationalism in the 1920s. The foundation of this program was advocacy of racially based cooperative economics. Cooperativist racial economics long had held an attraction for Du Bois. Both as an economic practicality and as a model for economic democracy, the cooperative recommended itself to him.[13] After World War I, though, Du Bois credited two realizations with gradually pushing the consumer-cooperative organization idea to prominence. In the postwar environment he felt that the slogans of political democracy developed a hollow ring; the pressing problems were then economic rather than political "in an oligarchic world."[14] Thus was he prepared to emphasize a strategy of economic organization. Although he had little support from the NAACP, by 1930 Du Bois was convinced that the organization needed to adjust its program to meet needs generated by "economic dislocation."[15] Simultaneously, he came to appreciate the extent to which deep-seated complexes and subrational behaviors shape public attitudes.[16] From this perspective he decided, as he reflected in 1940, that the "present attitude and action of the white world is not based solely upon rational, deliberate intent. It is a matter of conditioned reflexes; of long followed habits, customs and folkways; of subconscious trains of reasoning and unconscious nervous reflexes. To attack and better all this calls for more than appeal and argument. It needs carefully planned and scientific propaganda."[17]

What this meant, in his view, was that there needed to be a shift of emphasis in black uplift activity. Previously, when Du Bois had assumed rational motivations to explain racial prejudice and exclusion, the focus of his activism was directed toward education and changing whites' attitudes. Once he determined that the bases of much racial prejudice are nonrational, his stress moved away from education and propaganda among whites—which had not by any means been Du Bois's only previous concern anyway—to what he identified as his post-1928 strategy; that is, "[s]cientific investigation and organized action among Negroes, in close cooperation, to secure the survival of the Negro race, until the cultural development of America and the world is willing to recognize Negro freedom."[18]

In the meantime, in Du Bois's view, simple good judgment called for fortifying such black institutions as existed behind the walls of segregation. That practical viewpoint at times forced him into conflict with doctrinal foes of segregation, as when he supported the chartering of Cheyney State College in Cheyney, Pennsylvania, as a black school. Du Bois made clear that, although he opposed segregation as a principle, when confronted with the choice between a black school and no school, the black school would have to be supported. Indeed, when faced with already segregated institutions, he was left with a "paradox": "We must oppose segregation in schools; we must honor and appreciate the colored teacher in the colored school. . . . We recognize one thing worse than segregation and that is ignorance."[19] The consumer-cooperative organization strategy, however, was not only defensive; the consumer movement could develop into a powerful vehicle for social transformation as well. He maintained, "The consuming public, who should also be the real working producers of the world, must resume its logical and rightful place as the final directing force in industry. This can be done without violence or revolution."[20] Consumer groups then would be able to take over production, filling their own needs, breaking the chain of external dependence, and installing industrial democracy.[21] Nor was the consumer model restricted to the United States; Du Bois explored its possibilities for "freeing thought and action in the colonial areas."[22]

The consumer-cooperative organization strategy never really took off; in part its failure recalls a tragic aspect of political thought. As other than ideology for group mobilization, the strategy likely was too late when proposed. A "new industrial democracy established on a firm basis of individual knowledge and initiative built up to contest the occupation of the industrial field with the present individualists, monopolists, high-binders, and free-booters"[23] probably faced overwhelmingly bad odds in 1939. However, as a mobilization ideology, the consumer-cooperative organization that Du Bois advocated also resonated with the legitimation needs of the Afro-American elite as Du Bois saw them. He indicated that the program was designed, among other things, to answer the following question: "Can ten million Negroes, led by cultured classes numbering less than a million, achieve efficient and voluntary democracy without force, without police power, without the domination of wealth and capital?"[24]

Du Bois was concerned, however, about the black elite's readiness to shoulder its group responsibility in what he saw as a "long siege against the strongholds of color caste."[25] He expressed the basis for his concern:

> The upper class Negro has almost never been nationalistic. He has never planned or thought of a Negro state or a Negro church or a Negro school. This solution has always been a thought up-surging from the mass, because of pressure which they could not withstand and which compelled a racial institution or chaos. Continually such institutions were founded and developed, but this took place against the advice and best thought of the intelligentsia.[26]

He reminded them, however:

> When the NAACP was formed, the great mass of Negro children were being trained in Negro schools; the great mass of Negro churchgoers were members of Negro churches; the great mass of Negro citizens lived in Negro neighborhoods; the great mass of Negro voters voted with the same political party; and the mass of Negroes joined with Negroes and cooperated with Negroes in order to fight the extension of this segregation and to move toward better conditions. What was true in 1910 was still true in 1940 and will be true in 1970. But with this vast difference: that the segregated Negro institutions are better organized, more intelligently planned and more efficiently conducted, and today form in

themselves the best and most compelling argument for the ultimate abolition of the color line.[27]

He continued:

> To have started out in this organization with a slogan "no segregation," would have been impossible. What we did say was no increase in segregation; but even that stand we were unable to maintain. Whenever we found that an increase of segregation was in the interest of the Negro race, naturally we had to advocate it. We had to advocate all sorts of organized movement among Negroes to fight oppression and in the long run end segregation.[28]

Despite the elite's reluctance, Du Bois was consistent throughout the period of his active commitment to this nationalistic, or race-solidaristic, organizational strategy—roughly through World War II—on the importance of the elite's role; he was emphatic about the need for "trained" leadership.[29]

Although, as has been noted, he seems always to have been committed without reservation to black leadership of blacks, his experience with the white-dominated NAACP at least reinforced his disposition toward black self-organization. As his antagonism toward the NAACP's board grew over the issue of editorial autonomy for the *Crisis,* Du Bois's advocacy of the nationalistic program became more and more insistent.[30] Finally, he challenged the NAACP board to acknowledge the utility of segregation as a support for positive black institutions.[31] In the fervor to make his point, he even stooped to endorse black fraternities and sororities as exemplars of the racially useful side of segregation.[32]

Although his nationalistic program was the specific issue that precipitated Du Bois's departure from the organization, his course had not meshed well for some time with the thrust defined by the white liberals in the NAACP's leadership. Francis L. Broderick points out that the latter supported none of his post–World War I initiatives, noting that one Republican director even resigned over Du Bois's support of Robert Marion La Follette in the 1924 presidential election.[33] It is not unlikely that this experience with the apparent incongruence of black and white agendas for black uplift strengthened Du Bois's resolve for arguing the primacy of intraracial initiative as the appropriate strategy for realization of the ultimate objective of an integrated society.[34]

Du Bois's fundamental commitment to an interracial world civilization was teleological, and his teleology was one quite common among liberal (and radical) intellectuals of his cohort. He stated his view of this aspect of the trajectory of history emphatically in his critical assessment of Marcus Garvey's movement. Garvey, Du Bois noted, had failed in part because he did not realize that

> "[h]ere is a world that for a thousand years, from the First Crusade to the Great War, had been breaking down the barriers between nations and races in order to build a world-wide economic unity and cultural solidarity. The process has involved slavery, peonage, rape, theft, and extermination, but it is slowly uniting humanity. It is now proposed to turn back and cut out of this world its black eighth or its colored two thirds. Not only is this virtually impossible, but its attempt to-day would certainly involve the white and colored worlds in a death-

struggle whose issue none can surely foretell. The power of the yellow, black, and brown worlds to-day is the economic dependence of the white world on them, and the power of the white world is its economic technic and organization. The super-diplomacy of race politics tomorrow is to transmute this interdependence into cultural sympathy, spiritual tolerance, and human freedom. Not in segregation, but in closer, larger unity lies interracial peace.[35]

The "nationalism" which Du Bois embraced, therefore, assumed a broader context of genuinely *international* world unity, at least as an ideal and goal. To some extent his advocacy of organizing behind racial lines was tactical; as I have shown, he saw cultivation of all-black institutions as a necessary concession to the reality of segregation and a necessary element in the struggle against it. Du Bois saw other merits in black-controlled institutions. They could provide prophylaxis against racial humiliation; he observed that "if social contact can be had only at the cost of . . . racial degradation . . ., then the Negro race is almost forced to ask for its own teachers and to support its own colleges and universities—or to demand State aid for Jim Crow higher training."[36] And, although he steadfastly maintained his universalist teleology, he remained pessimistic regarding possibilities for honest interracial interaction in the present, as is indicated in his biting eulogy for Carter G. Woodson. After recounting and praising Woodson's accomplishments, Du Bois noted: "No white university ever recognized his work; no white scientific society ever honored him. Perhaps this was his greatest reward."[37]

Yet black-controlled racial institutions were attractive to Du Bois for purely positive reasons as well. He argued that "separation" had fostered for the Negro the rise of "cultured individuals in his own group who were not only able to impart the elements of civilization to others but were able to do it in much more pleasant and more effective ways than most white people."[38] In this context blacks developed an active preference for being ministered to by their own professionals. Moreover, this dynamic merely brought Afro-Americans into step with the march of world history:

Separation, for the most part, not only ceased to hinder the race from making any cultural advance, but even helped it forward. But forward toward what? Exactly the same thing was happening in Negro America that happened in Germany when she discovered resources within her own soul that made her independent of French culture; the same thing that happened in Ireland when she decided that to be Irish was even more desirable than to be English.[39]

He broke off the analogy dramatically short of a call for an independent Afro-American nation, and—given that this article appeared only a year after his universalistic "Back to Africa" essay—it is unlikely that he would have wanted to endorse such a stance. Instead, Du Bois's notion of racial particularism was more pluralistic than separatist. In fact, his universalist teleology shared features with the views of Horace Kallen, perhaps the most important early-twentieth-century advocate of cultural pluralism in the United States.[40] As appears most clearly in his proposals for a postcolonial Pan-African unity (see below), Du Bois

envisioned movement toward a world rationally and homogeneously administered but constituted of cultural units that would retain their distinctiveness. He
differed from Kallen, though, in the extent to which he saw pluralism as subordinate to a transcendent ideal of "civilization."

David Levering Lewis notes, in an examination of black and Jewish elite
responses to Americanization ideology in the early twentieth century, that Du
Bois believed that "[e]thnic pride . . . could be sublimated in the dogma of
unexceptionable public conformity to the best ideals and behavior of white
Anglo-Saxon Protestant (WASP) America—the better to guarantee private space
for retention of what was most precious in minority culture."[41] That stance is
quite like Kallen's call for the United States to be reconstituted as a "federal
republic," in which the "common language of the commonwealth, the language
of its great tradition, would be English, but each nationality would have for its
emotional and involuntary life its own peculiar dialect or speech, its own individual and inevitable esthetic and intellectual forms."[42] Du Bois, however, because of his teleological evolutionism, stressed the role of universal principles of
progress, and, correspondingly, was more inclined than Kallen to sacrifice ethnic
particularities on the altar of the cosmopolitan telos.[43]

Du Bois saw the dynamics of race and culture as at the same time pluralistic
and evolutionist; although the two perspectives need not conflict, in his case
they underwrote an embrace of ideals and rhetoric that were simultaneously
relativistic and hierarchical. The common root of these coexisting commitments
was his persisting affinity for reform-Darwinist premises in his theory of history.[44]
After World War II, when he was seventy-seven years old, he judged the Nazi
Holocaust to have been particularly horrendous because of the "cultural accomplishments of [the Jews], the gifts they have made to the civilization of the
world."[45] Contribution to that world civilization was for Du Bois the standard
for assessing the worth and significance of various social groups—classes, races,
nations. Unlike ideologues of Western supremacy, however, he called for recognizing the value and contributions of "primitive" cultures. However, his own
notion of the barometer of civilization was, despite his insistence on construing
it as universal and transcendent, very much defined by Western modernity. Not
only was his acknowledgment of the virtues of the "primitive" usually betrayed
by a rhetoric of condescension; he also never cut himself loose from seeing the
world as consisting of "backward" and "advanced" peoples. He allowed that "vast
numbers of backward peoples have made notable cultural advance under the
colonial regime"[46] even as he advocated a vigorous antiimperialism.

An unreflective acceptance of the self-referential, universalistic claims of
European cultural ideology was not unique to Du Bois; as Wilson J. Moses
observes, that disposition was ironically common among early black nationalists.[47] In general, that ironic tendency reflects the hegemonic power of the ideologies that have shaped the framework of conventions underlying cultural and
political discourse in the West. For Du Bois specifically, the outcome was a
perspective which—despite his own relativistic protests—saw the West as bearer
of the principle of cultural evolution and thus as a model for the backward

peoples. Although he believed that non-Western, Dionysian or primitive peoples could enrich—through their own racial-cultural "messages"—the main lines of progress in world civilization, he never questioned that the trajectory of civilization, as it evolved toward perfection, was leading toward a unitary world dominated by principles of planning and rational administration.[48] His cultural pluralism, therefore, was ultimately subordinate to the universalizing requirements of progress, and the ideal world which he envisaged was harmoniously integrated. The notions of progress and civilization which grounded his teleology—and which were to hold the unified world together—were virtually pure projections of a rhetorical and ideological orientation current among Western intellectuals.[49] Du Bois's failure to recognize that orientation's historical partiality and specificity led him to ontologize its categories into a universalistic philosophy of history. To that extent, he succumbed to a precisely Lukacsian false consciousness which gave his cultural relativism an ultimately hollow, defensive ring.

Pan-Africanism

The motif of stepping back into intragroup organization as a step toward realizing universalist objectives also helps to bring into focus the place of Pan-Africanism in Du Bois's thought.

Pan-Africanism appears in his writing first in relation to his proposals for decolonization in Africa. However, his commitment to Pan-African unity and self-determination was tempered from the outset by his distinction of the blacks who had appropriated the characteristics of "civilization" from those who had not. The former, in his view, should be responsible for the administration and guidance of the latter. In his program for dispensation of former German colonies after World War I, Du Bois acknowledged that the "principle of self-determination . . . cannot be wholly applied to semi-civilized peoples." Therefore, he argued, those colonies should have been placed "under the guidance of organized civilization," with special consideration given to the administrative opinions of the "chiefs and intelligent Negroes among the twelve and one-half million natives of German Africa [and the] twelve million civilized Negroes of the United States." Direct governance of the colonies, he proposed, should be assumed by an "International Commission [representing] not simply governments, but modern culture—science, commerce, social reform and religious philanthropy."[50]

This construction of the Pan-African mission reveals in yet another domain Du Bois's confidence in the capacity of the race's elite elements to define and realize the interests of the black world. Over at least the period of the first four Pan-African Congresses after World War I, he maintained detailed proposals for disposition of the colonial territories. The general program was directed in essence toward "preparing" African colonial territories for self-determination through gradual, supervised extension of autonomy. This gradual preparation was to include participation in colonial administration by indigenous peoples, as well as West Indian and North American "civilized" and "educated" blacks. Education of the indigenous population was to be extended and with it the franchise, which Du Bois considered the basis of political participation.

The key in the early program goes back to Du Bois's persisting distinction between the "civilized" and the "uncivilized." The resolutions of the first Pan-African Congress stated in part:

> The natives of Africa must have the right to participate in the Government as far as their development permits in conformity with the principle that the Government exists for the natives, and not the natives for the government. They should be allowed to participate in local and tribal government according to ancient usage, and this participation shall gradually extend, as education and experience proceeds, to the higher offices of State, to the end that, in time Africa be ruled by consent of Africans. . . . Whenever it is proven that any African natives are not receiving just treatment at the hands of any state or that any state deliberately excludes its civilized citizens or subjects of Negro descent from its body politic and culture, it shall be the duty of the League of Nations to bring the matter to the civilized world.[51]

The relevant social actors for Du Bois in this period were blacks from North America and the West Indies, and the indigenous elites generated by the colonial system. Those groups represented within the African world the bearers of civilization and were to function as the carriers of the Enlightenment to Africa.

Du Bois soon modified his position to explore what he perceived to be a chauvinistic impulse toward Africa on the part of blacks in the Western hemisphere and his own manifestations of that impulse.[52] He felt constrained to point out that, while reiterating that Africa should be administered by blacks, that position did not mean "that Africa should be administered by West Indians or American Negroes." He declared that the latter groups "have no more right to administer Africa for the native Africans than native Africans have to administer America."[53] Moreover, he contended that qualified opportunity did exist in Africa for Western blacks "with capital, education and some technical or agricultural skills, who have the courage of pioneers, good health, and are willing to rough it,"[54] but that the continent "has no place for empty-headed laborers . . . sick people or old people or orators or agitators."[55]

The mediation of leadership by Western blacks was made clearly unnecessary for decolonization in Africa; as Du Bois reflected in 1961:

> Africans began to demand more voice in colonial government and the Second World War had made their cooperation so necessary to Europe that at the end actual and unexpected freedom for African colonies was in sight.
>
> Moreover, there miraculously appeared Africans able to take charge of these governments. American Negroes of former generations had always calculated that when Africa was ready for freedom, American Negroes would be ready to lead them. But the event was quite opposite. The African leaders proved to be Africans. . . . American Negroes for the most part showed neither the education nor the aptitude for the magnificent opportunity which was suddenly offered. Indeed, it now seems that Africans may have to show American Negroes the way to freedom.[56]

Still, the civilizing mission remained, and in this respect the significance of Du Bois's Pan-Africanism as it faced Africa lay in the way that he saw it as an element of a modernization strategy. From that perspective, the most efficient governmental or social unit among a common group is that which is able to administer to and plan for the entire group, thereby minimizing duplication of effort, contradiction in policy, and other forms of social waste. As part of development into the "modern world," to the extent that Africa could be seen as a basically common cultural unit, the requirements of rational social administration would suggest combination and unification.

This rational-utilitarian view was enhanced by Du Bois's embedded teleology and theory of history, which emphasized harmonious social organization and progress through advances of civilization. Precolonial Africa appeared in his reconstruction as a series of societies moving in lockstep toward collective teleological goals. Similarly, he paid little attention to likely internal conflicts within his contemporary African unity,[57] and took for granted both the existence and progressive function of a coordinating apparatus, a continental state. Indeed he maintained:

> If Africa unites, it will be because each part, each nation, each tribe gives up a part of its heritage for the good of the whole. That is what union means; that is what Pan-Africa means. . . . When the tribe becomes a union of tribes, the individual tribe surrenders some part of its freedom to the paramount tribe. . . .
>
> When the nation arises, the constituent tribes, clans and groups must each yield power and some freedom to the demands of the nation or the nation dies before it is born. Your local tribal, much-loved languages must yield to the few world tongues which serve the largest number of people and promote understanding and world literature.[58]

This statement reflects the predatory and solipsistic optimism that arises from the rational-administrative outlook. The flippancy with which Du Bois dispatched intra-African particularity not only indicates the naïveté typically shown by the relatively more homogeneous Afro-Americans and West Indians concerning such matters, but also demonstrates the centrality of the universalist and homogenizing assumptions of social engineering in his thinking. The necessity of sacrificing provincial languages to the "world tongues" indicates the commitment of Du Bois's Pan-Africanism to an ultimately universalist goal. Where can history as increasing administrative rationality lead, other than to a united and coordinated world? Provincialisms that retard such development must be jettisoned in favor of progress.

The universalist grounding of his Pan-Africanism is hardly only an inference from Du Bois's text; for, in his own words, "[t]he broader the basis of a culture, the wider and freer its conception, the better chance it has for the survival of its best elements. This is the basic hope of world democracy. . . . Peace and tolerance is the only path to eternal progress. Europe can never survive without Asia and Africa as free and interrelated civilizations in one world."[59] Another aspect of his Pan-Africanism is of interest here. Pan-Africanism for Du Bois, in addition to being part of a strategy for decolonization and modernization in Africa, also represented a mechanism for constitution of an international black elite and its consciousness: "Pan-Africa means intellectual understanding and cooperation among all groups of Negro descent in order to bring about at the earliest possible time the industrial and spiritual emancipation of the Negro peoples."[60] One of the planks in his program for Africa in the early 1920s, in addition to promoting education among the natives and "industry, commerce and credit among black groups," entailed bringing together "for periodic conference and acquaintanceship the leading Negroes to the world and their friends."[61]

In this respect, his Pan-Africanism is directed more toward the United States than toward Africa. From the beginning of his involvement with and agitation for Africa, Du Bois, unlike others in the Pan-African pantheon, granted the fundamental Americanness of Afro-Americans. He clarified his position early: "Once for all let us realize that we are Americans. . . . there is nothing so indigenous, so completely 'made in America' as we."[62] Yet he saw Africa as offering "a chance for the colored American to emigrate and to go as a pioneer to a country which must, sentimentally at least, possess for him the same fascination as England does for Indian-born Englishmen,"[63] and Pan-Africanism as a mechanism for development of a consciousness among the Afro-American elite appropriate to the historical tasks required of it:

> I tried to say to the American Negro . . . there are certain things you must do for your own survival and self-preservation. You must work together and in unison; you must evolve and support your own social institutions; you must transform your attack from the foray of self-assertive individuals to the massed might of an organized body. You must put behind your demands, not simply American Negroes, but West Indians and Africans, and all the colored races of the world.[64]

Pan-Africanism, then, was for Du Bois largely a means. Although he built his Pan-Africanist vision on a foundation that stressed the spiritual ties binding people of African descent, Pan-Africanism constituted for him at most a basis for wide-scale racial organization within the context of a global pluralism. In this sense, his Pan-Africanism differed from the emigrationist-redemptionist orientation of Garveyism and the millenarian-tinged revolutionism of the post–Black Power American Pan-Africanism.[65] Unlike those other tendencies, Du Bois saw Pan-Africanism as an expression among blacks of the developmental logic of modern society. Although, for example, he suggested that the institutional foundation for a self-determining Africa would be a "socialism founded on old African communal life," he pointed out at the same instant that "Pan-African socialism seeks the welfare state in Black Africa."[66] Perhaps as a reflection of the cavalier or superficial attitudes about ethnic culture that abound in Afro-American thought, or perhaps as another expression of his "two-ness," at the same time that Du Bois called for "sacrifice" of intra-African particularity on the altar of progress, he insisted that "Pan-Africa will seek to preserve its own past history."[67] Pan-Africa ultimately was to Du Bois the African form of pluralist participation in a global socialist order that he saw as the highest expression of rational social organization. Du Bois assured that "[g]radually, every state is coming to this concept of its aim."[68] It is at this point that Du Bois's Pan-Africanism converged with his conception of socialism.

Socialism

The place of socialism in Du Bois's thinking is another area about which conventional wisdom is not as conventional as it appears; everyone agrees that Du Bois died a socialist, but few agree on when he became one or on what kind of socialist he was. Broderick, for example, sees Du Bois as having made "advances to socialism in 1907, although in early 1908 he affirmed his attachment to the principles of the Republican party."[69] Elliott M. Rudwick's view is less ambivalent: He contends that by the earlier year Du Bois was under socialist influence; and to support his claim, Rudwick adduces Du Bois's advocacy of "cooperation in capital and labor, wider distribution of capital."[70] Alan Sigmund Cywar, however, maintains that in the early part of this century Du Bois advocated a sort of leftwing Social Darwinism,[71] and that his "decisive swing to the left would begin to become evident in the pages of the *Crisis* only after World War I."[72] Eugene C. Holmes asserts that as "a materialist, it was only natural that ethically and economically Dr. Du Bois's sympathies were always along socialist lines of thinking."[73] Bernard Fonlon[74] and Julius Lester[75] agree that Du Bois opted for socialism in 1907, whereas W. Alphaeus Hunton[76] and Truman Nelson[77] emphasize Du Bois's commitment to socialism in general. Gerald Horne claims that Du Bois was a socialist "all of his adult life."[78]

A problem common to all these interpretations is the failure to account for the mercurial content that the term *socialism* had in the United States in the early twentieth century. Indeed, among students who address the issue of Du Bois's early *socialism*, only Manning Marable and Wilson J. Moses take into account the ambiguity of the label during the years before 1917 in the United States. Marable maintains, correctly, that when Du Bois joined the Socialist party in 1911, the "decision did not mark any significant turn to radicalism," and he suggests that the socialism with which Du Bois identified was the conservative variety endorsed by Charles Edward Russell, Mary White Ovington, Jane Addams, and other members of the NAACP board rather than the radical tendency of Eugene Debs and Bill Haywood.[79] Moses, also noting the preferences of other NAACP socialists, sees Du Bois as having "toyed with the idea of nonrevolutionary white-collar socialism of the domestic variety,"[80] and he links Du Bois's socialism and his technocratic-elitist commitments.[81]

Socialism was identified variously with support of trusts, public ownership of utilities, corporate regulation, municipal reform, trade unionism, industrial unionism, or any of a myriad of other social and economic policies.[82] Determination of whether Du Bois, or any other agent active at that time, should be considered a socialist, therefore, depends on which of the variety of socialist tendencies the critic takes as authentically socialist. Either that or the identification is so vague as to tell us very little.

This impasse of defining socialist authenticity, an intellectually feckless activity, can be circumvented. James Gilbert's focus on collectivism as an overarching rubric which has encompassed a number of industrial-era American ideologies (see chapter 2) is helpful in this regard.[83] This vantage point illuminates and subsumes theoretical continuities that unite the various social programs advocated by twentieth-century reform-oriented intellectuals, whether they embraced Marxism, other sorts of socialism, or progressivism.

Although he observes that socialist and progressivist visions are in retrospect often difficult to distinguish theoretically, Gilbert contends that socialism constitutes a central theme around which other collectivist ideologies have oscillated.[84] Therein lies the strength of his formulation for the present purpose; notwithstanding Gilbert's attempt to differentiate Marxism qualitatively from other collectivist ideologies,[85] collectivism suggests a way around the basically scholastic and probably futile debate over when and whether Du Bois became a Marxist or any other kind of socialist.[86]

Argument concerning whether "Marxist" influences on Du Bois's thought were dominant, or whether Pan-Africanism or non-Marxist socialism constituted the central orienting principle of his ideas, is beside the point. The ensemble of the Marxist, non-Marxist socialist, and Pan-African perspectives converged on a distinctive response to elements of the development of industrial capitalism as a national and global system in the twentieth century. The future of Du Bois's Pan-Africa was broadly socialist; his consumer-cooperative organization likewise was a step toward realization of an integral collectivist society, and official Marxism represents perhaps the apotheosis of collectivism.[87] In this sense, the collectivist perspective offers the advantage of dissolving superficial antagonisms among the strategies toward which Du Bois was drawn by locating common properties that highlight their status as ideological and programmatic elaborations of a coherent if not systematically articulated political outlook.

In considering these programmatic themes in relation to the problem of political agency, Du Bois's texts express an assumption of the rational movement of historical forces along a continuum of progress, the terminus of which is already knowable, at least in general terms. Thus socialism, defined as "the assertion by the community of its right to control business and industry; the denial of the old assumption that public business can ever be a private enterprise,"[88] stands as the unequivocal long-term goal of social development. That Du Bois saw his socialist ideal as a point on the continuum along which Western society is advancing teleologically is hinted at both by his insistence that the path to socialism must not be led by proletarians, who are untutored and without the capacity for making judgments about the thrust of civilization,[89] and by his view that transformation must be sought by evolutionary rather than disruptive means.[90]

He observed shortly after World War I that the great question facing the world concerned distribution of the wealth created by modern technique, that is, the issue of rationalizing the distributive system of large-scale capitalism.[91] Socialism, in this 1920 perspective, constituted the challenge to private ownership in "property and tools" and the call for elevation of need over the perquisites of power in distribution of the social product.[92] Moreover, he condemned monopoly primarily because of its irrationality, for under monopoly "it is not the Inventor, the Manager, and the Thinker who today are reaping the great rewards of industry, but rather the Gambler and the Highwayman."[93] His proposal for rectification was an interesting amalgam of work ethic and social rationalization—perhaps indicative of the behavioral preferences of intellectuals or other petit bourgeois. Du Bois wrote, "Present Big Business—that Science of Human wants—must be perfected by eliminating the price paid for waste, which is Interest, and for Chance, which is Profit, and making all income a personal wage for service rendered by the recipient."[94] The fact that monopoly hegemony refuses to acknowledge technical interests sufficiently should not be taken lightly:

> Today the scientific and ethical boundaries of our industrial activities are not in the hands of scientists, teachers, and thinkers; nor is the intervening opportunity for decision left in the control of the public whose welfare such decisions guide. On the contrary, the control of industry is largely in the hands of a powerful few, who decide for their own good and regardless of the good of others.[95]

The problem of twentieth-century capitalism was, therefore, that its laudable technical capacities had developed beyond the rational limits of its institutional steering apparatus.[96] The task before the world, then, was to move to correct the disjunction. However, that charge implies two questions, *who* and *how.* Du Bois, the careful analyst, strained with only limited success to answer those questions.

Du Bois early discarded the proletariat as the lever of social transformation. He was left without an effective agency even as he proclaimed class struggle to be a reality.[97] Although his writings toward the latter years of the interwar period are dotted increasingly with references to the need for democracy to "fan out from politics to industrial life,"[98] he persisted in distinguishing—apparently with such self-assurance as to feel no need to argue the matter—a "logical social hierarchy" from one that can be penetrated only by wealth, with the strong implication that only the latter is unacceptable.[99] Moreover, it is suggestive in this regard that the Soviet Union was his enthusiastically held model for the vision of economic democracy. Perception of Russia as being in the lead "for realizing industrial democracy in the world"[100] was not uncommon among intellectuals in the United States, especially before the Stalin trials.[101] Du Bois retained his enthusiasm, however; he noted, as World War II drew to a close, that "Russia . . . still is to my mind, the most hopeful land in the modern world."[102]

Certain indications of how he would resolve the agency problem are sprinkled throughout Du Bois's interwar texts. Notwithstanding his charge that the "workers of the world must have voice not only on conditions of work but also as to what kinds of goods shall be produced and what methods of production used,"[103] he maintained that "distribution of wealth and services by plan, emphasizing ability and deserts, and especially the public weal; and guarding mankind from ignorance and disease must be a primary object of civilization."[104]

A tension exists between his two stated concerns, a tension that does not surface for direct consideration in his writing. Even though Du Bois by no means lacked sophistication in his critical attention to socialism,[105] he never seemed aware (or at least was not sufficiently troubled to engage the issue formally) of the intrinsic tension between centralized planning—as the expression of macrological, technical interests—and democratic decision making.

His focus on the Soviet model, it turns out, was not fortuitous. Du Bois's agency revealed its identity through comparison with its Bolshevik confreres. In discussing steps necessary to build a cooperative economy in the Afro-American community, he broke the spell of invisibility. The "Talented Tenth," the natural leadership of the black population, he tells us, must "subject" black labor to its guidance in the same way that survival of the Soviet Union "involves vast regimentation, unquestioning obedience until the cumbersome superhuman economic machine can run in rhythmic order."[106] The invisibility of the agency, then, appears to be more a matter of class unconsciousness than of simple confusion on Du Bois's part. Moreover, it indicates an essential continuity in his view of socialism even through his period of association with Bolshevism.

Writing after he finally had joined the Communist Party (USA) (CPUSA) and left the United States permanently, he responded to the question, What is socialism?: "It is a disciplined economy and political organization in which the first duty of a citizen is to serve the state; and the state is not a selected aristocracy, or a group of self-seeking oligarchs who have seized wealth and power. No! The mass of workers with hand and brain are the ones whose collective destiny is the chief object of all effort."[107]

For his part, Du Bois's dictatorship of the proletariat seems not to have been too dissimilar from industrial democracy:

> Thus it is clear today that the salvation of American Negroes lies in socialism. They should support all measures and men who favor the welfare state; they should vote for government ownership of capital in industry; they should favor strict regulation of corporations or their public ownership; they should vote to prevent monopoly from controlling the press and the publishing of opinions. They should favor public ownership and control of water, electric, and atomic power; they should stand for a clean ballot, the encouragement of third parties, independent candidates, and the elimination of graft and gambling on television and even in churches.
>
> The question of the method by which the socialist state can be achieved must be worked out by experiment and reason and not by dogma. Whether or not methods which were right and clear in Russia or China fit our circumstances is for our intelligence to decide.[108]

Consonant with Gilbert's general critique of collectivism, Du Bois's social-ism and his gravitation toward the CPUSA orbit indicate not so much the as-sumption of revolutionary consciousness at eighty years of age as the conver-gence of Soviet and New Deal ideological stances in the postwar period. American Communism reached its nadir during those years and was forced in-creasingly to tail behind ordinary civil rights and other popular front-type pro-grams, only by then without much "boring from within."[109] Du Bois's affinity for the Communist agenda was one of the movement's few bright spots after 1948; for Du Bois, who had been ostracized from mainstream black institutions, the CP was a port in an endless storm.[110]

From the collectivist perspective, Du Bois did not really have to move much at all from the positions he had held for five decades to accommodate his Com-munist turn. As his continuing enthusiasm in the pages of the *Crisis* over the Russian Revolution indicated, he had always felt a certain fascination with Bol-shevism's Jacobinist element.[111] Furthermore, given the exigencies of the new atomic age and the consuming weakness of the Communists in the United States, Du Bois was not required even to revise his long-standing commitments to nonviolence and reason as the means of social transformation. He maintained in 1946: "We cannot escape the clear fact that what is going to win in this world is reason if this ever becomes a reasonable world. The careful reasoning of the human mind backed by the facts of science is the one salvation of man. The world, if it resumes its march toward civilization, cannot ignore reason."[112]

Again in 1957 he described his outlook thus:

> I should call myself a Socialist, although that isn't a very definite term. But I mean I believe in the welfare state. I believe that business should be carried on not for private profit but for public welfare. I believe in many of the steps which are usually associated with socialism. . . . The Communist state will come about by the increase of socialism, by the change in our attitude toward each other, by making an individual American think of the progress of America and the welfare of America rather than thinking of his own advantage over his fellows, by ceasing to make the butt of our jokes the person who has suffered injury . . . by the extension of sacrifice and of love and of sympathy for our fellow beings. . . . I think it will come about democratically, not by violence . . . the violence that accompanies revolution is not the revolution. The revo-lution is the reform, is the change of thought, is the change of attitude on the people who are affected by it."[113]

Du Bois's Communist theoretical turn can be seen in part as an attempt to resolve the perennial problem of agency in the American Left by revising his expectations of the black elite as bearers of black collective subjectivity and assigning transformative responsibilities to the international proletariat. His revi-sion of the role assigned to the black middle class reflects disappointment at the latter's Cold War opportunism, especially as his "Talented Tenth" failed to sup-port him during his persecution. Similarly, the rise in prominence of the prole-tariat in Du Bois's view does not appear to indicate a qualitative shift in his outlook. His faith did not rest with empirical proletarians inside lived history.

He noted that American workers, for example, were not up to their task.[114] The proletariat in which Du Bois had faith was a collective subject whose empirical and historical embodiment was constituted in the Party. As a core principle of Bolshevism, the Party stands above the proletariat, represents its collective will, and thus constitutes a true universal subject. The Party, therefore, is in effect a central planning directorate for the proletariat. When consideration is given that the ruling circles within the Party are both centralized and composed overwhelmingly of intellectuals and intelligentsia, it seems that in turning to the proletariat as his last hope for realization of reason in the social world, Du Bois in principle only rationalized and streamlined the commitment to the hegemony of the "new class" elite with which he had been identified over the previous half century.

In fact, the "radical" socialism which he articulated at the end of his life differed little from the distributivist, technocratic variant he had embraced before the Great Depression. In 1945 he declared:

> The social sciences have been remiss in not pointing out a natural realm of dictatorship to which all government must bow; that is, the physical laws governing the constitution of materials, the application of natural force, and the availability of certain techniques in using matter and force, which are all subject to law and cannot be changed by popular vote. Thus the production of goods and to some degree their distribution is not a matter of argument, decision, or majority opinion, but an inexorable system which men must follow under the trained guidance of managers and technicians if they would get the necessary results.
>
> On the other hand, questions as to the kind of goods to be produced and their distribution among nations, classes, and individuals for consumption, and most questions of personal service, as to both recipient and servant, are questions where democratic argument and democratic decision are absolutely necessary to the widest human happiness.[115]

He was just as likely as in 1920 or even 1900 to link popular participation to a meritocratic standard of competence, noting that "democracy has proceeded slowly because the mass of people do not have the intelligence, the knowledge, or the experience to enable them to bear the responsibility of rule."[116] Five years before his death he endorsed the conviction—teleologically construed—that

> government must increasingly be controlled by the governed; that the mass of people, increasing in intelligence, with incomes sufficient to live a good and healthy life, should control all government, and that they would be able to do this by the spread of science and scientific technique, access to truth, the use of reason, and freedom of thought and of creative impulse in art and literature.[117]

His essentially Fabian view remained intact even as he was on the threshold of joining the Communist Party. "As knowledge and efficiency increased," he interpreted Marxism to promise, "democracy would spread among the masses and they would become capable of conducting a modern welfare state."[118] And he still used the term "socialism" to refer interchangeably to regimes and political economies as disparate as Mao's China, India, Scandinavia, the U.S.S.R., and the welfare state.[119]

Conclusions

Du Bois's racial pluralism, his Pan-Africanism, and his socialism came together around a distinct view of the world. Socialism was desirable for Du Bois ultimately because it promised to realize the principles of administrative rationality and meritocratic equality. Pan-Africanism similarly was a mechanism for rationalizing Africa's participation in an integral world order. His racial pluralism reflects a focus on elite-driven mass organization and group competition,[120] and this pluralism was for Du Bois an instrument for enhancing black membership in an integral society. The coherence of Du Bois's political thought is disclosed in its components' convergence around the unifying principles of the collectivist outlook characteristic among reform-oriented industrial-era intellectuals.

Those principles, and the outlook that they indicate, seldom are discussed directly in Du Bois's work, because they were generally shared through the discursive arena within which he operated. Because they were not controversial, and were in fact part of the least common denominator of conventional attitudes that made reform dialogue possible, there was little reason for those principles ever to be discussed elaborately. Therefore, they are accessible to us, the inhabitants of a different discursive situation, mainly through a reading that is sensitive to his texts' location in relation to their audiences and the shared understandings that cement that relation. Still, those organizing principles are not totally invisible in Du Bois's writing, as I have shown; they often have been obscured or simply ignored by analysts more concerned to project their theoretical or ideological programs onto Du Bois at the expense of his own.

It is more than likely, moreover, that similar principles have undergirded Afro-American political discourse throughout the industrial era. This certainly seems to be the case in the famed Washington–Du Bois controversy, in which both sides demonstrate commitment to a project of "Americanizing" the rank-and-file black population by subordinating it to the imperatives of industrialization.[121] In any event, the search for structuring assumptions at the base of black social thought could disclose important meanings characteristically obscured in narrowly textualist or superficially biographical analyses of writers' views on such theoretically pregnant issues as intraracial stratification, the nature of leadership or spokesmanship, and definition of community. Perhaps a useful heuristic is the simple question, seldom asked of black political figures, What sort of society would they create if they could restructure the world according to their own designs?

Du Bois's "Double Consciousness"

Race and Gender in Progressive-Era American Thought

After the Egyptian and Indian, the Greek and Roman, the Teuton and Mongolian, the Negro is a sort of seventh son, born with a veil, and gifted with second-sight in this American world,—a world which yields him no true self-consciousness, but only lets him see himself through the revelation of the other world. It is a peculiar sensation, this double-consciousness, this sense of always looking at one's self through the eyes of others, of measuring one's soul by the tape of a world that looks on in amused contempt and pity. One ever feels his two-ness,—an American, a Negro; two souls, two thoughts, two unreconciled strivings; two warring ideals in one dark body, whose dogged strength alone keeps it from being torn asunder.

—W. E. B. Du Bois, *The Souls of Black Folk*

THE EPIGRAPH to this chapter is probably—excepting perhaps his statement designating the "color line" as the twentieth century's distinctive problem— the most widely known and most frequently cited statement of any in Du Bois's entire corpus.[1] Indeed, it is quite likely one of the most familiar in all of Afro-American letters. The passage's enduring resonance derives from its verisimilitude in expressing a core lament of the Afro-American condition. It has been a distinctly attractive template for the articulation of both interpretive and substantive, academic and hortatory arguments concerning the race's status. For that reason, Du Bois's double-consciousness construct and the ways it has figured into subsequent intellectual work warrant special attention. In this chapter I shall consider the significance of the two-ness theme by examining the main approaches that scholars and other commentators have taken to it and by proposing a different, more richly contextualized perspective that situates Du Bois within the matrix of Progressive-era intellectual life.

Specifically, I argue that Du Bois's double consciousness was embedded most significantly in the neo-Lamarckian thinking about race, evolution, and social hierarchy that prevailed in a strain of reform-oriented, fin-de-siècle American social science. To that extent, I demonstrate that, in appropriating the no-

91

tion, sundry intellectuals misread Du Bois ahistorically and instead project their own thinking onto him. In the process I comment on certain key conceptual and methodological issues bearing on interpretation in the study of Afro-American thought.

The "double-consciousness" or "two-ness" image has been a remarkably, but variously, evocative characterization of the black American condition for several generations of observers identified with widely different intellectual and political projects. These appropriations have clustered, roughly chronologically, around three ideological programs: an integrationist-therapeutic motiv from the 1920s to the mid-1960s, a nationalist-therapeutic one from the mid-1960s to the early 1980s, and an academic race-celebratory one since.

August Meier, for example, has maintained that in the double-consciousness image Du Bois more explicitly than anyone else "revealed the impact of oppression and of the American creed in creating ambivalent loyalties toward race and nation in the minds of American Negroes."[2] Harold R. Isaacs similarly credited Du Bois with having crystallized recognition that "Negro identity has remained blurred, obscured behind the veil of alienation, ambivalence, confusion, and duality."[3] In an article first published in 1923, Robert Ezra Park cited it as an expression of "the enigma of the Negro's existence . . . how to be at once a Negro and a citizen."[4] For Park's Chicago colleague Everett V. Stonequist, it captured "with eloquence and poignancy . . . [t]he psychological dilemma" of the northern mulatto, whose "identification with the white race has been more complete, with the consequence that failure of full acceptance has been more disturbing" than for the southern mulatto.[5] St. Clair Drake focused on Du Bois's imagery of the veil as having disclosed a generically black "sense of isolation from 'the mainstream' . . . [which] not only generates distorted perceptions of the total society and occasionally bizarre definitions of situations, but . . . also results in cognitive crippling."[6] Perhaps most significantly in this "mark of oppression" mode, Gunnar Myrdal (see my discussion of Myrdal in chapter 1) ended his revealing "Negro Popular Theories" chapter by quoting Du Bois to underscore the tragedy of the "dual pull [which] is the correspondence in the Negro world to what we for the white world have called the American Dilemma," that is, the tension between the reality of race relations and the "American Creed."[7]

With development of the Black Power stance and militant ethnic pluralism in the late 1960s, views of the normative significance of Du Bois's two-ness image began to shift, though it retained its force as a metaphor for a putatively collective Afro-American condition. Robert Blauner enlisted Du Bois on behalf of an argument for radical status group pluralism by first defining "existential 'two-ness' " as a dilemma posed by coexisting imperatives of integration and nationalism and then generalizing the phenomenon to all "third world people in the United States."[8] Charles Valentine, less flamboyantly, extrapolated from Du Bois's image to a more elaborate social scientific notion of how Afro-American ethnicity operates in the American cultural system.[9] Similarly, Carol B. Stack cited the image as a definitive expression of the "conflicting and warring identities between being a Black and an American in a white world"; after observing that subsequent black artists and social scientists had drawn frequently on this "theme of a black identity and the conflict between racism and the ideology of the American Dream," she construed it as an undergirding premise of contemporary scholarship—including Valentine's—attacking claims that there is a debilitating "culture of poverty." Stack sought primarily and insistently to authenticate a notion of autonomous black culture and to rescue it from the rhetoric of pathology; at the same time, she attempted to draw moral force and empathy from a Myrdalian focus on the demoralizing effects of the conflict between aspirations and opportunities.[10] Robert Staples, however, pushed normative revision of the image further by elevating it to an epistemic principle; he adduced Du Bois's formulation also in amending Valentine's "biculturation" concept explicitly to stress positive valorization and foregrounding of the black pole.[11] Similarly, Harold M. Baron accepted the two-ness image as an accurate representation of black life and defined "black pride" and "black consciousness" rhetoric as assertions of the "validity of Du Bois' darker self" against those who "see the damage wrought by oppression without being able to recognize the strength born amidst suffering."[12]

Nathan I. Huggins indicated a still sharper turn toward celebratory race consciousness in his use of two-ness. He noted that Du Bois's "remarkable and profound statement fails only to make explicit an important corollary: this 'double consciousness' opens to the Negro—through his own quest and passion—a unique insight into the vulnerable and unfulfilled soul of that other world; a possibility which, once grasped, liberates one forever from the snarls of that other world's measuring tape."[13] For George E. Kent proper celebration and liberation of black authenticity derived not so much from transcendent insight as from a more emphatic "dissociation of sensibility from constraining definitions enforced by white middle-class culture"; Kent viewed that project, which he grounded in the Harlem Renaissance, as an entailment of Du Bois's recognition of a "black selfhood . . . under threat from the black's double consciousness: the consciousness enforcing white definitions upon him; and the part that desired a full embrace of the universe."[14] Others, such as Larry Neal, John O'Neal, and Hoyt W. Fuller, after affirming Du Bois's characterization, took the next logical step and called for rejection of American identity altogether.[15] By 1972, Houston A. Baker Jr. even had decided that "the sense of 'two-ness' that Du Bois handles so skillfully in *The Souls of Black Folk* is fast disappearing as cultural nationalism grows stronger"; Baker reported happily that the "doubts, speculations, and reflections are falling into a clear and ordered pattern, and we realize that America is something apart. . . . The numbing electric shocks are at an end, and we are feeling completely well."[16]

Another shift in the mode of appropriating Du Bois's passage as a universalistic claim about empirical Afro-American life occurred mainly over the 1980s. This modification seems linked to the institutionalization of Afro-American Studies as an academic specialty and the decline of points of reference for an aggressive nationalist politics outside the university—to the limited extent, that is, that the nationalism of the 1960s and 1970s ever had generated an independent base for intellectual activity in the first place. While continuing to celebrate a distinctive blackness, these recent appropriations are more elaborately learned than the earlier nationalist views. Even though the interpretive stances to which Du Bois is annexed remain shaped by a language that treats racial or cultural identity and politics more or less interchangeably, occasionally hinting of *Kulturkampf*, calls for elimination of alien elements have all but disappeared. Resolution of the duality appears—if at all—as synthesis and distant objective rather than as immediate, cathartic imperative. Indeed, the double consciousness tends to be seen naturalistically, as an essential fact of Afro-American existence in the here and now.

Sterling Stuckey's career spans the two periods, and he was identified with the earlier nationalist scholarship. Although he credits Du Bois with the "important advance" of recognizing black Americans' two-ness as a "crisis [that] should be identified and treated," Stuckey's interest lies more in "distinguishing between that which is African and that which is American in the black ethos" than in wholesale purging of influences of the "larger society."[17] Manning Marable, showing his peculiar inventiveness, treats Du Bois's formulation as a creative tension: "the basis of the struggle to attack institutional racism, racial segregation and all forms of inequality, as well as of that internal collective effort to engender cultural and social structures specific to the Afro-American experience."[18] Bettye J. Gardner and Waldo E. Martin also simply accept the reality of the condition and note its salubrious entailments. For Gardner, blacks' two-ness "gave rise to the study and teaching of Afro-American history."[19] Martin characterizes it in pluralist terms, as a "historic tension between their racial and national identities [which] . . . most blacks have sought to reconcile . . . through humanism and assimilationism."[20] Even Maulana Karenga, the old nationalist warhorse, has padded the bromides onto which he grafts Du Bois with a rhetoric drawn from ego psychology and references to Marx, Hegel, and Gramsci, conceding that resolution of the alleged problem of "defective . . . derivative and split consciousness" lies in a millennial future.[21]

This revised focus on Du Bois's dictum reflects in two closely related ways the recent process of incorporation of Afro-Americanist interests into mainstream academic life. First, despite their tendency to employ an evocatively politicized terminology of "emancipation," "liberation," or "struggle," the contemporary appropriators usually advance arguments that are more purely contemplative than those of their predecessors. They do not intend to inform national social-policy debates or to influence public opinion about race relations, as did the proponents of double consciousness prior to the civil rights–Black Power era. Nor are their arguments strategically oriented toward enhancing more radically oppositional or otherwise counterhegemonic agendas outside the university, as was the norm in the 1960s and '70s. Second, the double-consciousness notion is typically called upon to help articulate relatively complex interpretations with pretenses to high theoreticism, in what amounts to a blackening of global social theory and/or a legitimation of Afro-American intellectual activity in its terms. That is, the insurgent objectives to which Du Bois is affixed—notwithstanding genuflections toward more secular concerns—center on assertion of black presence within hermetically constituted communities of academic discourse. Lucius Outlaw credits Du Bois with identifying a "continuing confusion with respect to our identity" and goes on from that point to present a critical explication of "various complexes of thought and praxis . . . which have guided African American struggles through the years."[22] However, that critique is actually only an instrument of another objective: to understand "particular African-American intellectual legacies as philosophy and to grasp them as such in their racial/ethnic particularity." This in turn will pose "major challenges to the hegemonic disciplinary/discursive practices that have dominated European and Euro-American philosophy . . . [make] a lie of the denials and disregard of the existence of African-American philosophy and [force] a redefinition of 'philosophy' through an extension of its denotative range."[23] Robert C. Williams also harnesses Du Bois to an effort to define a "black philosophy"; Williams declares that recognizing Afro-Americans' double consciousness "is indispensable for articulating the totality of the American—and the black—experience" and is therefore "relevant and necessary to any viable program in American philosophy."[24] Thomas F. Slaughter Jr. takes double consciousness, which he accepts as an empirically accurate description of a collective racial state ("Blackness begins in double-consciousness"), as an entry point to demonstrating that phenomenology as a "species of philosophical description tends primarily to disclose for us what is already before us in a new and sometimes deeper light." From that vantage point:

> double-consciousness is precisely the expression of the contradiction posed by this immovable immediacy of my lived-body on the one hand, and the society's apparently irresistible compulsion, on the other, to fashion my physiognomic degradation. My duality of consciousness is the psycho-spatial dynamic spanning the socio-physical gap between my own sense of me and the culturally contrived ignominy surrounding my body.[25]

Slaughter, who does not tie his exercise to intellectual ambitions concerning the status of a black philosophy, expresses in this essay no particular nonacademic objective at all. His apparently exclusive intention is to reinterpret a familiar construction of Afro-American psychological orientation in the language of phenomenology of the body.

Like Slaughter, Cornel West enlists Du Bois in an effort to recast commonplace ideas about the black American condition within the rhetorical structures of Continental high social theory; he also seeks to authenticate or found (West's claims repeatedly confound the two objectives) an "Afro-American philosophy." Du Bois's formulation is a cornerstone of the latter enterprise. West maintains that Du Bois "eloquently described . . . the dialectic of black self-recognition [that] oscillated between being in America but not of it, from being black natives to black aliens." He trumps the double-consciousness image, however, by asserting its location within a "broader dialectic of being American yet feeling European, of being provincial but yearning for British cosmopolitanism, of being at once incompletely civilized and materially prosperous, a genteel Brahmin amid uncouth conditions." In the breeze of West's elevated perspective, therefore, two-ness is only part of the story. Black Americans have experienced a "triple crisis of self-recognition . . . comprised of African appearance and unconscious cultural mores, involuntary displacement to America without status, and American alienation from the European ethos complicated through domination by incompletely European Americans."[26] This phenomenon is linked historically to a "process of cultural syncretism which combined indigenous African and provincial American life."[27] Thus:

> Afro-American philosophy expresses the particular American variation of European modernity that Afro-Americans helped shape in this country and must contend with in the future. While it might be possible to articulate a competing Afro-American philosophy based principally on African norms and notions, it is likely that the result would be theoretically thin. Philosophy is cultural expression generated from and existentially grounded in the moods and sensibilities of a writer entrenched in the life-worlds of a people. The life-worlds of Africans in the United States are conceptually and existentially neither solely African, European, nor American, but more the latter than any of the former.[28]

For West, two-ness—or, as he amends it, three-ness—constitutes the immutable core of black American existence. His intellectual program, therefore, is not directed toward overcoming that condition, and its secular ramifications are remote and inchoate. Instead, despite a copious sprinkling of political clichés, his Afro-American philosophy's substantive agenda consists in quite conventionally academic calls for "a genre of writing, a textuality, a mode of discourse"[29] and "genealogical inquiry into . . . cultural and linguistic roots . . . theoretical reconstruction and evaluation . . . [and] dialogical encounter."[30]

The practice of appropriating Du Bois's construct for a purely academic program reaches its apotheosis in the work of Henry Louis Gates Jr. Gates folds Du Bois into his theorization of a black literary-tradition linked by texts which are "double-voiced in the sense that their literary antecedents are both white and black novels."[31] Gates takes up double consciousness—which as a "trope of dualism figured initially in black discourse" in Du Bois's usage[32]—as an instance of "tropological revision," that is, "the manner in which a specific trope is repeated, with differences, between two or more texts."[33] He is emphatically clear that his intellectual project is hermetically academic;[34] he distances himself explicitly from those who would assert social activist criteria onto critical scholarly endeavor and endorses the "attempt to take the 'mau-mauing' out of the black literary criticism that defined the 'Black Aesthetic Movement' of the sixties and transform it into a valid field of intellectual inquiry once again."[35] Though he understands Du Bois's two-ness as a "metaphor for the Afro-American's peculiar psychology of citizenship,"[36] Gates is concerned with it only as a literary device. In fact, he annexes the entirety of *The Souls of Black Folk* to his literary-theoretical project by contending that the volume is a " 'classic' not because of the phase of Du Bois's ideological development that it expresses but because of the manner in which he expressed his ideology."[37]

The shifting patterns of appropriating Du Bois that I have outlined are meaningful in several respects for the study of his thought, and, by extension, for the study of Afro-American thought writ large. First, and most generally, the fact and nature of the changes are evidence that the ways we relate to ideas in the past are shaped by our own historicity. As E. H. Carr observed in the early 1960s, "[W]e can view the past, and achieve our understanding of the past, only through the eyes of the present." [38] We can see in each mode of appropriation the stamp of debates and intellectual orientations that were vital or prevalent among the appropriators' contemporaries. In each case Du Bois's formulation is instrumentalized to support some current strategic argument about blacks and/ or race relations.

A second point of significance is a corollary of the first. That the types of interpretation cluster in periods suggests their embeddedness in communities of discourse, that is, in groups of scholars and others who share concern with an overlapping set of problems or questions and thus constitute a universe of intellectual exchange and debate. [39] These discursive communities help to shape scholarly and commonsensical interpretations of the past no less than of the present. Their purposive orientation around a specific set of questions leads investigation of the past to push certain agents, ideas, and events into relief and shades historical reconstruction with tones of present interests. From this vantage point, I have described modes of appropriating Du Bois's double consciousness that are characteristic to three distinct discursive communities: (1) that organized around a broad *problematique* of racial adjustment or race relations management with a vision of eventual assimilation of blacks into a putative mainstream of American life; (2) that which came together in the late 1960s, in tandem with the "Black Power" articulation of civil rights activism, around a project of asserting the authenticity and legitimacy of Afro-American identity; and (3) that constituted by post-segregation-era academics concerned primarily with the status of blacks as personnel and subject matter within academic institutions and disciplines.

A third point has to do with a continuity among the modes of appropriation and is therefore rather different from the first two. Each way of employing Du Bois accepts as a settled fact what should be seen as at most a hypothesis and then uses it as cornerstone and legitimation for a strategic program of one or another sort. Annexation of Du Bois's exalted reputation gives an aura of noncontingent truth to a proposition that might be controversial—that black Americans universally (or even typically) experience bifurcated identity. Noting that Du Bois declaimed on double consciousness at the turn of the century, furthermore, enhances the claim's apparent strength by positing its enduring reality. Thus the references function to circumvent the need for argument and evidence.

Finally, all the appropriations are naive about or inattentive with respect to matters of history and context in rehearsing the two-ness formulation. They presume an unchanging black essence and do not consider the possibility that Du Bois's construction bears the marks of historically specific discursive patterns, debates, and objectives. That blindness, moreover, underlies the tendency to treat Du Bois's text as clear fact and conceals from its appropriators their own historical and discursive contingency.

Of course, partisans seeking to advance specific agendas predictably attempt to validate them by asserting links to an estimable past. We cannot reasonably expect such rhetorical strategies to accommodate that colonized past's integrity. Their polemical thrust derives from prior certainty of direction and has only instrumental objectives; to that extent their interest lies in grafting on images from the past as legitimizing symbols of continuity, not in examining it as a potential source of clarification of the present. The problem in this case, however, is that respectable scholarship is not less likely than self-conscious polemics to approach history instrumentally, with dubiously anachronistic, uninterrogated presumptions. This tendency toward naive anachronism handicaps the study of Afro-American thought because, in denying the need for historical contextualization, it removes an important source of interpretive discipline from discussion of black thinking and debate.

Present interests do inescapably shape reconstruction of the past, and we probably never can recover earlier mental states or authorial intentions with definitive accuracy. Yet we can recognize that different interpretations are more or less anachronistic, more or less careful and rich, more or less plausible as representations of the content and structure of past ideas or controversies. Acknowledgment that interpretation is contingent upon contemporary purposes does not eliminate the need to confront past thinking as much as possible on its own terms, and that need entails situating it within historical context. On that score the appropriations of double consciousness have failed badly.

Certainly, not all who have drawn attention to Du Bois's image have taken it as a simple reflection of empirical reality. Some, like Francis L. Broderick and Jack B. Moore, have seen it as an expression of biographically or psychologically idiosyncratic aspects of Du Bois's life and upbringing, even as they link the image to larger structures of meaning.[40] Others have taken the formulation as illustrative of lines of thinking prominent within his black intellectual world. Lawrence W. Levine connects it to a spreading fear among Du Bois's articulate black contemporaries of the dangers of "an excessive degree of assimilation."[41] For Wilson J. Moses, the double-consciousness idea helps to position Du Bois in relation to the strain of civilizationist nationalism common among black intellectuals at the end of the nineteenth century.[42]

Still others have emphasized locating the notion's relation to an American, or more broadly Western, theoretical or philosophical canon. Robert Gooding-Williams examines the two-ness passage as an expression of what he argues is Du Bois's unconfessed Hegelianism.[43] Arnold Rampersad mines that passage for possible traces of the thinking of James McCosh, William James, and Oswald Kulpe; Rampersad goes on to note resonances of Johann Gottfried von Herder, Ralph Waldo Emerson and other likely influences in *The Souls of Black Folk.*[44] Werner Sollors connects Du Bois to Josiah Royce (and through Royce to Randolph Bourne and Horace Kallen) and more directly to Emerson, as well as to a broader set of American "ethnic writers."[45] As part of an effort to situate him within a larger "genealogy" of American pragmatism, Cornel West not only links Du Bois to Emerson but also claims that he "attempts to turn the Emersonian theodicy inside out" in *The Souls of Black Folk*.[46]

In principle, such attempts to locate Du Bois biographically or canonically are legitimate, though the specific exemplars I have cited represent a sample of uneven quality. (In addition, I should point out that my categorizations in some cases do not do justice to complex scholarship that overlaps the boundaries artificially imposed by my categories. Rampersad considers Du Bois's relation to the ideas of Alexander Crummell and other of his black contemporaries, and Moses is quite clear in tying his black subjects to the theories of Herder and others.) Each can contribute in important ways to understanding Du Bois. The standard determining the propriety of one or another approach—bracketing the issue of relative success in formulation and execution—should be purposive. That is, the different ways of focusing interpretation help to shed light on different sorts of relationships, and the usefulness of any given approach is a function of the connection between what it puts into relief and what we want to know at a given point. Biographical or psychologistic interpretations, for example, cannot help to locate Du Bois within a larger intellectual matrix, but such interpretations usually do not seek that objective.

The canonical interpretations, on the other hand, are more problematic. While they do strive to place Du Bois in a broader context of ideas and certainly can claim the legitimacy of well-established scholarly practice, they depend on a notion of linear tradition that approaches discrete subjects principally as artifacts of the lineage. This approach biases interpretation in two directions: (1) toward idealism, because it reifies and animates ideas, and (2) toward ahistoricism, because it is blind to the importance of changing social context in the constitution of ideas and their meanings. These biases combine to divorce individuals' thought from their roles as social actors and to obscure the crucial point that the same language can be used in quite different ways and to mean quite different things. Specifically with respect to Du Bois, this canonical orientation—notwithstanding its possible merits for literary studies—produces a procrustean form of account that is both so narrow as to court misrepresentation and too thin to illuminate either the depth and complexity or the ideological entailments of his links to larger patterns of American intellectual life and political debate. This problem appears most clearly on interrogation of the assertion that a trajectory of influences from Emerson and James lies behind Du Bois's double-consciousness idea.

Emerson/James/Du Bois

Du Bois certainly was familiar with Emerson, and his long-standing relationship with and sense of intellectual indebtedness to James are well known. On examination, however, his specific usage of double consciousness seems to share little with theirs besides the label. Emerson deployed the double-consciousness image to affirm the existence of a higher spiritual, religious realm within the human soul. He characterized the state as a "distinction of the inner and the outer self," assuring us that "within this erring passionate mortal self, sits a calm immortal mind, whose powers I do not know, but it is stronger than I am. I seek counsel of it in my doubts; I repair to it in my dangers; I pray to it in my undertakings. It is the door of my access to the Father. It seems to me the face which the Creator uncovers to his child."[47] To Emerson the dilemma of double consciousness was that "the two lives, of the understanding and of the soul, which we lead, really show very little relation to each other; never meet and measure each other."[48] Eventually, he found a solution to the dilemma, one that became grist for Mary Baker Eddy, Norman Vincent Peale, and other "positive thinkers." He proposed that one "must ride alternately on the horses of his private and public nature." Thus, when afflicted with misery or discomfort, one should "rally on his relation to the Universe, which his ruin benefits."[49] Where Du Bois's notion pointed to a specific product of black American experience, Emerson's indicated a generic human condition, prior to and outside history. Where Du Bois's "two thoughts, two souls, two unreconciled strivings" existed in the same domain, Emerson's "two states of thought" represented different spheres of existence— one superficial, the other profound. Where Du Bois's double consciousness blocked its victim from attaining "true self-consciousness, but only lets him see himself through the revelation of the other world," for Emerson "propounding" it was the source of real self-knowledge and inner harmony.

James's connection to theories of double or multiple consciousness is more complicated, but his ruminations on that theme scarcely more than Emerson's resemble Du Bois's construction. Consciousness figured prominently for James in three discrete concerns, though his views often seemed less than precise and possibly inconsistent.[50] In his psychological work he grappled first of all with the status of consciousness as a substantial entity. James reacted against idealist psychology's claims that "mental states are composite in structure, made up of smaller states conjoined"; he noted that those claims require the presence of some empirically questionable "mind-stuff" or "mind-dust."[51] Instead, he was more inclined to view consciousness as simply the product of selective attention within a stream of experience.[52] It was in this context that he found the fields-of-consciousness idea appealing.

> The expression "field of consciousness" has but recently come into vogue in the psychology books. Until quite lately the unit of mental life which figured most was the single "idea," supposed to be a definitely outlined thing. But at present psychologists are tending, first, to admit that the actual unit is more probably the total mental state, the entire wave of consciousness or field of objects present to the thought at any time; and, second, to see that it is impossible to outline this wave, this field, with any definiteness.
>
> As our mental fields succeed one another, each has its centre of interest, around which the objects of which we are less and less attentively conscious

fade to a margin so faint that its limits are unassignable. Some fields are narrow fields and some are wide fields. Usually when we have a wide field we rejoice, for then we see masses of truth together, and often get glimpses of relations which we divine rather than see, for they shoot beyond the field into still remoter regions of objectivity, regions which we seem rather to be about to perceive than to perceive actually. At other times, of drowsiness, illness, or fatigue, our fields may narrow almost to a point, and we find ourselves correspondingly oppressed and contracted.[53]

A second way in which consciousness was a focal point of James's psychological theory seems at least superficially more pertinent to Du Bois's two-ness formulation. James was a serious student of research on paranormal and pathological psychology, particularly the condition that "organized systems of [association-] paths can be thrown out of gear with others, so that the processes in one system give rise to one consciousness, and those of another system to another simultaneously existing consciousness."[54] His interest was largely clinical and physiological, reflective of a concern with brain functions and their connections with mental activity. He concluded his consideration of cases of various "perversions of personality":

> I think we ought not to talk of the doubling of the self as if it consisted in the failure to combine on the part of certain systems of ideas which usually do so. It is better to talk of objects usually combined, and which are now divided between the two "selves," in the hysteric and automatic cases in question. Each of the selves is due to a system of cerebral paths acting by itself. If the brain acted normally, and the dissociated systems came together again, we should get a new affection of consciousness in the form of a third "self" different from the other two, but knowing their objects together, as the result.[55]

This focus on multiple personality, especially as demonstrated in psychic phenomena, linked James's scientific and mystical interests. As Gerald E. Myers notes, "discovery of the subconscious by abnormal psychology, psychical research and mind-healing excited James for its potential applications; it promised to revise traditional theories of mind and consciousness and possibly to explain the phenomenon that James often hailed, the sudden upsurge of energy or renewed vitality which seems sometimes to invade us from out of nowhere."[56] He was open to the possibility that even the existence of ghosts was only a radical extension of "the truth that the invisible segments of our minds are susceptible, under rarely realized conditions, of acting and being acted upon by the invisible segments of other conscious lives."[57] He believed that "we all have potentially a 'subliminal' self, which may make at any time irruption into our ordinary lives." While this subliminal self is minimally "only the depository of our forgotten memories[,] at its highest we do not know what it is at all."[58] In fact, he embraced the proposition that the subliminal consciousness could be a mechanism for connecting with a larger extrapersonal or cosmic consciousness. He judged views that locate the origins of consciousness in the brain to be inadequate inasmuch as they require some principle like spontaneous generation. Instead, James inclined to the belief that consciousness "does not have to be generated de novo in a vast number of places. It exists already, behind the scenes, coeval with the world." [59] Our capacities for transmitting that wider consciousness vary, and the variation can be explained at least in part—following Gustav Fechner— physiologically. The threshold of receptivity to transmission is lowered by "sense-action," which makes the receiving brain more "pervious." The more lucid or alert we are —the wider our field of consciousness—the lower the threshold for penetration by the larger consciousness.

Throughout, James insistently sought to establish mystical speculation on an empirical and physiological foundation. Even as he rhapsodized about "the continuity of our consciousness with a mother sea" whose "exceptional waves occasionally [pour] over the dam," he admitted, toughmindedly, that "the causes of these odd lowerings of the brain's threshold still remain a mystery on any terms." [60] Nevertheless, he accepted the premise that a deeper, spiritual world lay beyond ordinary human experience. He both attempted to demonstrate that world's reality by scientific method and characterized those who denied its existence as narrow-minded dogmatists. His skepticism ultimately was subordinate to—even an instrument of—his belief. That subordination is clearest in the third context in which he engaged the issue of consciousness, his considerations on religion. That is, moreover, the context in which he makes statements that appear most similar to Du Bois's.

The notion of a divided self was central to James's religious ideas. He identified as "the general basis of all religious experience, the fact that man has a dual nature, and is connected with two spheres of thought, a shallower and a profounder sphere, in either of which he may learn to live habitually." [61] Having recognized the "two lives, the natural and the spiritual," he declared flatly that "we must lose the one before we can participate in the other.[62] Despite the all-or-nothing ring of that statement, James contended that the "normal evolution of character" is a process of "straightening out and unifying . . . the comparative chaos within us . . . by forming a stable system of functions in right subordination." [63]

Although he believed that we all necessarily establish some such system, James maintained that some personalities seem naturally and effortlessly to demonstrate harmonious equilibrium, the state which he called "healthy-mindedness." He indicated a need to "distinguish between a more involuntary and a more voluntary or systematic way of being healthy-minded. In its involuntary variety, healthy-mindedness is a way of feeling happy about things immediately. In its systematical variety, it is an abstract way of conceiving things as good." [64] Where involuntary or natural healthy-mindedness—the " 'once-born' type of consciousness"—lives the condition in a way that appears "straight and natural, with no element of morbid compunction or crisis," [65] that which is voluntary chooses to construe "good as the essential and universal aspect of being [and] deliberately excludes evil from its field of vision." [66] The healthy-minded character tends toward a religion:

in which good, even the good of this world's life, is regarded as the essential thing for a rational being to attend to. This religion directs him to settle his scores with the more evil aspects of the universe by systematically declining to lay them to the heart or make much of them, by ignoring them in his reflective calculations, or even, on occasion, by denying outright that they exist. Evil is a disease, and worry over disease is itself an additional form of disease, which only adds to the original complaint. Even repentance and remorse, affections which come in the character of ministers of good, may be but sickly and re-laxing impulses. The best repentance is to up and act for righteousness, and forget that you ever had relations with sin.[67]

In contrast to those who naturally exhibit or cultivate the healthy-minded outlook, James noted, another character type—the "morbid-minded" or "sick soul"—"cannot so easily throw off the burden of the consciousness of evil, but [is] congenitally fated to suffer from its presence."[68] The sick soul must be "twice-born"—that is, must be reawakened spiritually "out of suffering and des-peration."[69] The sick soul, once reborn, embraces a religious consciousness deeper, if less cherubic, than that of the healthy-minded.

> One has tasted of the fruit of the tree, and the happiness of Eden never comes again. The happiness that comes, when any does come—and often enough it fails to return in an acute form . . .—is not the simple ignorance of ill, but something vastly more complex, including natural evil as one of its elements, but finding natural evil no such stumbling-block and terror because it now sees it swallowed up in supernatural good. The process is one of redemption, not of mere reversion to natural health, and the sufferer, when saved, is saved by what seems to him a second birth, a deeper kind of conscious being than he could enjoy before.[70]

The twice-born character, James believed, derived psychologically from "a certain discordancy or heterogeneity in the native temperament of the subject, an incompletely unified moral and intellectual constitution."[71] Drawing on cur-rent scholarship in psychology, he argued that the different character types ex-press inborn differences of "inner constitution" and suggested the possibility (without endorsing it) that the "heterogeneous personality" might even be inher-ited—"the traits of character of incompatible and antagonistic ancestors are sup-posed to be preserved along side of each other."[72] He also proffered a behaviorist description and explanation which rested on the premise that one's "ideas, aims, and objects form diverse internal groups and systems, relatively independent of one another."

> Each 'aim' . . . awakens a certain specific kind of interested excitement, and gathers a certain group of ideas together in subordination to it as its associates; and if the aims and excitements are distinct in kind, their groups of ideas may have little in common. When one group is present and engrosses the interest, all the ideas connected with other groups may be excluded from the mental field . . .
> Our ordinary alterations of character, as we pass from one of our aims to another, are not commonly called transformations, because each of them is so

rapidly succeeded by another in the reverse direction; but whenever one aim grows so stable as to expel definitively its previous rivals from the individual's life, we tend to speak of . . . a "transformation."

These alterations are the completest of the ways in which a self may be divided. A less complete way is the simultaneous coexistence of two or more different groups of aims of which one practically holds the right of way and instigates activity, while the others are only pious wishes, and never practically come to anything.[73]

This heterogeneous personality can, in the sick souls, produce "divided will, when the higher wishes lack just that acuteness, that touch of explosive intensity, of dynamogenic quality . . . that enables them to burst their shell, and make irruption efficaciously into life and quell the lower tendencies forever."[74] For such an individual the process of unification of the personality requires the dramatic experience of being twice-born. The regenerative experience can be either sudden or gradual. In either case, its trajectory begins with the *"fact that the conscious person is continuous with a wider self through which saving experiences come,"*[75] a variation on James's notion of the individual's continuity with a "mother sea" of consciousness. Not surprisingly, the subconscious or subliminal self is the "mediating term," the conduit for penetration and permeation by the unifying consciousness, or God.[76] James insisted that the unifying experience did not have to be—and in some cases could not be—religious; he also attempted to present his case more broad-mindedly than to equate the spiritual exclusively with religion or the latter exclusively with Christianity. Nevertheless, his concern with the twice-born is itself steeped in religious belief, and his interpretation speaks clearly of his own acknowledged preoccupation with faith, salvation, and contact with the divine.

> The individual, so far as he suffers from his wrongness and criticizes it, is to that extent consciously beyond it, and in at least possible touch with something higher, if anything higher exists. Along with the wrong part there is thus a better part of him, even though it may be but a most helpless germ. With which part he should identify his real being is by no means obvious at this stage; but when stage 2 (the stage of solution or salvation) arrives, the man identifies his real being with the germinal higher part of himself, and does so in the following way. *He becomes conscious that this higher part is conterminous and continuous with a MORE of the same quality. which is operative in the universe outside of him. and which he can keep in working touch with, and in a fashion get on board of and save himself when all his lower being has gone to pieces in the work.*[77]

Links and similarities between James and Emerson are clearly visible. James referred frequently to Emerson, taking him, for instance, as an exemplary advocate of healthy-mindedness. James's mother sea of consciousness is quite similar to Emerson's Over-Soul, "within which every man's particular being is contained and made one with all other."[78] James's divided self, torn by natural and spiritual forces, seems in one sense to be a restatement of Emerson's double consciousness in a gloomier key.

No such evidence joins James to Du Bois. James saw the divided self as alternately a psycho-physiological and a spiritual or mystical phenomenon; for Du Bois the idea was sociological and historical. To James, therefore, the condition and the path to transcending it were individual, even random, but to Du Bois both problem and remedy were bound up with the ascriptive lot of a racial collectivity. Although it in no way resembles James's "fields of consciousness" or his specific discussions of pathological and spiritual splitting of consciousness, one might argue that Du Bois's formulation may have been influenced by James's suggestion that heterogeneous personality could result from inheritance of "traits . . . of incompatible and antagonistic ancestors." Du Bois, however, makes no hint at biology at all in his two-ness claim. In addition, his essay proclaiming blacks' double consciousness appeared originally in the *Atlantic Monthly* in 1897, five years before James's publication of *The Varieties of Religious Experience*. Of course, James and Du Bois did communicate after the latter left Harvard, and it is possible that some of their interaction could have ranged to James's reflections on the divided self. Myers, though, notes that "James was skeptical about any automatic transfer of parental traits to children" and had begun to express his doubts no later than 1898.[79] In any event, attempts to establish direct links between James and Du Bois would require very elaborate arguments and layers of supposition and presumption. Nor would they— even if arguably successful in establishing some plausible, though remote tie— shed much light either on Du Bois's thinking or his relation to his contemporary world.

I have undertaken this examination of Emerson and James with two purposes in mind. The narrower, admittedly rather scholastic, one is to argue against assertions and intimations (usually made in a passing way) of a specific lineage encompassing Du Bois's and their ideas about consciousness. My broader purpose is to highlight pitfalls and limitations of what John Dunn has referred to as the interpretive tendency to focus on "what propositions in what great books remind the author of what propositions in what other great books."[80]

Limits of Canonical Focus

I have already criticized that tendency as it appears among Afro-Americanists as a species of a more general orientation toward racial vindicationism and for its embrace of a problematic notion of greatness as a category of intellectual history (see chapter 1). That kind of approach is defective in other important ways as well. First of all, those who trace patterns of influence typically fail to demonstrate them adequately. Such claims too often reduce to noting the presence of similar terms in texts by different authors and on that basis asserting the likely influence of the earlier author upon the later one, particularly if the two can be said in advance to be members of a common tradition. However, as Quentin Skinner has indicated, much more is required convincingly to demonstrate claims of influence. An effective case requires: "(i) that there should be a genuine similarity [i.e., deeper resemblance than use of similar language] between the doctrines of A and B; (ii) that B could not have found the relevant doctrine in any writer other than A; (iii) that the probability of the similarity being random should be very low (i.e., even if there is a similarity, and it is shown that it could have been by A that B was influenced, it must still be shown that B did not as a matter of fact articulate the relevant doctrine independently."[81] Skinner's standard may be too restrictively taxing or overly precise; there may very well be cases, for instance, in which it makes little difference whether A influenced B directly or indirectly through C or by some more circuitous route. Nevertheless, he does make clear, minimally, that claims of direct intellectual links must rest on more than superficial evidence. As examination of the putative Emerson/James/Du Bois connection illustrates, resemblance of concepts cannot be deduced from resemblance of terminology.

Making a credible argument for patterns of influence is a difficult enterprise that can require tedious exegetic, biographical, and bibliographical work that may or may not yield appropriate chains of evidence and reasonable inference. Proper attention to Skinner's first condition, moreover, shows that even then, the task is much more complicated and difficult than it might otherwise appear. And the difficulties associated with the need to satisfy that condition suggest that the focus on identifying influences may be—except in relation to certain strictly biographical objectives—a dubious way to approach the interpretive project.

The main reason that satisfying Skinner's first condition is so difficult is that different authors can use identical language in apparently similar ways to refer to very different concepts. The Emerson/James/Du Bois case is not anomalous. Daniel T. Rodgers has underscored, in his study of keywords in American political thought, how the substantive meanings of terms can change dramatically with changes in the purposive context in which they are used, even without overt revision of their denotative meanings.[82] In addition, as we have seen, the enlistment of Du Bois's two-ness passage to support quite different strategic programs in different periods points to a related problem.

Political ideas function pragmatically, as instruments of real-world objectives tied to historically specific debates and struggles. People adduce connection with past ideas rhetorically, to support stances and claims in and for their present. Because it centers on asserting fundamental continuities of meaning, the canonical focus on tracing influences abstracts away from that pragmatic dimension and inevitably diminishes the lived experience of the putatively influenced. It snatches historical subjects out of their contexts of action, disconnects them from their specific purposes and agendas, and severs them from the arenas of debate toward which their stances are tailored. Put more dramatically, the canonical orientation imposes an alien ideological force—either a transhistorical exchange among exemplary thinkers or, worse, the movement of disembodied ideas themselves—between interpreter and subject and between the latter and his or her own world.

This interpretive distortion artificially separates intellectual history from social and political history, rendering opaque the ways in which sedimented beliefs affect and are altered by current political debates and practices. From the elevated vantage point that gives transhistorical sweep, we overlook the complex dialectic through which ideas are formed and deployed—and gain constituencies—in relation to the practical concerns and "collective mentalities" that define discursive communities.[83] In losing sight of intellectual activity's roots in concrete historical situations, the canonical approach actually obscures rather than clarifies our understanding of the reproduction of political tradition.

In the study of Afro-American thought the impetus to trace out canonical lineages, when seen in this critical light, becomes ironically self-defeating. Shoehorning blacks into a chronology of exemplary thinkers is a subspecies of the vindicationist desire to establish the racial presence vis-á-vis a larger intellectual tradition. Yet that approach misses the deepest and most significant way that blacks figure into American intellectual life—through their participation in the historically specific networks of shared presuppositions and concerns that shape the environing political discourse at any given moment. Again, the Emerson/James/Du Bois nexus is instructive.

The issue of direct textual influences fades toward triviality when we see Du Bois's double-consciousness reference as a racially framed version of a sentiment common among his contemporaries. Of course, Du Bois certainly could have taken his precise language from Emerson or James; he shared with them also, for example, the metaphor of living behind or within a veil.[84] He could just as easily have taken the double-consciousness phrase, however, from Edward Bellamy, who was immensely popular in the late nineteenth century and whom Du Bois later recalled having "revered" in his youth.[85] In any event, the more interesting issue is that the sense of double consciousness, two-ness, or "alienage" was prominent among fin-de-siècle American intellectuals. Even if we were to presume that all who expressed those sentiments drew on Emerson, what led so many of them to find the specific image of fragmented consciousness a compelling metaphor for their own circumstances? Answering that question requires a synchronic focus rather than the diachronic telescopy of the canonical orientation. It also requires searching for the premises that Du Bois shared with his own peers rather than apparent doctrinal similarities with earlier (or later) luminaries.

Two-ness in the Progressive-Era Intellectual Milieu

Du Bois was part of a cohort of university-trained, reform-oriented, typically eastern intellectuals who mainly came to maturity during the last years of the nineteenth century and the first years of the twentieth and who shared a loosely defined outlook and intellectual and political *problematique*. In the terms which I have been using here, they constituted a reasonably distinct community of discourse. I have argued at various points in this volume that Du Bois's thinking—particularly in its structuring presuppositions—was embedded in discursive and ideological patterns characteristic to that cohort. Taking that link into account suggests an entirely different angle onto his lament concerning black Americans' purported double consciousness.

Expressions of liminality very similar to Du Bois's two-ness passage were common among his white intellectual contemporaries. Christopher Lasch, T. J. Jackson Lears, and Peter Conn are among those who have noted the prevalence of such expressions among American intellectuals around the turn of the century. Their interpretations focus on a largely generational response to what appeared to be rapid and radical cultural change.[86] Lasch related the common sense of liminality to the "growing isolation of the intellectuals as a class from the main currents of American life" as they formed for the first time a distinct social stratum.[87] He stresses their alienation from the "cultural style" of the old middle class "characterized by that combination of partiarchal authority and the sentimental veneration of women which is the essence of the genteel tradition."[88] The result was a generalized "sense of being in some way disabled or deformed" and of experiencing life at a remove.[89] For Lears liminality derived from disaffection with the process of social rationalization associated with a consolidating mass-industrial society. Many educated late Victorians "began half-consciously to perceive [modern culture's] limitations and contradictions, its failure to live up to its claim of perpetual progress and perfect autonomy." This spreading doubt precipitated a "crisis of cultural authority"[90] which individuals typically experienced as feelings of inauthenticity. In Conn's view intellectual life of the period was marked by "a profound internal dialectic, a conflict between tradition and innovation, between control and independence, between order and liberation."[91] Rather than appraising them a watershed or even necessarily a unique instance, though, he sees the two decades before World War I as a particularly luminous moment of an enduring "pattern of contrariety"[92] driven by a generational motor, the "simultaneity of future and past."[93] This "divided consciousness," Conn contends, was visible within individuals as well as the society at large.

Those interpretations, while clearly different, are not mutually exclusive. They very likely represent different angles onto the same phenomenon: that which lies at the nexus of the new middle class's "search for order" and the new intellectuals' search for meaning. These overlapping concerns grew within the entailments of the corporate industrialization of American society as described here in chapter 2. Focus on that phenomenon, however, does not go to the foundations of the intellectual temper under examination. The liminality that Lasch, Lears, and Conn identify was connected to shared presumptions about natural hierarchy, evolutionism, laws of knowledge and social organization, and the antinomies of human nature. They are traceable within and define the character of the essentially ideological response provoked by uncertainty and alienation — including perception of cultural or existential crisis.

The laments of his white contemporaries at times bore a striking resemblance to Du Bois's claim about racial two-ness. Inez Haynes Gillmore, writer and feminist, proclaimed in 1912: "For several years now I have felt myself alien to this world, and alien not because of race or color, but alien because of changing economic conditions. It seems to me that sociologically, so to speak, I hang in a void between two spheres—the man's sphere and the woman's sphere."[94] Charlotte Perkins Gilman in her early twenties defended her plans for spinsterhood by defining that course (which she did not actually take) as "the end of the long and tiresome effort to satisfy the demands of two opposing natures in myself."[95]

The experience of divided or fragmented consciousness was by no means restricted to representatives of marginalized and subordinate groups like blacks or women. The unadulterated patrician Henry Adams remarked:

> [T]he Bostonian could not but develop a double nature. Life was a double thing. . . . Winter and summer . . . were two hostile lives, bred two separate natures. Winter was always the effort to live; summer was tropical license. . . . The bearing of the two seasons on the education of Henry Adams was no fancy; it was the most decisive force he ever knew; it ran through life, and made division between its perplexing, warring, irreconcilable problems, irreducible opposites, with growing emphasis to the last year of study. From earliest childhood the boy was accustomed to feel that, for him, life was double. . . . The boy inherited his double nature.[96]

Lears, in fact, argues that while more than most "Adams was attuned to the pervasiveness of late-Victorian ambivalence as well as to the growing fascination with unconscious mind and multiple personality,"[97] the sense of fragmentation was widespread among the educated elite. Indeed, the therapeutic orientation Lears studies often aimed quite explicitly at helping to transcend "double-mindedness."[98]

That sense of fragmented consciousness also was expressed in the frequent complaint that one's experience of life was blocked, incomplete, or inauthentic. Lears quotes Vida Scudder's confession that from childhood she "had encountered too much at second hand," had lived an "imitative life." He relates that she was haunted by a "puzzling, distressing sense of unreality" and all her adult life prayed that God would "make me a real person."[99] Similarly, Mabel Dodge Luhan, writer and salon-keeper for the bohemian set, recalled coming to terms with her decision to immerse herself in a putatively natural world in New Mexico:

> Was one to be forever reminded of something else and never to experience anything in itself at first-hand? . . . It had begun to appear to me that there had always been a barrier between oneself and direct experience; the barrier of other people's awareness and perceptions translated into words or paint or music . . . never leaving one free to know anything for oneself, or to discover the true essence in anything.[100]

Jane Addams as well spoke of her secondhand experience of life. Recalling the years between her completion of college and the opening of Hull House, she concluded: "During most of that time I was absolutely at sea so far as any moral purpose was concerned, clinging only to the desire to live in a really living world and refusing to be content with a shadowy intellectual or aesthetic reflection of it."[101] She contrasted the condition of women of the previous generation favorably with her own:

> I gradually reached a conviction that the first generation of college women had taken their learning too quickly, had departed too suddenly from the active, emotional life led by their grandmothers and great grandmothers, that the contemporary education of young women had developed too exclusively the power of acquiring knowledge and of merely receiving impressions; that somewhere in the process of "being educated" they had lost that simple and almost automatic response to the human appeal, that old healthful reaction resulting in activity from the mere presence of suffering or of helplessness; that they are so sheltered and pampered they have no chance even to make "the great refusal."[102]

Her decision to found Hull House developed in part from a desire to provide therapy for victims of such alienation: "I gradually became convinced that it would be a good thing to rent a house in a part of the city where many primitive and actual needs are found, in which young women who had been given over too exclusively to study might restore a balance of activity along traditional lines and learn of life from life itself."[103]

The yearning for intense, authentic experience was common, and its link to therapeutic ideology often was direct. Lears sees the yearning as a source of the appeal that various manifestations of "anti-modern vitalism" held for many educated Americans. He takes James's fascination with mysticism as illustrative of a broader tendency to seek the key to profound experience that could transcend alienation.[104] Occultism and self-help religion of many sorts flourished in that milieu; Peale—later a pope of positive thinking—considered himself a disciple of James and Emerson.[105] James was in fact an early enthusiast of mind cure and asserted its roots in Emersonian transcendentalism.[106] Donald Meyer, moreover, examines mind cure advocates' appropriation of both Emerson's double-consciousness notion and James's related idea of fields of consciousness.[107]

Of course, Du Bois expressed no interest in mind cure or other therapeutic ideologies, and he certainly would not have wanted to be associated with them. Yet the therapeutic disposition rested on and was articulated in relation to deeper, more generally shared constructions of essential hierarchies of social groups, values and meaning. Those essentialist constructions are visible beneath the variety of expressions of the fragmentation metaphor, and explicating them and their sources brings Du Bois's own normative moorings more sharply into view.

Mind cure was only one of a panoply of responses to a common perception in the milieux of the educated bourgeoisie and petite bourgeoisie that American life exhibited the effects of overcivilization. The sense of being "suffocated by the stale gentility of modern culture"[108] propelled ostensibly disparate enthusiasms, from mind cure, mysticism, and Anglo-Catholicism to arts and crafts and militarism. Even Addams, as we have seen, justified social reform activity in part as a remedy for overcivilized young women, and she complained of "being cultivated" as a barrier to the real experience of life.[109] Similarly, Gillmore, reflecting on her college years, recalled that her female cohort—unlike men, she imagined—never realized that "we were studying a second-hand world, that we were getting our life in translation, that we never really had a face-to-face encounter with it."[110] That syndrome, she felt, had not been simply an artifact of her youth; even at thirty-five she had "never seen life in the raw."[111]

The specific conditions against which Addams and Gillmore reacted derived from the forms of structural, institutional, and ideological subordination to which women of their station were subjected. Gillmore was explicit about that point, linking her sense of "alienage" to the prevailing gender-based double standard of experience. In Addams's complaint the heavy hand of gender oppression is visible indirectly, within what she treated as settled conventions regulating the proper upbringing and comportment of genteel women. Nevertheless, in her case no less than Gillmore's the feeling of being blocked from real participation in life was bound up with the particular situation—including the contradiction between intellectual aspiration and socially acceptable conduct—of upper status women in their era.[112]

Their perception of their own lives as unreal, though, was predicated not only on the constraints of gender; it also presumed a sentimentalized view of lower-status "others" considered less complex or cultivated. Gillmore, for example, compared the downwardly mobile circumstances of her childhood unfavorably to the lives of the genuinely impoverished, which she simultaneously aestheticized and imagined to be more vital than her own. "We were poor enough to be dull," she noted, "but not poor enough to be picturesque . . . not poor enough to enjoy the hearty, vulgar social promiscuity of the frankly poverty-stricken."[113] Addams acknowledged a preference in her work for recent immigrants over second- or third-generation ethnics because the former were "more natural and cast in a simpler mold."[114] She also maintained a nostalgic image of women's lot in peasant villages, asserting and lauding its organic simplicity and mourning the loss of the "freedom and beauty of that life" in the immigrant experience.[115]

In a similar vein, Randolph Bourne feared that the new immigrants would lose their "native culture" and have their "distinctive qualities . . . washed out into a tasteless, colorless fluid of uniformity."[116] He assessed more harshly than Addams the stereotypically half-assimilated second and third generations. He recoiled from their "insipidity—masses of people who are cultural half-breeds . . . who retain their foreign names but have lost the foreign savor."[117] Bourne's sharp distaste for those "hyphenates" no doubt was connected with the fact that he viewed the immigrants principally as sources for revitalization of an indigenous bourgeois culture that he judged stagnant.[118]

Luhan saw a similar, but more dramatic and esoteric path to countering the sterility of bourgeois overcivilization. She found an effective antidote among the Native Americans and Mexican-Americans in the Southwest. In a paean of unabashed objectification, she romanticized their poverty and imagined them possessed of a superior, stoical essence that melded them into the local ecology.[119] She convinced herself that the Native Americans were animated by a collective tribal "over-soul," which she saw as analogous to the "group spirit in the flock, in the herd, and in the swarm."[120] In that environment, dominated by overarching spirituality, she believed it was possible to shatter the wall of intellection that blocked pure, immediate experience. "I had a sudden intuition right then that here in this country life could come to one more concretely than in other places, and that meanings that were shut up in words and phrases out in the world could incorporate themselves in living forms and move before one. Ideas here might clothe themselves in form and flesh, and word-symbols change into pictured living realities."[121] Luhan's rhapsodies bore the marks of conversion, certainly, and she employed that experience's language of rebirth. Not only did she believe that the organic simplicity of her Mexicans and Indians would satisfy her deep cravings for embeddedness and personal fulfillment; she also found in it a proper alternative to the "decadent unhappy world, where the bright, hot, rainbow flashes of corruption were the only light high spots."[122]

Luhan and Bourne were by no means unique in the belief that the putative traits of peoples generally held to be inferior or simpler could be mined to remedy the effects of overcivilization. Fin-de-siècle middle-class Americans commonly believed that "Oriental people, the inhabitants of the tropics, and the colored peoples generally" knew how to relax; emulating them could help combat excesses of "moral and intellectual strenuosity."[123] Henry Adams, for instance, found Samoans invigoratingly "spontaneous, healthy, free from our idiotic cant about work" and enthused that he had "never lived in so unselfconscious a place."[124] James followed Theodore Parker in taking the "heathen" consciousness as exemplary of the healthy-minded state.[125]

Prevailing adherence to theories of cultural evolution underwrote a notion of the "primitive" that included both contemporary inferiors and romantic constructions of earlier societies. The appeal of the primitive as an ideal, however, did not depend on the allegedly pacific qualities of simpler folk, either past or present. The less-evolved others were exalted also as more visceral. Gillmore's desire to see life "in the raw" was not idiosyncratic. Lears recounts the common view of medieval figures as "big children" who represented instinctual vitality both physical and emotional.[126] Frank Norris looked back to the Middle Ages to extol a savage authenticity drenched in Anglo-Saxon racism and pornographic violence.[127] James—on detailing the merciless inexorability of Homeric brutality—concluded that the "integrity of the instinctive reactions, this freedom from all moral sophistry and strain, gives a pathetic dignity to ancient pagan feeling."[128] More was at stake in this assessment, however, than nostalgic reconstruction of a classical past without ambivalence. "Our ancestors," James felt, "have bred pugnacity into our bone and marrow, and thousands of years of peace won't breed it out of us."[129] Therefore, he feared that a "pacific cosmopolitan industrialism" was inadequate as an object of properly enthusiastic patriotism. He called instead for fortifying pacifist principles with redefined martial virtues to produce the requisite basis for proper "civic passion." "Martial virtues," he maintained, "must be the enduring cement; intrepidity, contempt of softness, surrender of private interest, obedience to command, must still remain the rock upon which states are built."[130]

This turn to martial imagery discloses another layer of meaning in the concern with overcivilization. It was enmeshed in a profoundly gendered logic. We have seen how for women like Addams and Gillmore the pangs of overcivilization stemmed directly from oppressive conventions circumscribing genteel women's activities. More deeply, though, lay a tendency to cast the social and natural worlds—even knowledge itself—in explicitly gendered categories. James, for example, distinguished between the "scientific-academic mind and the feminine-mystical mind"[131] as parallel forms of knowing. His romanticized image of our pugnacious ancestors, typical to such warrior myths, incorporated women simply as property, the spoils of pillage.[132] As with the larger martial image, his scheme for contemporary revitalization only beveled off the crude edges of that objectification. Revitalization was to occur through making "new energies and hardihoods continue the manliness to which the military mind so faithfully clings."[133] The young men who were thus to "get the childishness knocked out of them" would count among their rewards that "the women would value them more highly."[134] When devotees of martial virtue saw women as more than prizes for male heroism, they typically associated the female character with social decay and decadence. Norris, for example, viewed feminization as a major source of "moral and physical weakness" and counseled resistance by "rekindling male potency."[135]

This gendered dualism, of course, was not restricted to martial ideology; its premises were widespread among educated—particularly male—Americans. In self-criticism George Herbert Mead described himself as weak and "rather of a feminine cast of mind."[136] Van Wyck Brooks defined the basic tension in American life as that between " 'masculine' business and 'feminine' culture."[137] Unlike Norris, he sought to blend the two principles—tough-minded calculation and emotional sensibility—to form a healthy mean. Similarly, G. Stanley Hall, who actively opposed education for women in general, warned especially of the dangers of coeducation, arguing that it would harm boys by "feminizing them when they need to be working off their brute animal element."[138] However, like Lester F. Ward and others, Hall was attracted to Johann Jakob Bachofen's theory of matriarchal origins and exalted an idealized female essence as the nurturant basis of social order. He argued, therefore, that exposure of adolescent males—temporarily and in the protective brute animality of the same-sex environment, of course—to a curriculum emphasizing the feminine principle ("repose, leisure, art, legends, romance, idealizations, in a word, humanisms") would put a calming and vitalizing polish on their preparation for adulthood.[139]

The idea of an essentialist dichotomy articulated in gendered terms was not an exclusively male or antifeminist premise.[140] Feminists and antifeminists differed mainly with respect to the centrality and character of biologistic or evolutionist elements in formulations of the dichotomy. In *Beyond Separate Spheres* Rosalind Rosenberg details the efforts of academic women to refute the orthodoxy that presupposed innate, sex-based differences in temperament and mental ability. Many feminists, however, accepted the premise that such differences existed and disputed only claims that their sources were biological or that they necessarily implied female inferiority. Indeed, activists frequently traded on essentialist stereotypes to support arguments for enlarging female participation in public life.[141] Addams, among others, invoked the common belief in specific female province in arguing for the "Utilization of Women in City Government":

> From the beginning of tribal life women have been held responsible for the health of the community, a function which is now represented by the health department; from the days of the cave dwellers, so far as the home was clean and wholesome, it was due to their efforts, which are now represented by the bureau of tenement-house inspection; from the period of the primitive village, the only public sweeping performed was what they undertook in their own door yards, that which is now represented by the bureau of street cleaning. Most of the departments in a modern city can be traced to woman's traditional activity, but . . . so soon as these old affairs were turned over to the care of the city, they slipped from woman's hands.[142]

With respect specifically to voting, Addams observed that women were constitutionally suited to form a particularly responsible electorate because civic duty is only an extension of domestic virtue, a view expressed in the phrase of the day "municipal housekeeping."[143] She indicated no hesitation in assuming the gendered dualism of temperament:

> To turn the administration of our civic affairs wholly over to men may mean that the American city will continue to push forward in its commercial and industrial development, and continue to lag behind in those things which make a city healthful and beautiful. After all, woman's traditional function has been to make her dwelling-place both clean and fair. Is that dreariness in city life, that lack of domesticity which the humblest farm dwelling presents, due to a withdrawal of one of the naturally cooperating forces? If women have in any sense been responsible for the gentler side of life which softens and blurs some of its harsher conditions, may they not have a duty to perform in our American cities?[144]

Advocates of suffrage and other agendas we would now call feminist commonly argued that women's domestic duties would not suffer and even could be enhanced by an enlarged role in civic affairs. As a rule, that is, they did not challenge the premise that domestic and humanistic virtues (and obligations) were intrinsically female.[145]

Even Gilman—who insisted that women's inferiority was the product of historical subjugation, not biology, and who sought, via the professionalization of housework, to redefine the distinction between public and domestic realms—operated within the essentialist logic. Despite the mainly economistic and functionalist character of her account of "sexuo-economic" evolution, she held a view of the dichotomous temperaments that verged on mysticism.

Maternal energy is the force through which have come into the world both love and industry. It is through the tireless activity of this desire, the mother's wish to serve the young, that she began the first of the arts and crafts whereby we live. While the male savage was still a mere hunter and fighter, expressing masculine energy, the katabolic force, along its essential line, expanding, scattering, the female savage worked out in equally natural ways the conserving force of female energy. She gathered together and saved nutrition for the child, as the germ-cell gathers and saves nutrition in the unconscious silences of nature. She wrapped it in garments and built a shelter for its head as naturally as the same maternal function had loved, clothed, and sheltered the unborn.[146]

Gilman embraced a modified form of Ward's "gynaecocentric" theory, which posited original matriarchy, and in her utopian "Herland," the female principle shaped the social order.[147]

The color line seems to have made little difference on this score. Anna Julia Cooper, in arguing for higher education for women averred that

there is a feminine as well as a masculine side to truth; that these are related not as inferior and superior, not as better and worse, not as weaker and stronger, but as complements—complements in one necessary and symmetric whole. That as the man is more noble in reason, so the woman is more quick in sympathy. That as he is indefatigable in pursuit of abstract truth, so is she in caring for the interests by the way—striving tenderly and lovingly that not one of the least of these "little ones" should perish.[148]

Education of women and their expanded participation in public life would enrich civilization by establishing harmony between the masculine and feminine principles throughout the social fabric. Like Addams and others, Cooper felt that contemporary social problems resulted from (or at least reflected) imbalance between the two; she promised that "you will not find the law of love shut out from the affairs of men after the feminine half of the world's truth is completed."[149] Also like Addams, she accepted female domestic responsibility in stride, reassuring that while "the untrammeled development of woman . . . gives her to the world and to civilization, [it] does not necessarily remove her from the home and fireside."[150] On the contrary, in Cooper's frame of reference the goal of broadened participation for women amounted to generalization of the province of domesticity, as she charged her gender with being guardians and tutors of society's "manners and morals."[151]

Certainly, this gendered logic's popularity as conventional wisdom derived largely from its congeniality to the prevailing ideology of male supremacy. Women operated within a community of intellectual discourse whose legitimating boundaries were set by sedimented presumptions of male preeminence, and notions of gender essentialism enshrined that preeminence by representing it as noncontingent. Historians from Marx to Daniel T. Rodgers have shown how insurgents develop within a constraining, hegemonic frame of reference and attempt, at least initially, to bend its premises to ends subversive of the institutional arrangements and social relations they had theretofore legitimated. That advocates of feminist agendas embraced essentialist views, therefore, should be neither dismissed as evidence of false consciousness (indeed, Cooper considered women who did not see themselves in essentialist terms to be victims of self-deception)[152] nor defensively glossed as clever strategy. Instead, women and men, defenders and enemies of feminist aspirations equally were inclined to proceed from essentialist assumptions about gender because essentialist beliefs and conventions suffused and joined the discursive universe in which they all participated and which shaped their ideas. Essentialist constructions of various sorts appealed to both common religious notions of divine or natural law and the nomological pretensions of the period's scientistic enthusiasms. Even the most careful scholarly discourse blurred the lines separating biology and sociology, heredity and environment, ontogeny and phylogeny.

The many different expressions of "alienage," fragmented consciousness, and anxieties about overcivilization were articulated within an outlook that hypostatized dichotomous, essentialist categories as fundamental determinants of human existence. Typically, the categories represented a dynamic tension between nature and culture. The former was broadly understood to be the domain of the feminine and the primitive; the latter, defined by rational calculation and instrumental action, was the masculine (and prototypically Western) province.

The masculine principle was the source of progress and social evolution—as can be seen clearly in the social theorizing of Ward, the pioneer sociologist and mentor to Gilman. Ward maintained that "shrewdness, diplomacy, strategy and the like are preeminently male characteristics; they are the active, positive, and progressive elements of society." The "male trunk" of mental development "may be conceived as devoted to the active increase, development, and advancement, and the female to the passive stability, permanence, and persistence of type."[153] He defined "inventiveness" as a male characteristic and juxtaposed it to a "female intuition," which he tied to women's characteristic conservatism.[154] Although he insisted that the two principles were of equal importance to society and that male "courage" needed to be balanced by female "prudence,"[155] Ward nonetheless assessed male inventiveness as the "real civilizing agent." "Civilization," he asserted, "consists in the utilization of the materials and forces of nature, and the exclusive means by which this is accomplished is human invention."[156]

Ward's theory of original matriarchy, in fact, underpinned a common view—at least suggestive of Lamarckianism—of male aggressiveness as the source of variation and racial and cultural evolution. G. Stanley Hall noted that the "male is the agent of variation and progress, and transmits variations best, so that perhaps the male cell and sex itself originated in order to produce variation." Hall also observed that in all types of society women are more primitive than men and that "woman is far nearer childhood than man."[157] William I. Thomas similarly categorized the female as "the animal norm from which the male departs by further morphological and physiological variations."[158] He also found women to be "intermediate in development between the child and the man" and endorsed the claims that "woman is always a growing child and that her brain departs from the infantile type no more than the other portions of her body."[159]

The identification of women as relatively primitive and infantile reveals the hierarchical presumption underlying the dichotomized masculine and feminine principles. Thomas, moreover, shows that the dichotomy supported a far broader perception of hierarchy. The ways in which women were primitive or underdeveloped were not only childlike; they were also generic markers of inferiority. He noted that "the lower human races, the lower classes of society, women and children show something of the same quality in their superior tolerance of surgical disease."[160] Female anatomy, he assured, "resembles the child and the lower races, i.e. the less developed forms."[161] The male principle of variation was an integral feature of this hierarchical order as both cause and classificatory evidence.

> Morphological differences are less in low than in high races, and the less civilized the race the less is the physical difference of the sexes. In woman the reproductive function fixes the form with relative definiteness at an early period; but the further variation and fixation of physical traits in man is conditioned by a multifarious activity, and it results that in the higher races men are both more unlike one another than in the lower races, and at the same time more unlike than the women of their own race; and the less civilized the race the less is the physical difference of the sexes. A similar relation holds between the higher and lower classes of the same society.[162]

At bottom, the distinction was between those groups held to be active, aggressive, self-consciously purposive, and goal-directed versus those considered to be passive, reactive, impulsive, and present-oriented. Thomas went so far as to seek the foundation of this distinction in essential metabolic differences. He suggested that

> males are more katabolic than females, and that maleness is a product of influences tending to produce a katabolic habit of body. If this assumption is correct, maleness and femaleness are merely a repetition of the contrast existing between the animal and the plant. The katabolic animal form, through its rapid destruction of energy, has been carried developmentally away from the anabolic plant form; and of the two sexes the male has been carried farther than the female from the plant process . . . woman stands nearer to the plant process than man, representing the constructive as opposed to the disruptive metabolic tendency.[163]

Edward A. Ross's version of the active/passive dichotomy was not so ruthlessly biologistic, but his sociohistorical theory was no less essentialist than the others. Although race was his pivotal unit, he argued that definitive racial qualities are formed, not given. The crucial distinction among racial groups, he believed, concerned their energy levels. Aggressive races are the product of migrations and the breeding of adventurous individuals with the resolve and ingenuity required to survive in unfamiliar or adverse conditions.[164] The more energetic races are future-oriented in Ross's view. They value foresight and the ability to defer gratification. By contrast, to "live from hand to mouth taking no thought of the morrow, is the trait of primitive man generally, and especially of the races in the tropical lands where nature is bounteous, and the strenuous races have not yet made their competition felt."[165] Instrumental rationality and "stability of character" also were critical attributes of advanced, "winning" races. "Primitive peoples," on the other hand, Ross noted, "are usually over-emotional and poised unstably between smiles and tears. They act quickly if at all, and according to the impulse of the moment."[166] Such a "race of impulsivists absorbed in sensations, and recollections or anticipations of sensations" is destined to give way before races driven by "lively imagination of remote experiences to come . . . self-control that can deny present cravings, or resist temptation in favor of the thrifty course recommended by reason." Thus Ross proposed another form of the dichotomy of experience: "the sensori-motor moved by sense-impressions and by sensory images, and the ideo-motor moved by ideas."[167]

What Ross propounded as the basis of racial stratification, Hall described as the biologically grounded substance of sex differentiation. Hall maintained that the female, in line with her anabolic nature, "works by intuition and feeling; fear, anger, pity, love, and most of the emotions have a wider range and greater intensity. If she abandons her natural naivete and takes up the burden of guiding and accounting for her life by consciousness, she is likely to lose more than she gains, according to the old saw that she who deliberates is lost."[168] He alleged also:

> Her thought is more concrete and individual and she is more prone to associations in space, and man in time. Men are more prone to bring things under general rules and with regard to symmetry. Her logical thought is slower, but her associations quicker than those of man, she is less troubled by inconsistencies, and has less patience with the analysis involved in science and invention.[169]

Park brought together racial and gendered versions of the dichotomy in his 1918 characterization of Negro temperament, which he declared "consists in a few elementary but distinctive characteristics, determined by physical organizations and transmitted biologically."

> These characteristics manifest themselves in a genial, sunny, and social disposition, in an interest and attachment to external, physical things rather than to subjective states and objects of introspection; in a disposition for expression rather than enterprise and action. . . . Everywhere and always [the Negro's racial temperament] has been interested rather in expression than in action; interested in life itself rather than in its reconstruction or reformation. The Negro is, by natural disposition neither an intellectual nor an idealist, like the Jew; nor a brooding introspective, like the East African; nor a pioneer and frontiersman, like the Anglo-Saxon. He is primarily an artist, loving life for its own sake. His metier is expression rather than action. He is, so to speak, the lady among the races.[170]

Beneath the several constructions of hierarchies of temperament lay a distinction between acting upon nature and living within it. The "male" principle stood for the former, the "female" for the latter. The view that systematic action upon nature—that is, culture—was the source of human progress was not unique to the fin de siècle context; nor was the corollary practice of stratifying modes of human existence according to their supposed capacities for or levels of cultural complexity. As L. J. Jordanova notes, for example, prevailing notions of progress during the Enlightenment already centered the narrative of human history on "the growth of culture through the domination of nature [characterized by] the increasing assertion of masculine ways over irrational, backward-looking women."[171] Progressive-era discourse, though, did give the nature/culture dichotomy a particular, historically specific grounding as a trope encoding legitimated stratification. The frame of biological and cultural evolution imbued extant hierarchy with the impersonality of positivist law and inscribed it among the core tenets of an organicist teleology.[172]

Several aspects of evolutionist thought—especially in its Lamarckian tendencies—came together to give the fin de siècle version of the nature/culture dichotomy its specific character and a respectable intellectual foundation. The notion that evolution was propelled by a logic of increasing differentiation and complexity provided an apparently objective, scientific basis for assigning populations to one or the other category. Recapitulationism—the theory that ancestral adult stages are repeated in embryonic or juvenile stages of descendants—accommodated the belief that characteristics of less advanced forms existed subsidiarily in the more advanced. This view obviously grew from and reinforced the practice of assigning groups to places on a scale of relative distance from a "natural" or animal state, and it gave intellectual authority to claims that equated women, primitives and (white) children. It also gave standing within educated and enlightened circles to the notion that individuals could experience atavistic impulses or yearnings. (As an indication of the extent of recapitulationism's legitimacy, Stephen Jay Gould notes that it was the conceptual foundation of Freud's entire psychoanalytic enterprise—a foundation, moreover, on which he stood until his death.)[173] The prevalent concern with overcivilization was fed by a judgment that the contemporary bourgeois world had been too successful in suppressing those impulses and could be reinvigorated by giving vent to them, albeit in contained or indirect ways.

The Lamarckian belief in inheritance of acquired characteristics also buttressed hierarchical essentialism; by underwriting what George W. Stocking Jr. has characterized as a "vague sociobiological indeterminism," it hopelessly obscured the lines between biological and social theory.[174] Ironically, neo-Lamarckians may have tended more than others to argue that backward groups could advance in the proper environment. Nevertheless, in propounding a "behavioral theory of biological evolution,"[175] the Lamarckian tendency actually made it possible to treat highly dubious behavioral stereotypes as if they had the force of biological law. Finally, a corollary of the Lamarckian view of inheritance—the belief that common environments produce collective, heritable temperaments—ensconced essentialism deeply within evolutionist discourse, as we have seen in Ross's and Park's ideas about racial temperament. It also opened the path to situating the double-consciousness phenomenon in biological territory. Gilman argued in a revealing way that gender stratification weakened the race by stunting half of its pool of hereditary qualities.

> The largest and most radical effect of restoring women to economic independence will be its result in clarifying and harmonizing the human soul. With a homogeneous nature bred of two parents in the same degree of social development, we shall be able to feel simply, to see clearly, to agree with ourselves . . . instead of wrestling in such hopeless perplexity with what we have called "man's dual nature." Marry a civilized man to a primitive savage, and their child will naturally have a dual nature. Marry an Anglo-Saxon to an African or oriental, and their child has a dual nature. Marry any man of a highly developed nation, full of the specialized activities of his race and their accompanying moral qualities, to the . . . rudimentary female creature he has so religiously maintained by his side, and you have as a result . . . the human soul in its pitiful, well-meaning efforts, its cross-eyed, purblind errors, its baby fits of passion, and its beautiful and ceaseless upward impulse through all this wavering.[176]

Du Bois's famous lament takes on heretofore unexplored meaning when cast within this evolutionist frame, and both textual and biographical evidence strongly support such an interpretation. Du Bois certainly was conversant with prominent intellectual constructs of nascent social science and operated quite naturally within them. And Stocking has indicated that environmentalist evolutionism of a Lamarckian sort was the norm among American social scientists at the turn of the century.[177] Du Bois even expressed discomfiture—as did many others—at the potentially reactionary implications of August Weismann's attack on the principle of inheritance of acquired characteristics; he feared that a strictly biological theory of heredity would promote "a lessening of faith in what human training may accomplish, and a general tendency to sit back and watch the lower classes and the lower races waver and wander on, unhelped and with little sympathy from above."[178]

Du Bois's basic views on race at the time of his initial "two-ness" statement proceeded explicitly from the conventions of neo-Lamarckian social science. He rejected strictly physical or anatomical classifications because "the wonderful developments of human history teach that the grosser physical differences of color, hair and bone go but a short way toward explaining the different roles which groups of men have played in Human Progress."[179] In that judgment Du Bois reflected contemporary social scientists' disposition to minimize the significance of gross anatomical features in explaining racial differentiation. Thomas, for example, argued against the usefulness of such approaches and invoked considerable scientific authority as support.[180] Even Ross—hardly the avatar of universal brotherhood—saw physical differences as largely the products of social conditions and subordinated them to moral or temperamental traits in his classificatory rubric.[181]

Du Bois, of course, did not deny the existence of essential racial differences; he simply grounded the "subtle, delicate and elusive" forces of differentiation within the dynamics of sociohistorical evolution:

> While these subtle forces have generally followed the natural cleavage of common blood, descent and physical peculiarities, they have at other times swept across and ignored these. At all times, however, they have divided human beings into races, which, while they perhaps transcend scientific definition, nevertheless, are clearly defined to the eye of the Historian and Sociologist.
>
> What, then, is a race? It is a vast family of human beings, generally of common blood and language, always of common history, traditions and impulses, who are both voluntarily and involuntarily striving together for the accomplishment of certain more or less vividly conceived ideals of life.[182]

This construction has led Anthony Appiah properly to identify Du Bois's view of race as sociohistorical; Appiah is also correct in judging that view unscientific in relation to presentist biological standards.[183] Implicit application of similar standards provoked Moses to charge Du Bois with being "dreadfully inconsistent" and operating with "reckless abandon" conceptually. "The basis of Du Bois's raciological theory," he concluded, "was not rational, but mystical; it was not grounded in reason, but in something akin to faith."[184] When seen in relation to what his contemporaries understood to be scientific knowledge and reason, however, Du Bois's construction does not seem to warrant Moses's assessment. Nor does it support Appiah's claim that Du Bois "explicitly sets [his sociohistorical view] over against the scientific conception."[185] On the contrary, Du Bois was unambiguously in step with the conceptual orthodoxy defined by the Lamarckian social science of his day.

Thomas, a founder of American sociology, had articulated a view quite similar to Du Bois's in 1896. He argued that, although physical differences among races were not especially revealing:

> the formation of artificial or historic races, through the influence of *milieu* and the diffusion of a common fund of beliefs, sentiments, ideas, and interests among a heterogeneous population brought by hap and chance into the same geographical zone, is taking place before our eyes at the present moment, and is a matter of history; and we are safe in assuming that in this the process of the formation of true races is repeating itself.[186]

Du Bois read the development of existing races in terms almost identical to Thomas's.

> The age of nomadic tribes of closely related individuals represents the maximum of physical differences. They were practically vast families, and there were as many groups as families. As the families came together to form cities the physical differences lessened, purity of blood was replaced by the requirement of the domicile . . . i.e., there was a slight and slow breaking down of physical barriers. This, however, was accompanied by an increase of the spiritual and social differences between cities. This city became husbandmen, this merchants, another warriors, and so on. The ideals of life for which the different

cities struggled were different. When at last cities began to coalesce into nations there was another breaking down of barriers which separated groups of men. The larger and broader differences of color, hair and physical proportions were not by any means ignored, but myriads of minor differences disappeared, and the sociological and historical races of men began to approximate the present division of races as indicated by physical researches. At the same time the spiritual and physical differences of race groups which constituted the nations became deep and decisive.[187]

What Thomas called "true" and "artificial" races, Du Bois treated as settled and emergent moments of a process. For both Thomas and Du Bois the process was driven principally by sociohistorical forces which drew upon, produced, realized, and refined themselves through physical characteristics. Like Thomas, Du Bois believed that "the same natural laws" governed the development of all races.[188] In his 1901 *Annals* essay, he allowed that "there are many delicate differences in race psychology, numberless changes that our crude social measurements are not yet able to follow minutely, which explain much of history and social development."[189]

Du Bois did not attempt to detail the biochemical mechanisms through which alleged racial characteristics were generalized and solidified within populations, as Thomas and others did. Taking account of the controlling intellectual orientation toward "sociobiological indeterminism," however, renders that distinction less significant than it might appear to a more presentist reading. More important is recognition that Du Bois's embeddedness within the prevailing discursive conventions extended to his acceptance of their evolutionist model of racial/cultural hierarchy.

As I have shown elsewhere in this volume, Du Bois defined blacks as comparatively primitive and undeveloped as a race. He referred only pages after the two-ness reference to their "credulous race-childhood,"[190] and there is no need to belabor his attachment to the principle of "civilization" (see chapters 4 and 5). He listed blacks among the "world's undeveloped peoples" in need of civilizing tutelage.[191] Beneath his defense of the race's capacity for civilization, moreover, lay an acceptance of the familiar notion that human social life was stratified on a vertical continuum rising from existence within nature. "Like all primitive folk," he averred in describing the distinctive qualities of the sorrow songs, "the slave stood near to Nature's heart."[192] In characterizing blacks' state as "race-childhood" he reproduced the common equation of ostensible primitives and children. His description of black essentiality was steeped in what contemporary observers uniformly would have recognized as the feminine principle. At the defining core of black life Du Bois found a "deep emotional nature which turns instinctively toward the supernatural . . . a rich tropical imagination and a keen, delicate appreciation of Nature."[193] Even as he articulated the "two-ness" phenomenon in terms of concrete social relations he pointed to the race's "innate love of harmony and beauty."[194] At least five years after he began accommodating to the critique of Lamarckian views of racial heredity, he could still declare matter-of-factly that "the Negro is essentially an artistic being, whose rich emotional nature can be made to contribute much to the world's enjoyment and appreciation of beauty." [195]

Of course Du Bois's perception of black Americans' double consciousness rested on an analysis of specific social conditions. He saw it arising broadly from blacks' contradictory and marginal position in American society, just as Gillmore rightly understood her sense of hanging between two spheres as a direct consequence of the contradictory status of women of her class. He bemoaned the plight of the black artisan, professional, and scholar forced to negotiate between a relatively lofty set of aspirations appropriate to the advanced, white world on the one hand and his race's thoroughly mundane, backward agenda on the other. The latter, in addition, threatened constantly to corrupt and debase by virtue of its taints of ignorance and poverty. [196] He portrayed the condition as a result of the blocked striving "to be a co-worker in the kingdom of culture," the bitter fruit of racial subordination. [197] But he also associated it with blacks' low level of cultural development, their being "swept on by the currents of the nineteenth while yet struggling in the eddies of the fifteenth century." [198] In communicating the angst of the black artist, he implied that a moral or spiritual equivalence pertains between competing black and white race ideals.

> The innate love of harmony and beauty that set the ruder souls of his people a-dancing and a-singing raised but confusion and doubt in the soul of the black artist; for the beauty revealed to him was the soul beauty of a race which his larger audience despised, and he could not articulate the message of another people. This waste of double aims, this seeking to satisfy two unreconciled ideals, has wrought sad havoc with the courage and faith and deeds of ten thousand people,—has sent them often wooing false gods and invoking false means of salvation, and at times has even seemed about to make them ashamed of themselves. [199]

In the end, however, despite yoking it to an appeal for securing civil rights, Du Bois's version of normative equivalence only rehearsed the dichotomy that underlay the fears of overcivilization; he embraced

> the ideal of fostering and developing the traits and talents of the Negro, not in opposition or contempt for other races, but rather in large conformity to the ideals of the American Republic, in order that some day on American soil two world-races may give each to each those characteristics both so sadly lack . . . all in all, we black men seem the sole oasis of simple faith and reverence in a dusty desert of dollars and smartness. Will America be poorer if she replace her brutal dyspeptic blundering with light-hearted but determined Negro humility? or her coarse and cruel wit with loving jovial good-humor? or her vulgar music with the soul of the Sorrow Songs? [200]

From the contextual vantage point I have proposed, Du Bois's double-consciousness formulation seems less a deliberate metaphor than an earnest attempt to characterize—within the limits of hegemonic social theory—the actual situation of blacks in American society. Knowing what we do about Du Bois's faith in science and the nature of social scientific discourse about race during the era in question, it should not be too surprising to see that he operated within the parameters of mainstream academic conventions. The fact that, for all its prominence in *The Souls of Black Folk*, the double-consciousness notion by and large disappeared from Du Bois's writing after 1903—he does not even mention it in subsequent reflections on *Souls*—supports this contextualist interpretation. By 1904 he had begun revising his thinking about race in ways that were incompatible with the neo-Lamarckian resonances surrounding the double-consciousness idea.[201]

Du Bois's reconstruction in *Dusk of Dawn* of the development of his thinking about race is revealing in this regard. Although he recalled himself to have been rather more skeptical about them than his writings from the period indicate, he described the states of learned thinking about race that prevailed within his fin de siècle intellectual milieu:

> At Harvard . . . I began to face scientific race dogma: first of all, evolution and the "Survival of the Fittest." It was continually stressed in the community and in the classes that there was a vast difference in the development of the whites and the "lower" races; that this could be seen in the physical development of the Negro . . . Eventually in my classes stress was quietly transferred to brain weight and brain capacity, and at last to the "cephalic index."
>
> In the graduate school at Harvard and again in Germany, the emphasis again was altered, and race became a matter of culture and cultural history.[202]

Given those options, it is not surprising that Du Bois would gravitate toward the latter, which—as he noted in his 1904 address to Washington, D.C., school-teachers—at least held out the possibility of improvement. "I could accept evolution and the survival of the fittest," he recalled, "provided the interval between advanced and backward races was not made too impossible. I balked at the usual 'thousand years'."[203]

He noted further that he had been "born in the century when the walls of race were clear and straight; when the world consisted of mutually exclusive races; and even though the exact edges might be blurred, there was no question of exact definition and understanding of the meaning of the word."[204] He then specifically situated the construction of race from which he had proceeded in the *Conservation of Races* essay within that historical context, and he judged that construction inadequate.[205] He argued instead that the foundations of race are socioeconomic and ideological. He capped this argument with the powerful apothegm: "the black man is a person who must ride 'Jim Crow' in Georgia."[206]

This vantage point on Du Bois seriously undercuts two main claims made by contemprary scholars concerning the double-consciousness notion: (1) that it was a definitive element, a key organizing principle of his thought, and (2) that it is a moment in the articulation of a distinctively black social-theoretical discourse or tradition. It also weakens the foundation for the view that the notion describes an existential condition generic among Afro-Americans. Of course, that claim is an empirical one and can be resolved ultimately only in such terms. Nevertheless, evidence that Du Bois's formulation was both historically contingent and not unique to a black sensibility destabilizes the claim's conceptual basis, especially since invocation of Du Bois typically substitutes for empirical evidence of the racial "two-ness."

The double-consciousness idea's apparent resonance is, nevertheless, a revealing facet of contemporary black intellectual discourse. As a proposition alleging a generic racial condition—that millions of individuals experience a peculiar form of bifurcated identity, simply by virtue of common racial status—the notion seems preposterous on its face. Yet, the image has become especially popular and evocative among post-segregation-era black intellectuals; moreover, its appeal, as recent estimations indicate, reflects a striking, new reading of the significance of *The Souls of Black Folk* and particularly troubling premises concerning the substance and objectives of Afro-American intellectual history and historiography. In chapters 8 and 9 I shall examine these developments and consider their implications for both the state of contemporary black politics and the study of the history of Afro-American political thought.

"Tradition" and Ideology in
Black Intellectual Life

D u Bois dropped the double-consciousness idea early in his career. Why has
it suddenly become fashionable among students of Afro-American
thought? The answer lies in the notion's appeal to contemporary ideological
sensibilities.

In 1989 and 1990 at least three new editions of *The Souls of Black Folk*
were published in the United States, and it was excerpted in at least one collection of "African-American Classics." An earlier wave of reissues had occurred,
not surprisingly, during the 1960s, and the introductory essays accompanying
editions in the different periods present a revealing contrast. No reference to the
double-consciousness passage appears in either Saunders Redding's introduction
to the 1961 Fawcett edition[1] or Nathan Hare's and Alvin Poussaint's introductions to the 1968 Signet edition.[2] Nor does John Hope Franklin mention it in
his introductory essay to the 1965 *Three Negro Classics*[3] collection which includes *Souls*. In a 1989 Penguin edition, however, Donald B. Gibson construes
the double-consciousness tension as a central element of Du Bois's volume.[4]
John Edgar Wideman, introducing a 1990 edition, considers it to be one of the
"[m]aster metaphors and tropes" that unify the book.[5] In the 1989 Bantam edition, Henry Louis Gates Jr.'s introduction pivots on the two-ness passage, which
he judges "Du Bois's most important gift to the black literary tradition . . .
without question."[6] Anthony Appiah begins his introductory essay in the 1990

Bantam *Early African-American Classics* anthology by quoting the passage; "Of Our Spiritual Strivings," the essay in which it appears, is Appiah's only selection from *Souls* for this collection.[7]

Attention to the Washington–Du Bois controversy marks the second major distinction between earlier and subsequent discussions of the volume. Redding centers the Washington essay in his assessment of the book's power and significance, as do Franklin and Hare. Among the introductions to the more recent editions, though, only Gibson—who in fact presents it as central—emphasizes the critique of Washington. Gates makes only a passing reference (not even mentioning the basis of the disagreement), and neither Wideman nor Appiah even alludes to it. In part this difference may reflect the professional influence of literary studies. Gates, for example, focuses his consideration on Du Bois's "rhetorical mastery, his superb command of the English language"[8] and prizes those of the book's reviewers who had "been able to see 'past' or 'through' the political or sociological content of a black author's work to proclaim its primarily *aesthetic* merits as literary art, as a sublime use of language."[9] Yet Redding was, and Gibson is, also a scholar of literature. Moreover, Gates and Appiah, at least, do not simply overlook the Washington essay's importance; they go out of the way to avoid it.

Gates cites *Souls* reviewers and others among Du Bois's contemporaries to support his view of the book's principally literary significance. He draws on Aptheker's[10] survey of reviews selectively, however, not mentioning the extent to which they—as Aptheker notes—revolved around Du Bois's challenge to Washington. Gates also adduces William Ferris's, Langston Hughes's, and James Weldon Johnson's reflections on the book's importance for themselves and for black Americans generally in the early twentieth century.[11] He observes that Ferris judged *Souls* to be blacks' "political bible," but he glosses over the fact that Ferris linked the book's significance explicitly to its role in consolidating anti-Washington sentiments.[12] Similarly, though he quotes Hughes's recollection that "my earliest memories of written words are those of Du Bois and the Bible," the sentences immediately following those which Gates quotes hardly convey an image of aesthetic contemplation: "My maternal grandmother in Kansas, the last surviving widow of John Brown's Raid, read to me as a child from both the Bible and *The Crisis*. And one of the first books I read on my own was *The Souls of Black Folk*."[13] Johnson not only praised *Souls* for its unique "effect upon and within the Negro race in America," as Gates indicates; that effect, Johnson makes clear at another point in the same text, had to do precisely with its serving as a clarion for the forces of opposition to Washington.[14]

Gates, moreover, quotes Redding's observations, from the 1961 introduction, that *Souls* "is more history-making than historical" and that the volume succeeds in "expressing the soul of one people in a time of great stress, and showing its kinship with the timeless soul of all mankind." Gates asks: "How can a work be 'more history-making than historical'? It becomes so when it crosses that barrier between mainly conveying information, and primarily signifying an act of language itself, an object to be experienced, analyzed and enjoyed aesthetically."[15] Perhaps, but Redding's view was rather more concrete and political. For Redding, *Souls* was "history making" ultimately because it

> may be seen as fixing that moment in history when the American Negro began to reject the idea of the world's belonging to white people only, and to think of himself, in concert, as a potential force in the organization of society. With its publication, Negroes of training and intelligence, who had hitherto pretended to regard the race problem as of strictly personal concern and who sought individual salvation in a creed of detachment and silence, found a bond in their common grievances and a language through which to express them.[16]

Appiah's treatment of Washington and Du Bois is even more revealing. He discusses both men's biographies without hinting at their celebrated conflict, and his silence definitely seems calculated. He maintains it even when enlisting Du Bois to buttress a description of Washington's prominence as an historical figure. Appiah quotes Du Bois's observation that "[e]asily the most striking thing in the history of the Negro since 1876 is the ascendancy of Mr. Booker T. Washington," and he indicates that the statement appears "at the start of the third essay of *The Souls of Black Folk*."[17] But Appiah does not acknowledge either that that "third essay" is "Of Mr. Booker T. Washington and Others" or that the statement he quotes is prefatory to Du Bois's attack.

Appiah, Gates, and Wideman certainly need not be constrained by earlier interpretations in locating meanings in Du Bois's text. In discounting the attack on Washington and emphasizing the double-consciousness formulation, though, they not only depart from the previous generation of introductory essays. They also break with a much older conventional understanding of *Souls*'s significance in Afro-American intellectual and cultural history—one that identifies the attack on Washington as the book's key moment and scarcely notices the double consciousness construct.[18] W. T. Fontaine was rare among earlier practitioners of Afro-American intellectual history in stressing the double-consciousness idea in *Souls*; yet he defined it as an artifact of the defeat of black aspirations for full citizenship after Reconstruction and tied it to Du Bois's criticism of Washington's capitulationist agenda.[19] Nellie Y. McKay credits Arnold Rampersad with initiating an expansion of the scope of commentary on *Souls* beyond the Washington–Du Bois debate,[20] but Rampersad nonetheless maintains that " 'Of Mr. Booker T. Washington and Others' is the key to the book's political intent" and examines the essay at considerable length.[21]

The radically new assessment presented in the recent introductions tells us more about contemporary black intellectual life than about Du Bois. The shift reflects an outlook that—in its focus on delineating a distinctive and coherent tradition in Afro-American thought—smoothes out important elements in the constitution of black intellectual and cultural history. It abstracts away from concrete debates, historically specific, enveloping patterns of discourse in the society as a whole, and the pragmatic concerns that inevitably shape perception. In its purview, differentiation, tension, and conflict among black Americans recede into a dim background. This outlook, I shall argue in chapter 9, arises from and reinforces an ideological current within the post-segregation-era black petite bourgeoisie that is troubling because of its fundamentally conservative and depoliticizing effects on black American intellectual life.

This orientation to the history of Afro-American thought is linked most immediately to the prominence of literary studies in contemporary Afro-Americanist scholarship. The disciplinary practice of contemporary literary studies centers on construction and examination of text-based notions of tradition, or canons. To that extent it underwrites an approach to intellectual history that is idealist and ahistorical. This approach produces typically "thin" accounts that emphasize purportedly transhistorical relations of writers and texts. In Afro-Americanist scholarship, moreover, this tendency has unhelpfully blurred the distinction between cultural history and the history of social and political thought, such that the former has tended to substitute for the latter. A result has been to trivialize the idea of the political by deploying it as a generic allusion— an all-purpose rhetorical symbol of legitimacy (or illegitimacy) and urgency— and by obfuscating the character of politics as an autonomous domain of social activity. As reinventions of *The Souls of Black Folk* without the Washington controversy indicate, this diffuse conception of politics can accommodate—and may even give rise to (after all, if politics can be anything, it need not be anything in particular)—accounts of Afro-American thought that are, from the standpoint of more conventional and bounded conceptions of the political, strikingly depoliticized.

Yet this interpretive tendency is intrinsically ideological. Its simultaneous inflation of political language (for example in casual propagation of such constructs as "cultural politics," "politics of interpretation," and the like) and depoliticization of the narrative of black intellectual history—again, as shown in the recent assessments of *Souls*—devalues discourse and action directed toward intervening either specifically in the exercise of public authority or more generally on the reproduction of given patterns of social relations. This intellectual historiography—as, for example, in Gates's dismissal of *Souls*'s political agenda in assaying the volume's importance—reduces to ephemera strategic arguments concerning mobilization for willful, collective action in public life. It also, relatedly, gives short shrift to critical reflection and debate bearing on social structure, political economy, and the staples of political theorizing, such as legitimacy, justice, obligation, the meaning of equality, or the nature of the polity. The narratives that result are ironically compatible in this regard with the broader rhetorical tendency in the Reagan-Bush-Clinton era to diminish the significance of politics as a consequential endeavor in American society. The compatibility, moreover, may not be purely serendipitous. The substantive interpretations proffered in those narratives have embedded within them politically conservative strains that occasionally erupt into explicitness in commentary that addresses issues in contemporary black life. These are rather provocative charges, and I shall specify them through a critique focused on the writings of the main representatives of this approach to Afro-American intellectual historiography—Houston A. Baker Jr. and Henry Louis Gates Jr.

Houston A. Baker Jr.: Cultural Politics and the Rehabilitation of Booker T. Washington

From his affiliation with the "Black Aesthetic" ideology of the late 1960s and early 1970s to the present, Baker has attempted to posit racial or cultural traditions in order to formulate notions of black authenticity.[22] His more recent excursions into commentary on Afro-American intellectual history simultaneously proceed from and seek to defend—albeit with shifting conceptual categories and idiosyncratic yet unexplicated appropriations of conventional usages—versions of authentic black tradition.

Baker's constructions of black authenticity rely first on subsumption of all of Afro-American intellectual history into literary history. He routinely invokes the former as if it were homologous with the latter.[23] Thus he is able to derive a vision of black intellectual tradition from claims about forms of artistic expression or modes of cultural performance. This move has two important consequences. First, it justifies an approach that is ahistorical, acontextual, and idealist in that it characterizes tradition as the elemental persistence of definitive forms—the constitutive idea of blackness—through all concrete environments. Baker indeed expressly rejects contextualist and historicist interpretations because they deny "the very possibility that sophisticated verbal art is an *always already present* feature of the Afro-American landscape."[24] Second, in abstracting away from historically specific discursive contexts, Baker's formalist construction overlooks real tensions and differences and trivializes the substance of real debates among black Americans; to that extent it grounds Afro-American intellectual history on a false unity. Presumption of that fundamental unity of experience leads Baker to assert a racial principle of masking—intentional, Aesopian misrepresentation—as a way of accommodating apparently conflicting tendencies within his black tradition.[25]

In addition to its troubling substantive aspect—Baker advances this idea initially on behalf of his attempt to rehabilitate Booker T. Washington as a race-nationalist hero—the masking principle creates a major interpretive problem for his project. If "x" and "not-x" equally can be taken as expressions of the black tradition, then how can we tell what does not qualify as representative? If we must assume that every artifact—even those that appear antagonistic to one another, produced by an Afro-American necessarily somehow reflects the tradition, then the argument is premised on a circularity that cannot bear skeptical scrutiny: we can demonstrate the tradition only because we already assume its existence. If expression of the tradition cannot be deduced automatically from group membership, identification of proper representations must depend on either esoteric knowledge or intersubjective standards of evidence. The latter are not immediately apparent, and Baker does not elaborate any. In explicating his underlying notion of black authenticity, however, he reveals how he can avoid the dilemma of circularity. In Baker's view the authentic black tradition is rooted in vernacular expression, which he maintains is organized around a sensibility formed in slavery and observable in the blues: "The metaphoric dimensions that arise in Afro-American discourse from sagging cabins, felt blues, and fastidious style must be apprehended in their vertical (or synchronic) completeness if one wishes to elaborate exacting accounts of Afro-American history and Afro-American literary history."[26]

He employs other constructions as well; for example, he advances a notion that modern black culture exhibits distinctive traits he labels "mastery of form" and "deformation of mastery,"[27] and he posits the force of an overarching category of "spirit work."[28] Nevertheless, the vernacular blues sensibility remains his fundamental classificatory unit. Yet Baker never provides a clear description of this sensibility. Furthermore, his account begs the question as to why—granting for the moment that a blues sensibility actually exists—the meter of black American authenticity begins running with the slave experience rather than at some other point. What makes the blues-informed vernacular the definitive black tradition? Baker anticipates this question, and his clarification inclines toward hubris: it is authentic because he has decided that it is.

> Afro-American expressive culture appears in its complex continuity and genuine cultural authenticity when it is analyzed according to the model that I have proposed in my foregoing discussions. "Authenticity" is a sign that can connote powers of certification and invoke a world of rarefied connoisseurship—and a desire, as well, for only the genuine and the original. What I intend by the term, however, is not a *raffiné* ARTWORLD projected by institutional theories of expression, but rather an everyday world occupied by our grand, great-grand, and immediate parents—our traceable ancestry that judged certain select sounds appealing and considered them efficacious in the office of a liberating advancement of THE RACE.[29]

However, this explanation is transparently arbitrary and circular, and it poses still another critical question. As it might be phrased in his hallowed vernacular, Who died and left Houston Baker in charge of designating black authenticity?

Any construction of cultural or racial authenticity would founder on that same problem, in part because the idea of the authentic is always hortatory rather than descriptive. It is an attempt to impose a boundary on the intrinsically fluid, syncretic, pragmatic processes that are the substance of human social existence. Notions of cultural authenticity reify culture by construing it as a set of properties whose ownership is established by proof of origination (though "cultural borrowing" may, in some tellings, confer rights of usufruct). Beneath this view typically lie presumptions of definitive group essences, evocations of the old belief in racial natures or temperaments, as in identification of groups—all too frequent in contemporary discourse—by their alleged possession of traits such as family structure, orientations toward work, spirituality, thrift, and so on.[30]

Baker is in no way coy about his essentialist commitments. He declaims unabashedly on the existence of an "Afro-American racial genius."[31] He assures us that "Afro-Americans—from Jamestown's first disembarkation of "twenty negres" to the era of Run-DMC—have been deconstructionists par excellence. They have continuously shaken (or solicited) Western discourse with *spirit work*".[32] He lauds Vincent Harding, Stephen Henderson, and Hoyt W. Fuller for their "explicit and unshakable trust in the value of their *own* explicitly racial instincts and experiences," and he contends that "*race* carries distinctive expressive cultural incumbencies."[33]

Baker himself links his principle of authenticity to a notion of racial essence in exhorting us to "assume that there is a field of 'particular' or vernacular imagery unique to the Afro-American imagination."[34] Even the apparent specificity of the Afro-American experience dissolves into a larger, generically racial essentialism: "Somehow, I cannot persuade myself that a black person in America, or South Africa, or the Caribbean, or anywhere else in today's world is anything other than a *black* person—a person preeminently and indisputably governed, in his life choices and expectations, by a long-standing and pervasive discourse called race."[35] Allowance for gender difference among blacks, moreover, does not at all mitigate his racial essentialism. He simply tacks a subsidiary "Afro-American women's expressivity" onto an otherwise unaltered collective racial essence.[36]

Baker's essentialist view of black Americans and his corollary, artistically inflected notion of authenticity connect with the perverse ways in which he thematizes politics in his characterizations of black intellectual life. I have already noted that the presumption of a unitary black experience imposes a false homogeneity on Afro-American intellectual history. It also supports reduction of politics to the expression of group identity. Baker contends, for instance, that the *telos* of black racial advocacy has always been "the establishment of a mode of *sounding* reality that is identifiably and self-consciously black and empowering."[37] This view allows him to allege a common political project advanced by (among others) Countee Cullen's and Langston Hughes's poetry, Frederick Douglass's abolitionism, the civil rights movement, late-sixties black cultural nationalism, the folkloric figure of the trickster, Alain Locke's New Negro rhetoric, urban uprisings, minstrelsy, Morris Day's pop music, Charles Chesnutt's and Paul Laurance Dunbar's fiction, and the music of the rap group Run-DMC.[38] Such a chronologically and substantively disparate array of individuals, activities, and artifacts can be united only by the most banal abstractions.

No doubt some of the problem with Baker's construction of politics is a function of his penchant for denominating categories and fashioning eccentric uses of conventional terminology—most often without any attempt to defend them or even to assign them clear meanings. He waxes on through at least three books about an "economics of slavery," by which he apparently intends to posit an evolving ideological narrative articulated through all specific contexts of black subordination from 1619 to the present; this narrative is produced by a consciousness formed in a three-century interaction with the phenomenon of "commercial deportation," or slavery and its consequences. These formulations appear first in association with the similarly amorphous notion, "blues sensibility," in Baker's *Blues, Ideology and Afro-American Literature*.[39] Then, in *Modern-*

ism and the Harlem Renaissance, he adds to them a chiasmic dyad: the "mastery of form" which seems to refer to the appropriation of restrictive, demeaning stereotypes for racially ennobling ends, and the "deformation of mastery," which Baker presents as a more direct, racially assertive, and emphatic—but no less cultivated—rhetorical strategy that in some unarticulated way "implies an altered definition of economics."[40] Blending of those two strategies produced, Baker avers, yet another vaporous category, "Afro-American modernism," which he claims was born in Washington's infamous September 18, 1895, speech at the Atlanta Cotton States and International Exposition.[41] Subsequent constructions add categories labeled "spirit work"[42] and "metalevels of cultural negotiation,"[43] again with no explication or suggestion as to how the new grafts connect with the earlier ones.

Baker's constantly shifting categorical fog completely obscures the ground of historical and social fact; as a result, he has neither means nor warrant to constrain the flight of his narrative imagination. Absence of constraint can yield expression of grandiloquent ignorance, as it does most clearly in Baker's remarkable treatment of Washington, which also makes strikingly clear the disturbing implications his views about tradition and authenticity hold for interpretation of the history of Afro-American political thought.

Baker's apologia combines a claim about Washington's intentions with one about the exculpatory significance of his larger agenda. Baker defends Washington's public acquiescence to blacks' disenfranchisement and relegation to second-class-citizen status by arguing that the stance was not genuine but was a cleverly adapted instrument of a higher purpose. In this view Washington's posture exemplified the "mastery of form"; it was a ruse through which he only appeared to endorse the rhetoric of racial subordination in order to "earn a national reputation and its corollary benefits for the Afro-American masses" via his program for institution building at Tuskegee.[44]

Baker's defense is in three major ways faulty. First, the "mastery of form" argument depends entirely on his own will to believe and thus demonstrates the circularity intrinsic to his notion of masking. He offers no evidence to support his contention that we should distinguish between Washington and "Washington's narrator." This distinction, which Baker simply posits in a formalistic discussion of rhetorical structure in *Up from Slavery,* is all that lies beneath his call to see Washington as striving "to reconcile whatever he thinks of as an 'authentic' self with demands of a larger world from which he must secure venture capital."[45] But why should we make such a distinction except to salvage an image of Washington as a legitimate race man? From an intellectual-historical standpoint, moreover, how far should we go in distancing a public figure from his or her acts by interposing a differently motivated, supposedly more "authentic," private self? Why would such a self be more authentic than the public, official one? Would the existence of a contrary, private self sanitize an agent's public acts, override their possibly objectionable public force? Baker addresses none of these issues, and his avoidance of them is symptomatic of a second problem with his defense.

Baker fails to consider the social and political consequences of Washington's strategy, the ways his public acts were received by his contemporaries and the agendas they furthered. He apparently accepts on Washington's word that the Tuskegee enterprise was a "skills center," leading the way to racial uplift,[46] and in doing so he illustrates both the paucity of his own historical understanding and the inadequacies of trying to read out the history of political thought from literary analysis of texts. James D. Anderson's rich scholarship has demolished the myth of Washington as trickster-nationalist. The Tuskegee model—only a blackface version of the Hampton model pioneered by General Samuel Chapman Armstrong, Washington's mentor—was never about real vocational training; like Hampton, Tuskegee actually functioned as a normal school designed to impart the barest rudiments of basic education and ideological training. As Anderson shows, "Hampton and Tuskegee were not trade schools, nor academic schools worthy of the name, but schools that attempted to train a corps of teachers with a particular social philosophy relevant to the political and economic reconstruction of the South."[47] That social philosophy "requested black southerners to eschew politics and concentrate on economic development" and focused on developing "black teachers and leaders who would prepare the black masses for efficient service in racially prescribed occupational niches."[48]

In his defense of Washington, Baker seems oblivious to the reality of the "black Eden at Tuskegee," about which he rhapsodizes as a "modernist" image. Later, however, he disparages "the turn-of-the-century training of blacks for vocational/technical jobs that they could not possibly hope to occupy in a segregated economy."[49] Although he makes no specific reference, the object of this criticism is the Tuskegee model of industrial education. In fact, as Anderson argues convincingly, industrial schools characteristically were barred by their public and philanthropic sponsors from undertaking any course that would bring blacks into direct competition for "white" jobs.[50] Still, the criticism discloses a revealing contradiction. How can Baker justify Washington's conciliationism by appeal to a greater goal which he then deems misguided?

He sidesteps this difficulty by separating praise for Washington as a spokesman from the substance of his spokesmanship; moreover, he eludes the discrepancy in his utterances by not acknowledging the links between them. (Not only does he get lost in his categorical fog, it also provides him hiding places.) Thus his reduction of Afro-American thought to artistic expressiveness gives vent to an indiscriminate exercise in racial celebration and allows Baker—never once blushing in his posture of stylized radicalism—to embrace the most central black henchman of the white supremacist juggernaut since Emancipation. Because Baker dismisses historicist and contextualist perspectives, he is able to enthuse over even the nefarious "Atlanta Compromise" address. What he lauds as a "Promethean cultural appropriation" and brilliant maneuver on behalf of black empowerment,[51] however, is historically and politically significant for giving an appearance of black approval to the New South regime explicitly predicated on black social and economic subordination and expulsion from civic life.[52] On the one hand Baker, ironically, understates Washington's agency in American politics. The Tuskegee Principal did not merely respond to a fait accompli; his active support helped to implement the new regime and to define a new orthodoxy in race relations. On the other hand Baker exalts Washington as the embodiment of collective black will, thereby vesting him with strategic agency for the entire race; in doing so Baker discloses the third fundamental inadequacy in his account.

Baker proceeds from a naive, extraordinarily simplistic notion of the relation between Washington and the larger black population whose interests he purported to represent. In Baker's purview there are only white elites to be cajoled and manipulated, Washington, and the inert, programmatically mute black "masses." White power is reified and naturalized as an unchallengeable environmental force, and Washington's leadership "emerges from a mass of southern black folk who sought ways beyond factionalism, uncertainty, oppression and minstrel nonsense that marked their lives during thirty uneasy years from emancipation to the dawn of a new century."[53] Having presumed a confused or benighted passivity as the popular black political condition and Washington as the sole source of strategic coherence, Baker is predisposed to perceive the interests of leader and led as identical. Benefit to Washington is ipso facto benefit to the Afro-American masses. So, he observes, Washington's "mind is undoubtedly always fixed on some intended gain, on a mastery of stories and their telling that leads to Afro-American advancement."[54]

Baker can maintain that view only because he does not inquire into black responses to Washington's program. Instead, he relies on the affinities of his father, uncle, and in-laws as proof of Washington's popular legitimacy.[55] If he had cast his net more widely, however, he should have found a more complex situation. Anderson shows that considerable black opposition to the Hampton-Tuskegee Idea always existed, and he documents a pattern of local protest against efforts to impose that model from the mid-1870s into the post–World War I era—well after Washington's death.[56] Moreover, Baker misrepresents black reaction to the Atlanta Compromise, asserting that the speech had been an "overwhelming success with black and white alike."[57] Louis Harlan, Washington's biographer, catalogs a "black response to the speech, from the beginning [that] was more varied and ambivalent than that of whites."[58] Anderson also describes elements of the great controversy that Washington's speech generated among blacks, and Rydell records that there had been substantial black opposition—both in Atlanta and elsewhere—to participation in the Atlanta Exposition at all because of its endorsement of Jim Crow both ideologically and organizationally.[59]

The synecdoche through which Baker evinces his family to stand for black America is instructive. He slides without hesitation from an excursus on certain of his own kin to a generically racial construction of "our family's sounding strategies" and a call to undertake the "hard and ofttimes painful journey back to ancestral wisdom in order to achieve a traditional (family) goal."[60] He can so easily assume his family to be a cellular representation of the race because he holds an image of the Afro-American population as an organic entity. The racial family imagery evokes a sort of *Volksgemeinschaft* in which individual and collective interests are identical and status relations are naturalized. His racial essentialism underwrites a slightly different organicist tendency that also appears in his synecdochic formulation. If black Americans possess distinctive qualities and interests that are purely racial, then those can be assumed to be reflected in any one authentically black individual. Any such individual, therefore, can be taken as accurately representative of collectively racial perspectives and aspirations. To that extent, racial leadership plausibly can be seen as rising naturally and unproblematically from the collectivity.

The essentialist and organicist strains in Baker's view of black Americans allow him to expatiate on politics and leadership without giving any consideration to issues bearing on accountability, legitimacy, or popular participation. His premise of the organic collectivity speaking with one voice is, when all is said and done, viscerally antidemocratic. His argument for the strategic importance of the Atlanta Compromise speech suggests the depth of his distaste for democratic participatory activity; he prefers order of any sort—even under the aegis of segregationist whites (though he tries to escape this extent of his preference through the passive voice)—to the messiness of popular mobilization.

> I designate Washington's speech as the point at which an agreed upon (by those whites in power, or by these empowered by whites in power) direction was set [!] for a mass of black citizens who had struggled through the thirty years since emancipation buffeted on all sides by strategies, plans, hopes, and movements, organized by any number of popular, or local, black spokespersons, without before 1895 having found an overriding pattern of *national* leadership or approved plan of action that could guarantee at least the industrial education of a considerable sector of the black populace.[61]

Baker's fetishizing of order and uniformity may be in part a vestige of his cultural nationalist commitments; it may reflect a more general trait of a politics merged with aesthetics.[62] It also lays bare a view of really existing black Americans that is—beneath all the ahistorical, aestheticized idealizations—empirically false and demeaning. In validating Washington's desire to "train the Afro-American masses in a way that would ensure their inestimable value to a white world," Baker also affirms Washington's depiction of an incompetent black population in need of elite tutelage to "enable them to survive."[63] Nor does Baker see popular black defectiveness only in the past. When he pronounces on the plight of the black poor in contemporary inner cities, he adopts automatically the prevailing frame of punitive moralism that defines problems in terms of the putative behavior of poor people themselves. He draws on the standard litany of "underclass" pundits, invoking the "spiraling rates of teenaged pregnancies in today's black inner cities," female-headed households, and "collapse of the black family." He even cites the authority of the scurrilously victim-blaming Bill Moyers television special, "The Crisis of the Black Family."[64] This retrograde frame is both wrongheaded and wrong. Black rates of teenaged childbearing declined steadily through at least the 1970s and 1980s. Collapse of the family is a mean-ingless, purely ideological category devoid of any content except patriarchal nos-talgia which similarly operates in defining the female head of household as a problem.[65]

Baker's objectionable pronouncements on contemporary black social life need not flow directly from a decontextualized, organicist approach to interpre-ting Afro-American intellectual history. All too many others rehearse bromides comparable to the former—which are, after all, conventions of Reagan-Bush-Clinton-era discourse on racial inequality—without the hermeneutic scaffolding of the latter. As his account of Washington shows, though, Baker's orientation certainly disposes him toward an authoritarian, antipopular view of the history of political thought among black Americans. Insofar as it pivots on an inevitably essentialist notion of racial or cultural authenticity, that view is fundamentally antidiscursive. That is, the premise of a unitary racial perspective does not pro-vide space for a politics, or therefore a trajectory of political thought, driven by open-ended debate and legitimate controversy. Thus Baker apprehends the pe-riod between Emancipation and the rise of Washington as a time of dysfunc-tional uncertainty; he sees in one of the two moments of the greatest popular democratic mobilization in Afro-American history only disorderliness, a pointless inefficiency that Washington's installation supposedly overcame. To that extent, Baker's account is actually the opposite of an interpretation of the history of political thought; it is a brief against the very idea of political discourse *among* black Americans. As his treatment of Washington also illustrates, only the decon-textualized idealism warranted by his elision of the distinction between the con-cerns of literary history and those of the history of political thought obscures this troubling feature of his approach.

Henry Louis Gates Jr.: From the Signifying Monkey to the Vital Center

Henry Louis Gates Jr.'s efforts to authenticate an Afro-American intellectual tra-dition and canon are considerably more complex than Baker's, in part because Gates wants to avoid racial or cultural essentialism. He is also more explicitly concerned than Baker to establish the black tradition on an academic plane of high intellectuality. Despite his greater care and concern, though, he does not escape the essentialist and ahistorical pitfalls implicit in his quest. Like Baker, Gates also relies on elision of distinctions between intellectual and cultural his-tory and—his explicit claims to the contrary notwithstanding—between politics and politically ambivalent cultural expression, as well as between aesthetic and anthropological notions of culture. Even more than Baker, as Gates moves to comment on contemporary affairs he betrays an often strikingly conservative political perspective.

Gates seeks the distinctiveness of "the black tradition" in the formal charac-teristics of rhetorical practice. He construes this tradition as one "not defined by a pseudoscience of racial biology, or a mystically shared essence called blackness, but by the repetition and revision of shared themes, topoi, and tropes, a process that binds the signal texts of the black tradition into a canon just as surely as separate links bind together into a chain."[66]

This "black tradition of figuration"[67] is preeminently literary; its engine and embodiment is a two-centuries-long "concern to depict the quest of the black speaking subject to find his or her voice."[68] This tradition's literariness presumes the need for and existence of a specific canon of texts. In Gates's view, moreover, this canonical foundation grounds the tradition in sociohistorically concrete, artistic practice and to that extent rescues it from racial or cultural essentialism. He argues that

> the existence of a black canon is a historically contingent phenomenon; it is not inherent in the nature of "blackness," not vouchsafed by the metaphysics of some racial essence. The black tradition exists only insofar as black artists enact it. Only because black writers have read and responded to other black writers with a sense of recognition and acknowledgment can we speak of a black literary inheritance, with all the burdens and ironies that has entailed. Race is a text (an array of discursive practices), not an essence.[69]

To this point, one might wonder how Gates's construction of Afro-American literary tradition bears at all on the concerns of the history of political thought. It does in two significant respects. First, beneath his formal, rhetorical characterization of black tradition lies a notion of cultural authenticity rooted in vernacular expression. This in turn implies an ontological claim about a definitive blackness. Second, Gates's interpretive project from the outset overtly swallows politics into literary artistry and criticism, a move that has its own political implications for both historical interpretation and contemporary ideological program.

Gates contends that black "canonical texts have complex double formal antecedents, the Western and the black."[70] He notes that black literature is more like than unlike the "Western textual tradition" but maintains that "black formal repetition always repeats with a difference, a black difference that manifests itself in specific language use."[71] The source of this difference is visible in vernacular expression. "By supplanting the received term's associated concept," Gates argues, "the black vernacular tradition created a homonymic pun of the profoundest sort, thereby marking its sense of difference from the rest of the English community of speakers."[72] Thus "the literary discourse that is most consistently 'black' . . . is the most figurative."[73] Vernacular expression, therefore, is the touchstone of black particularity; it occupies "the singular role as the black person's ultimate sign of difference, a blackness of the tongue."[74]

Gates is like Baker in seeking black distinctiveness in vernacular discourse, but the ends to which they employ the notion differ significantly. For Baker that vernacular operates mainly to confer a folkish authenticity; it is a theoretical elaboration of a populist nationalism animating the Black Arts ideology that he had long embraced. For Gates also the vernacular functions as an authentication, but a more overtly scholastic one; he emphasizes the vernacular as the source of a culture and a "tradition," and, therefore, of a canon. The Signifying Monkey is in this respect the equivalent of *Beowulf*. However, Gates's idea of the vernacular does more than that.

Rooting his notion of black authenticity on popular discursive practices allows Gates to assert that he has established it on a nonessentialist basis. He can make that assertion because he construes essentialism narrowly, as inhering only in claims for the existence of definitive group characteristics that are biological or otherwise obviously suprasocietal. From that perspective, representing definitive black difference as the product of historically specific and contingent practices avoids essentializing racial characterizations.[75] But this is only a tautological sleight-of-hand.

As I showed in chapter 7 with respect to Victorian ideology, racial essentialism does not necessarily depend on biological arguments. After World War II discovery of the Nazi death camps made biologically based justifications of racial hierarchy unfashionable in liberal American intellectual life. Therefore, "culture" gradually replaced biology as the metaphor characterizing the source of essential traits that supposedly define and separate human populations.[76] Gates's contention that "'race' is not an essence but a trope for ethnicity or culture"[77] is entirely consistent with this strain of nonbiologistic racial essentialism. As it has become hegemonic, moreover, this strain has made clear the extent to which prevailing notions of race, ethnicity, and culture function interchangeably as templates for essentializing claims about social groups.[78]

The inadequacy of Gates's narrowly stipulated category of essentialism points to the deeply problematic character of his own formulation of a contingent, yet elemental, quality of blackness. Credulity is overtaxed to imagine a collective attribute that could be simultaneously contingent and elemental. And his attempts to demonstrate such a trait's existence only underscore his position's impossibility.

At first glance Gates does seem to evince a notion of black particularity that is historically specific. He maintains that the black vernacular's definitive role has arisen "since slavery,"[79] a view that is affirmed by his repeated evocation of a two-centuries long project of collective expression. More directly still he argues,

> Free of the white person's gaze, black people created their own unique vernacular structures and relished in the double play that these forms bore to white forms. . . . That the myths of black slaves and ex-slaves embody theories of their own status within a tradition is only one of the more striking instances of what Ralph Ellison calls "the complexity" of the Negro's existence in Western culture.[80]

Nevertheless, Gates fails to avoid the essentialist pitfall, not least because his efforts to escape it are more apparent than real. Although he refers extensively to sociolinguistic scholarship on black Americans,[81] his notion of the black vernacular actually centers on formalized cultural production—both folkloric and literary, with the occasional allusion to music. He presents objects of folklore (toasts, mythological narratives) and literary texts as stand-ins for the vernacular discourse that carries such a heavy existential burden in his argument for a black particularity grounded in popular practice. This move elides a distinction between aesthetic and anthropological notions of culture—a distinction, that is, between culture as a compendium of fixed and specialized artifacts and the formal principles governing them and culture as the pragmatic processes of social life.

While quotidian culture—ways of living and the meanings constructed around them—certainly has an aesthetic dimension, it is also fluid, various, and always syncretic. Those characteristics, which reflect the messy autonomy and open-endedness of social existence, are the more pertinent for claims such as those Gates wants to make about popular practices. Yet they have no place in the fundamentally Arnoldian view that Gates exposes.[82] Culture for Gates is ultimately, as it was for Arnold and generations of his epigones, rarefied and aestheticist. Art promises a summary elegance that trumps all else as source and statement of group meaning.

Like Baker, Gates reifies artistic production as an unproblematic expression of definitively black characteristics. This reification in turn supports the premise of a collective racial subject. Thus he can ensconce the artist as "point of consciousness, or superconsciousness of his or her people"[83] and treat the fiction of Zora Neale Hurston, Ishmael Reed, and Alice Walker as direct representations of a collectively black expressive culture. This reified vision allows him as well to propose neatly circumscribed formulations like the "classic confrontation between Afro-American culture and American culture" or a dichotomy like "the Western and the black," which treat "cultures" as bundles of identifiable properties inhering in and marking clearly bounded populations—a variant, that is, of Victorian notions of racial ideals.

Gates's emphasis on historical contingency in his construction of black distinctiveness also collapses in short order. He presents the definitive black vernacular simultaneously as a product of the slave experience in the New World and as indigenously African, predating and outside the social system of Western Hemispheric slavery and its ideological entailments. To that extent, his vernacular black authenticity is transcontextual and even transhistorical. He posits an "unbroken arc of metaphysical presuppositions and patterns of figuration shared through space and time among black cultures in West Africa, South America, the Caribbean and the United States."[84] At the same time that he acknowledges the existence of discrete black "cultures" and "traditions" in the New World, he treats them as instances of a singular, "extraordinarily self-reflexive tradition" originating in Africa. This perspective sets the Afro-Americanist intellectual project. "Because of the experience of diaspora" he maintains, "the fragments that contain the traces of a coherent system of order must by reassembled."[85]

Gates recognizes that such constructs are freighted with the implication of a racial essence, which he tries to shed. On the one hand, he declares that

> Repetition and revision are fundamental to black artistic forms, from painting
> and sculpture to music and language use. I decided to analyze the nature and
> function of Signifyin(g) precisely because it *is* repetition and revision, or repeti-
> tion with a signal difference. Whatever is black about black American literature
> is to be found in this identifiable black Signifyin(g) difference.[86]

On the other hand, he attempts in the same breath to back away from that
claim's obviously essentialist foundation. "Lest that theory of criticism, however,
be thought of as only black," he hastens to reassure us, "let me admit that the
implicit premise of this study is that all texts Signify upon other texts, in motivated and unmotivated ways."[87] Yet how can both statements be true? Either
"Signifyin(g)" is authentically and distinctively black, or it is not. If he seeks to
argue for a distinctively black *form* of Signifying that marks the boundaries of
group particularity, he has only refined the idea of a black essentiality, not transcended or overcome it.

Gates's transhistorical claims are ironic and revealing, as well as badly
flawed on their own terms. He advances his thesis crucially by assertion, synecdoche, and calls to suspend disbelief. In seeking to establish what seem to be
quite tenuous links between the Esu figure in Yoruba mythology and the Signifying Monkey in Afro-American folklore, he attempts to slide past his lack of
evidence by admitting it in passing, yet proceeding, unhesitatingly, with his con-
tentions. Apparently, in Gates's view, noting that assertions are unwarranted
somehow makes them less so or preempts objection to them.[88] He glosses over
the evidentiary void with a veneer of lyrical analogy; he suggests that "the Signifying Monkey emerges from his mysteriously beclouded Afro-American origins
as Esu's first cousin, if not his American heir. It is as if Esu's friend, the Monkey,
left his side at Havana and swam to New Orleans. The Signifying Monkey remains as the trace of Esu, the sole survivor of a disrupted partnership."[89]

This construction makes sense only if we presume the connection between
Esu and the Monkey that Gates wants to demonstrate. When all is said and
done, he exhorts us to make a leap of faith based only on his own will to believe.
His argument reduces to purely arbitrary justification: "Whereas the rich parallels between Esu and the Monkey cannot be demonstrated historically, these
are the rhetorical figures and the critic's enterprise that I am positing a relation
between, a functional and rhetorical equivalency and complementarity."[90]

Equally problematic is Gates's synecdochic treatment of Africa in his zeal
to locate black distinctiveness and cultural tradition. He extrapolates Yoruba ritual and mythology to all of Africa and, through a similar elision, takes the "my-
thologies of Yoruba cultures found in . . . Brazil, Cuba and Haiti, among others" as representative of a generically diasporic black sensibility.[91] The logical
condensation of his gambit is thus: Esu is a tricksterlike figure in Yoruba mythology; Yoruba mythology reflects the "splendid . . . ancient . . . classic culture of
traditional West Africa" and a more general "African system of meaning and
belief";[92] these survive in the New World, as can be seen in Brazilian and
Caribbean retentions of Yoruba myths; the Esu figure in Cuba sometimes ap-

pears with a monkey; therefore, the Signifying Monkey trickster of Afro-American folklore derives from Esu.

In the absence of "archeological and historical evidence" Gates relies heavily on etymological claims to shore up this logically shaky chain of argument. The burden of his etymological analysis is twofold. He wants to uncover patterns of overt and sedimented meanings that link the West African, Caribbean, and Afro-American trickster figures by ascribed behavior and characteristics. He also wants to identify all the tricksters with functions related more or less obliquely to rhetorical strategies. He wants, that is, to show not only that the tricksters are related but also that they equally "function as focal points for black theories about formal language use."[93]

In pursuing this objective Gates centers on two words, apparent African retentions, that appear in Afro-Cuban trickster lore. He traces nuances of meaning associated with supposedly related words in several West, Central and East African languages. His execution of this effort, however, is driven by a fallacious presumption that similar combinations of letters in words indicate common derivation. In an offhand comment he succumbs to this fallacy with regard to words in a single language in suggesting "a possible French connection between *signe* ('sign') and *singe* ('monkey')."[94] The problem is magnified when extended across discrete languages. In attempting to trace Kikongo words into Kiswahili, Gates mistakenly identifies verb and noun roots and does not recognize that he must allow for both different noun prefixes and for historical sound shifts in roots. His specific error lies in assuming the Kikongo noun *nganga* ("one expert in medicine or magic") is linked to the Kiswahili verbs *ng'ang'ama* ("to clutch hold of, as of a swinging branch or tree") and *ng'ang'ania* ("to beg earnestly, beseech, until one attains a desired end") ostensibly on the strength of the shared *ngang* lettering. The link thus postulated is the main support for Gates's claim for a connection between Esu and monkey. This in turn is crucial to his argument for a diasporic black cultural tradition and sensibility. The Kikongo and Kiswahili words, however, are not evidently related. Gates does not acknowledge that related roots in different Bantu languages may not have exactly the same sound shape (Kikongo and Kiswahili are both Bantu languages). In this case, the related root in Kiswahili is the verb -ganga (from which the Swahili noun mganga is formed). -Ngagama and -nganganía are two other, independent Kiswahili verb stems, unrelated either to -ganga (in Kiswahili) or nganga (in Kikongo). Therefore the association he proposes is specious.[95] (This is not to consider whether such common etymological derivatives would meaningfully support his theories even if they could be shown convincingly to exist.)

Gates's trickster-based argument for a diasporic black particularity suffers from yet another potentially fatal flaw, one in part bound up with the absence of other persuasive evidence. Without the putative Esu–Signifying Monkey relation we have no compelling reason to assume that the Afro-American trickster is even a "pure" African retention at all. The trickster figure is common all over the world, and the Signifying Monkey could be an autonomously *Afro-American* entity. In addition, Native American trickster figures have been shown to be strikingly close in some instances to their Afro-American counterparts.[96] Moreover, Gates's interpretation begs questions—especially given the weakness of his diasporic claims and absence of direct examination of a certainly more varied Afro-American vernacular discourse—as to why the Signifying Monkey figure or, for that matter, the trickster trope writ large becomes definitive or constitutive of group sensibility.

I mentioned at the beginning of this critique of Gates that his arguments for a transhistorical black particularity are ironic and revealing as well as problematic on their merits. His position is ironic insofar as it amounts to a variant of the project of the Black Arts nationalism from which he has consistently sought to distance his own approach to Afro-Americanist scholarly inquiry. This vantage point also throws into relief a little-remarked but central aspect of Gates's intellectual enterprise, a concern to cleanse Afro-Americanist scholarship of its association with nonacademic political agendas and ideological programs.

Gates's commonality with Black Arts nationalism comes into focus through his insistence on rooting black distinctiveness in Africa. He pursues this task even though doing so, as I have shown, not only requires him to strain against a manifest lack of evidence but also fatally undermines his equally insistent claim to an historically contingent—and therefore putatively nonessentialist—formulation of black particularity. This is by no means to suggest that dropping the African link would automatically rescue his formulation, which is in principle oxymoronic. Historical contingency means flux, variation, and change; elemental group distinctiveness implies uniformity and persistence over time. Nevertheless, an argument, such as Gates seems at points inclined to make, for a common sensibility conferred by the material realities of the slave experience is, on its face at least, more plausible than one for a group particularity that is somehow both historically contingent and radically transhistorical. Indeed, other scholars have advanced accounts that treat slavery as the cauldron for creation of a distinctive black culture in the New World. Lawrence W. Levine, Eugene D. Genovese, and more recently Sterling Stuckey have published studies in this vein that are widely known and generally regarded as reasonable, whether or not they are ultimately persuasive.[97] Why is Gates not satisfied with this kind of interpretation, admittedly more modest but nonetheless grand in scope, and why does he persist instead with one that is both impossible to sustain on its own terms and incompatible with his other intellectual commitments?

The key to answering that question, I submit, lies in Gates's project of authenticating an autonomously black intellectual tradition and literary canon. His vigorous attempts to establish his claim on an African foundation, even without clear basis and on pain of mortal contradiction, may stem immediately from a more or less willful desire to have it both ways. Nevertheless, it is important for him to have it both ways—at least by holding onto the African foundation narrative—in part because of the value he attaches to notions of tradition and canon. These notions proceed from and loom so large because of premises that amount to a blend of Arnoldian and Black Arts nationalist perspectives, a blend that illuminates their overlapping features.

Throughout his career Gates has recurred to the significance of the ability to produce literature as an issue in eighteenth- and early-nineteenth-century debates about black people's status as full members of the human community and their actual, or even potential, equality with Europeans.[98] He laments the special, and unjust, burden that this artifact of the Enlightenment's exaltation of reason placed on black people. He also sees this "onerous burden of literacy"[99] as having distorted black writing, arguing that it has embedded as a "subtext of the history of black letters [the] urge to refute the claim that because blacks had no written traditions, they were bearers of an 'inferior' culture."[100] Gates traces this organizing subtext from eighteenth-century slave narratives through the contemporary tendency he describes as "race and superstructure" criticism, maintaining that its effect on literary studies in particular has been to circumscribe too tightly and inappropriately the compass of scholarly inquiry and criticism.[101] "Because of this curious valorization of the social and polemical functions of black literature," he observes, "the structure of the black text has been *repressed* and treated as if it were *transparent.*"[102]

Gates's critique resonates with others that have in varying ways drawn attention to a chronic problem in Afro-American intellectual life, typically formulated as a self-defeating racial defensiveness or a strait-jacketing, narrowly single-minded focus on race. Fontaine and L. D. Reddick in the 1930s and 1940s, for example, pointed to the limitations of a simplistic concentration on race that ironically blunts the development of knowledge about the black American situation. Ralph Ellison and James Baldwin in the 1950s and 1960s bemoaned the dominant presumption that black art should be evaluated primarily in relation to its status as an aid to social protest. Those arguments converge around a reaction against the stance I have characterized as racial vindicationism.[103] Gates is incisive and eloquent in his objection to the consequences of the vindicationist orientation in the study and practice of black literature.

> Not only the theory but also the practice of black literature has, for two hundred years, grown stunted within these dubious ideological shadows. The content of a black work of art has, with few but notable exceptions, assumed primacy in normative analysis, at the expense of the judgment of form. What's more, many black writers themselves seem to have conceived their task to be the creation of an art that reports and directly reflects brute, irreducible, and ineffable "black reality," a reality that in fact was often merely the formulaic fictions spawned by social scientists whose work intended to reveal a black America dehumanized by slavery, segregation, and racial discrimination, in a one-to-one relationship of art to life. Black literacy, then, became far more preoccupied with the literal representation of social content then with literary form, with ethics and thematics rather that poetics and aesthetics. Art therefore was argued implicitly and explicitly to be essentially referential. This theory assumed . . . that there existed a common phenomenal world, which could be

reliably described by the methods of empirical historiography or else by those of empirical social science . . . [and] that the function of the black writer was to testify to the private world of black pain and degradation, determined by a pervasive white and unblinking racism. Not only would creative writing at last make visible the face of the victimized and invisible black person, but it would also serve notice to the white world that individual black people had the requisite imagination to create great art and therefore to be "equal," an impetus, again, that we have traced to the eighteenth century.[104]

Unlike others who have made similar critiques, however, Gates wants to hold on to a notion of authentic blackness. This is one sense in which he wants to have it both ways, as we can see in his objection to the Black Arts/Black Aesthetic discourse in Afro-American studies—the contemporary manifestation of the race and superstructure tendency against which he defines his project. His concern has been "to take the 'mau-mauing' out of the black literary criticism that defined the 'Black Aesthetic Movement' of the sixties and transform it into a valid field of intellectual inquiry once again."[105] But Gates's problem with that discourse ultimately is just that it is theoretically low-tech and unsophisticated. He propounds a "new black aesthetic movement" whose interpretive orientation draws on poststructuralism and deconstructionist theorizing extrapolated from the black vernacular. He presents this as a corrective to a Black Arts/Black Aesthetic scholarship in which "art for art's sake was seen to be a concept alien to a pan-African sensibility."[106] He wonders, in responding to a nationalist critic:

> Who can disagree that there is more *energy* being manifested and good work being brought to bear on black texts by black critics today than at any other time in our history, and that a large part of the explanation for this wonderful phenomenon is the growing critical sophistication of black readers of literature? Or that this sophistication is not directly related to the fact that we are taking our work—the close reading, interpretation, and *preservation* of the texts and authors of our tradition—with the utmost *seriousness?*[107]

For his part Gates proclaims a desire "to lift the discourse of Signifyin(g) from the vernacular to the discourse of literary criticism."[108] And elsewhere he elaborates on his hyperprofessionalistic view of the task of Afro-American literary studies.

> We write, it seems to me, primarily for other critics of literature. Through shared theoretical presuppositions, the arduous process of "cultural translation," if not resolved, is not hindered. To maintain yet go beyond this split text milieu is our curse and, of course, our challenge, as is the fact that we must often resurrect the texts in our tradition before we can begin to explicate them. To render major contributions to contemporary theory's quest to "save the text," in Hartman's phrase is our splendid opportunity. Unlike critics in almost every other literary tradition, almost all that we have to say about our literature is new.[109]

What Gates offers is a version of the Black Arts perspective that has been refined by an infusion of high intellectuality and purified of its explicitly political intent. He sees a tabula rasa available to Afro-Americanists because in his view no previous criticism has approached the technical sophistication and transcendence of mundane politics—and the two are joined for him—to which current critics have access. In this circumstance he sees both intellectual maturation and a radically new interpretive context for an academic field.

Nevertheless, the claim to continuity with an African sensibility does the same work for him—albeit at the price of contradicting other central tenets—that it does for Black Arts nationalists. It provides a purely black foundation for a cultural tradition. Gates emphasizes that Afro-American expressive culture is the product of white as well as black influences, asserting that "every black canonical text is . . . 'two-toned' or 'double-voiced' ";[110] that point figures prominently in his criticism of the Black Arts school. Against its parochialism he argues:

> Black writers, like critics of black literature, learn to write by reading literature, especially canonical texts of the Western tradition. Consequently, black texts resemble other, Western texts. These black texts employ many of the conventions of literary form that comprise the Western tradition. Black literature shares much with, far more than it differs from, the Western tradition, primarily as registered in English, Spanish, Portuguese, and French.[111]

However, he sees the product of this influence not really as a hybrid or even as a smooth syncretism. For Gates, the outcome remains a conjunction of two distinct cultures, thus the *doubled* voice. He maintains that "the inscription of the black voice in Western literature has preserved those very cultural differences to be imitated and revised in a separate Western literary tradition, a tradition of black difference."[112] Indeed, a key question driving his approach to the study of Afro-American literature reflects a concern quite like that which inspires Black Arts inquiry. He asks, "If every black canonical text is . . . 'two-toned' or 'double-voiced,' how do we explicate the signifyin(g) black difference that makes black literature 'black'?"[113]

Tradition and its formal embodiment in a canon are pivotal for Gates—notwithstanding the weight he attaches to the black vernacular—because he ultimately assents to the view that takes the capacity to produce literature as a marker of racial accomplishment. This view rests on two premises: (1) that there are discrete characters, styles, or sensibilities that inhere to racial, ethnic, or national groups; and (2) that there are identifiable benchmarks indicating the extent of a group's cultivation. Having a sophisticated literary tradition that bears the distinctive marks of the group, then, supports a claim to black equality and worth. This imperative underlies the need to define a canon. Gates puts the issue clearly: "[I]f a peripheral ethnicity is to come into its own through the production of literature, the mechanisms of recognition—the 'selection of classics'—remains integral to the attainment."[114]

Gates's preoccupation with defining a black tradition has been present from the first in his scholarly writing. It has existed in a not uninteresting tension with his more cosmopolitan arguments against Black Arts ideology's conceptual narrowness that fails to account for nonblack influences on black texts. Over time, though, he has tended to resolve this tension increasingly in favor of the position of racial autonomy. In the process he reveals a similarity between the rarefied notions of high culture propounded by Arnold and modernist critics, on the one hand, and the meanings assigned to culture by Black Aestheticians on the other. Gates is indeed steeped in the former, as his emphasis on the problem of canonicity and his various defenses of *ars gratia artis* (for example, in his assessment of the significance of *The Souls of Black Folk,* noted above) reveal. He lobbies only for a separate but equal high culture. Kenneth W. Warren points out astutely that "[b]y conceding, as Gates does in *The Signifying Monkey,* a vision of white cultural ownership, of a Western tradition that has been 'created and borne in the main, by white men,' one purchases like ownership of a black tradition." [115]

Gates proposes what might be described as a neoliberal revision of the Black Aesthetic. He calls on Afro-Americanist critics to get up to technical speed, but in a language that bridges the imagery of sacred vocation deployed by modernist and other conventional aestheticisms and the strikingly similar rhetoric of the Black Arts movement:

> We have the special privilege of explicating the black tradition in ever closer detail. We shall not meet this challenge by remaining afraid of, or naive about, literary theory; we will only inflict upon our literary tradition the violation of the uninformed reading. We are the keepers of the black literary tradition. No matter what theories we seem to embrace, we have more in common with each other than we do with any other critic of any other literature. We write for each other and for our own contemporary writers. This relation is one of trust, if I may. How can any aid to close reading of the texts of the black tradition be inimical to our modes of criticism? [116]

In responding to Joyce Joyce's fatuous, Black Arts-inflected challenge to the racial legitimacy of his approach to the study of black literature, Gates reasserts almost verbatim this combination of neoliberal fetishism of technique and Arnoldian-modernist-nationalist pieties regarding the hallowed mission of the critic. In that context he specifies that by "we" he means "critics in the 1980s" and the "trust" becomes a "sacred" one. [117]

Gates even approximates the self-consciousness that (Maulana) Ron Karenga and (Imamu) Amiri Baraka displayed a generation earlier in calling for invention of a black tradition, but, again, from a more professionalistic orientation. In discussing his work on a *Norton Anthology of African-American Literature,* he enthuses, "We have at our disposal the means to edit an anthology that will define a canon of African-American literature for instructors and students at any institution which desires to teach a course in African-American literature. . . . A well-marked anthology functions in the academy to *create* a tradition, as well as to define and preserve it." [118] In defending his claim to a separate black tradition parallel to the "larger American tradition," he asserts that "nationalism has always been the dwarf in the critical, canonical chess machine. For anyone to deny us the right to engage in attempts to constitute ourselves as discursive subjects is for them to engage in the double privileging of categories that happen to be preconstituted."[119] Elsewhere he elaborates on this connection between nationalism and canon formation after proposing that the "selection of classics" is integral to the construction of nationality through literature: "Inevitably, the process of constructing a group identity, at the margins as at the very center, involves active expulsion and repudiation; self-identity requires the homogeneity of the self-identical. Ironically, then, the cultural mechanism of minority self-construction must replicate the mechanism responsible for rendering it marginal in the first place."[120]

Finally, he extols the "wonderful opportunity offered to our generation of critics as heirs to the Black Arts movement" and embraces Greg Tate's challenge to produce a "black critical theory as great as this greatest black art."[121] His trenchant call to "redefine 'theory' itself from within our own black cultures" brings to mind a Baraka, Karenga, or Don L. Lee (Haki Madhubuti) with a more finely honed academic professionalism.

> As deconstruction and other post-structuralisms, or even an aracial Marxism and other "articles of faith in Euro-Judaic thought," exhaust themselves in a self-willed racial never-never land in which we see no true reflections of our black faces and hear no echoes of our black voices, let us—at long last—master the canon of critical traditions and languages of Africa and Afro-America. . . . We must, in the truest sense, turn inward even as we turn outward to redefine every institution in the profession—the English Institute, the MLA, the School of Criticism—in our own image . . .
>
> . . . [U]ntil we free ourselves of the notion that we are "just Americans," as Ellison might put it, and that what is good and proper for Americanists is good and proper for Afro-Americanists, we shall remain indentured servants to white masters, female and male, and to the Western tradition, yielding the most fundamental right that any tradition possesses, and that is the right to define itself, its own terms for order, its own presuppositions. . . . When we mindlessly borrow another tradition's theory, we undermine [the] passage from the seen to the told—from what we see to how we tell it—this basis for our own black public discourse, this relation between cognition and utterance.[122]

Gates's association of literature and canon with nationalist imperatives, as well as his solemn rhetoric about critics as keepers of the cultural flame and artists as "points of consciousness" for their people, not only echoes the ponderous style and program of Black Arts nationalism. It also contains anachronistic resonances that suggest a perspective on his repeated discussion of two-centuries-old debates about blacks' capacities for literary production. This disposition might seem to be the product of either a peculiar obsession or extensive recycling of the same essays. However, taking account of his blend of Black Arts and formalist aestheticism discloses a layer of meaning in Gates's reconstruction of those early debates that imbues them with pivotal strategic importance for his intellectual agenda. They become the basis for a view that absorbs politics into literary analysis by merger.

To this point I have described Gates's interpretive stance as revolving in part around a call to transcend politics in or to purge political considerations from black textual interpretations. However, though he does complain fulsomely about the practice of subordinating formal analysis to immediate ideological or sociological concerns, he actually makes a more radical move. He wants instead to *redefine* political significance to give priority to literary expression and criticism as strategic action. This tack he pursues in two ways. First, he eliminates distinction between literary and political texts, subsuming the latter within the former. Second, correspondingly, he assigns to the production and formalist analysis of literature the most elemental and consequential role in advancing racial interests. He sees the black literary tradition as "broadly defined, including as it does both the imaginative and the political text."[123] Having incorporated both types of content into a general category of black writing, he then defines writing itself as the primordial political undertaking.

> The very act of writing has been a "political" act for the black author. Even our most solipsistic texts, at least since the Enlightenment in Europe, have been treated as political evidence of one sort or another, both implicitly and explicitly. And, because our life in the West has been one political struggle after another, our literature has been defined from without, and rather often from within, as primarily just one more polemic in those struggles. The black literary tradition now demands, for sustenance and growth, the sort of reading which it is the especial province of the literary critic to render; and these sorts of reading all share a fundamental concern with the nature and function of figurative language as manifested in specific texts.[124]

Anticipating objections, he actively defends the dissolution of politics into form by depicting figurative expression as both the quintessence of blackness and the most fundamental imperative of blacks' existence—thus, by implication their most basic politics—in the West.

> Given the obvious political intent of so much of our literary traditions, is it not somewhat wistful to be concerned with the intricacies of the figure? The Afro-American tradition has been figurative from its beginnings. How could it have survived otherwise? . . . Black people have always been masters of the figurative: saying one thing to mean something quite other has been basic to black survival in oppressive Western cultures. Misreading signs could be, and indeed often was, fatal. 'Reading,' in this sense, was not play; it was an essential aspect of the 'literacy' training of a child. This sort of metaphorical literacy, the learning to decipher complex codes, is just about the blackest aspect of the black tradition.[125]

This combination of claims amounts to something of a coup for the depoliticization of Afro-Americanist intellectual activity. Gates is able to construe literary studies as a self-contained, ahistorical enterprise impelled by formalist aestheticism. Yet he can simultaneously appropriate for that endeavor the cachet and sense of moral urgency that have legitimized Afro-Americanist scholarly pursuits purporting to bear more directly on secular politics and social affairs.

Invoking arguments by Hume, Jefferson, and others that hinged the question of blacks' status in the human community on the production of literature is rhetorically instrumental for this objective. Doing so—particularly because Gates reduces the totality of a controversy that ranged across many fronts (for example, biology and physiology, theology and species descent, capacity for scientific and mathematical reasoning, relative moral sense, capacity for self-government and complex social organization) to this one dimension[126]—supports equating production and criticism of literature with political action. By representing that debate as venerable and historically fundamental, and projecting it forward in time, he asserts the *political* primacy of the dynamics of expressive culture. This perspective helps to make sense of Gates's ahistorical and Procrustean reading that makes *The Souls of Black Folk*'s artistic qualities paramount for the book's significance and reputation. His commitment to having literary studies swallow politics and his aestheticism of the Arnoldian-modernist sort converge to overdetermine such a reading.

Gates exemplifies this move clearly in his response to Joyce Joyce's puerile attack. On the one hand, he announces: "I do not think that my task as a critic is to lead black people to 'freedom.' My task is to explicate black texts. That's why I became a critic. In 1984, I voted for Jesse Jackson for President: if he stays out of literary criticism, I shall let him continue to speak for me in the political realm."[127] Immediately thereafter, on the other hand, he offers this assessment:

> And who is to say that Baker's work or mine is not implicitly political because it is "poststructuralist"? How can the demonstration that our texts sustain ever closer and sophisticated readings *not* be political, at a time in the academy when all sorts of so-called canonical critics mediate their racism through calls for "purity" of "the tradition," demands as implicitly racist as anything the Southern Agrarians said? How can the deconstruction, as it were, of the forms of racism itself . . . not be political?[128]

Gates discusses a "classic confrontation between Afro-American culture and American culture" that "is both political and metaphysical," a struggle "defined by the politics of semantics." He specifies it as a "(political, semantic) confrontation between two parallel discursive universes: the Black American linguistic circle and the white . . . a protracted argument over the nature of the sign itself, with the black vernacular discourse proffering its critique of the sign as the difference that blackness makes within the larger political culture and its historical unconscious."[129]

In assessing the Joyce-Gates-Baker exchange, Theodore O. Mason Jr. suggests that "Gates is actually making an argument not against politics and ideology as general concerns, but rather is mounting an attack on a specific political ideology, the liberationist movement of the sixties."[130] That point is central. As Mason also notes, Gates in fact shares Joyce's concern with "the need for a protective solidarity to defend black culture and the black critical tradition from the depredations of the surrounding racist environment" and joins her—and, I

would add, Black Arts nationalists generally—in "assuming the mantle of libera-
tor and custodian."[131] Like the Black Arts theorists, Gates romanticizes an artist's
(and by extension a critic's) role in mythopoeically "forging value, . . . solidifying meaning," translating "experience into meaning and meaning into belief
. . . incorporating experience into [the] people's pantheon of value."[132] He di-
verges from them precisely in that he rejects their political focus because of its
mundaneness.

> Because of the nature of black poetic expression . . . the black poet is far more
> than a mere point of consciousness of the community. He or she is a point of
> consciousness of the entire language. In the former role—especially in black
> America—one is often bogged down by far too many political considerations.
> The latter role, however, though based in part on political reality, allows the
> poet to transcend his or her political reality and arrive at the core of the com-
> munity's values and way of life. It is debilitating for a people's art to be tied
> merely to its immediate political reality. That which individuates a way of life
> is not only the set of principal goals a people hold but, more important, their
> central beliefs about happiness and suffering (above all, about death) which
> play their part in determining choice and motivating action—indeed, in de-
> termining value.[133]

From this perspective, Gates clearly fails to escape the essentializing ideological
tendency that he laments in race and superstructure criticism, the presumption
of a mimetic function for black artistic production. He simply shifts the locus of
the warranted mimesis from content to form. He also presumes that black art
transparently reveals an essential black social reality; his claim is that the black
experience authentically reflected is a definitive mode of expression rather than
features of demography, social psychology, political economy, or public opinion.
He even shares the reflex that impels nationalists' fetishism of African origins.
In this regard, the narrative of a putative Esu–Signifying Monkey connection,
as well as the undergirding desire to reconstitute poststructuralist literary theory
as an African retention, is Gates's version of Afrocentrists' Egyptology.[134]

The shift from content to form, including the related subsumption of politics into literature, has serious implications for inquiry into Afro-American intellectual history and historiography. This shift is nested ideologically with a political quietism that affects conceptualization of the history of ideas and illuminates
the homology between Gates's interpretive program and neoliberal political ideology. The parallels stem from his desire to dehistoricize and depoliticize black
intellectual history. They become especially obvious on considering his perspective on *The Souls of Black Folk* as a positive expression of the sensibility reflected in his brief against Black Arts criticism.

Where Gates objects to "race and superstructure" critics' isolation of social
or political content as the basis for critical appraisal, he proposes that the real
significance of Du Bois's text appears when we "see 'past' or 'through' the political or sociological content" to its "primarily *aesthetic* merits as literary art."[135]
The focus on literary form turns attention away from both the practical issues
and the substantive arguments that animate the text. "Long after the social issues

with which Du Bois wrestled so intently and so passionately have become chapters in the chronicle of African-American history," he enthuses, "students and their professors continue to turn to *The Souls* to experience the power of its lyricism, the 'poetry' of its prose."[136]

In the same vein, he lauds *Souls* as "an urtext of the African-American experience," in part because it "succeeds, somehow, in 'narrating' the nation of Negro Americans at the turn of the century, articulating . . . the *cultural particularity* of African-Americans."[137] This assessment of the text is consistent with Black Aestheticians' interpretive predisposition; both pivot on reflection of a generically authentic blackness as a criterion for membership in the racial canon. Gates dissents only with respect to identification of the racially definitive substance, and in the process sidesteps a conundrum that characteristically has beset black nationalist intellectual historiography—the problem of accommodating real conflict and incompatibility among representatives of the tradition. If canonical authors represent a unitary blackness, how can historiography handle their disagreements with one another? In relocating the site of black authenticity to the formal aspects of expression, and in explicitly rejecting explicit politics as a criterion, Gates abstracts away from this problem. So, for instance, he can gloss over the Washington–Du Bois controversy with polite demurral; politics is ephemeral in relation to aesthetics in defining the black intellectual tradition.

The combination of depoliticizing transcendence and aestheticist technicism that shapes Gates's interpretive program also yields a suggestive similarity to the "scriptures of modernism," which, David A. Hollinger notes, functioned to create

> a base free from the obligation to specify and to take a stand upon the political, moral, and metaphysical. . . . The modern canon was thus a vital tool in the reconsideration of liberalism that figured prominently in the intellectual history of the 1940s and 1950s. . . . Now, literature was to be about society but not subject to it: *of* the world, but not *in* it. This suspended quality in the "modernism" embodied in the canon was often expressed through the notion of "aesthetic." The texts were presumed to be capable of filling cultural space once occupied by philosophy, theology, and political theory *without losing their distinctive aesthetic quality*, and becoming, in themselves, subject to the rules of argument appropriate for philosophy, theology, and political theory.[138]

Hollinger is rather circumspect about the intrinsically conservative, politically quietistic entailments of the stance advocated by this formalism, but Paul Lauter remarks on "how fully formalist criticism and McCarthyite politics had buried ideas about the social functions of writing."[139]

Despite its official professions of Black Power rhetoric, Black Arts/Black Aesthetic ideology proceeds from a view that is in its fundamental features similarly quietistic. In idealizing transcendent roles for artists as a caste of priestly culture-keepers and art as the suprahistorical domain for definition of the group and its essential values, the Black Aesthetic reproduced in a different rhythm and key modernist ideologues' radical separation of art from concrete social life. This effect indeed runs throughout black cultural nationalism, even when it purports to political activism, because it is moved by a formalistic, ultimately aestheticized view of black people, and therefore of black interests and the means to realize them.[140] As a program for political action, Black Arts ideology's "populist modernism" reduces to efforts to cultivate authentically black aesthetic sensibility for a popular audience: the talking drums play an Africanized, inner-city version of the theme to *Masterpiece Theater.*

Gates recognizes that the Black Aesthetic rests on this concatenation of markedly different features—a pious aestheticism that amounts to a claim for a distinctively black high-cultural critique and the romantically populist rhetoric characteristic to Black Power politics. He notes that "conservative black academic critics and professors" such as Charles T. Davis often looked favorably on the formalist-critical possibilities of the Black Aesthetic while rejecting its ostensibly radical politics.[141] Gates himself has effected the complete separation, showing that the two moments are not necessarily interdependent. In doing so he reflects in his interpretive theory the utter collapse of the extra-academic black political mobilization that had warranted the hybrid of populist modernism in the first place. He simultaneously suggests a link between the aestheticism that he advocates and his own explicitly conservative political centrism.

Gates has expatiated in the public realm much more frequently and fulsomely than Baker on politics and politically charged matters. Especially in the 1990s has he commented often on topical, political issues in the *New York Times, Newsweek, Forbes,* the *New Yorker,* the *New Republic,* and elsewhere. His having pursued this course poses a peculiar irony. Gates, after all, acquired his academic renown principally on the basis of militant argument for depoliticized inquiry into black life. He has then used the visibility thus attained as a platform from which to pontificate about politics. At the very least, by the force of his own theoretical narrative, the expertise that made him a public figure by itself cannot qualify him to function in the sort of "public intellectual" role he increasingly occupies.

Gates's activity as a public intellectual is suggestive and problematic; it raises concern not because he is a scholar of literary studies who deigns to speak for the record on public affairs. He is hardly unique in that position. Edmund Wilson, Raymond Williams, Edward Said, Irving Howe, and Lionel Trilling are only the first few names that come immediately to mind. More broadly, Noam Chomsky, E. P. Thompson, Stephen Jay Gould, and the late Linus Pauling are among the most accomplished examples outside literary studies who have used their prominence in unrelated specialty areas to comment visibly on political and social issues. Gates differs, though, insomuch as the thrust of his scholarship has been to reinforce the boundary between academic and civic pursuits. Others may operate in separate spheres with no overlap—chemistry and antimilitarism, linguistics and anti-imperialism, Shakespeare and socialist activism. Gates stands out because his public intellectual and academic stances are not simply unconnected; they appear to contradict each other. His intellectual program seems not just apolitical but *anti*political through and through.

This may be a real contradiction of which Gates is not aware or by which he is untroubled. It may also express nothing deeper or more complicated than the "that was there, this is here; that was then, this is now" quality so common in his writing. (He has published at many, quite different ideological compass points, giving each readership doses of its own comforting truths.) But Gates himself provides a clue to an alternative view of his apparent contradictoriness, one that implies compatibility if not coherence. "The political authority that came to Du Bois after 1903," he observes, "was generated in large part by the rhetorical authority that he revealed in *The Souls of Black Folk*."[142] This assessment suggests a perspective that in either (or both) of two ways comports with his elevation of the aesthetic in Afro-American intellectual history. The more benign reading follows from Gates's elevation of the aesthetic to a transcendent status that makes it the site of the profoundest politics. If aesthetics is a metapolitics that subsumes politics of the more conventional sort, then his perception of the trajectory of Du Bois's stature seems reasonable. Demonstration of rhetorical prowess is the paramount legitimation; recognition as a political voice is an entailment of the more meaningful admission to the "republic of letters." A less benign reading raises the spectre of careerism and self-promotion. Gates is candid about this aspect of his new role: "At one time I wanted to grow up and be Jacques Derrida. Now I want to grow up and be Edmund Wilson. I always wanted to write for *The New Yorker*, and now I do. If I publish an essay in *Time* magazine, or the *New York Times*, I get dozens of letters. . . . Every afternoon I answer my mail, and it's generally people responding to something that I've written. That's wonderful."[143] Gates might have decided to follow a course similar to that which he reads into Du Bois—or might have read it into Du Bois after having chosen it for himself. To that extent he could quite appropriately shift gears abruptly from the one role to the other. This view may help to make sense of Gates's otherwise curious switch in tone. Where he had become increasingly assertive and trenchant in a race-nationalist way in the late 1980s, suddenly thereafter—as he began to publish "social commentary" in mainstream organs of opinion—he adopted a more temperate, Archimedean voice.[144]

Of greater concern than the relation between Gates's academic and political roles, however, is the substance of the latter. The piece of political ground he has staked out for himself emits several familiar and quietistic themes and resonances. Above all else, he wants clearly to establish his political centrism. Evoking the Cold War liberalism of Arthur M. Schlesinger Jr., Gates endorses the ideal of seeking the "vital center,"[145] announces his desire to "search for a middle way,"[146] and bemoans "the sharp ideological oppositions through which we parse political discourse."[147] He shilled for President-Elect Clinton just after the 1992 election, retailing the conservative Democratic Leadership Council's line on the requirements of American politics and praising Clinton's centrism, which, according to Gates, "is not the centrism of caution: it reflects, rather, a heartfelt negotiation between creeds that are bitterly in conflict but do not have to be so."[148]

This centrist commitment is not idle. Gates has articulated it directly and indirectly through critical essays on other topics. Not surprisingly, the *New Republic* has been a receptive forum. (His coinage of "muscular humanism" to describe his perspective consciously evokes that magazine's "muscular liberalism.") In 1992 he constructed a reminiscence of Baldwin to support his ideal of political moderation. Baldwin, on Gates's idiosyncratic reading, lost his discerning critical eye, and thus his power as a public moral force, when he became overtly politicized and accepted the role of spokesman for the movement in the late 1960s.[149] This is, first of all, a dubious perspective on Baldwin, who—despite his protestations—had functioned as a race spokesman in his writing and public appearances throughout the civil rights era. Gates even discusses his early repudiation of Malcolm X, which was by definition an act of engagement in black political debate.[150] Baldwin was no more—or less—an "official" spokesman for the movement in 1970 than he had been a decade earlier. Though Gates is certainly right in arguing that Baldwin lost his acute purchase on American society and race relations after the mid-1960s, he has to overlook or deny key features of the earlier period to provide an account that blames the siren of activism for deterioration of Baldwin's critical vision. More likely, Baldwin only demonstrated earlier and more visibly than others how inadequate received ways of seeing were for making sense of the changing character of racial politics and the challenges facing black Americans in the postsegregation era.

The real point of Gates's essay, however, is not so much to situate Baldwin as it is to counsel quietism dressed up as judicious moderation. He places his hopes in "a new generation of readers that has come to value just those qualities of ambivalence and equivocality, just that sense of the contingency of identity, that made [Baldwin] useless to the ideologues of liberation and anathema to so many black nationalists." Gates attacks caricatures of irrational radicalism, a "populist left," then and now. He presents first Eldridge Cleaver's and Baraka's homophobic attacks on Baldwin and then "urban activists who would rather picket Korean grocery stores than crack houses" as the substance of radicalism.[151]

In a 1993 *New Republic* cover article that trades on the currently popular canard of juxtaposing the warrants of the First and Fourteenth Amendments, Gates makes a yet more spirited and direct statement of his ideological position. He is properly troubled by the flawed psychologism that undergirds a strain of critical race theorists' support for regulating hate speech, although he advances his case against them in part in a less than principled way. He links them by association with Catherine MacKinnon and then takes MacKinnon's argument for prohibition of pornography as a proxy for the others—even though the question of harm in the hate speech issue is burdened with contextual complexities that do not similarly complicate the pornography debate. To that extent, he creates a straw opponent through sleight-of-hand.[152] (This is a common rhetorical move for Gates. His response to Joyce's attack revolves around his imputing an "implied presence of the word *integrity*" to her essay.[153] And he more than once blithely invokes the existence of a "silent second text"—a construction that can take absence as proof of presence—to justify claims of influence in the face of a lack of evidence.)

In this essay as elsewhere in his new public intellectual guise, Gates resorts to a substantively legitimate criticism that is nonetheless a familiar device of those who counsel quietism. He chides the critical race theorists for not paying attention to political economy, poverty, and class differentiation among black Americans.[154] On the merits this is a fair and reasonable criticism. Yet it can also be a smokescreen, a handy way to change a disagreeable topic by pointing to—but not engaging systematically—a different, supposedly more urgent area for concern. Gates certainly provokes skepticism with his high-minded charge, steeped in implication of hypocrisy or irresponsibility, that those who pursue agendas he criticizes do not focus on "such 'real social problems' as the disintegration of American cities and the failure of the public schools."[155] Gates himself has never addressed such issues in his scholarly or public intellectual pursuits; he only invokes them to reject other programs by impugning their proponents' sincerity or clearheadedness. He is thereby able to evade confronting the views he opposes on their own terms.

Gates's criticism seems disingenuous both because of the disjunction of his preachment and practice and because the tendencies he thus rejects share a common element: they all position themselves as oppositional alternatives to some academic or political orthodoxy. He has leveled this attack, which is actually an appropriation of the 1960s' "mau mau" style, at Afrocentrism and poststructuralism as well as critical race theory. Although each of these tendencies has very disturbing if not damning features and eminently sensible grounds exist for rejecting each, what Gates objects to ultimately is their aspirations to radicalism. And this principle stands out most of all when he does remark on what he flippantly calls "the politics of politics."[156]

In this regard Gates's celebrated attacks on "black anti-Semitism" take on a less than salutary cast.[157] While anti-Semitism is no less reprehensible among blacks than others, it is by no means clear that there is a particularly virulent, distinctively black form that warrants special designation and denunciation. Gates indeed might have taken up that issue in some of his public breast-beating. There is a potentially dangerous political subtext to the invention of the black-anti-Semitism category, one that aims to undermine demands for social justice by imputing to them a tarnished moral foundation and to deflect discussion of black politics away from the problem of inequality. For Gates to join the chorus of denunciation on the op-ed pages without addressing that problem is less an act of courage than a militant endorsement of neoconservative ideologues' conventional wisdom.

In "Let Them Talk," Gates embraces Isaiah Berlin's thinly ahistorical and narrowly individualist formulation of negative liberty as the essence of liberalism and posits it as a standard against which to judge attempts to compel behavior through state power. Predictably, that standard predisposes him against "sweepingly utopian rhetoric [that invites] a regime so heavily policed as to be incompatible with democracy."[158] As with much of Gates's social commentary, he defines himself against a straw alternative. Who would speak for a sweepingly utopian, heavily policed regime? He does not specify the conditions that would qualify for that characterization. But in presenting it as the polar and sole alternative to Berlin's negative liberty, Gates both leaves the impression that whatever deviates from Berlin's thin, fundamentally conservative notion of liberalism is suspect and gives himself room to deny intending to leave that impression.

The posture of courageous tough-mindedness in defending centrist convictions is a key trope in Gates's commentary. In a single essay he, incredibly without hint of self-criticism, castigates "massively totalizing theories that marginalize practical political action as a jejune indulgence"; and objects to "the historiographical tradition that depicts America univocally as a force of reaction in a world of daisy-fresh revolutionary ferment."[159] After issuing a disclaimer that he does not wish to trumpet a new Pax Americana, he asks: "Should the global circulation of American culture always be identified as imperialism, even if imperialism by other means? In an era of transnational capital, transnational labor, and transnational culture, how well is the center-periphery model holding up?"[160] He draws on Arjun Appadurai's contention that a "new global cultural economy" has rendered center-periphery theories, and thus theories positing an overarching American imperialism, obsolete. Gates thereby illustrates the depoliticizing tendency within postmodernist cultural studies' inattentiveness to, or dismissal of, political economy and the state system as domains crucially structuring power relations. In an essay published as the Bush administration—fresh from invading Panama—was unleashing its military might on Iraq, Gates maintains that "the spatial dichotomies through which our oppositional criticism has defined itself prove increasingly inadequate to a cultural complex of traveling culture." As the International Monetary Fund's structural-adjustment policies impose dislocations that send people moving around the globe like sharecroppers, hoping in vain that Lagos or Delhi will be better than the countryside and that New York or London will be better than Lagos and Delhi, postmodernists exult in what they see myopically only as "a complex, overlapping, disjunctive order."[161]

Yet it is in his ruminations on Afro-American politics and social life that the conservative thrust of Gates's commentary is clearest. At times he verges on the flatly reactionary. In his love note to Clinton he defends the president-elect's support for workfare and capital punishment, justifying those positions by noting support for them in "black public opinion."[162] He asserts that poverty "can take on a life of its own, to the point that removing the conditions that caused it can do little to alleviate it."[163] Appropriately, his rightist inclination is most transparent in an essay in *Forbes*. Writing in a special seventy-fifth-anniversary issue on the theme "Why We Feel So Bad When Things Are Going So Good," Gates lays out his take on intraracial stratification. He notes that "it's time for the black middle class to stop feeling guilty about its own success while fellow blacks languish in the inner city of despair. Black prosperity does not derive from black poverty: Those who succeed are those whose community, whose families, *pre-*

pared them to be successful." He pulls out a black neoconservative chestnut in announcing that "[t]he time has come for honesty within the black community." And what does honesty decree but admission—in *Forbes* no less—that "[t]he causes of poverty within the black community are both structural and behavioral . . . [and] it's time to concede that, yes, there *is* a culture of poverty. How could there not be? How could you think that culture *matters* and deny its relation to economic success?"

He rehearses a Rush Limbaughesque stereotype of black poverty: "In general a household made up of a 16-year-old mother, a 32-year-old grandmother and a 48-year-old great-grandmother is not a site for hope and optimism." He polishes this argument off in fine, Victorian form, raising the spectre of the lazy, sturdy beggar: "It's also true that not everyone in any society wants to work, that not all people are equally motivated. There! Was that hard to say?"[164] Well, no, it is not at all hard to say in *Forbes*. In another version of this essay Gates deletes that provocative expletive and rhetorical question, replacing them with a less bombastic but perhaps more revealing sentence: "The commitment to redress a legacy of economic violence does not require a fantasy of economic egalitarianism."[165]

Even the set of specific programs he lauds come from the conservative repertoire—"tax breaks to generate new investment in inner cities, youth apprenticeships with corporations, expanded tax credits for earned income and tenant ownership of inner-city property." And his accusatory conclusion could have come from Thomas Sowell or Glenn Loury:

> To continue to repeat the same old stale formulas—to blame, in exactly the same ways "the man" for oppressing us all, to scapegoat Koreans, Jews or even Haitians for seizing local entrepreneurial opportunities that have, for whatever reason, eluded us —is to fail to accept moral leadership. Not to demand that each member of the black community accept individual responsibility for their behavior—whether . . . gang violence, unprotected sexual activity, you name it—is another way of selling out a beleaguered community.[166]

Gates in fact depicts a situation in which, in effect, racial discrimination is the principal source of difficulty and inequality only for upper-status blacks; the "underclass" suffers most conspicuously as the consequence of its own deficiencies, whether bad behavior or lack of human capital.[167] And that picture highlights the class character of Gates's vision. It also connects the approach to Afro-American intellectual history that he and Baker represent and the current popularity of the "double-consciousness" formulation to larger ideological currents within the post-segregation-era black petite bourgeoisie. Gates repeatedly calls up a nostalgic image of organic solidarity in black communities under Jim Crow. He cannot decide exactly how solidaristic segregated black life was. In one moment he scolds that blacks "have *never* been members of a single social or economic class."[168] In another he contends that "the effect of the Civil Rights Era . . . was to create two classes in the black community."[169] Nevertheless, he is convinced that the " 'black' community, as we knew it before 1965, simply does not exist any longer."[170]

This community's supposed passing is a source of consternation. Dissipation of the enforced proximity of segregation has allowed the growth of both opportunity and anxiety within the black petite bourgeoisie, which finds itself in a "no-man's land of alienation and fragmentation [among] white colleagues at school, in our mostly white neighborhoods and in the workplace."[171] This sense of "alienation and fragmentation" fuels nostalgia for a supposedly more connected setting in which it was possible "to be a part of a community, of something 'larger' than ourselves."[172] But this nostalgia is a class dream; it bears a striking resemblance to white baby boomer counterparts' romantic wistfulness for the Victorian and Edwardian petit bourgeois worlds. The yearning is for a simpler, organic community in which the petite bourgeoisie's status was secure and its cultural authority was hegemonic and deferred to automatically. Gates's nostalgic vision centers Du Bois's "Talented Tenth," of which—as his first-person-plural pronoun discloses—he reads himself as a product.

> This was a colored world then. . . . It was a world that in some sense has shaped and nurtured many of us, a world in which both our purpose and our enemies were clear. We were to get just as much education as we possibly could, to stay the enemies of racism, segregation, discrimination. . . . It was a world in which comporting ourselves with dignity and grace, striving to "know and test the cabalistic letters" (as Du Bois put it) of the white elite and acknowledging and honoring those of us who had achieved were central to being a colored person in America. . . . We, too, were a people of the Book.[173]

In considering "the meaning of blackness for my generation of African-American scholars," he makes a definitively revealing announcement: "I want my own children to grow up in the home of intellectuals, but with black middle-class values as common to them as the air they breathe."[174]

Gates's memoir is particularly instructive in this regard. He confesses his own sense of double consciousness ("Bach *and* James Brown. Sushi *and* fried catfish") in a preface written to his daughters "because a world into which I was born, a world that nurtured and sustained me, has mysteriously disappeared."[175] The memoir—which from its rhetorical structure could have been titled *Up from Slavery on Lake Wobegon, or Booker T. Washington Meets Garrison Keillor*—is a reminiscence on "a village, a family, and its friends. And of a sort of segregated peace." His narrative is a lovesong to the ancien régime. He bemoans what he perceived as "late sixties and early seventies" radicalism's presumption that "enlightened politics" required loss of "our sense of humor."[176] By his own account, his experience of the Jim Crow world was sheltered and protected, in part by his youth but mainly by his class position. Moreover, much of his fond remembrance is predicated upon his family's relatively prestigious standing in the black social hierarchy. And not unrelatedly, the crucial loss is not the *Gemeinschaft* of the "village" but the dissolution of the segregated institutional apparatus within which that status system was embedded.

Only later did I come to realize that for many of the colored people in Pied-
mont—and a lot of the older Colemans [his mother's prominent family] in
particular—integration was experienced as a loss. The warmth and nurturance
of the womblike colored world was slowly and inevitably disappearing, in a
process that really began on the day they closed the door for the last time at
Howard school, back in 1956.[177]

We might only wonder how those less fortunately placed experienced the
passing of the old order. The book resolves to a reflection on the last segregated
annual family picnic that the town's principal employer, a paper mill, sponsored
for its black workers. Gates, despite disclaimers along the way, proffers a tale of
desegregation experienced primarily as unintended, unpleasant consequences
for blacks, effected by a reluctant, paternalistic employer trying to avoid the
punitive action of a distant and impersonal state: "Nemo's corn never tasted
saltier, his coffee never smelled fresher, than when these hundreds of Negroes
gathered to say good-bye to themselves, their heritage, and their sole link to
each other, wiped out of existence by the newly enforced anti–Jim Crow laws.
The mill didn't want a lawsuit." [178]

If Gates's reflections on the demise of Jim Crow bring to mind Washington's
sentimentalized account of freedpeople's reluctance about Emancipation, it is
for good reason. Nor is it simply because both figured out that mainstream
recognition as a black voice (or public intellectual) requires dramatic and repeated endorsement of centrist or conservative orthodoxy. Gates has proposed a
version of bootstrap, self-help social policy consonant with a Washingtonian vision. He asserts that black impoverishment will persist "[u]ntil we own things."

> That's one of the things I like about the Nation of Islam. Elijah Muhammad
> was very clear about the fact that you have to own a chunk of it, you have to
> own things, you have to be self-sufficient. You're always going to be interdepen-
> dent economically in this society, but you have to control your local institu-
> tions. Black people are . . . thirty-three million, and if we consider the fact
> that there are twenty-six million Canadians, we're a nation. We *are* a nation.
> Instead of mau-mauing each other with disagreements about cultural authentic-
> ity, asking, "Mirror mirror on the wall, who's the ideologically blackest one of
> all?"—rather [if we] start to pool our ideological and economic resources, I
> think we'd have a lot more power. Paradoxically, America presently has the
> largest black middle class in history and the largest black underclass in history.
> The middle class wants to do something about the underclass. That kind of
> pooling and group economic thinking is certainly a much more positive way to
> go than manifestations of guilt about our success. . . . We need to use group
> political and economic power in this country if we really want to do something
> about the other half of the black community.[179]

So we come full circle. This is the outcome of Gates's depoliticized essentialism, what Warren insightfully describes as his "wish to end up with a more
or less unproblematic 'we' [and] his belief that 'professionalism'—rather than
functioning within, or, as an ideology—can provide a refuge from it." [180] In his
role as public intellectual he endorses precisely the position that he built his

academic career attempting to purge from Afro-American intellectual historiography in the name of a new-Black Aesthetic: simplistic Black Power ideology. In the process he displays the ahistoricism and conservatism of both stances, as well as that of the post–Jim Crow petit bourgeois consciousness from which they spring.

From Historiography to
Class Ideology

THE HISTORIOGRAPHICAL TENDENCY that Baker and Gates exemplify has attained prominence partly for institutional reasons. Its popularity reflects the broader appeal of literary studies—and lines of inquiry rooted in the concerns of literary studies—in the academy of the 1980s and 1990s. This appeal has been notable in Afro-Americanist scholarship, which has become sharply inflected toward the study of literature and associated interpretive rubrics. As in other academic pursuits, this development is most immediately the product of a familiar professional dialectic. The interpretive orientation that emerged in literary studies in the 1980s, typically under the flags of deconstruction and poststructuralism, has several features that support its proliferation. It is a self-contained discourse that, not unlike Straussianism in the history of political thought, has its own relatively esoteric lexicon and an elaborate canon of critical texts—characteristics that impose entry costs high enough to confer a technicistic legitimacy. Yet militant antipositivism and skepticism regarding linear argument or grand narrative undermine both internal and external consistency as criteria for evaluation. Successful interpretation, therefore, is not simply a function of straightforward application of method, and adjudication of interpretive claims necessarily is idiosyncratic.

The result is accommodation of a relatively high level of controversy among practitioners on any issue. Thus the technical requirements for entry into the discourse do not operate as a filtering mechanism that screens participation on grounds of methodological proficiency. Pretty much anyone willing to put in the time required to appropriate the lexicon can play the game. Moreover, the sociological milieu that has developed around this discourse is aggressively expansionist, tending to redefine other scholarly disciplines' topical domains in line with the practices of literary theory—which, often cast, revealingly without modification, as "theory," in effect displaces all other forms and areas of theoretical or interpretive endeavor. The combination of an elaborate, esoteric intellectual apparatus, weak guild controls on entry into the discursive community, and disciplinary expansionism overdetermines academic popularity, particularly once beachheads have been established in prestigious departments and universities. (Rational-choice theory, which is similarily esoteric, formalist, and expansionist, makes an illustrative contrast. Because its formalism derives from the more closed methodological system of mathematical modeling, and because of its scientistic ideological commitments, the rational choice community screens membership on the basis of proficiency in mathematical analysis. Nevertheless, although insistence on technical rigor limits access to the universe of functionally certified practitioners, it does not—as Donald Green and Ian Shapiro have demonstrated[1]—produce interpretive outcomes with any greater empirical force or purchase on the social world.)

In addition, the new discourse's claims to subvert, even invert, received canonical and interpretive hierarchies vest it with a politicized aura likely to find a congenial audience among proponents of feminist, minority, and other insurgent academic interests. As both subject matter and personnel, those interests remained marginalized in the academy into the 1980s. The poststructuralist and deconstructionist orientation became, as rhetorical posture and substantive program, a weapon in the institutional war of position. Moreover, that politicized rhetoric, in part as an expression of disciplinary expansionism, typically elides distinctions between the "politics of interpretation" or the status of marginalized interests in the academy on the one hand, and extramural politics on the other. As I have argued in chapter 8, this elision has attractive ideological entailments for adherents. Chief among these is access to a language of moral urgency not typically applicable in debates surrounding status and legitimacy within academic regimes.

In the Afro-Americanist field this elision's benefits also extend to the conceptual realm, as my examination of Baker and Gates has shown. Substituting literary history for the history of political thought glosses over the fundamentally problematic character of the claim to a smooth, coherent black intellectual tradition. This claim's appeal stems in part from its relation to attempts to legitimize Afro-American studies theoretically and institutionally. But institutional imperatives alone seldom fully account for the vagaries of academic fashion. Academic discourses are not pristine in relation to currents of thought that strike responsive chords in other spheres of social life. Professors, after all, are embedded in social structures broader than the university. They live, consume, vote, desire, fear, and pay taxes like everyone else, and they do so, by and large, in ways that reflect middle- to upper-middle-class habits of mind and perspectives. Specifically, the idea of a coherent black tradition that is both essentialist and depoliticized has become popular in Afro-Americanist scholarly circles also because it expresses the sensibility of at least a fraction of the post-segregation-era black petite bourgeoisie.

The idea of a reified black tradition and the imagery of double-consciousness connect particularly with the middle-class stratum that operates in largely integrated career environments, especially those professional milieux—including elite colleges and universities—in which work and social networks overlap. The mindset that grows from this stratum's social position is predisposed to find the double-consciousness trope resonant and familiar. As was true in its original Victorian formulation, the trope's power presumes a model of identity constructed from monads such as femaleness, blackness, whiteness, gayness, and the like. The presumption that group identities are monadic entities—essences—persists broadly as an organizing feature in American discourse. The boundaries may be construed as more or less permeable, but the crucial point is that Americans generally continue to apprehend salient group affiliations such as race/ethnicity, class, gender, and, more recently, sexual orientation as unitary properties that are in effect primordial and that confer corresponding states of feeling and perceiving. Double consciousness attains its affective force as an expression of the sensibility of those who embrace this monadic discourse and experience their situation as not adequately accounted for by any one of its reified categories of identity.[2]

Trey Ellis's manifesto for a "New Black Aesthetic" explicitly theorizes this sensibility as a class phenomenon. In fact, Ellis luxuriates in class status in a way that brings to mind the hyperbolic self-congratulation for which E. Franklin Frazier berated an earlier black bourgeoisie and its publicists. Ellis presents himself as an avatar of the new sensibility.

> I grew up in predominantly white, middle and working-class suburbs around Ann Arbor, Michigan, and New Haven, Connecticut, while my mother and father worked their way through the University of Michigan and Yale. At public elementary school in Hamden, Connecticut, my sister and I were the only blacks not bused in from New Haven. It wasn't unusual to be called "oreo" and "nigger" on the same day. After going to private junior high and high school in New Haven, I transferred to Phillips Academy, Andover, in the eleventh grade. . . . I won't pretend to be other than a bourgie black boy . . . who hadn't lived around a lot of other black people except my own family until I moved into Ujamaa, Stanford's black dorm.[3]

He defines himself as a "cultural mulatto," a member of a black status group "educated by a multi-racial mix of cultures [who] can navigate easily in the white world. And it is by and large this rapidly growing group of cultural mulattoes that fuels the NBA [New Black Aesthetic]."[4] But his formulation conflates class and a racialized notion of culture. He praises Lisa and Kellie Jones for having chosen to identify as black despite having been "raised primarily by their

Jewish mother" and having attained elite academic pedigrees. "Never before," he announces, "have individual, educated blacks had the ability to assimilate so painlessly, yet both Jones sisters didn't."[5] Being raised in largely white environments and the markers of privileged education converge, reinforcing each other as signs of hybridity.

Class celebration ultimately drives Ellis's exultation in the cultural mulatto status he proclaims. His "New Black Aesthetic" is—as was the "New Negro" projected nearly two-thirds of a century earlier, and with almost identical rhetoric—at bottom a manifesto for a new petit bourgeois stratum.

> For the first time in our history we are producing a critical mass of college graduates who are children of college graduates themselves. Like most artistic booms, the NBA is a post-bourgeois movement driven by a second generation of middle class. Having scraped their way to relative wealth and, too often, crass materialism, our parents have freed (or compelled) us to bite those hands that fed us and sent us to college. We now feel secure enough to attend art school instead of medical school.[6]

Ellis praises the Black Filmmaker Foundation as "one of the first black-arts organizations that couples the creativity of the new black artists themselves with the insider's knowledge of high finance from the current flood of young black investment bankers and lawyers." He lauds the filmmaking Hudlin brothers as "some of the most traditionally middle class of the NBA. Artful black yuppies ('buppies'), they don't dress like either hiphop B-boys or punkish hepcats. And they aren't ashamed that many of their friends are lawyers and bankers." At the same time he effuses that the films of Reginald Hudlin (a Harvard man, as Ellis apparently feels it important to point out) "realistically, relentlessly, and hilariously portray contemporary black working-class life" and approvingly quotes Hudlin's observation that black films should attempt to be "culturally authentic."[7] But how, one might ask, does the exaltation of "cultural mulatto" status comport with a notion of cultural authenticity?

Ellis only begs this question and seems oblivious to the contradiction his stances suggest. This contradiction runs throughout his argument. He proclaims that "[n]ationalist pride continues to be one of the strongest forces in the black community and the New Black Aesthetic stems straight from that tradition."[8] In responding to critics he proffers his cohort's "leftist, neo-Nationalist politics."[9] Yet nowhere does he suggest how this supposed nationalism, with its implications of an essentialist construction of black authenticity, even coexists with— much less derives from—the condition of hybridity that also defines his New Black Aesthetic sensibility.

Similarly, Ellis claims that this sensibility "is not an apolitical, art-for-art's-sake fantasy," and follows with an allusion to contemporary black suffering. Yet in the next breath he praises as sophistication a posture that seems at least as likely to reflect a smug individualism that is politically quietistic.

> For us, racism is a hard and little-changing constant that neither surprises nor enrages. Robert Townsend, 31, puts it this way, "You can't sit around and com-

plain about the white man until you're blue in the face. . . ." So he took the dominant culture's credit cards and clobbered it with a film. Terry McMillan "thinks life's a bitch no matter what color you are. You can't blame the world." We're not saying racism doesn't exist; we're just saying it's not an excuse.[10]

How these views diverge from those of "black conservatives such as Thomas Sowell . . . or Stanley Crouch"—from whom Ellis seeks to differentiate his New Black Aesthetic just one paragraph earlier—is not immediately clear. As with Baker and Gates, when Ellis reaches toward specificity in his comments on the political exigencies of the moment, his reflex is not to indict inequality and social injustice; instead he invokes a cheap, empty gesture and the need for behavioral purification. "We realize that a poem, no matter how fiery, isn't going to feed a homeless black child or make a black junkie clean his syringe."[11] Ellis is like Gates in embracing black conservatives' stock-in-trade political orthodoxy as intrinsically virtuous. He boasts of his group's "postliberated aesthetic," their willingness to deviate from the "official, positivist black party line," and he generally commends them for having the self-confidence to present unflattering or racially satirical portrayals of black life.[12]

Of course merely employing imagery popularized by conservative ideologues does not necessarily indicate similar commitments. However, Ellis offers no substantive evidence that would gainsay a suspicion that he shares more of their perspective than he would like to be recognized as sharing. His reflexive view of social responsibility as largely centering on rectifying objectionable black behavior fuels such suspicion, as does his unabashed class celebration.

Considering the composition of the New Black Aesthetic's audience in relation to the self-justifying goal of disturbing black conventions accentuates the tension between Ellis's "leftist, neo-Nationalist" posturing and his overlap with a black conservative perspective. Ellis glosses over this ticklish matter by naturalizing the white audience. He praises the NBA particularly for not being "afraid to flout publicly" the conventions of nationalist politics through parody. But he is able to construe the nose-thumbing stance toward black conventions of depiction as either avantgardist or requiring special courage only because he treats that "public" as an exogenous abstraction. The fact is that the NBA's popularity and critical acclaim—on which Ellis dilates fulsomely—means that their audience is largely white, and that fact undermines any contention that making fun of black conventions is an especially risky endeavor in this context. Ellis circumvents this problem for his praisesong by characterizing the audience only in the abstract, as "the world"—a world which, revealingly, "is not only now accustomed to black faces in the arts, but also hungers for us."[13] Yet it is not the "world" that awards the Pulitzers, MacArthurs, Nobels, and other prizes that Ellis takes as transparent ratifications of virtuosity; those are conferred by the same white cultural establishment whose precepts historically have legitimized exclusion and disparagement of black cultural production and whose standards he, reasonably enough, otherwise feigns to reject or at least distrust. Moreover, what Ellis and the NBA project as a courageous break with black conventions fits very comfortably with the bourgeois cultural establishment's opposition to politicized populist sentimentalism. This opposition rests as much on the premise that thematizing the political is in principle artistically illegitimate as it does on the formalist shortcomings from which such work typically suffers.

Ellis presents nationalism as the marker of black political authenticity, a position he claims to endorse. However, reducing the scope of activist politics to this iconic nationalism (itself a troubling move) and then belittling the nationalist style parodically repeats a depoliticizing trope that ran through 1970s blaxploitation films. Comically inept or out-of-touch black militants were a common feature of those films, and their existence bespoke the futile inappropriateness of seeing politics as an arena for defining and pressing black Americans' desires to improve social conditions. Thus dissent from conventions in the racially politicized black domain amounts to acceptance of conventions in the white upper-middle to highbrow domain, and the latter is that which confers recognition, acclaim, and the material benefits accruing thereto.

The cast of mind that careers between rejection and affirmation, militant posture and quite ordinary aspiration leads to an extraordinary muddle of self-contradiction and sophistry. Ellis maintains that

> the new unflinching way NBA artists are looking at black culture is largely responsible for their popularity. No longer are too many black characters either completely cool and fearless . . . or completely loving and selfless. . . . Says Spike Lee, "The number one problem with the old reactionary school was they cared too much about what white people think." And it is precisely because Mr. Lee isn't afraid of what anyone else thinks that he dares to show his world warts and all.[14]

One hardly needs to endorse the vapid, intellectually oppressive insistence that only "positive images" of blacks be depicted to see something problematic in this stance. Treating unattractive depictions of blacks as somehow threatening to white opinion is absurd in a way that borders on dishonesty of precisely the sort that propels black conservatives' rhetoric. In the great cauldron of black petit bourgeois ideology, this strange view is even compatible with the concern to present positive racial images. John Singleton's films, for instance, manage to combine all the seemingly contradictory strains of racial uplift—nationalist sentimentalism, victim-blaming, glorification of the upwardly mobile as positive role models, and self-righteous claims to uncompromisingly race-conscious, personally risky dissent from orthodoxy—to synthesize a racialized version of a perspective that is "left in form, right in essence."

Ellis is an unabashed propagandist, but he echoes less trendy social-scientific chroniclers in describing this new black class fraction. In the early 1980s Martin Kilson discussed the emergence of a black middle class that was "acquiring social, professional, and political attitudes that are more class-linked than race-linked, resembling what may be found among upper status whites."[15] Kilson linked this development to expansion of middle-class employment opportunities beyond the confines of the segregated job market. Because of the effects of "residual racist practices," however, the new upper-status group's integration into mainstream networks is incomplete, and that circumstance has limited the extent of its "status deracialization."[16] As a result, Kilson contended, the stratum's members occupy a liminal "insider/outsider" social position that makes for a collective identity marked by ideological ambivalence and ambiguity akin to a "split personality." Specifically, this tendency appears in the group's simultaneously liberal and conservative political dispositions. In Kilson's view, however, the concatenation of liberal and conservative inclinations is not random or arbitrary. He sees a fundamental coherence inasmuch as "the interplay between conservative and liberal feelings among the black bourgeoisie revolves around whether social and political issues are viewed as class-linked or race-linked. If viewed as class-linked, upper-strata blacks are likely to respond as conservatives. If seen as race-linked, they respond as liberals."[17]

Kilson's overall view of the new elite's significance is filtered through a teleological assumption that the black middle class is evolving toward absorption into the "mainstream," away from the ethnic parochialism of its predecessors. From that perspective he sees the new class fraction's liminality as transitional, an artifact of its movement toward full incorporation. However, one need not accept Kilson's evolutionist view, a reflection of his perception of American race relations through the lens of modernization theory, to appreciate his account of the stratum's peculiar social and ideological position. Indeed, seeing the new petite bourgeoisie as a discrete historical and sociological phenomenon, rather than as an incompletely formed point in a process, gives access to the central role of the sense of cultural ambivalence in this cohort's experience of mutual recognition. Ambivalence is a key metaphor around which the stratum congeals as a distinct identity; it is a condensation symbol that mediates the movement from abstract statistical aggregate to self-conscious reference group.

Ellis's articulation of a "cultural mulatto" voice seeks overtly to constitute the new middle class as a stratum-for-itself by theorizing and positively valorizing its liminal status. As a way of enunciating a distinct black middle class experience, though, the trope of ambivalence is much more widely resonant, and its expressive power and verisimilitude do not depend on explicit ideological affiliation or political program. In addition to those who actively laud the condition as the font of a superior, uniquely sophisticated consciousness, others represent it as a red-black-and-green badge of courage, the special burden of a particular combination of racial and economic status. Almost universally the trope is bound up with assertions regarding the black middle class's racial authenticity, and those assertions typically proceed—even when formulated in a language of interracialism—from essentialist constructions of group identity. In some versions the metaphor is a lament accompanying a willfully nasty intraracial class politics, a call for the elite to take priority as the genuinely representative black identity and fulcrum of political propriety.

The impulse is clearest when conservatives like Shelby Steele or Deroy Murdock complain that poor, uncultivated, and disreputable blacks have monopolized the public image of racial authenticity.[18] Others embrace a somewhat softer, and ostensibly more sympathetic, variant of conservatives' frustration that the wrong populations define authentic blackness. Much of the basis for construing the absence of proper "role models" as a problem in inner cities derives from a belief that black youth in particular are mired in self-defeating notions that treat aspirations for conventional upward mobility as denials of racial identity.[19] Like the black conservatives, proponents of this view seek less to challenge the premise of monadic racial authenticity (though conservatives tend to give lip service to this objective) than to project the respectable petite bourgeoisie as the normative representation of black Americans. In fact, it is the pandemic appeal of the rhetoric of authenticity—as is exemplified in the persisting conventional usage in scholarly, journalistic, and colloquial parlance of a "black community" construct that functions as the subject of singular verbs—that accounts for the ambivalence imagery's resonance. The image refers to a sense of straddling two uniform and bounded entities, into neither of which one fits neatly.

Instructively, even those who actively attempt to problematize the categories, to deconstruct the reified entities, find doing so very difficult. Lorene Cary's memoir *Black Ice* is a singularly intelligent and sensitive reflection on her experiences as an early integrator of an exclusive New England prep school. Cary interrogates the subtle, complex processes of personal transformation that ensued from the liminal social position she entered. Her narrative is grounded in the realm of concrete social relations, and the people and interactions that carry it along retain human depth and multidimensionality. Thus Cary not only grapples usefully with the multifarious, crosscutting ways that race and class—and gender—swirl together to form experience and self-perception; she also exposes the inadequacy of the essentializing shorthand so prevalent in the rhetoric of group identity. Cary considers how the notions of blackness that provided existential and solidaristic comfort for her cohort were fashioned largely out of reified images drawn from artistic representation and popular culture. And in recalling an episode of deepest adolescent angst she captures the way that the experience of liminality itself rests on presumptions that identity is built from fixed, monadic conceptions of groupness: "Over and over and over I had said to Jimmy, and to other friends, that I did not want to be trapped in one world. I wanted to be black, to be part of our group, to draw nourishment from it and give back, and yet I wanted to be free to come and go."[20]

Although Cary problematizes and struggles against this kind of monadic construction, she nonetheless resolves her narrative into a dyadic configuration in which a basically folkish principle of blackness collides with (ultimately to be expanded and enriched by) a "white American education."[21] In finally adopting that construction she inadvertently indicates how deeply the rhetoric of black liminality is embedded on reified, essentialist premises. Her resort to a juxtaposition of folkishness and cultivation evokes older versions of the nature/culture dichotomy; it also reflects a common ambivalence surrounding the race/class nexus that in less nuanced and humanely progressive hands supports the punitively elitist impulse in black politics.

The tension that concludes Cary's memoir pervades the new black middle class's self-reflection and underwrites the recent popularity of Du Bois's double-consciousness passage. Discussing black social scientists, Jacquelyn Mitchell writes:

> In pursuit of our goals, it was easy to overlook how extended interactions with white colleagues and exposure to different ways of thinking could alter our world view and change the way we think. Some of us became the prodigal sons and daughters in our communities, returning to our grassroots only to discover painfully that we have changed and are now strangers—marginal members within our ethnic group and communities. "What usually happens is that blacks become detached from their own . . . ethnic world, and alienated from the black masses." (Noble, 1978, p. 149)
>   What ensues is a state of double marginality. . . . It is of little consequence that we may be recognized and respected for our contributions and scholarship; our ever-present visibility never allows us to experience complete membership in white academia. At the same time, these marginal feelings begin to affect our ethnicity as well. We thus experience double marginality, belonging to and feeling a part of two worlds, yet never at home in either.[22]

Ellis glories in this experience as a form of protean transcendence, and Cary puzzles with it as a practical fact of life that has both useful and frustrating features. Mitchell, though, is arguably nearer the norm in apprehending it as simultaneously a marker of elevated status and an artifact of the racial burden borne uniquely by elite nonwhites. To that extent she reveals the double-consciousness trope's particular attraction: it expresses in the same instant celebration and complaint.

This combination permeates the ruminations by contributors to Gerald Early's anthology of reactions to the double-consciousness image. Several of the essays proceed from the view that, as Stephen L. Carter puts it, to "be a black professional is to lead a dual existence."[23] Carter makes sure we recognize his own solidly petit bourgeois circumstances, noting that he lives in a white elite world and comports himself appropriately ("I shop mostly at Brooks Brothers"). And he illustrates how whites' petty racial discrimination can be blind to class markers. On the other hand, he assures us that "[r]acial solidarity, in the sense of self-love, is the key to our survival in a frustratingly segregated integrated professional world, just as it is the key to our survival in a frustratingly oppressive nation."[24] His summary thesis is clear. "To succeed in a profession, one adopts the profession's ethos, its aesthetic, its culture. One remakes significant aspects of oneself. It should be possible to adapt to this professional aesthetic and yet retain one's cultural identity."[25]

The structure of this narrative recurs in many of the contributions. Several in addition muse nostalgically about an organic black universe that has been superseded by the disenchanted world into which their (and the race's) success has thrust them. They fret about how their own purchase on blackness will differ from that of their still more solidly petit bourgeois and mainstream children.[26]

Nor is this fixation on the nexus of ambivalence and authenticity, success and suffering only the province of academic intellectuals.

Isabel Wilkerson of the *New York Times* laments with Ellis Cose "the incredible burden of living this dual life," and Cose reports that "the fear of being forced to shed one's identity in order to prosper is not at all uncommon."[27] The trope has made its way into popular media. A *Time* feature on the new black middle class quotes Du Bois and takes the frame "Between Two Worlds."[28] A *Chicago Tribune* puff piece invokes Du Bois's formulation to express John Edgar Wideman's situation as a successful writer with working-class black origins.[29] Perhaps most revealing, *Newsweek* enlists Du Bois to characterize O. J. Simpson's supposed "twoness—the higher he reached for the trappings of the white world, the more he distanced himself from his beginnings."[30] For *Newsweek* the trope's overlap with the nature/culture dichotomy is no longer implicit, tentative, or nuanced. Instead, the lament about the tensions connected with being black and middle class is reduced to its hoary foundation: "black" = visceral, uncultivated, savage; "middle class" = white. This reduction actualizes middle-class fears that folkish or populist notions of black authenticity support racist stereotypes and demonization.

The legitimate basis for this fear appears in more mundane ways as well. Many of Cose's informants report—and this is routine in anecdotal black professional-managerial-class experience—white colleagues' observations that they are not "really" black because they do not conform to some "ghetto" stereotype.[31] Thus an objectively grounded concern with racial denigration merges with the logic of class consolidation to support a discrete, petit bourgeois ideological program. This convergence is a factor impelling the production of a genre of scholarly and popular literature that charts and celebrates the black middle class's place in Afro-American history. Along with the generically American penchant for uplifting stories of individual (or group) triumph against adversity as well as the black form of the contemporary sensibility that enthralls professional-stratum whites with images of Victorian and Edwardian bourgeois life, the concern to establish the black middle class's racial authenticity (if not primacy) fuels proliferation of biographies of distinguished, race-conscious ancestors, historical memoirs of upper-status families, and histories stressing the race-serving roles of elite organizations. Perhaps because the area of interest has gathered momentum in this ideological environment, the effort to construct an autonomous black women's history, ironically, seems particularly congenial to the genre.[32]

Nowhere are the tensions, anxieties, and political contradictions that undergird the double-consciousness image's popularity more sharply laid out than in Leanita McClain's posthumously collected essays, *A Foot in Each World*.[33] McClain was a wunderkind at the *Chicago Tribune* and a success story of rapid upward mobility. She had grown up in a black working-class family in the Ida B. Wells housing project and attended the inner-city Chicago State University. Her star began its rapid ascent with graduate study at Northwestern University's journalism school, from which she went immediately to the *Tribune*, where she remained until her suicide in 1984 at age thirty-two.

Significantly, McClain's career began its steepest incline in 1980 when she published an opinion piece in *Newsweek* titled "The Middle-Class Black's Burden." This essay was something of a cri de coeur on behalf of what her former husband and posthumous editor, Clarence Page, describes as the "emerging class of black professional baby boomers" of her sort.[34] She begins by establishing the stratum's ambivalent social position and protesting its frustrations: "I am a member of the black middle-class who has had it with being patted on the head by white hands and slapped in the face by black hands for my success."[35] After pointing out that middle-class blacks have the same material aspirations as their white peers and complaining about their being berated as "Oreos" by "those we left behind," she writes:

> It is impossible for me to forget where I came from as long as I am prey to the jive hustler who does not hesitate to exploit my childhood friendship. I am reminded, too, when I go back to the old neighborhood in fear—and have my purse snatched—and when I sit down to a business lunch and have an old classmate wait on my table. . . . My life abounds in incongruities. . . . But I am not ashamed.[36]

She most closely approximates Du Bois's language at the most revealing points of her narrative, such as: "I run a gauntlet between two worlds, and I am cursed and blessed by both. . . . I have a foot in each world, but I cannot fool myself about either. . . . I know how tenuous my grip on one way of life is, and how strangling the grip of the other way of life can be."[37]

McClain's anxiety about the fragility of her upward mobility is clear; she also focuses that anxiety toward blacks, whom she sees challenging her right to be petit bourgeois: "As for the envy of my own people, am I to give up my career, my standard of living, to pacify them and set my conscience at ease? No I have worked for these amenities and deserve them, though I can never enjoy them without feeling guilty."[38]

McClain also embodies Kilson's hypothesis about her stratum's combination of liberal and conservative politics. Repeatedly in her essays she declaims passionately in support of a liberal political disposition and agenda with respect to strictly racial issues. Her approach to intraracial stratification, though, is saturated in paternalism and class prejudice.

> The greatest commitment now in the civil rights struggle must come from the black middle class, which at the same time must guard its own sliver of the economic pie. . . . And it will be triply hard without the very dollars-and-cents programs that helped them, programs that have been stripped bare by the Reagan administration. They could not have achieved what they did alone, and they cannot now do for others without that assistance.
>
> It will be black self-help that will have to save the underclass, to educate and call for an end to rampant teenage pregnancy, to offer reforms in welfare

that will allow fathers to stay home, to decrease criminal recidivism, to demand better schools and community services.[39]

McClain's visits to her old South Side neighborhood stir within her a victim-blaming scorn that prompts an intensely punitive illiberalism. As is common in such interpretations, a nostalgic tale of decline from an organic golden age shores up the self-righteousness required to make harsh judgments of people in circumstances objectively so similar to those of her own past. On returning to her old high school, Lucy Flower Vocational, she observes:

> While I found the building much the same, the students were not. There is no dress code. Far worse, there is little of a moral code, and the true "young ladies" are by far outnumbered by girls who are proud of their pregnancies and so uninterested in an education that they skip class and boldly just sit outside the school door playing cards. Trouble-making young men, drawn to Flower like bees to honey loiter outside in souped-up jalopies.[40]

Her paternalistic concern with moral rectification leads her to a reactionary approach to social policy worthy of Thomas Sowell, Charles Murray, or Phil Gramm. Of the inner-city schools she attended, she complains that they "took on too much that was black oriented but also tried to do too much of everything. . . . Out went dress codes and corporal punishment; in came permissiveness and students' rights. Out went the standards, the great American cookie cutter everyone was supposed to pass through."[41]

She singles out the "free-meals program" as especially corrosive because it reinforces poor people's expectations that things should just be "given to them." She pauses to reflect that she would have qualified for the free lunch program if it had been offered when she was in school, but nostalgic elevation of the moral fiber of the community of her youth establishes—indeed forces—the distance needed to preempt the taint of hypocrisy. "Yet I must remind myself that to be poor and to live in the projects is not the same any more, just as the schools are not the same. I can see the despair, the lost sense of self-sufficiency, when I go back to the old neighborhood."[42] (No doubt the apples also were sweeter, the music better, and the rooms bigger! It is worth noting, moreover, that McClain's tale of precipitous decline from the community of her youth appeared when she was less than thirty years old.)

McClain's punitive paternalism reaches its extremes in her vehement attack on civil libertarian impulses in inner-city schools. She castigates judicial and legislative interventions securing students' and parents' rights as having "gone to the extreme to undermine teacher authority, and at the very time that other traditional authority figures in a student's life also are declining." Predictably, she evokes a Reaganite image of the simple virtue and benign tonic of a teacher's backhanded slap across (someone else's) face.[43]

McClain, apparently, was in a variety of ways a deeply troubled person, and I would not suggest that her suicide be seen as a case of terminal class/race ambivalence. Nevertheless, the palpable experience of tension, ambiguity, and ambivalence in her social and ideological position condensed a malaise whose sources no doubt were more complicated into a single, distinctly resonant metaphor. Like others who express the sense of being trapped between two worlds or identities, she both struggled to reject yet could not transcend the limitations of the essentialist conceptions of blackness (and other identities) on which such formulations inevitably depend.

To some extent the difficulty in breaking with the essentialist mystifications that underlie the double-consciousness sensibility reflects the force of intellectual habit. Essentialist premises are solidly ensconced in the conventions shaping discourse about black Americans—without regard to level of intellectual sophistication or point on the ideological spectrum. Habits of mind, however, are sustained and reinforced by the social realities that they interpret and thus partially constitute. This effect is likely to be especially durable if the interpretive orientation firmly supports pragmatic interests. That is the case with the black petit bourgeois commitment to essentialist constructions of black identity.

At a minimum, the persistence of racial discrimination works in two ways to validate essentialist notions of blackness as common sense. On the one hand, the reality of discrimination buttresses impressions of shared suffering; on the other hand, the programmatic remedies for discrimination proceed from an assumption that common racial classification implies common social condition. At the same time, particularly for the black professional cohort that Kilson characterizes as relatively "cosmopolitan," the demand for racial justice is partly a demand for equal capacity to realize class privilege. This fuels the apparent dissonance that Kilson observes between this class fraction's race-inflected liberalism and class-inflected conservatism, which runs the gamut from the ideological underpinnings of Gates's and Baker's intellectual historiography through McClain's pathetic lament. To the extent that derogatory, class-tinged racial stereotypes are experienced as undermining petit bourgeois aspirations through guilt by association, the effect is further to strengthen a nasty, victim-blaming intraracial class politics, whose distasteful features are typically shrouded in a rhetoric of noblesse oblige.

Certainly other, less immediately material factors help to reproduce the essentialist perspective that underlies the double-consciousness conundrum. For instance, it comports with the nostalgic yearning for a mythical past of organic racial community that both mediates petit bourgeois status anxiety and eases accommodation to a rightward shift in the ideological context within which incremental political agendas and prevailing models of respectable middle-class opinion are constructed. This nostalgic current becomes all the more salient as the postwar baby boom—the first age cohort to grow into the new professional-managerial stratum—settles evermore into middle age. The yearning for restoration of supposedly lost organicism and wholeness in fact appears in multiple forms. In addition to wistful reinvention of community in the Jim Crow South (a vision against which Charles Burnet's film *To Sleep with Anger* emphatically exhorts), this yearning is articulated in middle-class adoption of invented traditions like Kwanzaa, embrace of Afrocentricity, Egyptology and other sorts of mysticism, propagation of religiosity as the wellspring of black authenticity, and assertion of the racialized ideology of patriarchal restoration that lurks within the rhetoric of special crisis of supposedly "endangered" black males.

When seen in this light, the black middle-class appropriation of the double-consciousness trope gives off a familiar glow. As a metaphor that voices and grounds class consciousness and identity, it has much in common with the similar mindset that pervaded the white upper middle class at the end of the nineteenth century. Both rest on essentializing rhetoric rooted in the nature/culture dichotomy. Both tend to mediate status anxiety through idealization of myths of past or present organicism. As a malaise, the ambivalence bemoaned by contemporary black petit bourgeois sufferers is conceptually quite similar to the old fretting about the threat of overcivilization—an ailment that simultaneously certifies elevated class standing and elicits sympathy for suffering. Double consciousness, therefore, is the neurasthenia of the black professional-managerial class at the end of the twentieth century.

Conclusion

A Generativist Approach to the History of Political Thought

THAT RECENT INTEREST in Du Bois is so bound up with the double-consciousness formulation is deeply ironic. The sensibilities to which the formulation appeals hardly could differ more from the central premises and driving concerns of Du Bois's career. As I showed in chapters 8 and 9, the double-consciousness metaphor figures into contemporary popular and scholarly discourse about black Americans as part of a strain that depoliticizes and dehistoricizes accounts of the Afro-American experience. This appropriation has, perhaps fittingly, a doubly dissonant relation to Du Bois.

First, Du Bois was one of the very most consistently and resolutely *political* of all twentieth-century black American intellectuals. This assessment rests not just on his movements back and forth between employment in academic and activist domains, though it is easy to lose sight of the fact that he held full-time academic appointments for only about a third of his postdoctoral lifetime and that he was an employee of the NAACP for more years than he was a professor. It is also the case that nearly all his writing—scholarly and otherwise—was shaped by his engagement with the controversies of the day. Du Bois's fundamental orientation to scholarly activity, his basic epistemic reflex, as I argued in chapter 4, linked inquiry to strategic political action. The links were more or less direct, more or less nuanced. In some venues, for example art, his disposition was crudely instrumental; in historical and social-scientific inquiry he was more sophisticated. Nevertheless, it would be barely an exaggeration to contend that all Du Bois's writing pivots on a concern to influence contemporaneous, explicitly political debates. His idea of politics, moreover, always centered unambiguously on the realm of government activity and public policy. His antiimperialism, his reinterpretation of Reconstruction, his vision of social transformation in the United States and elsewhere all proceed from recognition of the centrality of state power, both in the shaping of social life in general and as the crucial focal point for effective progressive theorizing and practice. Du Bois's insistence on the primacy of a state-centered politics in making sense of the black American situation was, most dramatically, the foundation of his critique of Booker T. Washington, the source of its eloquent sharpness.

The Washington controversy is also emblematic of the second way that the actual Du Bois is at odds with the sensibility that now appropriates him as an icon. That sensibility not only devalues politics as constitutive of the black experience; its own ideological inclinations are much nearer Washington's conservative moralism and privatistic bootstrap rhetoric than to Du Bois's perspective at any point in his mature life. Du Bois certainly was like those who now invoke him—and, for that matter, Washington—in perceiving the black population in a way that at least implies the primacy of the group's elite strata. However, even though his pro-elite bias prompted Du Bois to assign the "natural aristocracy" a tutelary function vis-à-vis the rest of the race, it never led him (at least not after 1900) to embrace the kind of politically quietistic and victim-blaming interpretation of that role that Washington advocated and current petit bourgeois nostalgia exalts. Even the racial celebration articulated in *The Negro, The Gift of Black Folk, Black Folk: Then and Now,* and *The World and Africa*—while romantically articulating the equivalent of the postsegregation era's "positive images" rhetoric—did not in Du Bois's view substitute in any way for aggressive, direct challenge to the political-economic and racial status quo. Here he differs markedly from today's nationalists and proponents of notions of a black "cultural politics," who rationalize the essentially quietistic retreat to celebration as therapy, a morale booster preliminary to or even as a novel form of political action. Similarly, for at least his last sixty years Du Bois did not elevate the task of correcting putative deficiencies within the black population to an equal status with the externally directed struggle for racial equality and broader social reorganization.

In noting Du Bois's inappropriateness as an avatar of the discursive tendency onto which he has lately been grafted, I do not wish to present him as a benchmark of propriety or authenticity against which those who now invoke him are to be judged and thus found wanting. Nor do I intend to imply where Du Bois might stand in relation to current political controversies among black Americans. Some possibilities, given what we know about his basic commitments and clarity, arguably would be more likely than others; it seems most unlikely, for instance, that he would have succumbed to the Reaganite ideological blitz and become an apostle of inward-looking quiescence or a free-marketeer. Nevertheless, we can never speculate confidently about how an individual formed through one historical context would respond to the imperatives, cleavages, and options that comprise another. Nor would it matter if we could. They lived their history; we must live ours.

Remarking on what Du Bois would think, say, or do if he were alive can be superficially effective rhetorically, but doing so is unsound on its own terms and reflects a distinctly unhelpful, if not counterproductive, way of thinking about the relation between past and present. The "if-x-were-alive-now" laments have a prelapsarian quality that posits a golden age of heroic antecedents purer, clearer, and smarter than ourselves. The cast of mind from which such statements arise is to that extent fundamentally ahistorical; it presumes the past to have been an order of existence intrinsically, and radically, different from our own, a world free from the partiality, contingency, and mundane, imperfect, and purblind choices that are our lot. This perspective converges with a naive reading of the old saw about learning from history to reify the past as a singular, empyrean realm that we can mine for allegorical lessons and the timeless wisdom of the ancients. Though it is by no means the only academic precinct so afflicted, Afro-Americanist scholarship is plagued by this mindset, whose appeal has been reinforced in the 1980s and 1990s by pro forma gestures of ancestor reverence as expressions of racial/cultural authentication.

As the recent appropriations of Du Bois demonstrate, the result undermines historical understanding. Beneath the sentimental reduction of history to a reservoir of inspirational anecdotes, heroic figures, and debaters' points lies a heavy presentist bias that obfuscates the past in the process of drawing on it. This points to a problem intrinsic to the rhetorical allusion to historical antecedents in service to presentist objectives. A common defense of the anachronism exhibited in such moves is that they proceed from purely pragmatic agendas that do not involve claims to historical interpretation at all. At first blush, this defense, and the corollary call for separate criteria for judgment, seem reasonable enough. In quoting, for instance, from Frederick Douglass's "West India Emancipation" address to counsel against the Democratic Leadership Council's capitulationist politics or John Locke in support of private property against a regulatory, social-democratic state, one is not intending a situated interpretation of Douglass or Locke. Besides, it would be both priggish and silly to insist that hortatory political activity be bound by the strictures of scholarly rigor. Political rhetoric operates in an entirely different field of discourse and on the basis of quite different pragmatic principles, and reinventing notable antecedents through presentist appropriation has been a staple ideological practice—itself an important object of intellectual historical inquiry—in the West at least since the Renaissance.

The relation between scholarly and hortatory projects, however, is more complicated in actual practice. Scholarly inquiry also springs from questions shaped by concerns and discourses anchored in the present. Therefore, it can never completely escape the influences of contemporary partisanship and invention. As proponents of what is often labeled the "linguistic turn" tirelessly announce, the real alternative to radical presentism is not a pure historicism that faithfully reconstructs the past entirely on its "own" terms, that recovers it as it "really" was. It is at the same time true, though less commonly noted, that even radical presentism makes at least implicit claims that are both historicist and strive for interpretive authenticity. One does not invoke Douglass or Locke, to return to my earlier example, at random from the rolls of the literate dead. Rather, adducing them functions rhetorically to annex their presumed cultural authority as prominent figures associated with one or another estimable tradition, to elicit from their reputations endorsements for the positions on behalf of which they are cited. One in effect says, "If Douglass were alive now, he also would dissent from the DLC's capitulationist agenda." One is claiming, that is, minimally: (1) that Douglass is a significant figure whose views should have weight with us; (2) that we know clearly what those views are and can extrapolate them accurately to the context of our own controversies; and (3) that opposition to the DLC is at least consistent with, perhaps a direct outgrowth of, a venerable tradition that Douglass exemplifies. Each of these claims presumes a historical interpretation, and each is subject to critical evaluation as such.

Once again, my point is not to indict the hortatory appropriation of prominent antecedents. I freely acknowledge finding it a quite useful gambit myself in polemical political writing and speeches, including drawing on Douglass in precisely the manner described here. I believe, though, that it is important to be self-conscious in one's rhetoric and to avoid savaging historical integrity, for example, by claiming associations that fly in the face of informed understandings of the views held by the figures appropriated. This concern no doubt partly expresses the guild mentality of a professional historian of political thought, just as artists have more exacting standards for constructing political posters and leaflets or carpenters and architects for remodeling party offices. Yet it also reflects a premise that—particularly at this historical moment and in discourse bearing on the character of Afro-American politics—the hortatory project ought to be leavened with pursuit of civic education. The latter objective entails, to whatever extent feasible in the given circumstance, clarifying, demystifying, or simply providing better alternatives to cracker-barrel or bowdlerized versions of political tradition. This conviction is linked to an argument that I shall make presently for a particular perspective on and approach to the study of the history of political thought, a perspective and approach that I believe are especially crucial with respect to Afro-Americanist intellectual interests. It is not likely that political activists will be much inclined to cultivate a sophisticated understanding of the history of Afro-American debate, and such an understanding is not an essential ingredient for creation of a vital, critical black politics. Nevertheless, clarity about the links between past and present discourses is one thing that engaged intellectuals can contribute to the larger political project.

In recent years we have seen instead, in the name of engaged scholarly intervention, proliferation of a problematic tendency to blend or confound the two objectives and the strategic imperatives that ensue from them. Afro-Americanist inquiry has from its origins been oriented simultaneously toward advancing scholarly understanding of black Americans and improving or protecting the race's position in the social order. These purposes occasionally have conflicted, which is not surprising, because one presumes an audience sympathetic to and already relatively knowledgeable about black Americans and the other presumes an audience that is either neutral or skeptical and generally uninformed. That condition has prompted scholars like Earl E. Thorpe, William T. Fontaine, L. D. Reddick, Joseph A. Bailey, and others to complain of a myopic focus on racial vindication, as I characterized it in chapter 1, that undermines rigorous investigation of the black experience through its dogmatic adherence to a restrictive metanarrative stressing propagation of only favorable accounts of the race. This metanarrative is the academic expression of the protest discourse that became hegemonic in black politics after the discrediting of Washington's accommodationism and that remained the animating perspective of black political activity for the duration of the struggle against Jim Crow segregation.

The institutional dynamics surrounding Afro-Americanist scholarship's entry into mainstream academic venues in the postsegregation era reproduced that metanarrative, buttressing it with the affective force of a rhetoric drawn from insurgent black activism outside the academy. The result has been to reinforce, if not intensify, the confounding of the scholarly and hortatory projects. This tendency has been further exacerbated by legitimation of a sensibility—associated with the related discourses of "cultural politics" and various strains of antifoundationalist social theory, chiefly postmodernism and poststructuralism—that devalues the concern to distinguish the two projects. This concatenation of tendencies has produced the class of ahistorical, sometimes perverse interpretations I have criticized in this book.

As I have indicated, it is not possible to isolate in practice either a pure historicism or a pure presentism, a scholarly inquiry unaffected by presentist concerns or a hortatory appropriation that avoids historical interpretation and, thus, judgment. To that extent the antifoundationalist sensibility's rejection of absolute distinctions is correct. Unfortunately, the antifoundationalist tendency goes further: it takes recognition of the impossibility of absolute criteria for interpretation as an invalidation of attempts to impose any objective or intersubjective criteria at all for evaluating claims about the past. This amounts to seeing the twenty-five-cent bet on the table in a poker game and raising it a thousand dollars. As we have seen, this approach makes for bad history and worse politics. What is required is adoption of criteria for historical interpretation that take into account the contingency, incompleteness, and inescapably presentist connections of any statement about the past. I have attempted in this book to exemplify an approach that rests on such criteria with respect to reconstruction of Du Bois's political thought. I shall now specify it in conceptual and historiographical terms and argue for its virtues for making sense of the history of political thought in general and the Afro-Americanist project in particular.

I propose what is perhaps best described as an evolutionist or a generative perspective on the history of political thought. By this I mean a vantage point that approaches examination of antecedent individuals and debates and the discourses within which they were embedded from an orienting concern to locate within them clues to sources of salient political problems and discursive tendencies in our present. The metaphor of open-ended evolution—minus the leftover Victorian teleology that implies hierarchical movement from less to more advanced—most effectively captures this perspective. The view I put forward rests on two premises regarding the nature of political discourses and ideologies: (1) that they arise pragmatically, from a dialectic of concrete events, issues, actions, disagreements, patterns of social relations (including existing alliances and cleavages), and received ways of conceptualizing the social and political world; and (2) that they evolve along with—shaping and being shaped by—those social contexts. Because political discourses, and the individuals and debates that instantiate them, are thus tied fundamentally to discrete historical situations, making sense of them requires interpreting them in terms of their formative, temporally autonomous complexes of meaning. These include the prevailing political vocabulary and semantics. It follows that, as I have asserted at various points in this study, this sort of inquiry into the history of political thought must proceed from immersion in the history in which the thought emerges, about which that thinking most immediately *is*. Political tendencies and principles become meaningfully visible through reconstruction of the premises, formulations, questions, and positions around which pragmatic discourses cohere in specific contexts. Explication and assessment of the thought of individuals similarly requires, as I hope to have accomplished here in the case of Du Bois, reading them through their situatedness in their discursive environments.

The generativist premise underscores the need for careful historical grounding. Assumptions that are made explicitly and arguments that are contested in one historical moment subsequently can become ensconced as the given background assumptions that limit the thinkable—tacitly channeling political debate and influencing its character. Construction of an evolutionary narrative requires examination of the ideological fossil record, excavation of discursive moments as fluid points in an open-ended dialectic in which the present emerges organically from the past and is the constraining raw material of the future. Close attention to each moment's constitutive context, moreover, is necessary to protect an evolutionist account from the everpresent temptation of teleology, the inclination to represent the history of political thought as an anachronistic chronicle of anticipations and shortfalls in an ineluctable unfolding toward current conventions. Ideological narratives evolve instead through the victory of some discrete tendencies and interpetations over others by means of varying combinations of persuasiveness and coercion. Those that win—often enough not in forms their proponents would choose—become naturalized as the common sense of the next historical moment and so on. The outcomes of this dialectic, in addition, are knowable only after the fact; political truth is made through contestation, not discovered.

A generative view of the history of ideologies overcomes the presentism/historicism conundrum pragmatically, by anchoring inquiry overtly to contemporary concerns while requiring thick historical grounding. On the one hand, this perspective avoids the historicist dilemma by not claiming to represent the past purely on its own terms. On the other hand, its commitment to historical contextualization imposes an interpretive coherence and the intellectual discipline of purposiveness that presentist accounts typically lack. This outlook, therefore, apprehends the social world on the basis of a contingent foundationalism, which I believe provides the most reasonable substantive view of how the social world works, as does this perspective's insistence that the roots and logic of political thought lie in its pragmatic relation to practical political debates and choices inside lived history.

This mindset has potentially useful entailments for the study of Afro-American political thought in particular. For the same reasons that it avoids the presentism/historicism problem this approach also resolves the tension between the scholarly and hortatory imperatives in Afro-Americanist intellectual life. Its objectives are probing and tough-minded academically and, simultaneously, directly linked to civic concerns. Seeing the history of Afro-American thought as the trajectory of a generative activity is especially important at this historical juncture, a period in which the dominant conceptual categories and narratives in black political discourse presume the superficially less complicated diagnostic and strategic vision that characterized the era of struggle against Jim Crow. In this context communitarian nostalgia for the organic simplicity that supposedly structured black life under segregation—a trope becoming hegemonic within the black petite bourgeoisie, even in the face of a rightist political counteroffensive that threatens to restore a modified form of Jim Crow—bespeaks a wish to amend the world to fit the interpretive categories available for comprehending it.

The inherited interpretive frames, which ultimately derive from the discourse of racial protest, were always incomplete and problematic in their inability effectively to conceptualize differentiation and dynamism among black Americans. This inadequacy remained generally invisible throughout the segregation era, when presumption of a monadic racial community of interest seemed plausible relative to the main political challenges toward which the discourse was articulated. However, the criticisms of its corrosive effect on scholarly inquiry into black life mounted by Thorpe, Fontaine, Reddick, and the others threw this problem into relief in ways that at least passingly commented on its political inadequacies as well. The latter critique came more forcefully, if mechanistically, from Marxists like the young Ralph Bunche and Oliver Cox. Nevertheless, buoyed by the postwar political successes embodied in the *Brown* decision and shifting public and elite sentiment toward opposition to Jim Crow, the protest discourse—despite its limitations—became the generic American frame for discussing black American politics. Its persistence can be seen in the dominant Afro-Americanist scholarly reflex that formulates the dictates of political engagement exclusively in line with the imperatives of racial vindication. This stance translates into not only a restrictive bias toward racial image management but also continuing legitimation-through-use of simplistically monadic, organicist constructions of black politics and institutional life. These formula-

184 W. E. B. Du Bois and American Political Thought

tions—which give us, for example, accounts of Afro-American politics that contain no autonomous politics among black people—are objectionably thin and increasingly unhelpful. They and the communitarian mystifications on which they rest spin further and further away from credible reflection of the social forces and world of mundane experience in which the black American population is enmeshed.

No intellectual approach is a panacea; any ideological or epistemic stance can be harmonized with virtually any specific interpretation or political position. The most general methodological commandment, as I suggested in chapter 1, cannot be more elaborate than the injunction not to be stupid or simplistic and to avoid anachronism. This neither provides a roadmap for nor carries guarantees regarding substantive interpretations. Nonetheless, a generative perspective opens conceptual possibilities for examination of Afro-American politics and political thought under current circumstances. A contextualist disposition in principle emphasizes the dynamism and tensions internal to black political discourse, which means that it also stresses ideological and programmatic differentiation. Its pragmatic view that connects political thought to concrete, historically specific political issues and action also opens space for consideration of differentiation by material political interests and structural position in the social order as a normal, consequential feature of black politics. And these possibilities have political as well as scholarly ramifications.

In reifying the past as an empyrean region hovering above, but connecting only allegorically with our own, the prevailing ways of thinking and writing about black political thought, in both popular and scholarly venues, profoundly depoliticize the history of Afro-American debate. To that extent they fail at the task of civic education, which thus reduces to platitudes about the wisdom of our predecessors, a larger-than-life cohort of Great Men and the occasional Great Woman. This tendency underwrites political passivity through supporting a defeatist rhetoric that bemoans the absence of such heroes in our time. By contrast, a generative or evolutionist perspective suggests folding the Greats back into history, situating them within discursive communities formed through grappling with concrete, historically specific problems. It establishes, that is, connections between them and ourselves—both by considering them and us as distinct yet related moments in a process and by bringing them down to earth as people just like us, the best of whom struggled in concert and debate with their peers to craft progressive visions and programs under adverse and uncertain conditions, with imperfect knowledge and constrained by the histories and *mentalités* through which they could construct meanings. The stress on the discursive constitution of political thought, moreover, can reinforce the importance of strategically organized, collective action for creating and sustaining political movements, a lesson that has receded from public consciousness, partly as an ironic consequence of the dominance of potted, bowdlerized versions of black political history that purport to just the opposite intent.

Although there is no methodological magic pill that guarantees construction of historical accounts that are true in the sense that they capture the past exactly "as it was," that does not mean that any sort of account is necessarily as good as any other. Interpretations differ qualitatively with respect to the extent to which they are reasonable and meaningful in historical terms. And, from the perspective I lay out here, the two criteria overlap. That past social actors responded to issues and concerns they and their peers found pressing provides one solid basis for evaluation: the extent to which an interpretation sensibly fits the contingent linguistic and empirical facts around which the arguments and positions under investigation cohered. Representation of Washington as a nationalist militant, based on a cleverly inventive, decontextualized reading of his Atlanta Compromise speech, is challengeable on grounds of historical fact, including the facts of the substantive ideological premises and beliefs structuring the discursive frames within which he operated.

The purposive orientation of inquiry also yields a corresponding basis for evaluation. Because past ideological discourses were constituted as responses to events and issues at least partly external to themselves, making historical sense of them requires examining them in relation to the ways they distort, misrepresent, or otherwise characterize an out-there reality whose pertinent features are at least contingently accessible. What determines pertinence in this regard is the configuration of the historian's perception—blessed by hindsight—of the aspects of the moment under investigation that were most consequential both at the time and for subsequent events and the presentist concerns that organize her inquiry. This vantage point not only supports judgment of contemporary accounts of past actors and ideologies by asking how well and how meaningfully an interpretation connects with the external reality as we understand it to have been important. It also makes possible evaluation of the political and normative character and entailments of positions and discourses articulated in the past by connecting them to political agendas and their consequences—examining the substance and effects of what they emphasized and overlooked, how they constructed and evaluated significant dimensions of their social reality. That is indeed a crucial way that generative, thick historical interpretation is particularly well suited practically to illuminate features of the present, its contribution to realization of the goal of engaged inquiry.

By contrast, the hyperrelativism propounded by radical antifoundationalism appears fatally contradictory, if not hypocritical. The claim that no single interpretation of the past can be intrinsically better than any other fails on at least two scores. First, insofar as this view rests on repudiation of the idea of interpreter's authority, it begs the question as to why we should acknowledge the implicit presumption of expertise on which that repudiation in turn rests. If scholarly specialization does not at least in principle justify a claim to interpretive expertise, then what basis exists for antifoundationalist professors' claims on jobs that by most standards in the American political economy are fairly comfortable and secure? The warrant ensuing from rejection of the idea that scholarly expertise confers contingent interpretive authority is that faculty positions bearing on such endeavors should be filled without regard to usual academic protocols, perhaps randomly. While no doubt some radical antifoundationalists would embrace this view officially, there is no evidence yet of a wave of faculty resignations in accordance with it. As the gospel lyric puts it, everybody wants to go to heaven, but nobody wants to die. Second, although the hyperrelativist view typically is associated with a rhetorical emphasis on the political aspect of interpretation, its own premises and practices actually depoliticize interpretation by severing it from the strictures of purposive evaluation. If everything is everything, nothing is anything. We are as a result left rudderless, without any pragmatic foundation for our undertakings. This is the opposite of engaged inquiry.

Finally, it may be especially fitting that this argument for a generative or evolutionary approach to inquiry into the history of political thought grows out of a study of Du Bois. Although his substantive interpretations of the world owed very little, if anything, to philosophical pragmatism, his practice spoke eloquently of the substantively pragmatic relation between knowledge and action. His career, moreover, embodied several of the main precepts of the perspective I propose. His simultaneous insistence on the purposive foundations of scholarly work and the need to inform action through rigorous, tough-minded inquiry is one instance. This enabled him to combine the scholarly and hortatory projects productively and self-consciously, at his best avoiding confounding them and using the imperatives of each to discipline the other. This in turn fed his deep commitment to civic education as an elemental part of both projects.

Du Bois is an apt background figure for this discussion in other ways as well. Mundanely, the fact of his longevity provides a ready point of emphasis of the dialectic of change and continuity in response to changing contexts that propels the evolutionist trajectory. As a principal proponent of the protest stance in the struggle against Washington who then became a foe of that stance's interpretive and programmatic strictures as it was articulated as an orthodoxy in the NAACP, Du Bois illustrates the way that the history we make is never final or completely under our control. And on the front of practical politics, making sense of Du Bois's political thought is especially important now, as a corrective to the rehabilitation of Washington's gospel of political quiescence and accommodation to racial inequality which proceeds around us.

Toward that end, with regard to the relation between the interpretation of the world and acting in it, perhaps the key point of connection with Du Bois is his militant and unyielding understanding that truth is made—under constraints and not as its agents choose, but made nonetheless. And the actual boundaries of possibility are knowable only through challenging them. This basically pragmatic notion of truth is consistent with the contingent foundationalism for which I have argued here. Each is an antidote to naive realism and the apocalyptic, equally naive antifoundationalism associated with the linguistic turn. Whether or not he would have embraced it theoretically, Du Bois's career realized as few others have the deepest *epistemological* significance of Marx's Eleventh Thesis on Feuerbach: "The philosophers have only *interpreted* the world, in various ways; the point is to change it."

Notes

Chapter 1

1. Arnold Rampersad, *The Art and Imagination of W. E. B. Du Bois* (Cambridge, Mass., 1976); Joseph P. DeMarco, *The Social Thought of W. E. B. Du Bois* (Lanham, Md., 1983). David Levering Lewis's *W. E. B. Du Bois: Biography of a Race, 1868–1919* (New York, 1993) also engages usefully and most intelligently with the foundations of Du Bois's thinking. Lewis's study is the definitive biography of Du Bois's first fifty years, but its principal focus is not examination of his political thought.

2. DeMarco claims erroneously, for example, that the "role of the Talented Tenth was dropped, by and large, from [Du Bois's] writing" shortly after 1907 (*Social Thought*, p. 54), and his reading of Social Darwinism (pp. 31, 69) is rather simplistic.

3. Adolph Reed Jr., review of *Prophesy Deliverance!: An Afro-American Revolutionary Christianity*, by Cornel West, *Telos* (summer 1984): 211–18. St. Clair Drake, "Anthropology and the Black Experience," *Black Scholar* 11 (September–October 1980): 2–31, also discusses the long-standing concern of black intellectual activity with a project of "racial vindication."

4. For discussion of these general problems, see J. G. A. Pocock, *Politics, Language and Time: Essays on Political Thought and History* (New York, 1971); David A. Hollinger, "Historians and the Discourse of Intellectuals," in John Higham and Paul K. Conkin, eds., *New Directions in American Intellectual History* (Baltimore, 1979); Ian Shapiro, "Realism in the Study of the History of Ideas," *History of Political Thought* 3 (1982): 535–78; two essays by Quentin Skinner: "Meaning and Understanding in the History of

Ideas," *History and Theory* 8 (first quarter 1969): 3–53, and "The Limits of Historical Explanations," *Philosophy* 41 (July 1966): 199–215; John G. Gunnell, "Interpretation and the History of Political Theory: Apology and Epistemology," *American Political Science Review* 76 (June 1982): 317–27; and John Dunn, "The Identity of the History of Ideas," in Peter Laslett, W. G. Runciman, and Quentin Skinner, eds., *Philosophy, Politics and Society* (New York, 1972).

5. Manning Marable, "The Black Faith of W. E. B. Du Bois: Structural and Political Dimensions of Black Religion," *Southern Quarterly* 23 (spring 1985): 15–33, and Marable, *W. E. B. Du Bois: Black Radical Democrat* (Boston, 1986). Compare Du Bois's statement concerning religion: "I cannot believe that any chosen body of people or special organization of mankind has received a direct revelation of ultimate truth which is denied to earnest scientific effort. . . . It may well be that God has revealed ultimate knowledge to babes and sucklings, but that is no reason why I, one who does not believe this miracle, should surrender to infants the guidance of my mind and effort. No light of faith, no matter how kindly and beneficent, can in a world of reason guide human beliefs to truth unless it is continually tested by pragmatic fact." He referred to religious belief as accepting "urgent desire, or myth and fairy tale, as valid truth" (Du Bois, *Color and Democracy: Colonies and Peace* [New York, 1945], p. 137. Lewis also is emphatic about Du Bois's aversion to religiosity; see *Biography of a Race*, pp. 65–66.

6. Marable, *Black Radical Democrat*, p. 47.

7. Francis L. Broderick, *W. E. B. Du Bois: Negro Leader in a Time of Crisis* (Palo Alto, Calif., 1959); Elliott M. Rudwick, *W. E. B. Du Bois: A Study in Minority Group Leadership* (Philadelphia, 1960). A revised version of Rudwick's study was published under the title *W. E. B. Du Bois: Propagandist of the Negro Protest* (New York, 1968). Unless otherwise indicated, references here are to the earlier edition.

8. R. Charles Key, "Society and Sociology: The Dynamics of Black Sociological Negation," *Phylon* 39 (March 1978): 35–48; see also two articles by Elliott M. Rudwick: "Notes on a Forgotten Black Sociologist: W. E. B. Du Bois and the Sociological Profession," *The American Sociologist* 4 (November 1969): 303–6, and "W. E. B. Du Bois as Sociologist," in James E. Blackwell and Morris Janowitz, eds., *Black Sociologists: Historical and Contemporary Perspectives* (Chicago, 1974), pp. 25–55.

9. Dan S. Green and Edwin D. Driver, "W. E. B. Du Bois: A Case in the Sociology of Sociological Negation," *Phylon* 37 (December 1976): 308–33.

10. Arthur L. Johnson, "The Social Theories of W. E. B. Du Bois," master's thesis, Atlanta University, Atlanta, Ga., 1949.

11. Charles H. Wesley, "W. E. B. Du Bois: The Historian," in John Henrik Clarke et al., eds., *Black Titan: W. E. B. Du Bois* (Boston, 1970), pp. 82–97; Jessie P. Guzman, "W. E. B. Du Bois—The Historian," *Journal of Negro Education* 30 (fall 1961): 377–85.

12. Eugene C. Holmes, "W. E. B. Du Bois: Philosopher," in Clarke et al., eds., *Black Titan*, pp. 76–81.

13. William T. Fontaine, " 'Social Determination' in the Writings of Negro Scholars," *American Journal of Sociology* 49 (January 1944): 302–13; see also Fontaine's: "An Interpretation of Contemporary Negro Thought from the Standpoint of the Sociology of Knowledge," *Journal of Negro History* 25 (January 1940): 6–13, and his "The Mind and Thought of the Negro of the United States as Revealed in Imaginative Literature, 1876–1940," *Southern University Bulletin* (March 1942): 5–50.

14. Many revisionist Americanists, especially social and cultural historians, have begun to overcome—often quite impressively, as in the work of James McPherson and Eric Foner—the ghettoization in the study of American life. By and large, however, revisionist intellectual history, perpetuates the presumption that "American" means "white." Other-

wise impressive recent scholarship—such as David Green, *Shaping Political Conscious-ness: The Language of Politics in America from McKinley to Reagan* (Ithaca, N.Y. 1987), and James T. Kloppenberg, *Uncertain Victory: Social Democracy and Progressivism in European and American Thought, 1870–1920* (New York, and London, 1986)—manages to reconstruct twentieth-century American political debate in ways which give no clue that either race or anyone other than whites (with the exception of Green's brief discus-sion of Martin Luther King Jr. as a national moral symbol) has figured into the picture at all.

Some signs of improvement do exist, however. Daniel T. Rodgers (*Contested Truths: Keywords in American Politics since Independence* [New York, 1987]) notes the power of racism as an enduring ideological current in American life. And Rogers M. Smith ("The 'American Creed' and American Identity: The Limits of Liberal Citizenship in the United States," *Western Political Quarterly* 41 [June 1988]: 225–51, and "Beyond Tocque-ville, Myrdal, and Hartz: The Multiple Traditions in America," *American Political Science Review* 87 [September 1993]: 549–66) argues that a racialist ideological orientation, which he calls "ethnocultural Americanism," or "ascriptive inegalitarianism," has been one of three fundamental currents—along with liberalism and republicanism—of Ameri-can political discourse since the revolutionary era. Other scholars have focused on the importance of race and ideologies about race in American history. (See, for example, George M. Frederickson, *The Black Image in the White Mind* [Middletown, Conn., 1971]; Edmund Morgan, *American Slavery, American Freedom* [New York, 1975], and Reginald Horsman, *Race and Manifest Destiny* [Cambridge, Mass., 1981]). Rodgers and especially Smith, though, stand out for their efforts to integrate that perspective into accounts of the main trajectories of American intellectual life. See also James Oakes, *Slavery and Freedom: An Interpretation of the Old South* (New York, 1990), and Mark Pittenger, *American Socialists and Evolutionary Thought, 1870–1920* (Madison, Wis., 1993).

15. For detailed discussion of this phenomenon and its implications see John Higham, *History: Professional Scholarship in America* (Baltimore and London, 1983), pp. 212–32, and Higham, Introduction to Higham and Conkin, eds., *New Directions in American Intellectual History*, pp. xi–xix.

16. Among the classic examples of this approach are Louis Hartz, *The Liberal Tradi-tion in America* (New York, 1955), and Daniel Boorstin, *The Genius of American Politics* (Chicago, 1953). Arthur M. Schlesinger Jr. managed during this period to publish a book on Jacksonian politics which does not refer at all to Native Americans—despite Jackson's pivotal role as shaper and enforcer of the genocidal consensus then prevailing among whites. See Arthur M. Schlesinger Jr., *The Age of Jackson* (Boston, 1945). This orienta-tion has had remarkable staying power, even in the face of a more than twenty-year counteroffensive undertaken by revisionist schools that seek to recover a more expansive view of American history and intellectual life. For an example of its persistence into the present, see especially the title essay in Michael Walzer, *What It Means to Be an Ameri-can: Essays on the American Experience* (New York, 1992).

17. Gunnar Myrdal, *An American Dilemma: The Negro Problem and Modern De-mocracy*, 2 vols. (1944; reprint, New York, 1962).

18. Gerald D. Jaynes, "Urban Policy and Economic Reform," *Review of Black Politi-cal Economy* 13 (summer–fall 1984): 103–15; *Report of the National Advisory Commis-sion on Civil Disorders* (New York, 1968), pp. 236–82.

19. See, for example, Arthur M. Schlesinger Jr., *The Vital Center* (Boston, 1949), esp. pp. 228–30. Mary Louise Dudziak carefully examines the Cold War's shaping of elite concern about domestic race relations in "Cold War Civil Rights: The Relationship

between Civil Rights and Foreign Affairs in the Truman Administration," Ph.D. dissertation, Yale University, New Haven, Conn., 1992.

20. Ralph Ellison, "*An American Dilemma*: A Review," in Ellison, *Shadow and Act* (New York, 1972), p. 315.

21. See, for example, Stephen Steinberg, *Turning Back: The Retreat from Racial Justice in American Thought and Policy* (Boston, 1995). In addition to the study of Afro-American thought, the pluralist turn in the social sciences—particularly political science—would be an especially interesting focal point for such research, as would the variants of the "culture of poverty" thesis in sociology and social psychology.

22. See, for example: August Meier, *Negro Thought in America, 1880–1915: Racial Ideologies in the Age of Booker T. Washington* (Ann Arbor, Mich., 1963); Howard Brotz, ed., *Negro Social and Political Thought, 1850–1920* (New York, 1966), pp. 1–33; August Meier, Elliott M. Rudwick, and Francis L. Broderick, eds., *Black Protest Thought in the Twentieth Century* (Indianapolis, 1971), pp. xix–lvi; Theodore Draper, *The Rediscovery of Black Nationalism* (New York, 1970).

23. Judith Stein, " 'Of Mr. Booker T. Washington and Others': The Political Economy of Racism in the United States," *Science and Society* 38 (winter 1974–75): esp. 423–63; Mack H. Jones and Alex Willingham, "The White Custodians of the Black Experience: A Reply to Rudwick and Meier," *Social Science Quarterly* 51 (June 1970): 31–36; Alex Willingham, "Black Political Thought in the United States: A Characterization," Ph.D. dissertation, University of N.C., Chapel Hill, N.C. 1974; and Eric Foner, "Reconstruction Revisited," *Reviews in American History* 10 (December 1982): esp. 87–90. See also Alex Willingham, "Ideology and Politics: Their Status in Afro-American Social Theory," in Adolph L. Reed Jr. ed., *Race, Politics and Culture: Critical Essays on the Radicalism of the 1960s* (Westport, Conn., 1986), esp. pp. 17–18.

24. Examples of valuable, though ultimately unsuccessful, attempts are Harold Cruse, *The Crisis of the Negro Intellectual* (New York, 1967), and S. P. Fullinwider, *The Mind and Mood of Black America* (Homewood, Ill., 1969). Cruse's and Fullinwider's accounts are limited by their own reliance on transhistorical dualisms, and Cruse's suffers as well from an excess of one of its strengths—i.e., a passion for the subject undermines intellectual discipline. Moses and Toll have gone still farther in the direction of providing historically contextualized interpretations that explore the theoretical dimensions of black debates. See Wilson J. Moses, *The Golden Age of Black Nationalism, 1850–1925* (New York, 1988), and William S. Toll, *The Resurgence of Race: Black Social Theory from Reconstruction to the Pan-African Conferences* (Philadelphia, 1979). It may be that a cohort of younger scholars finally will establish the history of Afro-American thought firmly on a foundation that apprehends both the internal dynamism of black debate and its rootedness in broader historical and discursive streams. See, for example, Jonathan Scott Holloway, "Confonting the Veil: New Deal African-American Intellectuals and the Evolution of a Radical Voice," Ph.D. dissertation, Yale University, New Haven, Conn., 1995; Dean E. Robinson, "To Forge a Nation, to Forge an Identity: Black Nationalism in the United States, 1957–1974," Ph.D. dissertation, Yale University, New Haven, Conn., 1995 and Michele Mitchell, "Adjusting the Race: Gender, Sexuality and the Question of African-American Destiny, 1877–1930," Ph.D. dissertation, Northwestern University, Evanston, Ill., 1977.

25. Myrdal, *American Dilemma*, vol. 2, p. 786.

26. Ibid., p. 784.

27. L. D. Reddick, "A New Interpretation for Negro History," *Journal of Negro History* 22 (January 1937): 27–28.

28. E. Franklin Frazier, "The Failure of the Negro Intellectual," in Frazier, *On Race Relations* (Chicago, 1968), p. 273.

29. Earl E. Thorpe, *The Mind of the Negro: An Intellectual History of Afro-Americans* (1961; reprint, Westport, Conn., 1970), p. xii.

30. Ibid., pp. 444–45.

31. Ibid., p. xi.

32. Earl E. Thorpe, *The Central Theme of Black History* (Durham, N.C., 1969), esp. pp. 18–32.

33. Myrdal, *American Dilemma*, pp. 783–84. More than twenty years after those words were written, Martin Luther King Jr. was attacked widely for being so audacious as to express a nonconformist opinion on the Vietnam War, which, he was reminded, was not a proper issue for black concern. See David Garrow, *Bearing the Cross* (New York, 1986), pp. 553–58.

34. Myrdal, *American Dilemma*, p. 784.

35. Cox similarly identifies the "American Creed" notion as a pivotal weakness in Myrdal's study, though from the standpoint of a somewhat mechanistic Marxism; see Oliver C. Cox, *Caste, Class and Race* (1948; reprint, New York, 1959), pp. 510–14. See also Smith, "Beyond Tocqueville, Myrdal, and Hartz."

36. Myrdal, *American Dilemma*, pp. 783–85.

37. I do not wish to argue that Myrdal is responsible for the constitution of the study of Afro-American thought as a field around an atheoretical approach to its subject matter. However, the conceptual foundation on which his study rested meshed readily with both the consensualism that overtook the study of American thought during the postwar years and the instrumentalism that organized the growing concern with race relations. To that extent *An American Dilemma* expresses, analytically at least, the convergence of those two intellectual tendencies. That circumstance no doubt helped Myrdal's view to become so influential. For thorough consideration of the study's impact see David W. Southern, *Gunnar Myrdal and Black-White Relations: The Use and Abuse of An American Dilemma, 1949–1969* (Baton Rouge, La., and London, 1987), and Walter A. Jackson, *Gunnar Myrdal and America's Conscience: Social Engineering and Racial Liberalism, 1938–1987* (Chapel Hill, N.C., 1990).

38. Hollinger, "Historians and the Discourse of Intellectuals," p. 43. For other elaborations of this point, see e.g.: William E. Connolly, *The Terms of Political Discourse* (Princeton, N.J., 1983); J. G. A. Pocock, *Politics, Language, and Time* (New York, 1971), and Rodgers, *Contested Truths.*

39. George W. Stocking Jr., "On the Limits of 'Presentism' and 'Historicism' in the Historiography of the Behavioral Sciences," in Stocking, *Race, Culture, and Evolution: Essays in the History of Anthropology* (Chicago, 1982), pp. 1–12.

40. Ibid., p. 4.

41. Recent examples of these tendencies are, respectively: Vincent Harding, *There Is a River: The Black Struggle for Freedom in America* (New York, 1981); and Sterling Stuckey, *Slave Culture: Nationalist Theory and the Foundations of Black America* (New York and London, 1987).

42. Foner, "Reconstruction Revisited," pp. 90–91.

43. Cornel West, *Prophesy Deliverance!: An Afro-American Revolutionary Christianity* (Philadelphia, 1982); Marable, *Black Radical Democrat.* Both studies seek to erect among Afro-American intellectuals coherent traditions comparable to those held to exist among whites. Marable, for instance, argues at length that Crummell's "influences" are more prominent in the early texts of Du Bois than are those of certain other, white

theorists, and West's volume is essentially a polemic on behalf of a claim that there is an autonomously grounded "Afro-American critical philosophy."

44. See Robert Gooding-Williams, "Philosophy of History and Social Critique in *The Souls of Black Folk*," *Social Science Information* 26 (1987): 99–114. Gooding-Williams argues somewhat convincingly that Du Bois held some views about history similar to those held by Hegel. On that basis, unfortunately, he characterizes Du Bois—without the latter's explicit complicity—as a Hegelian and contends that in sections of *Souls* Du Bois argues against his own unacknowledged Hegelianism. This approach does justice to neither Du Bois nor Afro-American thought, nor to Hegel. Lewis also points to apparently Hegelian traces in Du Bois's early writing, but he makes less of them than Gooding-Williams; see *Biography of a Race*, pp. 139–40, 165.

45. Hollinger, "Historians and the Discourse of Intellectuals," pp. 44–45.

46. Ibid., p. 43.

47. For discussion of some of these problems see Skinner, "Meaning and Understanding."

48. Pocock, *Politics, Language, and Time*, pp. 3–41. I do not wish to endorse the more elaborate arguments of Skinner or Pocock with respect to linguistic conventions and recovering authorial intentions in the study of the history of ideas. In the first place those arguments are struck at a level of procedural detail more specific than I care to engage in this or quite possibly any other context. In addition that linguistic approach has been criticized capably, and in ways that I do endorse, by Shapiro ("Realism in the Study of the History of Ideas") and Gunnell ("Interpretation and the History of Political Theory"). I share their view that the sharp linguistic turn proposed by Skinner, Pocock, and others leads into an interpretive blind alley and can result in an unproductive hyper-methodism. My own methodological prescriptions are no more detailed than Gunnell's charge that "what is required is sensitive textual analysis coupled with historical awareness and conducted with philosophical and political self-consciousness" (p. 327) and Shapiro's general defense of an "anthropological" approach which requires the historian of ideas also to be a "competent social, economic and political historian" (p. 578).

Chapter 2

1. Alfred D. Chandler Jr., *The Visible Hand: The Managerial Revolution in American Business* (Cambridge, Mass., 1977), pp. 331–34, and Gabriel Kolko, *The Triumph of Conservatism: A Reinterpretation of American History, 1900–1916* (New York, 1963), pp. 18–19; see also Martin J. Sklar, *The Corporate Reconstruction of American Capitalism, 1890–1916: The Market, The Law and Politics* (Cambridge, Mass., 1988).

2. Carol S. Gruber, *Mars and Minerva: World War I and the Uses of the Higher Learning in America* (Baton Rouge, La., 1975), p. 12.

3. David F. Noble, *America by Design: Science, Technology and the Rise of Corporate Capitalism* (New York, 1977).

4. Gruber, *Mars and Minerva*, p. 12.

5. Richard Hofstadter, in his *Social Darwinism in American Thought* (Boston, 1955), details the impact of the American appropriation of Darwinian theory as social science and ideology. See also Mark Pittenger, *American Socialists and Evolutionary Thought, 1870–1920* (Madison, Wis., 1993).

6. Arthur M. Schlesinger Sr., "A Critical Period in American Religion, 1875–1900," in John M. Mulder and John F. Wilson eds., *Religion in American History: Interpretive Essays* (Englewood Cliffs, N.J., 1978), p. 303.

7. Samuel P. Hays, *The Response to Industrialism: 1885–1914* (Chicago, 1957), p. 72. However, the new reform spirit did not strictly preclude religiosity. President Folwell of Minnesota, himself a reformer and new-breed academic, mobilized his powers of rational thought not only to effect his conversion, but also to lead him to a conviction that anyone with any sense must see the Protestant Episcopal course as God's exclusive Truth. See Burton J. Bledstein, *The Culture of Professionalism: The Middle Class and the Development of Higher Education in America* (New York, 1976), p. 199.

8. Gruber, *Mars and Minerva*, p. 12. See also Joel H. Spring, *Education and the Rise of the Corporate State* (Boston, 1972).

9. Gruber, *Mars and Minerva*, p. 14.

10. On the history of psychology in the United States, see L. Postman, *Psychology in the Making* (New York, 1962); E. G. Boring, *A History of Experimental Psychology* (New York, 1950); and R. S. Crutchfield and D. Krech, *A Source Book in the History of Psychology* (Cambridge, Mass., 1965). Gruber notes that the first professorship in this country in psychology alone was established at the University of Pennsylvania in 1891 (*Mars and Minerva*, p. 188). On the articulation of history of a discrete discipline, see Julian Herbst, *The German Historical School in American Scholarship: A Study in the Transfer of Culture* (Ithaca, N.Y., 1965); John Higham, *History: Professional Scholarship in America* (Baltimore and London, 1983); Merle Curti, ed., *American Scholarship in the Twentieth Century* (Cambridge, Mass., 1953); and Peter Novick, *That Noble Dream: The "Objectivity Question" and the American Historical Profession* (Cambridge and New York, 1988). On the social sciences, see Thomas L. Haskell, *The Emergence of Professional Social Science* (Urbana, Ill., 1977) and Dorothy Ross, *The Origins of American Social Science* (Cambridge and New York, 1991).

11. Gruber, *Mars and Minerva*, p. 14. For a view that emphasizes the diversity among academic responses to the changing environment see Laurence R. Veysey, *The Emergence of the American University* (Chicago, 1965).

12. See, for example, Samuel P. Hays, *Conservation and the Gospel of Efficiency* (Cambridge, Mass., 1959). A statement of this ideology by one who—though writing somewhat later, after World War I—elaborates its radical implications is Thorstein Veblen, *The Engineers and the Price System* (New York, 1963). See also Pittenger, *American Socialists.*

13. Noble, *America by Design*, pp. 257–324; Harry F. Braverman, *Labor and Monopoly Capital: The Degradation of Work in the Twentieth Century* (New York, 1974), pp. 155–83; C. Wright Mills, *White Collar* (New York, 1951), pp. 77–111.

14. Kolko, *Triumph*, pp. 1–10. Also see David W. Eakins, "The Origins of Corporate Liberal Policy Research, 1916–1922: The Political-Economic Expert and the Decline of Public Debate," in Jerry Israel, ed., *Building the Organizational Society* (New York, 1972), pp. 163–79, and Stephen Skowronek, *Building a New American State: The Expansion of National Administrative Capacities, 1877–1920* (Cambridge and New York, 1982).

15. Christopher Lasch, *Haven in a Heartless World: The Family Besieged* (New York, 1977), pp. 3–22; Alvin W. Gouldner, *The Future of Intellectuals and the Rise of the New Class* (New York, 1979), pp. 14–15; Pat Walker, ed., *Between Labor and Capital* (Boston, 1979). Lasch, in his earlier study *The New Radicalism in America, 1889–1963: The Intellectual as a Social Type* (New York, 1965), refers to this new "status group" generically as "intellectuals" (p. x); Gouldner uses the term "new class" to refer to a stratum of academic or humanistic intellectuals and technical intelligentsia. I employ the terms interchangeably without acceding to the extent of the theoretical claims that

Gouldner makes concerning the significance of the constitution of this stratum as a class.

16. Gouldner, *Future of Intellectuals*, pp. 5–6.

17. Ibid., p. 19.

18. Alvin W. Gouldner, *The Dialectic of Ideology and Technology: The Origins, Grammar, and Future of Ideology* (New York, 1976), pp. 253–57.

19. Cf. Sheldon Wolin, *Politics and Vision: Continuity and Innovation in Western Political Thought* (Boston, 1960), pp. 352–434. Simon H. Patten, a prominent spokesman among turn-of-the-century intellectual ideologues, wrote: "The final victory of man's machinery over nature's control of human society was the transition from anarchic and puny individualism to the group acting as a powerful, intelligent organism" (*The New Basis of Civilization* [1907; reprint, Cambridge, Mass., 1968], p. 43. See also James Gilbert, *Designing the Industrial State: The Intellectual Pursuit of Collectivism in America, 1880– 1940* (Chicago, 1972), pp. 8–9.

20. Gouldner, *Future of Intellectuals*, 11–15; Jurgen Habermas, "Technology and Science as 'Ideology,'" in Habermas, *Toward a Rational Society: Student Protest, Science and Politics* (Boston, 1970), pp. 81–122. Habermas details a critical view of the fundamental interest-groundedness of all knowledge and the ideological tendencies of both traditional philosophy and modern science to obscure their foundations in interestedness; see his *Knowledge and Human Interests* (Boston, 1979), pp. 301–17.

21. Gilbert, *Industrial State*, p. 6.

22. Ibid. p. 7. Pittenger stresses the significance of evolutionism in this loose consensus *(American Socialists)*.

23. Gilbert, *Industrial State*, p. 31.

24. Ibid., pp. 7–8.

25. Ibid., pp. 34–35.

26. Gilbert, *Industrial State*, p. 36.

27. Ibid., p. 18. Nowhere is the disappearance of socialism into progressivism much more pronounced than in the career of Charles Steinmetz, whom Gilbert discusses in detail. Ira Kipnis cites an article by Victor Berger, the Wisconsin Socialist party leader, titled "Socialism, the Logical Outcome of Progressivism" (Kipnis, *The American Socialist Movement: 1897–1912* [New York, 1952], p. 226).

28. Gilbert, *Industrial State*, p. 64.

29. Ibid., p. 66; see also Pittenger, *American Socialists*, and James T. Kloppenberg, *Uncertain Victory: Social Democracy and Progressivism in European and American Thought, 1870–1920* (New York and London, 1986).

30. Ibid.

31. Ibid. See also, for example, Richard T. Ely, *The Strength and Weakness of Socialism* (New York, 1894).

32. See Loren R. Graham, *Science and Philosophy in the Soviet Union* (New York, 1974), esp. pp. 443–50.

33. Karl Korsch, *Marxism and Philosophy* (New York, 1970).

34. Albrecht Wellmer, *Critical Theory of Society* (New York, 1971), pp. 67–119.

35. Alvin W. Gouldner, *The Two Marxisms: Contradictions and Anomalies in the Development of Theory* (New York, 1980).

36. See, for example, Rainer Traub, "Lenin and Taylor: The Fate of 'Scientific Management' in the (Early) Soviet Union," *Telos* (fall 1978): 82–92; François George, "Forgetting Lenin," *Telos* (winter 1973–74): 53–88; Russell Jacoby, "What Is Conformist Marxism?" *Telos* (fall 1980): 19–44; and Frederic J. Fleron, ed., *Technology and Communist Culture* (New York, 1977).

37. V. I. Lenin, *What Is to Be Done?: Burning Questions of Our Movement* (New York, 1943).

38. George Konrad and Ivan Szelenyi, *The Intellectuals on the Road to Class Power: A Sociological Study of the Role of the Intelligentsia in Socialism* (New York, 1979), p. 141.

39. Ibid., p. 142.

40. V. I. Lenin, *One Step Forward, Two Steps Back,* in Lenin, *Selected Works,* 3 vols. (New York, 1967), vol. 1, p. 412. See Rosa Luxemburg's critique of Lenin and the Bolsheviks on this view in "Organizational Question of Social Democracy," in Luxemburg, *Rosa Luxemburg Speaks,* ed. Mary-Alice Waters (New York, 1970), pp. 112–30. Konrad and Szelenyi point out that Lenin's organizational model disqualified workers from participating as party members and reduced them to recipients of consciousness from professionals (*Intellectuals,* pp. 140–41).

41. This legacy of the Enlightenment is traced critically by Max Horkheimer and Theodor W. Adorno, *The Dialectic of Enlightenment* (New York, 1972), and William Leiss, *The Domination of Nature* (Boston, 1973).

42. T. J. Jackson Lears, *No Place of Grace: Antimodernism and the Transformation of American Culture, 1880–1920* (New York, 1981), pp. 4–58.

43. Alan Trachtenberg, *The Incorporation of America: Culture and Society in the Gilded Age* (New York, 1982), p. 59.

44. Robert H. Wiebe, *The Search for Order, 1877–1920* (New York, 1967), p. xiii.

45. Ibid., pp. 19–20.

46. Ibid., p. 111. Wiebe notes that "in order to demarcate this national upper class new modes of identification such as a common educational experience in an exclusive boarding school and then in one of a select set of Eastern colleges assumed far greater importance. Aristocrats, in other words, made peace with an impersonal world by extending their familiar pattern of life" (ibid). Kenneth W. Warren examines elite concerns with establishing and maintaining social boundaries to provide insulation from presumed inferiors during this period, focusing on expression of such anxieties in realist literature; see his *Black and White Strangers: Race and American Literary Realism* (Chicago and London, 1993).

47. Wiebe, p. 112.

48. Ibid., p. 129.

49. Ibid., p. 113.

50. Ibid., p. 129.

51. Ibid., p. 52.

52. R. Jeffrey Lustig, *Corporate Liberalism: The Origins of Modern American Political Theory, 1890–1920* (Berkeley, Calif., 1982), p. 45. See also John L. Thomas, *Alternative America: Henry George, Edward Bellamy, Henry Demarest Lloyd and the Adversary Tradition* (Cambridge, Mass., 1983).

53. Gronlund's *The Cooperative Commonwealth in Its Outlines* was published in 1884, Bellamy's *Looking Backward* in 1888 and Lloyd's *Wealth against Commonwealth* in 1894. Lustig contends that the cooperative commonwealth idea "until the First World War expressed the indigenous American radicals' vision of a democratic future" (*Corporate Liberalism,* p. 72). See also Pittenger, *American Socialists,* esp. pp. 25–88.

54. Gilbert, *Industrial State,* p. 23. A far more ambitious attempt to link Bellamy with antidemocratic collectivism is Arthur Lipow's study *Authoritarian Socialism in America: Edward Bellamy and the Nationalist Movement* (Berkeley, Calif., 1982); Pittenger (*American Socialism,* pp. 65–71) also discusses this feature of Bellamy's vision,

noting that his utopian "vocabulary of desire holds no terms to express what human beings might yet become" (p. 67).

55. Lipow, *Authoritarian Socialism*, pp. 54–72; Pittenger, *American Socialism*, pp. 43–65.

56. Lears, *No Place of Grace*, p. 7.

57. Ibid., p. xiii.

58. Ibid., pp. 218–19. I shall detail this mindset and its relation to Du Bois's thought in chapter 7.

Chapter 3

1. W. E. B. Du Bois, *The Philadelphia Negro: A Social Study* (1899; reprint, New York, 1967). Gunnar Myrdal, in *An American Dilemma* (2 vols. [1944; reprint, New York, 1962]) lauded Du Bois's volume as a pioneering sociological work, and E. Digby Baltzell seconded that judgment in his introduction to the 1967 edition of Du Bois's study. Arthur J. Vidich and Stanford M. Lyman identify Du Bois's Philadelphia research as "the first American urban community study," the initial expression of American sociologists' efforts to link "the methods of urban research being developed in England and the ethnographic study of the urban community" (*American Sociology: Worldly Rejections of Religion and Their Directions* [New Haven, Conn., and London, 1985], pp. 75 and 127); see also Martin Bulmer, "W. E. B. Du Bois as a Social Investigator: *The Philadelphia Negro*, 1899," in Bulmer et al., eds., *The Social Survey in Historical Perspective, 1880–1940* (Cambridge, 1991).

2. W. E. B. Du Bois, *Autobiography: A Soliloquy on Viewing My Life from the Last Decade of Its First Century* (New York, 1968), p. 194. A pillar of the progressivist view on political reform was the claim that government could be run more "efficiently" were it not for the influence of the non-Anglo-Saxon immigrant groups who propped up the machines. In Philadelphia, which had one of the largest black populations among American cities at the turn of the century, considerable sentiment assigned blacks great responsibility for the maintenance of corruption. On the position of immigrants in progressivist political ideology, see Richard Hofstadter, *The Age of Reform* (New York, 1955), esp. pp. 178–81, Edward C. Banfield and James Q. Wilson, *City Politics* (New York, 1968), pp. 139–50, and Samuel P. Hays, "The Politics of Reform in Municipal Government in the Progressive Era," *Pacific Northwest Quarterly* 55 (October 1964): 157–69.

3. Du Bois, *Autobiography*, p. 197. Allison Davis claims that the university's interest stemmed from the fact that the black population "was beginning to encroach upon" the campus; see his *Leadership, Love and Aggression* (New York, 1983), p. 127. See David Levering Lewis, *W. E. B. Du Bois; Biography of a Race, 1868–1919* (New York, 1993), pp. 179–210, for the most thorough discussion of the Philadelphia study's genesis and conduct.

4. Du Bois, *Autobiography*, p. 206.

5. W. E. B. Du Bois, *The Conservation of Races* (Washington, D.C., 1897), p. 15. This tract shows Du Bois's affinity for reform Darwinism or Lamarckian social theory. See also Alfred O. Moss Jr., *The American Negro Academy* (Baton Rouge, La., 1980); Lewis, *Biography of a Race*, pp. 168–74.

6. Du Bois, *Philadelphia Negro*, pp. 6–8.

7. Elliott M. Rudwick, *W. E. B. Du Bois: A Study in Minority Group Leadership* (Philadelphia, 1960), pp. 29–30, and Baltzell, Introduction, to Du Bois, *Philadelphia Negro*, p. xvi. Baltzell and Rudwick, however, only mention Wharton's role in passing

and draw no implications from her association. Lewis notes that Wharton and Lindsay—reflecting the bent of the College Settlement Association with which they were affiliated—"represented more of the right wing's paternalism than the left wing's mobilizing fervor" (*Biography of a Race*, p. 188).

8. Vidich and Lyman discuss the origins of this strain in the Social Gospel movement and trace its development in the field. See *American Sociology*; see also Robert M. Crunden, *Ministers of Reform: The Progressives' Achievement in American Civilization, 1889–1920* (Urbana, Ill., 1984).

9. The Americanization movement and its impact on the family structure of immigrant populations are discussed in Stanley Aronowitz, *False Promises: The Shaping of American Working Class Consciousness* (New York, 1973), pp. 158–66; Stuart and Elizabeth Ewen, "Americanization and Consumption," *Telos* (fall 1978): 42–51. Each of these authors establishes the further link between the impetus to Americanization and the production and consumption requirements of the newly ascendant corporate capitalism. See also John Higham, *Strangers in the Land: Patterns of American Nativism 1860–1925* (New York, 1981), pp. 234–63.

10. Du Bois, *Philadelphia Negro*, p. 15.

11. Ibid., p. 55.

12. Ibid., p. 67.

13. Ibid.

14. Ibid., p. 97.

15. Ibid., pp. 192–93.

16. Ibid., p. 193.

17. Ibid., p. 193.

18. Ibid., p. 195.

19. Ibid.

20. Ibid., pp. 195–96.

21. Ibid., p. 196. Du Bois elsewhere and not too happily identified the church congregations as "the real units of race life" (*Some Efforts of American Negroes for Their Own Social Betterment* [Atlanta, 1898], p. 4).

22. It is worthy of note here that Du Bois, no doubt because of the room available for their cultural improvement, saw Negroes by and large as "a people comparatively low in the scale of civilization" (*Philadelphia Negro*, p. 66).

23. Ibid., p. 195.

24. Ibid.

25. Ibid., p. 390.

26. Cf. Christopher Lasch's discussions of Addams, Bourne, and others in his *The New Radicalism in America, 1889–1963: The Intellectual as a Social Type* (New York, 1965). Some feminists, like Charlotte Perkins Gilman, were prepared during the prewar years to displace family functions altogether in deference to progress in the form of Taylorist rationalization. See, for example, Gilman's article "The Waste of Private Housekeeping," *Annals of the American Academy of Political and Social Science* 48 (July 1913): 91–96. See also Simon H. Patten's enthusiasm over the prospects of extension of corporate rationalization to the nuclear family in the same issue of the *Annals* ("The Standardization of Family Life," pp. 81–90).

27. Du Bois pointed out early on that "the little shop, the small trader, the house industry have given way to the department store, the organized company and the factory" (*Philadelphia Negro*, p. 45). And again: "Today . . . the application of large capital to the retail business, the gathering of workmen into factories, the wonderful success of

trained talent in catering to the whims and taste of customers almost precludes the effective competition of the small store" (ibid., p. 123).

28. In spite of his awareness of the passage of the entrepreneurial phase from the society in general, he still maintained the value of entrepreneurship among blacks, who had not—because of the slave experience—assimilated the bourgeois virtues. "For a Negro, then, to go into business means a great deal. It is, indeed, a step in social progress worth measuring" (W. E. B. Du Bois, *The Negro in Business* [Atlanta, 1899], p. 5).

29. W. E. B. Du Bois, *The Quest of the Silver Fleece: A Novel* (Chicago, 1911). This tension has persisted in various guises among black intellectuals and appears at times to have had a reasonably clear material basis. I shall discuss this recurring tension in chapter 5 in relation to the Harlem Renaissance and the early attempts at consolidation of an elite within the black community.

30. Du Bois, *Philadelphia Negro*, p. 174.

31. Ibid., p. 161. Improper dressing, lack of understanding of the need to change wet clothes (not enough sense to come in out of the rain?!), superstitious fear of hospitals—these "bad habits" contributed to poor health, especially among southern migrants (ibid., p. 162).

32. Ibid., p. 161.

33. Ibid., pp. 283–84. The importance of "house and home and ward" here underscores Du Bois's concerns about building the nuclear family and stimulating neighborhood community.

34. Ibid., p. 221.

35. Sheldon Wolin, *Politics and Vision: Continuity and Innovation in Western Political Thought* (Boston, 1960), pp. 352–434. Samuel P. Hays maintains that an "organizational revolution" took off after the mid-1890s (*The Response to Industrialism, 1885–1914* [Chicago, 1957], pp. 48–50).

36. Du Bois, *Some Efforts of American Negroes*, p. 4. This statement recalls the tendency of collectivist intellectuals to assume the mantle of the society as a whole.

37. Du Bois, *Philadelphia Negro*, p. 284.

38. Ibid., p. 285.

39. Ibid., p. 315. These views imply both a specific model of how the Afro-American population should be structured and a special tutelary role for an organizational vanguard. In the last analysis, therefore, these are categories whose profoundly political character is concealed within the organizationalist terminology.

40. Ibid., p. 235.

41. Ibid.

42. George Mosse, *Toward the Final Solution: A History of European Racism* (New York, 1978), esp. pp. 77–93, discusses at length those theories he characterizes as efforts to wed science and racism in the latter nineteenth and early twentieth centuries—for example, phrenology and physiognomy. See also Stephen Jay Gould, *The Mismeasure of Man* (New York, 1981). The political and cultural climate associated with Reaganism has allowed reputable scholars once again to attempt to link criminality and biology. See James Q. Wilson and Richard Herrnstein, *Crime and Human Nature* (New York, 1985), and Richard Herrnstein and Charles Murray, *The Bell Curve: Intelligence and Class Structure in American Life* (New York, 1994); see also Adolph Reed Jr. "Looking Backward," *Nation*, November 28, 1994, pp. 654–62.

43. Indications of the persistence of this problem can be seen over the next two generations in William T. Fontaine, " 'Social Determination' in the Writings of Negro Scholars," *American Journal of Sociology* 49 (January 1944): 302–15, and Orlando Pat-

terson, "The Moral Crisis of the Black American," *Public Interest* (summer 1973): 43–69. See also my discussion of this problem in chapter 1.

44. Du Bois, *Philadelphia Negro*, pp. 254–56. Du Bois noted that more and more black convicts knew how to read.

45. Ibid., pp. 389–90.

46. Ibid., p. 373. He notes, however, that this debasement of electoral responsibility was not exclusive to blacks, though it may have been relatively more common among them.

47. Ibid., pp. 374–75 and 380–81.

48. Ibid., p. 382. He went on to point out that while this laudable conservatism may in part have been a function of "the inertia of ignorance," the point remained that the black voter usually was allied with the "better" and never with the "worst" political elements (ibid).

49. Ibid., pp. 136–39.

50. Ibid., p. 395.

51. Ibid., p. 129.

52. Ibid., pp. 129–31n and 331–32.

53. For a general discussion of Taylor and his experiments see Sudhir Kakar, *Frederick Taylor: A Study in Personality in Innovation* (Cambridge, Mass., 1971). More critical views are proffered by David F. Noble, *America by Design: Science, Technology and the Rise of Corporate Capitalism* (New York, 1977) esp. pp. 264–78, and Harry F. Braverman, *Labor and Monopoly Capital: The Degradation of Work in the Twentieth Century* (New York, 1974), esp. pp. 85–138. Taylor's ideas are best presented in his rather self-serving volume *The Principles of Scientific Management* (New York, 1967). Lewis also notes the Midvale-Taylor connection (*Biography of a Race*, p. 191).

54. Du Bois, *Philadelphia Negro*, pp. 126–27.

55. Ibid., pp. 138–39. Like Charlotte Perkins Gilman and Simon H. Patten (cited above, note 26), Du Bois advocated the "professionalization" of domestic work. Unlike the others, however, he mixed a healthy dose of paternalism in with his prescription by proclaiming servants to be "constituent members of the family and as such [to] have rights and privileges as well as duties." Among the reforms he proposed was an effort to reverse the trend toward having servants live off the premises. This regrettable situation left servants "free at night to wander at will, to hire lodgings in suspicious houses, to consort with paramours, and thus to bring moral and physical disease to their place of work." Moreover, the reform that was "imperatively needed" in this area would, he noted, "benefit white and black alike—the employer as well as the employed" (ibid., p. 141). With this kind of outlook predominant in the progressive social sciences, there is small wonder that Henry Ford was to find use for a Sociology Department!

56. Ibid.

57. W. E. B. Du Bois, "The Training of Negroes for Social Power," *Outlook* 75 (October 17, 1903): 409–14. Quotations here are from a typescript copy of the essay in the Countee Cullen–Harold Jackman Collection, Atlanta University, Collection No. 3, "Du Bois."

58. Ibid., p. 4.

59. Ibid., pp. 5–6. "An industrial school, however, does not merely teach technique. It is also a school—of moral influence and of mental discipline" (ibid., p. 6).

60. Ibid., p. 7.

61. Ibid., pp. 7–8.

62. Du Bois, *Philadelphia Negro*, p. 7. This view of the upper class as bearer of a

group's "realized ideal" also reflects Du Bois's embrace of a variant of racialist social theory prevalent among his educated, late Victorian contemporaries.

63. Ibid.

64. Ibid., p. 309.

65. Ibid., p. 310.

66. Ibid., pp. 310–11.

67. Ibid., p. 62n. He also deplored the practice among realtors of dumping "undesirable elements . . . from the slums" among black settlements (ibid., p. 194). The bluntness of his class prejudice should give pause to those who currently adduce *The Philadelphia Negro* as evidence for the persistence of a so-called black urban underclass—for example, Orlando Patterson, "Toward a Study of Black America," *Dissent* (fall 1989): 483.

68. Du Bois, *Philadelphia Negro*, p. 55n.

69. E. Franklin Frazier, "Durham: Capital of the Black Middle Class," in Alain Locke, ed., *The New Negro: An Interpretation* (1925; reprint, New York, 1968), pp. 333–40. In this essay Frazier anointed the new black elite for the sacred mission of uplift and advancement of the race as a whole. Unfortunately Spaulding, Pearson, Moore, and the other guiding lights of the North Carolina Mutual Life Insurance Company—not to mention the larger elite stratum and aspirants to it—did not heed the clarion but went about their chosen agenda of personal aggrandizement and conspicuous consumption.

70. Du Bois, *Philadelphia Negro*, p. 155.

71. Ibid., p. 177.

72. Ibid., p. 316.

73. Ibid., p. 318.

74. Ibid., p. 317.

75. Ibid., p. 177.

76. Ibid., p. 318.

77. Ibid., p. 177.

78. Lester F. Ward, *Pure Sociology: A Treatise on the Origin and Spontaneous Development of Society* (New York, 1907), p. 205.

79. Du Bois, *Conservation of Races*, p. 7.

80. Ibid.

81. See, for example, Howard Brotz, ed., *Negro Social and Political Thought, 1850–1920* (New York, 1966).

82. Du Bois, *Conservation of Races*, p. 8. Lewis notes the echoes of German romantic race theory in Du Bois's writing in this period (*Biography of a Race*, pp. 165–66).

83. Du Bois, *Conservation of Races*, p. 9. Appiah and Fergerson note that Du Bois's writings—as was common among his contemporaries—were ambiguous during those early years with respect to whether race is defined ultimately by biology or history. In part this ambiguity stems from the prevailing naïveté (i.e., prior to the "rediscovery" of Mendelian theory) about genetics and thus about heredity. Indeed, race and class typically were discussed in a language that was at the same time categorically vague and at least evocative of biological determinism. See Anthony Appiah, "The Uncompleted Argument: Du Bois and the Illusion of Race," *Critical Inquiry* 12 (autumn 1985): 21–37; Gerard Fergerson, "Race, Science, and Medicine in the Late Nineteenth Century: W. E. B. Du Bois and the Health and Physique of the Negro American," master's thesis, Yale University, New Haven, Conn., 1987; George W. Stocking Jr., *Race, Culture, and Evolution* (Chicago, 1982), esp. pp. 42–68 and 161–94; Greta Jones, *Social Darwinism and English Thought: The Interaction between Biological and Social Theory* (Atlantic High-

lands, N.J., 1980), pp. 140–59; Mark Pittenger, *American Socialists and Evolutionary Thought, 1870–1920* (Madison, Wis., 1993). I shall return to this issue in chapter 7.

84. Du Bois, *Conservation of Races*, p. 10. The "advance guard" of the race in Du Bois's view were the Afro-Americans. Perhaps West Indians and Africans would have seen things differently.

85. Ibid., p. 12. This specific proposal of course reflects an attempt to promote the newly formed group that published Du Bois's monograph. See note 5 above.

86. Ibid., p. 13.

87. Ibid. "The Academy," Du Bois proposed, "should seek to gather about it the talented, unselfish men, the pure and noble-minded women, to fight an army of devils that disgraces our manhood and womanhood" (ibid., p. 14).

88. Du Bois, "The Problem of Amusement," *Southern Workman* 27 (September 1897): 184.

89. Du Bois, "The Study of the Negro Problems," *Annals of the American Academy of Political and Social Science* 11 (January 1898): 21.

Chapter 4

1. See, for example, the following works by Du Bois: *The Philadelphia Negro* (1899; reprint, New York, 1967); *The Negro* (1915; reprint, New York, 1970 *Black Folk: Then and Now* (New York, 1939); *The World and Africa: An Inquiry into the Part Which Africa Has Played in World History* (1947; reprint, New York, 1965). See also Francis L. Broderick, *W. E. B. Du Bois: Negro Leader in a Time of Crisis* (Palo Alto, Calif., 1959), pp. 48–49, and Joseph P. DeMarco, *The Social Thought of W. E. B. Du Bois* (Lanham, Md., 1983), pp. xi–xiii; David Levering Lewis, *W. E. B. Du Bois: Biography of a Race, 1868–1919* (New York, 1993).

2. W. E. B. Du Bois, *Dusk of Dawn: An Essay toward an Autobiography of a Race Concept* (1940; reprint, New York, 1968), p. 63.

3. Elliott M. Rudwick points out in this regard that Du Bois "hoped to use the Negro university . . . to train a brain trust" (*W. E. B. Du Bois: A Study in Minority Group Leadership* [Philadelphia, 1960], p. 37).

4. The studies were published by Atlanta University as proceedings of the annual conferences on the "Negro problem" that Du Bois organized. He continued his role with the conferences and the studies for five years after his departure from the university. The series included, among others, the following volumes: *Social and Physical Condition of Negroes in Cities* (1897), *Some Efforts of American Negroes for Their Own Social Betterment* (1898), *The Negro in Business* (1899), *The College-Bred Negro* (1900), *The Negro Common School* (1901), *The Negro Artisan* (1902), *Some Notes on Negro Crime, Particularly in Georgia* (1904), *The Health and Physique of the Negro American* (1906), *Economic Cooperation among Negro Americans* (1907), *The Negro American Family* (1908), *Efforts for Social Betterment among Negro Americans* (1910), *The Common School and the Negro American* (1912), *The Negro American Artisan* (1913), *Morals and Manners among Negro Americans* (1915).

5. Du Bois began to collect and annotate his papers at the age of fifteen. Broderick, *Negro Leader*, p. 4.

6. After indicating that their ultimate purpose was to determine "how much of natural law there is in human conduct," Du Bois argued that the Atlanta University studies of the Afro-American community offered to sociology insights to questions such as: "What

is human progress and how is it emphasized? How do nations rise and fall? What is the meaning and value of certain human actions? Is there rhythm and law in the mass of the deeds of men—and if so how can it best be measured and stated?" (Du Bois, "The Atlanta Conferences," *Voice of the Negro* 1 [March 1904]: 85).

7. Du Bois, "The Study of the Negro Problems," *Annals of the American Academy of Political and Social Science* 11 (January 1898): 1–23.

8. Henry Lee Moon perceptively notes the connection between Du Bois's faith in scientific expertise and his assertion of the duty of the intellectual elite (Moon, Introduction to W. E. B. Du Bois, *The Emerging Thought of W. E. B. Du Bois*, Henry Lee Moon, ed. [New York, 1972]).

9. Du Bois's affinity for positivist science as a model for understanding social life has been noted by several analysts. See for example Eugene C. Holmes, "W. E. B. Du Bois: Philosopher," in John Henrik Clarke et al., eds., *Black Titan: W. E. B. Du Bois* (Boston, 1970); Julius Lester, Introduction to W. E. B. Du Bois, *The Seventh Son: The Thought and Writings of W. E. B. Du Bois*, Julius Lester, ed. (New York, 1971), esp. pp. 54, 58; William Allison Davis, *Du Bois and the Problems of the Black Masses* (Atlanta, 1974); Bernard R. Boxill, "Du Bois and Fanon on Culture," *Philosophical Forum* 9 (winter–spring, 1979): 326–38; and Dan S. Green and Edwin D. Driver, Introduction to Du Bois, *W.E.B. Du Bois on Sociology and the Black Community*, Green and Driver, eds. (Chicago, 1978). Some of the zest with which these authors attempt to identify Du Bois with science may derive from a desire to legitimize or exalt his reputation among American intellectuals. The high value generally attached to science in this culture is such that "scientific" knowledge typically is held to be its highest expression, and each of the authors cited here writes in part from an intention to elevate Du Bois's role within the history of American ideas.

As an indication of his receptiveness to the scientism then coming into its own at the more prestigious universities, among his early Cambridge notes is the following syllogism: "Science is Mathematics. Mathematics is Identity. Science is Identity." Quoted in Francis L. Broderick, "The Academic Training of W. E. B. Du Bois," *Journal of Negro Education* 27 (winter 1958): 13; Lewis, *Biography of a Race*, pp. 95–96 also discusses Du Bois's early, exuberant scientism.

10. W. E. B. Du Bois, *Some Notes on Negroes in New York City* (Atlanta, 1905), p. 1.

11. Du Bois, "Atlanta Conferences," p. 85.

12. Ibid.

13. Du Bois, *Dusk of Dawn*, p. 50.

14. Ibid., p. 51. At the time of his early encounter with Spencer's work, however, Du Bois does not appear to have been quite so skeptical as this passage might suggest. Cf. Du Bois, *The Conservation of Races* (Washington, D.C., 1897).

15. Du Bois, *Dusk of Dawn*, p. 51.

16. Arthur L. Johnson, "The Social Theories of W. E. B. Du Bois," M.A. thesis, Atlanta University, Atlanta, Ga., 1949. Du Bois himself informs us that the Atlanta series received accolades for its scientificity from William James and other prominent scholars and reformers (*Autobiography: Soliloquy on Viewing My Life from the Last Decade of Its First Century* (New York, 1968), pp. 218–19.

17. Mark Pittenger, James Gilbert, R. Jeffrey Lustig, and Arthur Lipow all discuss the static and mechanistic biases operating in scientific reform activity during this period in, respectively, *American Socialists and Evolutionary Thought, 1870–1920* (Madison,

Wis., 1993), *Designing the Industrial State* (Chicago, 1972), *Corporate Liberalism* (Berkeley, Calif., 1982), *Authoritarian Socialism in America* (Berkeley, Calif., 1982). See also Dorothy Ross, *The Origins of American Social Science* (Cambridge and New York, 1991).

18. Elliott M. Rudwick, "W. E. B. Du Bois as Sociologist," in James E. Blackwell and Morris Janowitz, eds., *Black Sociologists: Historical and Contemporary Perspectives* (Chicago 1974), p. 26.

19. I have borrowed the phrase "background assumption" from Alvin W. Gouldner, *The Coming Crisis of Western Sociology* (New York, 1970), pp. 29–31. Gouldner defines background assumptions as the "unpostulated and unlabeled" assumptions out of which a theory in part emerges. These assumptions, furthermore, "are embedded in a theory's postulations . . . [and] . . . provide some of the bases of choice and the invisible cement" for linking postulations together.

20. Arthur J. Vidich and Stanford M. Lyman, *American Sociology: Worldly Rejections of Religion and Their Directions* (New Haven, Conn., and London, 1985), p. 307.

21. J. David Lewis and Richard L. Smith, *American Sociology and Pragmatism: Mead, Chicago Sociology, and Symbolic Interaction* (Chicago, 1980), p. 5.

22. Lustig, *Corporate Liberalism*, p. 168. Lustig suggests that pragmatism might even be seen as an attempt to extend positivism to new terrain: "An approach that is usually celebrated for admitting that social matter was informed by mind turns out to have actually provided a rationale for applying *to* mind a set of techniques proven useful in dealing with matter" (p. 169).

23. Arnold Rampersad, *The Art and Imagination of W. E. B. Du Bois* (Cambridge, Mass., 1976), p. 27. A notable and, I believe mistaken, alternative assessment is DeMarco's claim that social Darwinism "never occupied a strong role in [Du Bois's] thought" (*Social Thought of W. E. B. Du Bois*, p. 69). The basis for this faulty interpretation may be DeMarco's curious assertion that the principle of "advance through race loyalty," which he rightly attributes to Du Bois, conflicted with Social Darwinist precepts. However, Lester F. Ward, Thomas Nixon Carver, Edward Cummings and other early evolutionary sociologists found little difficulty in incorporating notions like race loyalty into their theoretical constructs. See Vidich and Lyman, *American Sociology*, pp. 28, 71–78. On Du Bois's persisting rationalism, see Lewis, *Biography of a Race*, pp. 438–41.

24. Of Bismarck, Du Bois stated: "The Fate of Europe is Germany and Germany is Bismarck. The Man of Iron, one of the strangest personalities the world has ever seen; brilliant, stubborn;—reckless, careful, a patriot, a despot: the Man of One Idea" ("Bismarck," Fisk University, June 1888, *W. E. B. Du Bois Papers at the University of Massachusetts*, Amherst, Mass., Reel 80 #7).

25. DeMarco, *Social Thought of W. E. B. Du Bois*, pp. 45–47. See also Du Bois, *Autobiography*, pp. 154–82; Francis L. Broderick, "German Influence on the Scholarship of W. E. B. Du Bois," *Phylon* 19 (December 1958): 367–71. Manning Marable emphasizes Alexander Crummell's racial theories in discussing the intellectual foundations of *The Conservation of Races* (Marable, *W. E. B. Du Bois: Black Radical Democrat* [Boston, 1986], pp. 31–35). Wilson J. Moses, though, notes that Crummell and Du Bois operated equally within a broader Germanically inflected discourse of racial romanticism (*The Golden Age of Black Nationalism, 1850–1925* [New York, 1988], p. 81). Lewis elaborates the latter view (*Biography of a Race*, pp. 163–69).

26. W. E. B. Du Bois, "Proposal for a Sociological Society," Atlanta University, 1897, *Du Bois Papers*, Reel 80 #84–94. In this draft Du Bois emphasized regularities as

the object of sociological study and argued that social scientific facts and expertise should have priority in reform efforts, racial and otherwise.

27. Dan S. Green and Edwin D. Driver, "W. E. B. Du Bois: A Case in the Sociology of Sociological Negation," *Phylon* 37 (December 1976): 313–17. Lewis's account is a solid corrective; see *Biography of a Race,* esp. chapter 9.

28. Du Bois, *Negroes in New York City,* p. 3.

29. Ibid., p. 2.

30. Ibid., pp. 2–3.

31. A flavor of this perspective is found in the following: Gilbert, *Industrial State*; ed., Jerry Israel, *Building the Organizational Society: Essays on Associational Activities in Modern America,* (New York, 1972); Robert H. Wiebe, *Search for Order* 1877–1920 (New York, 1967); Lipow, *Authoritarian Socialism*; Pittenger, *American Socialists.*

32. See, for example, Ira Kipnis, *The American Socialist Movement, 1897–1912* (New York, 1952); Lipow, *Authoritarian Socialism*; Aileen S. Kraditor, *The Radical Persuasion, 1890–1917: Aspects of the Intellectual History and the Historiography of Three American Radical Organizations* (Baton Rouge, La., 1981); James Weinstein, *The Corporate Ideal in the Liberal State, 1900–1918* (Boston, 1968); Lustig, *Corporate Liberalism.*

33. Gilbert, *Industrial State,* p. 31. The situation with legal theory, however, is somewhat more complex than Gilbert suggests. While proponents of sociological jurisprudence and legal realism certainly advocated reliance on the fruits and techniques of social science, they were not inclined to justify their project in terms of neutrality or impartiality. Indeed, they understood themselves to be reacting against the alleged impartiality associated with formalist doctrines. I am grateful to Rogers M. Smith for bringing this clarification to my attention. For discussion bearing on this issue, see his *Liberalism and American Constitutional Law* (Cambridge, Mass., 1985), pp. 75–78 and 154–57, and his "Constitutional Interpretation and Political Theory: American Legal Realism's Continuing Search for Standards," *Polity* 15 (summer 1983): esp. 492–97.

34. W. E. B. Du Bois, "Speech by Dr. William E. B. Du Bois, A.L.P. Candidate for U.S. Senator at A.L.P. Rally, Golden Gate Ballroom," in Du Bois, *Seventh Son,* vol. 2, p. 604.

35. W. E. B. Du Bois, "My Evolving Program for Negro Freedom," in Rayford W. Logan, ed., *What the Negro Wants* (Chapel Hill, N.C., 1944), p. 56.

36. W. E. B. Du Bois, *Darkwater: Voices from within the Veil* (1920; reprint, New York, 1969), p. 21.

37. Du Bois, *Dusk of Dawn,* p. 67. He also learned, so he tells us, that there was little demand for the research that he had been doing (ibid).

38. Du Bois, "My Evolving Program," p. 57.

39. Du Bois, "My Evolving Program." Despite this statement, Rampersad asserts emphatically that Royce had no influence on Du Bois (*Art and Imagination,* p. 29).

40. Broderick, *Negro Leader,* pp. 30–31. Cornel West similarly sees a pragmatist strain in Du Bois; see West, *The American Evasion of Philosophy: A Genealogy of Pragmatism* (Madison, Wis., 1989), pp. 142–43.

41. Alan Sigmund Cywar, "An Inquiry into American Thought and the Determinate Influence of Political Economic and Social Factors in the Early Twentieth Century: Bourne, Dewey, Du Bois, Nearing, Veblen, and Weyl," Ph.D. dissertation, University of Rochester, Rochester, N.Y., 1972, p. 315. Cywar also discusses apparent reform Darwinist influence in Du Bois's writing in this early period, pp. 330–31.

42. Rampersad, *Art and Imagination,* p. 65. See also Bruce Kuklik, *The Rise of American Philosophy: Cambridge, Massachusetts, 1860–1930* (New Haven, Conn., 1977),

esp. chaps 9, 14–17; Lewis and Smith, *American Sociology*, pp. 59–86; C. Wright Mills, *Sociology and Pragmatism* (New York, 1964), pp. 215–76; and William James, *Pragmatism* (Cleveland and New York, 1955). Despite these shared concerns, David Levering Lewis concluded, I believe correctly, that the extent of James's philosophical "imprint on Du Bois is somewhat less distinct than some recent students of ideas have believed," noting that there is no clear evidence that Du Bois embraced pragmatism's theoretical underpinnings either formally or substantively (*Biography of a Race*, p. 96).

43. W. E. B. Du Bois, "Education and Work," *Journal of Negro Education* 1 (April 1932): 64–65. Du Bois made clear in this essay that he was not unmindful either of the underlying sense in which this view of the purpose of education dovetails with the utilitarian objectives of vocational training. The differences were, first, that such vocational training as had been advocated was obsolescent and generally useless, and, second, that the vocational training advocates paid insufficient attention to the utilitarian character of the sensibility that can accompany college education.

44. Du Bois, *World and Africa*, p. xii

45. W. E. B. Du Bois, *The Gift of Black Folk: The Negroes in the Making of America* (1924; reprint, New York, 1970).

46. W. E. B. Du Bois, *Black Reconstruction in America, 1860–1880* (1935; reprint, New York, 1969) and *Black Folk: Then and Now* (New York, 1939).

47. Cf. Daniel Lerner and Harold Lasswell, *The Policy Sciences* (Stanford, Calif., 1965). See David W. Eakins, "The Origins of Corporate Liberal Policy Research, 1916–1922: The Political-Economic Expert and the Decline of Public Debate," in Israel, ed., *Building the Organizational Society*, pp. 163–179; David M. Ricci, *The Tragedy of Political Science: Politics, Scholarship and Democracy* (New Haven, Conn., and London, 1984); Raymond Seidelman, with the assistance of Edward J. Harpham, *Disenchanted Realists: Political Science and the American Crisis, 1884–1984* (Albany, 1985).

48. W. E. B. Du Bois, "Prospect of a World without Race Conflict," *American Journal of Sociology* 49 (March 1944): 456.

49. Ibid.

50. Ibid., p. 456.

51. Ibid.

52. Du Bois, *Negro in Business*, p. 1.

53. W. E. B. Du Bois, "The Training of Negroes for Social Power," *Outlook* 75 (October 17, 1903): 409–14. The quotation here is from a typescript copy of the essay in the Countee Cullen–Harold Jackman Collection, Atlanta University, Collection No. 3, "Du Bois," p. 10.

Chapter 5

1. Joseph P. DeMarco, *The Social Thought of W. E. B. Du Bois* (Lanham, Md., 1983), p. 54.

2. Gerald Horne, *Black and Red: W. E. B. Du Bois and the Afro-American Response to the Cold War, 1944–1963* (Albany, 1986), p. 7. It is possible for Horne to make this contention only because he does not consult Du Bois's major prewar writings and relies on Du Bois's own retrospective assessments of his earlier positions. Manning Marable goes so far as to reinterpret the "Talented Tenth" formulation as not really elitist after all, contending that it should be seen as "a strategy to win democracy for all black Americans" (*W. E. B. Du Bois: Black Radical Democrat* [Boston, 1986], p. 47). That Marable seems untroubled by this interpretation's manifestly Orwellian character may reflect the

hegemony of an antiparticipatory model of political action current in black civic discourse. This problem intensified over the 1980s with proliferation of an idea of leadership vested in individuals who represent group interests organically, without mediation or mechanisms of accountability. I have discussed this phenomenon at greater length in *The Jesse Jackson Phenomenon: The Crisis of Purpose in Afro-American Politics* (New Haven, Conn., and London, 1986) and in the forthcoming volume, *Stirrings in the Jug: Black American Politics in the Post-Segregation Era* (Minneapolis, 1998).

3. W. E. B. Du Bois, *Some Efforts of American Negroes for Their Own Social Betterment* (Atlanta, 1898), p. 43.

4. Ibid., p. 43.

5. Ibid., p. 36, cf. W. E. B. Du Bois, *The Conservation of Races* (Washington, D.C., 1897), pp. 12–14. I discuss Du Bois's earlier advocacy of an "intellectual clearinghouse" role for the American Negro Academy in chapter 3. On the history of the Academy see Alfred O. Moss Jr., *The American Negro Academy: Voice of the Talented Tenth* (Baton Rouge, La., 1980).

6. Du Bois, *Some Efforts*, p. 37, quoting Alexander Crummell, *Character: The Great Thing*, Tracts for the Negro Race, no. 2 (Washington, D.C., American Negro Academy, n.d.).

7. W. E. B. Du Bois, *The Negro in Business* (Atlanta, 1899).

8. W. E. B. Du Bois, *The College-Bred Negro* (Atlanta, 1900).

9. W. E. B. Du Bois, "The Study of the Negro Problems," *Annals of the American Academy of Political and Social Science* 11 (January 1898): 1–23. See also Du Bois, "Program for a Sociological Society" Atlanta University, 1897, *W. E. B. Du Bois Papers at the University of Massachusetts*, Amherst, Mass., Reel 80 #84–94.

10. W. E. B. Du Bois, "Possibilities of the Negro: The Advance Guard of the Race," *Booklovers Magazine* 2 (July 1903): 3.

11. W. E. B. Du Bois, "The Talented Tenth," in *The Negro Problem* (multiauthor collection) (1903; reprint, New York, 1969 p. 33. Despite Du Bois's atypically resolute support for women's rights, he almost certainly in such formulations meant to refer literally to men.

12. Ibid., p. 34.

13. Ibid., p. 54.

14. Ibid., p. 35.

15. Ibid., p 45. Arnold Rampersad also notes Du Bois's "trickle down" view of culture (*The Art and Imagination of W. E. B. Du Bois* [Cambridge, Mass., 1976], p. 87). Several years later, in the thick of the Washington controversy, Du Bois would assert that all youth in principle should receive "a training designed . . . to make them men of power, of thought, of trained and cultivated taste—men who know whither civilization is tending and what it means." However, he noted, the costs involved prohibited the universal dissemination of liberal education and decreed that only a few could benefit; to make the best of this unfortunate situation required that such opportunities as were available be reserved for the most talented. Du Bois, "The Hampton Idea," *Voice of the Negro* 3 (September 1906): 632–36. The quotation here is from a typescript copy in the Countee Cullen–Harold Jackman Collection, Atlanta University, Collection No. 3, "Du Bois." Du Bois's consistent emphasis on talent as a legitimizing principle of the elite conforms not only with the meritocratic ideological posture of reform liberalism but also with the circumstances of his own biography. He had grown up in poverty in the Berkshires only to be rescued by opportunities opened to him through the initiative of those who observed his intellectual ability.

16. Quoted by Du Bois in "The Talented Tenth," p. 41. This reference occurs in

the midst of a recounting of antislavery and prorace activism by early prominent blacks. Du Bois contented in his essay that pride in ethnicity by no means necessarily implies interracial populism or even exaltation of folkishness. His deprecation of what he saw as the backwardness of Afro-American social organization coexists with his high admiration of the racial pride exhibited by Benjamin Banneker and others (ibid., pp. 35–36).

17. Ibid., p. 42.

18. Ibid., pp. 45.

19. Francis L. Broderick contends that Du Bois was consistent from his 1896 talk to the American Negro Academy through Niagara and the NAACP in the conviction that blacks should challenge their physical and intellectual powers for self-organization (*W. E. B. Du Bois: Negro Leader in a Time of Crisis* [Stanford, Calif., 1959], p. 101). See also David Levering Lewis, *W. E. B. Du Bois: Biography of a Race, 1868–1919* (New York, 1993), pp. 398–99.

20. William Allison Davis, *Du Bois and the Problems of the Black Masses* (Atlanta, 1974), p. 16.

21. For example, in *Crisis* 2 (November 1911), the first advertisement for "Crisis-Maid" face powder appeared, with a photograph of a Crisis-Maid in *Crisis* 5 (December 1912), and shortly after an issue in which he had hailed the Bolshevik Revolution, Du Bois noted with "exceeding interest" the pleasure and beauty he had seen displayed at recent black elite balls (*Crisis* 18 [October 1919]: 285).

22. W. E. B. Du Bois, *Crisis* 7 (December 1913); 83. Several months later he took issue with the practice of designating talented blacks as " 'black Westers,' 'black Sousas' . . . black *this* and black *that*. Who ever heard of a 'white Fred Douglass,' a 'white Coleridge-Taylor' or even a 'white Jack Johnson'?" (*Crisis* 7 [April 1914]: 288).

23. W. E. B. Du Bois, *Crisis* 5 (January 1913): 130.

24. W. E. B. Du Bois, *Crisis* 9 (February 1915); 184.

25. W. E. B. Du Bois, *The Negro* (1915; reprint, New York, 1970), p. 138.

26. Alain Locke, ed., *The New Negro: An Interpretation* (1925; reprint, New York, 1968).

27. Charles S. Johnson, "The New Frontage on American Life," in Locke, ed., *New Negro*, pp. 278–98.

28. Kelly Miller, "Howard: The National Negro University," in Locke, ed., *New Negro*, pp. 312–322.

29. Robert R. Moton, "Hampton-Tuskegee: Missioners of the Mass," in Locke, ed., *New Negro*, pp. 323–32.

30. Johnson, "New Frontage," p. 297.

31. E. Franklin Frazier, "Durham: Capital of the Black Middle Class," in Locke, ed., *New Negro*, pp. 333–40.

32. W. E. B. Du Bois, *The Gift of Black Folk: The Negroes in the Making of America* (1924; reprint, New York, 1970), p. 178.

33. Ibid., p. 158.

34. W. E. B. Du Bois, *Crisis* 24 (May 1922): 8–9.

35. W. E. B. Du Bois, *Crisis* 24 (October 1922), 247–48.

36. Frantz Fanon describes this dynamic eloquently in *Black Skin, White Masks* (New York, 1967).

37. I shall discuss this issue in detail in chapter 7 as a feature of Du Bois's early acceptance of the Lamarckian race theory prominent at the end of the nineteenth century.

38. See the lengthy discussion of this relation in Harold Cruse, *The Crisis of the Negro Intellectual: From Its Origins to the Present* (New York 1967), pp. 11–63.

39. C. Vann Woodward, *Origins of the New South: 1877–1913* (Baton Rouge, La., 1951), pp. 356–60. See also Louis R. Harlan's biography *Booker T. Washington*, 2 vols. (New York, 1972–83) as well as Lewis, *Biography of a Race*, esp. chapters 9–15.

40. Du Bois, "The Talented Tenth," pp. 74–75.

41. J. Saunders Redding maintains that the volume "may be seen as fixing that moment in history when the American Negro began to reject the idea of the world's belonging to white people only, and to think of himself in concert, as a potential force in the organization of society" (Redding, "*The Souls of Black Folk:* Du Bois' Masterpiece Lives On," in John Henrik Clarke et al., eds., *Black Titan: W. E. B. Du Bois* [Boston, 1970], p. 49). See also William S. Toll, *The Resurgence of Race: Black Social Theory from Reconstruction to the Pan-African Conferences* (Philadelphia, 1979), p. 120. In this sense *Souls* was a manifesto of a rising black elite.

42. W. E. B. Du Bois, *The Souls of Black Folk* (1903; reprint, New York, 1907), pp. 29–30. This passage may be to some degree an escape into style that got carried away with itself. However, he also reflected that the freedman "had emerged from slavery,— not the worst slavery in the world, not a slavery that made all life unbearable, rather a slavery that had here and there something of kindliness, fidelity, and happiness,—but withal slavery, which so far as human aspiration and desert were concerned, classed the black man and the ox together" (p. 28). Such studied evenhandedness surely indicates that Du Bois's desired audience was in large part white.

43. Ibid., p. 56.

44. Ibid., p. 86.

45. W. E. B. Du Bois, *Dusk of Dawn: An Essay toward an Autobiography of a Race Concept* (1940; reprint, New York, 1968), p. 75. David Levering Lewis has provided a definitive account of the intricacies and specifics of the Washington–Du Bois conflict, including the lineaments of the patterns of political alliance within which it was embedded and which it shaped (see note 39 above). There is no need to rehearse that account here.

46. Mary Law Chaffee, "William E. B. Du Bois' Concept of the Racial Problem in the United States," *Journal of Negro History* 41 (July 1956): 242.

47. Robert L. Factor, "Booker T. Washington and the Transformation of the Black Belt Negro: Disorganization and Change," in Jerry Israel, ed., *Building the Organizational Society: Essays on Associational Activities in Modern America* (New York, 1972), p. 112. See also Harlan, *Washington*, as well as Lewis, *Biography of a Race*, and James D. Anderson, *The Education of Blacks in the South, 1860–1935* (Chapel Hill, N.C., 1988), pp. 33–110.

48. Toll, *Resurgence of Race*, p. 17; Judith Stein, " 'Of Mr. Booker T. Washington and Others': The Political Economy of Racism in the United States," *Science and Society* 38 (winter 1974–75): 422–63.

49. Toll, *Resurgence of Race*, p. 21.

50. Ibid., p. 58.

51. Ibid., p. 109. In this context Toll observes, insightfully, that the structural division between Du Boisians and Washingtonians spun more likely around an urban/rural axis than a northern/southern one.

52. Du Bois, *Crisis* 7 (December 1913): 84. Americanization, of course, during that period meant industrial socialization and acculturation.

53. As is true of the society as a whole, the story of the women involved in the genesis of this discourse of "race adjustment" remains largely untold. Much fruitful research can be done on the ideas of such figures as Mary Church Terrell, Ida Wells-Barnett, and others. Recent though theoretically uneven contributions are Paula Gid-

dings, *When and Where I Enter: The Impact of Black Women on Race and Sex in America* (New York, 1984); Thomas C. Holt, "The Lonely Warrior: Ida Wells-Barnett and the Struggle for Black Leadership," in John Hope Franklin and August Meier *Black Leaders of the Twentieth Century* (Urbana, Ill., Chicago, and London, 1982); and Hazel Carby, " 'On the Threshold of Woman's Era': Lynching, Empire, and Sexuality in Black Feminist Theory," *Critical Inquiry* 12 (autumn 1985): 262–77. Carby's account is the most directly intellectual-historical.

54. While Du Bois's inclinations in this regard have been discussed, the following passage from Washington should establish the extent to which he assimilated the dominant values of the order, even the logic of the incipient consumer culture: "[W]hat is needed is not only to have the individual educated in industry but to have his hand so trained that he will become ambitious. We should get the man to the point where he will want a house, where his wife will want carpet for the floor, pictures for the walls, books, a newspaper and a substantial kind of furniture. We should get the family to the point where it will want money to educate its children, to support the minister and the church. Later, we should get this family to the point where it will want to put money in the bank and perhaps have the experience of placing a mortgage on some property. When this stage of development has been reached, there is no difficulty in getting individuals to work six days during a week." Booker T. Washington, "The Economic Development of the Negro Race since Its Emancipation," in W. E. B. Du Bois and Booker T. Washington, *The Negro in the South: His Economic Progress in Relation to His Moral and Religious Development* (1907; reprint, Northbrook, Ill., 1972), pp. 56–57. August Meier also discusses the extent to which adjustment to industrialization was a central theme of black political discourse in the decades preceding World War I. See his account in *Negro Thought in America 1880–1915: Racial Ideologies in the Age of Booker T. Washington* (Ann Arbor, Mich., 1963). Washington and Du Bois equally advocated for much of the Afro-American population something very much akin to the Americanization initiatives to which European immigrants were subjected by northern progressives.

55. August Meier, Introduction to *Negro Problem*, pp. viii-ix. Julius Lester's claim that the disagreement between Du Bois and Washington struck so deep as "their concepts of the nature of Man and his function" seems extreme by contrast (Lester, Introduction to W. E. B. Du Bois, *The Seventh Son: The Thought and Writings of W. E. B. Du Bois*, Julius Lester, ed. [New York, 1969], p. 43). In fact, in the same year that *The Souls of Black Folk* appeared, Du Bois rendered a qualified but still laudatory assessment of Washington's work. Du Bois, "Possibilities of the Negro," p. 7.

56. Elliott M. Rudwick, *W. E. B. Du Bois: A Study in Minority Group Leadership* (Philadelphia, 1960), p. 59.

57. Ibid., p. 81.

58. Ibid., p. 63–64.

59. W. E. B. Du Bois, "The Twelfth Census and the Negro Problems," *Southern Workman* 29 (May 1900): 308. This recalls Du Bois's earlier call for organization of an "intellectual clearinghouse through the American Negro Academy," in his *Conservation of Races*, pp. 12–14.

60. Du Bois, *Autobiography*, p. 224. David Levering Lewis indicates that Schiff's lack of support resulted at least in part from Washington's veto (*Biography of a Race*, p. 325) and also discusses another, more humiliating rejection Du Bois suffered from the Carnegie Institution in 1906 (ibid., pp. 366–67).

61. Rudwick, *W. E. B. Du Bois*, p. 118.

62. Ibid., p. 298.

63. Robert L. Factor, pointing out the importance of the educational apparatus as a source of the elite's income and status, describes the tight control that the religious and other philanthropic organizations maintained over black education in the South (Factor, "Booker T. Washington," pp. 111–12. Kenneth Manning's *Black Apollo of Science* (New York, 1983) portrays brilliantly and poignantly the tragic experience of the black biologist E. E. Just in attempting to secure philanthropic support for his research; in the process Manning richly illuminates the defensive paternalism with which white philanthropists approached even nonpolitical black initiatives. On this relation see also James D. Anderson, "Philanthropic Control over Private Black Higher Education," in Robert F. Arnove, ed., *Philanthropy and Cultural Imperialism* (Bloomington, Ind., 1980), and Anderson, *The Education of Blacks in the South*; and John H. Stanfield, *Philanthropy and Jim Crow in American Social Science* (Westport, Conn., 1985).

64. Cited in Virginia Hamilton, *W. E. B. Du Bois: A Biography* (New York, 1972), p. 102. Reflecting on the philanthropic connection years later, Du Bois observed a source of the paradox. Most of the prominent philanthropists, while often relatives or friends of Abolitionists, were also capitalists and employers of labor who saw in blacks a way to restrain the demands of white labor (*Autobiography*, pp. 239–40).

65. Du Bois, *Souls of Black Folk*, p. 113. Atlanta, interestingly, was his model for this encroaching philistinism. *Plus ça change, plus c'est la même chose!* Wilson J. Moses claims that Du Bois attacked Washington from the standpoint of a backward-looking anti-capitalism which recoiled from the "values of an upstart burgher class" *The Golden Age of Black Nationalism, 1850–1925,* [New York, 1988] p. 137). However, Du Bois's critique was struck explicitly in the name of a *rising* stratum of young, cosmopolitan professionals. See also Lewis, *Biography of a Race*, pp. 297–342.

66. W. E. B. Du Bois, *The Social Evolution of the Black South* (Washington, D.C., 1911), p. 9.

67. Du Bois, *Dusk of Dawn*, p. 183.

68. Ibid., pp. 185–86.

69. Ibid., p. 189.

70. Ibid., p. 217.

71. Ibid., p. 219.

72. Rampersad, *Art and Imagination*, p. 209. The novel's hero, Matthew Towns, embraces as his revolutionary vision a society guided by an oligarchy of excellence. Rampersad rightly identifies the theme as Towns's "search for an aristocracy of merit" (p. 217) and notes—on the basis of a plot in which Afro-American struggle hinges on leadership by an assemblage of Third World revolutionaries—"Where Du Bois had seen the civilizing of Afro-Americans as a moral responsibility of the white world, he was now transferring the burden to darker but still foreign backs" (p. 210).

73. W. E. B. Du Bois, "What Is Wrong with the NAACP?" conference address, May 18, 1932, *Du Bois Papers*, Reel 80 #492–93.

74. Ibid.

75. The limitations of this kind of self-criticism were disclosed in their extremes to a later generation, which witnessed in the 1970s first Louis Althusser's intellectual contortions and then those of the American Maoists who squabbled over the carcass of the New Left. The latter, with each new ideological turn made and each new party proclaimed, engaged in a ritual of "summing up," in which no earlier positions were examined and transcended, only declared no longer appropriate for the "new stage." Russell Jacoby discusses these developments in "The Politics of Objectivity: Notes on the U.S. Left," *Telos* (winter 1977–78): 74–88.

76. W. E. B. Du Bois, *The Correspondence of W. E. B. Du Bois*, 3 vols., Herbert Aptheker, ed., (Amherst, Mass., 1973–78), vol. 2, p. 92.

77. W. E. B. Du Bois, "The Talented Tenth: The Re-Examination of a Concept," address to the Sigma Pi Phi Grand Boulé, Wilberforce, Ohio, August 12, 1948, *Du Bois Papers*, Reel 80 #1092.

78. Ibid., #1110–11.

79. Ibid., #1093. He also criticized them for repudiating the idea of a Negro culture, and raised the spectre of a large Negro "nation" in the United States in objecting to their course of "complete effacement and utter nirvana in another and foreign entity." As with most proponents of the idea of a politically significant racial culture in this century, that notion was intrinsically connected in Du Bois's thought with the special responsibilities—and special status—of the black elite. I have taken up the problem of this pivotal though often overlooked aspect of Afro-American nationalism in "The Black Revolution and the Reconstitution of Domination," in Reed, ed., *Race, Politics and Culture: Critical Essays on the Radicalism of the Sixties* (Westport, Conn., 1986).

80. *Du Bois Papers*, #1109–10. His construction tells more than his statement; the "mass" remains inert and amorphous, devoid of subjectivity and fit only to be administered.

81. Ibid., #1120.

82. Ibid., #1117.

83. Ibid., #1121. He also called for greater emphasis on art and culture in home life (#1120).

84. Ibid., #1111.

85. Ibid., #1112–13.

86. Ibid., #1119–20. If this were not sufficiently repressive, he reached back further into his progressivist roots to condemn gambling.

87. Ibid., #1121. It is very difficult to comprehend how Gerald Horne could refer to this text as an indication of Du Bois's disavowal of elitism Horne, *Black and Red*, p. 7).

88. W. E. B. Du Bois, "How United Are Negroes?" in Du Bois, *Seventh Son*, vol. 2 p. 630, *National Guardian*.

89. W. E. B. Du Bois, *In Battle for Peace: The Story of My 83rd Birthday* (New York, 1952), pp. 76–77.

90. Du Bois, "How United Are Negroes?" p. 632.

91. Ibid.

92. Du Bois, *In Battle for Peace*, p. 77.

93. Ibid.

94. W. E. B. Du Bois, "Speech by Dr. William E. B. Du Bois, A.L.P. Candidate for U.S. Senator at A.L.P. Rally, Golden Gate Ballroom," in Du Bois, *Seventh Son*, p. 604.

95. Du Bois, "How United Are Negroes?" p. 631. He continued to exhort the black intelligentsia to fulfill the mission he had set for it more than a half century earlier. See W. E. B. Du Bois, "The Negro and Socialism," in Helen Alfred, ed., *Toward a Socialist America: A Symposium of Essays by Fifteen Contemporary American Socialists* (New York, 1958), esp. p. 188.

Chapter 6

1. Exemplary, although unevenly successful, efforts to confront this general problem—in addition to the work of Arnold Rampersad and Wilson J. Moses—are Hanes Walton, "Black Political Thought: The Problem of Characterization," *Journal of Black*

Studies 1 (December 1970); 213–18; S. P. Fullinwider, *The Mind and Mood of Black America* (Homewood, Ill., 1969); Herbert Storing, Introduction to Storing, ed., *What Country Have I?: Political Writing of Black Americans* (New York, 1970); Alex Willingham, "Ideology and Politics: Their Status in Afro-American Social Theory," in Adolph L. Reed Jr., ed. *Race, Politics, and Culture: Critical Essays on the Radicalism of the 1960s* (Westport, Conn., 1986); William S. Toll, *The Resurgence of Race: Black Social Theory from Reconstruction to the Pan-African Conferences* (Philadelphia, 1979); and Harold Cruse, *The Crisis of the Negro Intellectual: From Its Origins to the Present* (New York, 1967).

2. This is not to say that interracialism was generally accepted among Du Bois's contemporaries; rather, in the system of relevance that structured the earlier political debates, the proper forms of interracial contact seldom surfaced as an issue for explicit discussion. Even though different writers might be shown to have held different implicit positions on the matter, it was not sufficiently meaningful in the context of their commonly conceived project of discourse to warrant contention.

3. Howard Brotz, in Brotz, ed., *Negro Social and Political Thought: Representative Texts* (New York, 1966). Wilson J. Moses also sees Du Bois as a nationalist, even a "racial chauvinist" (Moses, *The Golden Age of Black Nationalism, 1850–1925* [New York, 1988], pp. 144–45). Manning Marable, never to be outdone at piling up labels, sees Du Bois's outlook as a "synthesis of racial democracy, cultural pluralism, pan-Africanism and socialism" (*W. E. B. Du Bois: Black Radical Democrat* [Boston, 1986], p. 91).

4. Cruse, *Crisis of the Negro Intellectual.*

5. Sterling Stuckey, *Slave Culture; Nationalist Theory and the Foundations of Black America* (New York and London, 1987), p. 291.

6. Vincent Harding, "W. E. B. Du Bois and the Black Messianic Vision," in John Henrik Clarke et al., eds., *Black Titan: W. E. B. Du Bois* (Boston, 1970).

7. W. E. B. Du Bois, *The Gift of Black Folk: The Negroes in the Making of America* (1924; reprint, New York, 1970). Also see William T. Fontaine, "The Mind and Thought of the Negro of the United States as Revealed in Imaginative Literature, 1876–1940," *Southern University Bulletin* 28 (March 1942): 20–22.

8. Ibid., p. 158.

9. W. E. B. Du Bois, *The Souls of Black Folk* (1903; reprint, New York, 1907), pp. 85–86.

10. Ibid., p. 172.

11. Du Bois, *The Philadelphia Negro* (1899; reprint, New York, 1967), p. 317. Moses notes that an authoritarian component typically accompanied racial collectivist ideology among black American intellectuals during the early modern period (*Golden Age of Black Nationalism*, pp. 21–22).

12. Du Bois, *Philadelphia Negro*, p. 318.

13. See, for example, his two studies: W. E. B. Du Bois, *Some Efforts of American Negroes for Their Own Social Betterment* (Atlanta, 1898), and Du Bois, *Economic Cooperation among Negro Americans* (Atlanta, 1907).

14. W. E. B. Du Bois, "A Pageant in Seven Decades" (1938), in Du Bois, *W. E. B. Du Bois Speaks: Speeches and Addresses, 1920–1963*, Philip S. Foner, ed., 2 vols. (New York, 1970), vol. 2 p. 66.

15. W. E. B. Du Bois, *Dusk of Dawn: An Essay toward an Autobiography of a Race Concept* (1940; reprint, New York, 1968), p. 295.

16. Ibid., p. 296.

17. Ibid., pp. 171–172.

18. W. E. B. Du Bois, "My Evolving Program for Negro Freedom," in Rayford W. Logan, ed., *What the Negro Wants* (Chapel Hill, N.C., 1944), p. 70.

19. W. E. B. Du Bois, "The Tragedy of 'Jim Crow,' " *The Crisis* 26 (August 1923): 170. On Cheyney State, see ibid., p. 172. See also Du Bois, "The Dilemma of the Negro," *American Mercury* 3 (October 1924): 179–85.

20. W. E. B. Du Bois, "The Position of the Negro in the American Social Order: Where Do We Go from Here?" *Journal of Negro Education* 8 (July 1939): 565–66.

21. Ibid.

22. W. E. B. Du Bois, "Prospect of a World without Race Conflict," *American Journal of Sociology* 49 (March 1944): 456.

23. Du Bois, "Position of the Negro," p. 565. Du Bois advanced this view also as a criticism of individualistic black entrepreneurial activity; see Mark David Higbee, "W. E. B. Du Bois, F. B. Ransom, the Madam Walker Company, and Black Business Leadership in the 1930s," *Indiana Magazine of History* 89 (June 1993): 101–24.

24. Du Bois, "Position of the Negro," p. 569.

25. Du Bois, *Dusk of Dawn*, p. 296.

26. Ibid., p. 305. Moses, in identifying a strain of nationalistic thinking among prominent black "race men," demonstrates that Du Bois's charge was at best an exaggeration; see his *Golden Age of Black Nationalism*. Du Bois's objective here, however, is hortatory rather than analytical. It is understandable, therefore, that his narrative rests on the hyperbolic claims of a jeremiad rather than the cautious empiricism of a scholarly description. Judith Stein, in *The World of Marcus Garvey: Race and Class in Modern Society* (Baton Rouge, La., 1986), has argued persuasively that even the Garvey movement's social base was concentrated in the aspiring petite bourgeoisie.

27. Du Bois, *Dusk of Dawn*, pp. 309–10.

28. Ibid., p. 310.

29. See, for example, W. E. B. Du Bois, "On Being Ashamed of Oneself: An Essay on Race Pride," *Crisis* 40 (September 1933): 199–200, and Du Bois, "Prospect of a World."

30. See Du Bois's editorials in the *Crisis* 41.

31. W. E. B. Du Bois, *Crisis* 41 (May 1934): 149.

32. W. E. B. Du Bois, *Crisis* 41 (June 1934): 184.

33. Francis L. Broderick, *W. E. B. Du Bois: Negro Leader in a Time of Crisis* (Palo Alto, Calif., 1959), pp. 172–73.

34. It is significant here to note that Du Bois defined his conflict within the NAACP as "not an absolute difference of principle, but it was a grave difference as to further procedure" (*Dusk of Dawn*, p. 313).

35. W. E. B. Du Bois, "Back to Africa," *Century* 105 (February 1923): 546–47.

36. Du Bois, "Dilemma of the Negro," p. 184.

37. W. E. B. Du Bois, "As the Crow Flies," *Chicago Globe*, April 12, 1950.

38. Du Bois, "Dilemma of the Negro," p. 180.

39. Ibid.

40. See, for example, Horace M. Kallen, *Culture and Democracy in the United States* (New York, 1924), and Kallen, *Cultural Pluralism and the American Idea* (Philadelphia, 1956). For a perspective on the conceptual and practical limitations of cultural pluralism for black Americans, see Oliver C. Cox, "The Question of Pluralism," *Race* 12 (fourth quarter 1971): 385–400; John Higham, *Send These to Me: Jews and Other Immi-*

grants in Urban America (New York, 1975), pp. 203–8; and Werner Sollors, "A Critique of Pure Pluralism," in Sacvan Bercovitch, ed., *Reconstructing American Literary History* (Cambridge, Mass., 1986).

41. David Levering Lewis, "Parallels and Divergences: Assimilationist Strategies of Afro-American and Jewish Elites from 1910 to the Early 1930s," *Journal of American History* 71 (December 1984): 545.

42. Kallen, *Culture and Democracy*, p. 124. David A. Hollinger maintains that Kallen "was not so much for cross-fertilization as for the harmonious cooperation and mutual enrichment of clearly defined, contrasting, durable ethnic units" (*In the American Province: Studies in the History and Historiography of Ideas* [Bloomington, Ind., 1985], p. 65).

43. For comparisons of Kallen and Du Bois in this respect, see Werner Sollors, *Beyond Ethnicity: Consent and Descent in American Literature* (New York, 1986), pp. 181–88, and Higham, *Send These to Me*, pp. 209–12. William T. Fontaine also emphasizes Du Bois's subordination of racial particularity to a "broader *human* perspective" (*Reflections on Segregation, Desegregation, Power and Morals* (Springfield, Ill., 1967), pp. 12–13. From this vantage point Du Bois arguably had more in common with his statist Harvard classmate, Herbert Croly, than with Kallen. See Croly's *The Promise of American Life* (1909; reprint, Indianapolis, 1965); David Levy, *Herbert Croly of the New Republic* (Princeton, N.J., 1985); Charles Forcey, *The Crossroads of Liberalism: Croly, Weyl, Lippman, and the Progressive Era, 1900–1925* (New York, 1961), pp. 3–51; and R. Jeffrey Lustig, *Corporate Liberalism: The Origins of Modern American Political Theory, 1890–1920* (Berkeley, Calif., 1982), pp. 211–16.

44. Recent Du Bois scholarship has stressed his links to Alexander Crummell in seeking the sources of his racial views. (See, for example, Marable, Moses, and Stuckey.) Crummell most likely did influence Du Bois's early formulations of the specifically black variant of racial idealism. There are, however, at least three reasons for emphasizing instead the wider reform Darwinist and Lamarckian evolutionist tendencies' significance. First, Crummell's racial organicism was itself an instance of the broader orientation toward teleological evolutionism (see Moses, *Golden Age of Black Nationalism*, pp. 59–61). Second, Du Bois had absorbed a disposition toward that orientation through his Harvard and Berlin experiences prior to his close association with Crummell. Finally, although Du Bois's link to Crummell is no doubt salient biographically, that focus can obscure the extent to which both Crummell and Du Bois operated within a more general context of intellectual conventions. Not surprisingly, the scholars who have emphasized Crummell's influence on Du Bois have been concerned to establish the contours of autonomous Afro-American intellectual traditions. It is instructive that only Moses and David Levering Lewis, who are least inclined among them to argue for a wholly independent black philosophical orientation, seek to situate both subjects *within* contemporaneous intellectual currents. The most careful and reasonable efforts to situate Du Bois *and* Crummell, in addition to Moses's *Golden Age of Black Nationalism*, are Wilson J. Moses, "W. E. B. Du Bois's 'The Conservation of Races' and Its Context: Idealism, Conservatism and Hero Worship" *Massachusetts Review* (summer 1993): 275–94, and David Levering Lewis, *W. E. B. Du Bois: Biography of a Race, 1868–1919* (New York, 1993), pp. 161–70.

45. W. E. B. Du Bois, *Color and Democracy: Colonies and Peace* (New York, 1945), p. 70.

46. Ibid., p. 10.

47. Moses, *Golden Age of Black Nationalism*, p. 133.

48. Lewis describes Du Bois's effusions of rationalist optimism surrounding the 1911 Universal Races Congress in *Biography of a Race*, pp. 439–41.

49. Moses, *Golden Age of Black Nationalism*, p. 133.

50. W. E. B. Du Bois, "The Future of Africa—A Platform" (1919), in Du Bois, *Du Bois Speaks*, vol. 1 p. 273.

51. W. E. B. Du Bois, "The Pan-African Movement" (1945), in Du Bois, *Du Bois Speaks*, vol. 2 p. 166. Moreover, the second Pan-African Congress declared in part that, "The Negro race, through their thinking intelligentsia, demand . . . recognition of civilized men as civilized, despite their race or color" (ibid., p. 170). Stuckey nevertheless observes that Du Bois in his early years "underestimated the power of contemporary African cultures" but reassures us that the notion that Western blacks should lead Africa out of darkness was a "position from which [Du Bois] later backed away" (*Slave Culture*, p. 259).

52. "There are . . . in the United States today several commendable groups of young people who are proposing to take hold of Liberia and emancipate her from her difficulties, quite forgetting the fact that Liberia belongs to Liberia," W. E. B. Du Bois, "Pan-Africa and the New Racial Philosophy," *Crisis* 49 (November 1933): 247. Du Bois articulated this position in the context of accusations that the Americo-Liberian aristocracy was practicing slavery.

53. W. E. B. Du Bois, *Crisis* 23 (February 1922): 155. This criticism was directed specifically at Garveyism in general and Garvey's dispute with the Liberian elite in particular; Du Bois not unreasonably chose the Americo-Liberians over Garvey.

54. Ibid., p. 154.

55. Ibid.

56. W. E. B. Du Bois, "American Negroes and Africa's Rise to Freedom" (1961), in Du Bois, *The Seventh Son: The Thought and the Writings of W. E. B. Du Bois*, Julius Lester, ed., 2 vols. (New York, 1971), vol. 2, pp. 693–94.

57. That "tribalism" and its variants are mainly European colonial imports to Africa (see W. E. B. Du Bois, "The Saga of Nkrumah," *National Guardian*, July 30, 1956) and that "Pan-African socialism seeks the welfare state in Africa" (Du Bois, "A Future for Pan-Africa: Freedom, Peace, Socialism," in Du Bois, *Seventh Son*, vol. 2, p. 649) obviated any such attention.

58. Du Bois "Future of Africa," pp. 660–61. This passage suggests that the spirit of Du Bois's admiration of Bismarck never completely disappeared.

59. W. E. B. Du Bois, *The World and Africa: An Inquiry into the Part Which Africa Has Played in World History* (1947; reprint, New York, 1965). Even here, however, he genuflects toward cultural pluralism in according Asia and Africa the status of civilizations along with Europe.

60. Du Bois, "Pan-Africa and the New Racial Philosophy," p. 247.

61. Du Bois, *Crisis* 23 (April 1922): 251–52.

62. Du Bois, *Crisis* 17 (February 1919): 166.

63. Ibid.

64. Du Bois, *Dusk of Dawn*, p. 304.

65. For critical interpretations of Garveyite Pan-Africanism, see Stein, *World of Marcus Garvey*, and Adolph L. Reed Jr., "The Political Philosophy of Pan-Africanism: A Study of the Writings of Du Bois, Garvey, Nkrumah and Padmore and Their Legacy," M.A. thesis, Atlanta University, 1975. Post–Black Power Pan-Africanism is analyzed systematically in Charles Hopkins, "Pan-Africanism: A Theoretical Examination of Contemporary Afro-American Involvement," M.A. thesis, University of North Carolina, Chapel Hill, N.C., 1974. See also Adolph L. Reed Jr.: "Pan-Africanism: Ideology for Liberation?" *The Black Scholar* (September 1971), and Reed, "Pan-Africanism as Black Liberalism:

Du Bois and Garvey," in Ofuatey-Kodjoe, ed., *Pan-Africanism: New Directions in Strategy* (Lanham, Md., 1986).

66. Du Bois, "Future for Pan-Africa," p. 649.

67. Ibid. Preservation in this context evokes the appropriate image—that of the fossilized museum piece.

68. W. E. B. Du Bois, "The Future of Africa" (Address to the All-African People's Conference, Accra, Ghana, December 22, 1958), in Du Bois, *Seventh Son*, vol. 2, pp. 658–59.

69. Broderick, *Negro Leader*, p. 123.

70. Elliott M. Rudwick, *W. E. B. Du Bois: A Study in Minority Group Leadership* (Philadelphia, 1960), p. 51.

71. Alan Sigmund Cywar, "An Inquiry into American Thought and Determinate Influence of Political Economic and Social Factors in the Early Twentieth Century: Bourne, Dewey, Du Bois, Nearing, Veblen, and Weyl," Ph.D. dissertation, University of Rochester, Rochester, N.Y., 1972, pp. 330–31.

72. Ibid., p. 340.

73. Eugene C. Holmes, "Du Bois: Philosopher," in Clarke et al., eds., *Black Titan*, p. 80.

74. Bernard Fonlon, "The Passing of a Great African," in Clarke et al., eds. *Black Titan*, p. 220.

75. Lester, Introduction, to Du Bois, *Seventh Son*, vol. 1, p. 137.

76. W. Alphaeus Hunton, "W. E. B. Du Bois: The Meaning of His Life," in Clarke et al., eds., *Black Titan*, p. 176.

77. Truman Nelson, "W. E. B. Du Bois as a Prophet," in Clarke et al., eds., *Black Titan*, p. 145.

78. Gerald Horne, *Black and Red: W. E. B. Du Bois and the Afro-American Response to the Cold War, 1944–1963* (Albany, 1986), p. 5.

79. Marable, *Black Radical Democrat*, p. 83.

80. Moses, *Golden Age of Black Nationalism*, p. 139.

81. Ibid., p. 140; see also Lewis, *Biography of a Race*, pp. 143, 543.

82. See Ira Kipnis, *The American Socialist Movement, 1897–1912* (New York, 1952); James Weinstein, *The Decline of Socialism in America, 1912–1925* (New York, 1969).

83. James Gilbert, *Designing the Industrial State: The Intellectual Pursuit of Collectivism in America, 1880–1940* (Chicago, 1972); Mark Pittenger, *American Socialists and Evolutionary Thought, 1870–1920* (Madison, Wis., 1993).

84. Gilbert, *Industrial State*, p. 64.

85. Ibid. Pittenger also stresses the concern of a reform tendency to construct a socialist vision shorn of Marxism's radical implications and propagation of a rhetoric of necessary social conflict *(American Socialists)*.

86. Marable, for example, contends that Du Bois was always essentially a "radical democrat" *(Black Radical Democrat*, p. 195). Moses sees him as having been a "radical liberal" *(Golden Age of Black Nationalism*, p. 144) and maintains, furthermore, that his attraction to Communism rested on "black nationalistic rather than on Marxist grounds" (ibid., p. 140). By contrast, the burden of Horne's entire interpretation of Du Bois is validation of the premise that he was always a Marxist—even before recognizing it *(Black and Red*, e.g. pp. 289–90). Lewis's account locates—correctly, in my view—Du Bois's early socialist affinities as outcroppings of his rationalist and scientistic commitments *(Biography of a Race*, pp. 144, 338).

87. Du Bois affirmed his belief that "the end of economic reform is socialism, or as some would call it 'collectivism'; but I also just as firmly believe that the next step toward this is consumers' co-operation and that for the American Negro it is the only step" (Du Bois, *Pittsburgh Courier*, March 28, 1936). For theoretical discussion of the convergence of Marxism and liberal collectivism see Russell Jacoby, "What Is Conformist Marxism?" *Telos* (fall 1980): 19–44; Alvin W. Gouldner, *The Two Marxisms: Contradictions and Anomalies in the Development of Theory* (New York, 1980); and Michael Urban, *The Ideology of Administration: American and Soviet Cases* (Albany, 1982).

88. W. E. B. Du Bois, *Crisis* 22 (September 1921): 199–200.

89. W. E. B. Du Bois, *Crisis* 22 (October 1921); 245.

90. Ibid., p. 246.

91. W. E. B. Du Bois, *Darkwater: Voices from within the Veil* (1920; reprint, New York, 1969), p. 98.

92. Ibid., p. 100.

93. Ibid., p. 101.

94. Ibid., p. 103.

95. Ibid., p. 157.

96. Du Bois observed that the "essential difficulty with liberalism in the twentieth century was not to realize the fundamental change brought about by the worldwide organization of work and trade and commerce" ("Pageant in Seven Decades," p. 64).

97. W. E. B. Du Bois, "Marxism and the Negro Problem," *Crisis* 40 (May 1933), p. 103.

98. Du Bois, *Dusk of Dawn*, p. 289. Also, after citing inequitable taxation, imperialism, fluctuation in gold prices, and myriad indicators of the "fundamental unsoundness" of industrial capitalism, he observed, "Beyond all this lies the great fact that income is a social product and not simply the result of individual effort. Income is and must be divided by human judgment. That judgment must eventually be determined by social ethics and controlled by wider and more intelligent democracy in all industry" (*Crisis* 37 [December 1930]: 426).

99. Du Bois, *Dusk of Dawn*, pp. 189–90.

100. W. E. B. Du Bois, *Crisis* 32 (June 1926): 64.

101. See, for example, John P. Diggins's two volumes: *Up from Communism: Conservative Odysseys in American Intellectual History* (New York, 1975) and *The American Left in the Twentieth Century* (New York, 1973); Daniel Aaron, *Writers on the Left* (New York, 1961).

102. Du Bois, "My Evolving Program," p. 60. As Broderick (*Negro Leader*, p. 193) observes, that Du Bois in the interwar period tended to support Trotsky and Radek over Stalin has little bearing here. At issue is the outlook that the three Soviet antagonists shared, commitment to a model of a command society of mass mobilization.

103. Du Bois, *World and Africa*, p. 256.

104. Ibid.

105. Du Bois detected early, along with and presumably independently of his German contemporaries associated with the Frankfurt Institute, the fundamental homology uniting Fascism, Bolshevism, and the New Deal (*Dusk of Dawn*, p. 288); he expressed a need to adjust the orthodox critique of capitalism to account for the rise of a "new class of technical engineers and managers" and other internal systemic changes in the twentieth century ("Marxism and the Negro Problem," p. 104), and he demonstrated a sense of the significance of the mass-culture apparatus, planned obsolescence and intensified

marketing in the contemporary social management synthesis (*World and Africa*, pp. 254–56). See also his discussion of the growth of a permanent white-collar class in "The American Negro and the Labor Movement," Reel 80 #894, *Du Bois Papers*.

106. W. E. B. Du Bois, *Pittsburgh Courier*, June 5, 1937. He expressed a need for the black "mass" to "be induced to submit itself to the dictatorship which is best and quickest for bringing . . . an economic development which is primarily for the benefit of [that] laboring mass" (ibid). William E. Cain notes the persistence of Du Bois's attraction to "comprehensive organization, centralized authority, rational planning on a massive basis, exhaustive gathering and sifting of facts, and highly disciplined, tightly controlled attitudes toward work," from his youthful fascination with Bismarck to his support for Stalinism; see Cain, "From Liberalism to Communism: The Political Thought of W. E. B. Du Bois," in Amy Kaplan and Donald E. Pease, eds., *Cultures of United States Imperialism* (Durham, N.C., 1993), p. 466. Cain attempts to determine when Du Bois became a Marxist, with no greater success than others who have undertaken to chart that transition.

107. Du Bois, "Future of Africa," pp. 658–59.

108. W. E. B. Du Bois, "The Negro and Socialism" in Helen L. Alfred, ed., *Toward a Socialist America: A Symposium of Essays* (New York, 1958), pp. 190–91.

109. For detailed examination of the atrophy of the CPUSA in this period, see Joseph R. Starobin, *American Communism in Crisis, 1943–1957* (Berkeley, Calif., 1972). On the decline of a Left opposition in the postwar West more generally, see C. Wright Mills, *Power Politics and People: The Collected Essays of C. Wright Mills*, Irving Louis Horowitz, ed. (New York, 1963); Peter Clecak, *Radical Paradoxes: Dilemmas of the American Left, 1945–1970* (New York, 1973); and E. J. Hobsbawm, *Revolutionaries* (New York, 1973).

110. Although Horne argues that Du Bois enjoyed considerable support from black elites during his persecution in the postwar years, he almost certainly overstates his case. One of his own sources, for example, while noting that Du Bois's black supporters were ardent, pointed out also that they "were very few" (*Black and Red*, p. 257).

111. Du Bois had declared during the Depression that "Russia would welcome an autonomous Negro state within her boundaries. Are there no Negroes young or old who have the guts to leave America?" (*Pittsburgh Courier*, February 29, 1936.

112. W. E. B. Du Bois, "Behold the Land," in Du Bois, *Seventh Son*, vol. 2, p. 583.

113. "Interview with Dr. W. E. B. Du Bois," in Du Bois, *Seventh Son*, vol. 2, pp. 701–3.

114. "The American worker himself does not always realize [his mission]. He has high wages and many comforts. Rather than lose these, he keeps in office by his votes the servants of industrial exploitation so long as they maintain his wage. His labor leaders represent exploitation and not the fight against the exploitation of labor by private capital" (W. E. B. Du Bois, "Hail Humankind!" in Du Bois, *Du Bois Speaks*, p. 318.

115. Du Bois, *Color and Democracy*, pp. 83–84.

116. Ibid., p. 73. He went on to indicate that the lack of intelligence and experience derived from poverty (p. 74).

117. Du Bois, "Negro and Socialism," p. 180.

118. Ibid., p. 183.

119. Ibid., p. 179.

120. Gilbert, *Industrial State*, pp. 7–8, and Louis Lindsay, "The Pluralist Persuasion in American Democratic Thought," *Social and Economic Studies* 22 (December 1973): 479–513; see also Lustig, *Corporate Liberalism*, pp. 120–49.

121. See, for example, Toll's discussion of the structuring principles of black discourse in this period in *The Resurgence of Race*. The theme of adjustment to industrialization is also visible in August Meier's account in *Negro Thought in America, 1880–1915: Racial Ideologies in the Age of Booker T. Washington* (Ann Arbor, Mich., 1963); and, in a more limited compass, Kevin Gaines, "Black Americans' Racial Uplift Ideology as 'Civilizing Mission': Pauline E. Hopkins on Race and Imperialism," in Kaplan and Pease, eds., *Cultures of United States Imperialism*.

Chapter 7

1. The text of the epigraph appears on p. 3 of *The Souls of Black Folk* (1903; reprint, Chicago, 1907).

2. August Meier, *Negro Thought in America 1880–1915: Racial Ideologies in the Age of Booker T. Washington* (Ann Arbor, Mich., 1963), p. 190.

3. Harold R. Isaacs, *The New World of Negro Americans* (New York, 1963), p. 97. Isaacs repeated this appropriation of Du Bois over a decade later, asserting the persistence of a collective black struggle "to shake the blur into some single or coherent image" (Isaacs, *Idols of the Tribe* [New York, 1975], p. 198).

4. Robert Ezra Park, *Race and Culture: Essays in the Sociology of Contemporary Man* (New York, 1950), p. 291.

5. Everett V. Stonequist, "Race Mixture and the Mulatto," in Edgar T. Thompson, ed., *Race Relations and the Race Problem: A Definition and an Analysis* (Durham, N.C., 1939), p. 266.

6. St. Clair Drake, "The Social and Economic Status of the Negro in the United States," in Talcott Parsons and Kenneth B. Clark, eds., *The Negro American* (Boston, 1967), p. 34. Versions of most of the essays in this volume, including Drake's, had appeared in the fall 1965 and winter 1966 issues of *Daedalus*.

7. Gunnar Myrdal, *An American Dilemma: The Negro Problem and Modern Democracy*, 2 vols. (1944; reprint, New York, 1962), vol. 2, p. 809. Before quoting Du Bois, Myrdal also quotes Bertram Schrieke on black Americans' "double consciousness." Schrieke was a Dutch colonial official and anthropologist who, rather like Myrdal himself, had been hired in the early 1930s by the Julius Rosenwald Fund "to make a study of Negro life and education, especially in the Southern states, on the basis of [his] extensive but quite different experience with race relations in the Orient" (Bertram F. O. Schrieke, *Alien Americans: A Study of Race Relations* [New York, 1936], p. vii). Although Schrieke does not cite Du Bois for the double-consciousness reference, *The Souls of Black Folk* does appear in his bibliography.

8. Robert Blauner, *Racial Oppression in America* (New York, 1972), pp. 69–70. Thomas L. Blair also, though without the rhetorical flourish of the colonial analogy, attached Du Bois's "two-ness" to the integration/nationalism dichotomy; see his *Retreat to the Ghetto* (London, 1977), pp. 25–26.

9. Charles A. Valentine, "Deficit, Difference and Bicultural Models of Afro-American Behavior," *Harvard Educational Review* 41 (May 1971): 143–44.

10. Carol B. Stack, *All Our Kin: Strategies for Survival in a Black Community* (New York, 1974), pp. 26–27.

11. Robert Staples, *Introduction to Black Sociology* (New York, 1976), pp. 67–68.

12. Harold M. Baron, "The Web of Urban Racism," in Louis L. Knowles and Kenneth Prewitt, eds., *Institutional Racism in America* (New York, 1969), pp. 173–74.

13. Nathan I. Huggins, *Harlem Renaissance* (New York, 1971), pp. 244–45.

14. George E. Kent, "Patterns of the Harlem Renaissance," in Arna Bontemps, ed., *The Harlem Renaissance Remembered* (New York, 1972), p. 50.

15. Larry Neal, "And Shine Swam On," in LeRoi Jones and Larry Neal, eds., *Black Fire: An Anthology of Afro-American Writing* (New York, 1968), pp. 640–41; John O'Neal, "Black Arts: Notebook," in Addison Gayle Jr., ed., *The Black Aesthetic* (Garden City, N.Y., 1971), pp. 48–50; Hoyt W. Fuller, "The New Black Literature: Protest or Affirmation," in Gayle, ed., *The Black Aesthetic*, pp. 348–50.

16. Houston A. Baker Jr., *Long Black Song: Essays in Black American Literature and Culture* (Charlottesville, Va., 1972), p. 17.

17. Sterling Stuckey, *Slave Culture: Nationalist Theory and the Foundations of Black America* (New York, 1987), pp. 274–75. Stuckey's construction of black authenticity does, however, endorse a principle of selective repudiation of alien influences.

18. Manning Marable, *Black American Politics: From the Washington Marches to Jesse Jackson* (London, 1985), p. 56. Elsewhere, Marable asserts that the "essential duality" Du Bois identified is the source of the "most fundamental characteristics of modern Black political life" (Marable, "The Contradictory Contours of Black Political Culture," in Mike Davis et al., eds., *The Year Left 2: Toward a Rainbow Socialism: Essays on Race, Ethnicity, Class and Gender* [London, 1987], p. 1).

19. Bettye J. Gardner, "The Teaching of Afro-American History in Schools and Colleges," in Darlene Clark Hine, ed., *The State of Afro-American History: Past, Present and Future* (Baton Rouge, La., 1986), p. 172.

20. Waldo E. Martin, *The Mind of Frederick Douglass* (Chapel Hill, N.C., 1984), p. 106.

21. Maulana Karenga, "Society, Culture, and the Problem of Self-Consciousness: A Kawaida Analysis," in Leonard Harris, ed., *Philosophy Born of Struggle: Anthology of Afro-American Philosophy from 1917* (Dubuque, Iowa, 1983), pp. 214–15.

22. Lucius Outlaw, "African-American Philosophy: Social and Political Case Studies," *Social Science Information* 26 (first quarter 1987): 80–83.

23. Ibid., 77–78.

24. Robert C. Williams, "W. E. B. Du Bois: Afro-American Philosopher of Social Reality," in Harris, ed., *Philosophy Born of Struggle*, p. 17.

25. Thomas F. Slaughter Jr., "Epidermalizing the World: A Basic Mode of Being Black," in Harris, ed., *Philosophy Born of Struggle*, pp. 283–84.

26. Cornel West, *Prophesy Deliverance!: An Afro-American Revolutionary Christianity* (Philadelphia, 1982), pp. 30–31.

27. Ibid., p. 31. Paul Gilroy expands on West's already broad view of the phenomenon by extrapolating it to the entire Atlantic region, contending that double consciousness is the "resolution of a familiar problem which points towards the core dynamic of racial oppression as well as the fundamental antinomy of diaspora blacks" (*The Black Atlantic: Modernity and Double Consciousness* [Cambridge, Mass., 1993], p. 30).

28. West, *Prophesy Deliverance!*, p. 24.

29. Ibid., p. 15. Because West consistently refers without clarification to Afro-American "philosophy," "critical philosophy," "critical thought," and "religious philosophy" when discussing his program, my use of "secular" here may seem ambiguous. I use the term to denote activity and phenomena situated outside self-contained, specialized discursive communities associated with academic disciplines and subdisciplines.

30. Ibid., p. 23.

31. Henry Louis Gates Jr., *The Signifying Monkey: A Theory of Afro-American Literary Criticism* (New York and Oxford, 1988), p. xxiii.

32. Henry Louis Gates Jr., *Figures in Black: Words, Signs and the "Racial" Self* (New York and Oxford, 1987), p. 276. Other scholars of Afro-American literature recently have made use of Du Bois's formulation in arguments concerning the status and character of black literary tradition. Michael Awkward sees double consciousness as "the merging of the binary opposites 'spirit' and 'matter' for which the Afro-American strives" and as a precursor of Toni Morrison's "dual voices of narrator and protagonist" in *The Bluest Eye*; see Awkward, *Inspiriting Influences: Tradition, Revision and Afro-American Women's Novels* (New York, 1989), p. 12. Barbara Johnson endorses the premise of a distinctive racial two-ness; she then criticizes Du Bois and James Weldon Johnson for having assumed the black voice's maleness, noting that women also have been forced to be two-voiced; see her "Metaphor, Metonymy and Voice in *Their Eyes Were Watching God*," in Henry Louis Gates Jr., ed., *Black Literature and Literary Theory* (New York and London, 1984), pp. 214–15.

33. Gates, *Signifying Monkey*, p. xxv. Tropological revision is one of four types of "double-voiced textual relations" that Gates identifies in the black tradition.

34. Gates, *Figures in Black*, pp. 56–57.

35. Ibid., p. 44.

36. Gates, *Signifying Monkey*, p. 207.

37. Henry Louis Gates Jr., Introduction to W. E. B. Du Bois, *The Souls of Black Folk* (1903; reprint, New York, 1989), p. xiv.

38. Edward Hallett Carr, *What Is History?* (New York, 1961), p. 28.

39. See my discussion of this notion in chapter 1. It is noteworthy that, despite the extensive appropriations of Du Bois's passage in support of arguments about black people's empirical condition in the United States, the formulation until very recently had gone virtually unnoticed among Afro-Americanist intellectual historians. I discuss this issue at length in chapter 8.

40. Francis L. Broderick, *W. E. B. Du Bois: Negro Leader in a Time of Crisis* (Palo Alto, Calif., 1959), pp. 102–3; Jack B. Moore, *W. E. B. Du Bois* (Boston, 1981), pp. 68–69. Peter Conn both asserts the source of the two-ness reference in Du Bois's personality and credits him with having discovered a generic racial condition; see Conn, *The Divided Mind: Ideology and Imagination in America, 1898–1917* (Cambridge and New York, 1983), pp. 148–49.

41. Lawrence W. Levine, *Black Culture and Black Consciousness: Afro-American Folk Thought from Slavery to Freedom* (New York, 1977), p. 151.

42. Wilson J. Moses, *The Golden Age of Black Nationalism, 1850–1925* (New York, 1988), pp. 136–37. Though he does not focus on the two-ness notion, William S. Toll also provides a very useful account which situates *The Souls of Black Folk* in an enveloping black discursive community; see his *The Resurgence of Race: Black Social Theory from Reconstruction to the Pan-African Conferences* (Philadelphia, 1979), pp. 118–19; see also David Levering Lewis, *W. E. B. Du Bois: Biography of a Race, 1868–1919* (New York, 1993), esp. pp. 265–96.

43. Robert Gooding-Williams, "Philosophy of History and Social Critique in *The Souls of Black Folk*," *Social Science Information* 26 (first quarter 1987): 106–8. Gilroy also claims to find Hegelian roots for the double-consciousness passage (*Black Atlantic*, p. 134). Lewis notes Du Bois's general fondness for Hegel but resists claiming unique lines of influence; see *Biography of a Race*, pp. 134, 139–140, 165.

44. Arnold Rampersad, *The Art and Imagination of W. E. B. Du Bois* (Cambridge, Mass., 1976), p. 74; see also his "Biography and Afro-American Culture," in Houston A. Baker Jr. and Patricia Redmond, eds., *Afro-American Literary Study in the 1990s* (Chi-

cago, 1989), p. 200. Eric Sundquist similarly asserts James's influence; see *To Wake the Nations: Race in the Making of American Literature* (Cambridge, Mass., 1993), pp. 487, 571; also see Dickson D. Bruce Jr., "W. E. B. Du Bois and the Idea of Double Consciousness," *American Literature* 64 (June 1992): 299–309.

45. Werner Sollors, *Beyond Ethnicity: Consent and Descent in American Culture* (New York and Oxford, 1986), pp. 186–88 and 249. Kimberly Benston also indicates an Emersonian connection via William James in his "I Yam What I Am: The Topos of (Un)naming in Afro-American Literature," in Gates, ed., *Black Literature*, p. 170n.

46. Cornel West, *The American Evasion of Philosophy: A Genealogy of Pragmatism* (Madison, Wis., 1989), pp. 142–43.

47. Ralph Waldo Emerson, "Religion and Society," in Emerson, *Young Emerson Speaks*, Arthur Cushman McGiffert, ed. (Boston, 1938), p. 200.

48. Ralph Waldo Emerson, "The Transcendentalist," in *The Portable Emerson*, Carl Bode, ed. (New York, 1981), p. 106.

49. Ralph Waldo Emerson, "Fate," in *Portable Emerson*, pp. 372–73. He observed that "by the cunning co-presence of two elements, which is throughout nature, whatever lames or paralyzes you draws in with it the divinity, in some form, to repay."

50. For a discussion of the ambiguities in James's considerations of consciousness and related issues, see Gerald E. Myers, *William James: His Life and Thought* (New Haven, Conn., and London, 1986), esp. pp. 54–80 and 344–86.

51. William James, *The Principles of Psychology* (1890; reprint, Cambridge, Mass., 1983), pp. 148–49.

52. See, e.g., William James, "Does Consciousness Exist?" in *The Writings of William James*, John J. McDermott, ed. (Chicago, 1977), pp. 169–83; Bruce Kuklick, *The Rise of American Philosophy: Cambridge, Massachusetts, 1860–1930* (New Haven, Conn., and London, 1977), pp. 169–70, and Myers, *William James*, pp. 72–80.

53. William James, *The Varieties of Religious Experience* (1902; reprint, New York, 1961), p. 190.

54. James, *Principles of Psychology*, p. 377.

55. Ibid., pp. 377–78. In exploring the extent to which the "splitting up of the mind into separate consciousness may exist in each one of us"—that is, in critically examining Pierre-Marie-Félix Janet's claim that it appears only in mental disorder—James took an experimental, empiricist route. He argued, albeit tentatively, that normal subjects demonstrate a similar, though less extreme, process: "namely, an active counting out and positive exclusion of certain objects" (ibid., p. 209). His argument was rigorously empirical and physiological: "The mother who is asleep to every sound but the stirrings of her babe, evidently has the babe-portion of her auditory sensibility systematically awake. Relatively to that, the rest of her mind is in a state of systematized anesthesia. That department, split off and disconnected from the sleeping part, can none the less wake the latter up in case of need. . . . As glands cease to secrete and muscles to contract, so the brain should sometimes cease to carry currents, and with this minimum of its activity might well coexist a minimum of consciousness. On the other hand, we see how deceptive are appearances, and are forced to admit that part of consciousness may sever its connections with other parts and yet continue to be" (p. 210).

56. Myers, *William James*, p. 376. See also James, *Essays in Radical Empiricism and A Pluralistic Universe* (New York, 1971), pp. 262–64.

57. William James, *The Will to Believe* (1897; reprint, New York, 1956), pp. 320–21.

58. Ibid., p. 321.

59. William James, *Human Immortality* (1898; reprint, New York, 1956), pp. 22–23.

60. Ibid., pp. 24 and 27. See also Myers, *William James*, pp. 383–86.

61. James, *Varieties of Religious Experience*, p. 92.

62. Ibid., p. 143.

63. Ibid., p. 146. James acknowledged that religion is not the only way to establish that unity. He noted that "the new birth may be away from religion into incredulity; or it may be from moral scrupulosity into freedom and license; or it may be produced by the irruption into the individual's life of some new stimulus or passion, such as love, ambition, cupidity, revenge, or patriotic devotion" (ibid., p. 150).

64. Ibid., p. 85.

65. Ibid., p. 81.

66. Ibid., p. 85.

67. Ibid., p. 114. James recognized mind cure as an instance of this sort of religion (ibid., p. 90).

68. Ibid., pp. 118–19.

69. Myers, *William James*, p. 468.

70. James, *Varieties of Religious Experience*, p. 135.

71. Ibid., p. 144.

72. Ibid., pp. 144–45.

73. Ibid., pp. 163–64.

74. Ibid., p. 148

75. Ibid., p. 398.

76. Ibid., p. 396.

77. Ibid., pp. 393–94.

78. Ralph Waldo Emerson, "The Over-Soul," in *Portable Emerson*, pp. 210.

79. *William James*, p. 19. Of course it is possible that James changed his mind after influencing Du Bois or that Du Bois may have accepted the idea over James's skepticism, or perhaps that Du Bois found the notion useful or attractive as a trope that stimulated him to formulate his own nonbiological idea of race. Each of those possibilities, however, requires assumption warranted only by acceptance of the proposition which is to be demonstrated. If accepted, moreover, each possibility posits conditions which beg questions as to whether "influence" reasonably describes the relation between the two ideas or the extent to which they reasonably can be viewed as similar.

80. John Dunn, "The Identity of the History of Ideas," in Peter Laslett, W. G. Runciman, and Quentin Skinner, eds., *Philosophy, Politics and Society* (New York, 1972), p. 160. Lewis makes a similar complaint specifically regarding the double-consciousness issue, criticizing those who have asserted James's influence on Du Bois for "their readiness to infer connections between ideas largely because of similarity, possibility of contact, or plausible nexus, in the absence of sufficient documentary evidence available from the subject's life" (*Biography of a Race*, p. 603). Sundquist (*To Wake the Nations*, pp. 570–71) and Bruce ("Du Bois and Double Consciousness," p. 304) base their claims entirely on similarity of a few terms and the facts of personal connection to draw inferences for which they have no subtantive textual basis. Both rest their claims on the circular assertion that Du Bois must have been familiar with current psychological research, in effect suggesting his use of the double-consciousness term as evidence. This position, though, presumes what is to be demonstrated. It also requires reading into Du Bois's essay a psychological argument that, as I have shown here, is in no way visible in the text. Bruce is in such thrall to this putative chain of influence that he maintains that

Du Bois must have intended a medical-psychological foundation, basing this claim on a reference to James's usage and the latter's role as Du Bois's "mentor."

81. Quentin Skinner, "Meaning and Understanding in the History of Ideas," *History and Theory* 8 (first quarter 1969): 26. This essay has been reprinted—along with others by Skinner, several criticisms and his reply—in James Tully, ed., *Meaning and Context: Quentin Skinner and His Critics* (Princeton, N.J., 1988). Skinner's argument concerning imputations of influence has not provoked the sort of critical debate or dissent among historians of ideas as have other of his methodological views.

82. Daniel T. Rodgers, *Contested Truths: Keywords in American Politics since Independence* (New York, 1987). In a critique of Raymond Williams's *Keywords*, which provided some of the inspiration behind Rodgers's exemplary study, Skinner stresses the distinction between different forms of politically significant contestation over proper use of terms (over whether agreed-upon meanings are being applied to the proper practices, whether the normative appraisal of an agreed-upon meaning should change, etc.) and their differing implications for the conceptual and ideological content of the contestation. Unfortunately, Skinner overstates the need for and usefulness of speech-act theory as a technique for making such interpretive distinctions. See "Language and Social Change," in Tully, ed., *Meaning and Context*, pp. 119–32. Among others, Ian Shapiro has criticized effectively the intellectual inadequacies and conservative (i.e., depoliticizing) bias in Skinner's approach in his "Realism in the Study of the History of Ideas," *History of Political Thought* 3 (November 1982): 535–78; see also Shapiro's review of *Meaning and Context* in *Canadian Philosophical Reviews*, vol. 10 (1990), p. 291.

83. Laurence R. Veysey, "Intellectual History and the New Social History," in John Higham and Paul K. Conkin, eds. *New Directions in American Intellectual History* (Baltimore, 1979), pp. 11–19.

84. In this case as well, Emerson's and James's references have more in common with each other than either's does with Du Bois's. See Emerson, "Over-Soul," p. 221; James, *Human Immorality*, p. 26 and Du Bois, *Souls of Black Folk*, p. 3. For Emerson and James the veil surrounds transcendental inner experience; for Du Bois it is the wall of racial exclusion.

85. Du Bois, *The Autobiography of W. E. B. Du Bois: A Soliloquy on Viewing My Life from the Last Decade of Its First Century* (New York, 1968), p. 168. Julian West, the protagonist of Bellamy's much-read magnum opus, observes: "The idea that I was two persons, that my identity was double, began to fascinate me with its simple solution of my experience" (Edward Bellamy, *Looking Backward* [1888; reprint, New York, 1982], p. 78).

86. Christopher Lasch, *The New Radicalism in America, 1889–1963: The Intellectual as a Social Type* (New York, 1965); T. J. Jackson Lears, *No Place of Grace: Antimodernism and the Transformation of American Culture, 1880–1920* (New York, 1981); Conn, *Divided Mind*.

87. Lasch, *New Radicalism in America*, p. 101.

88. Ibid., p. xiii.

89. Ibid., pp. 100–101.

90. Lears, *No Place of Grace*, p. 26.

91. Conn, *Divided Mind*, p. 1.

92. Ibid., p. 4.

93. Ibid., p. 13.

94. Inez Haynes Gillmore, "Confessions of an Alien," *Harper's Bazaar* 46 (April 1912): 170.

95. Cited in Mary A. Hill, *Charlotte Perkins Gilman: The Making of a Radical Feminist, 1860–1896* (Philadelphia, 1980), p. 74.

96. Henry Adams, *The Education of Henry Adams* (Boston, 1918), p. 9. Lears quotes Adams's complaint to his father about his "double personality" (*No Place of Grace*, p. 264).

97. Ibid., p. 290.

98. Ibid., p. 75.

99. Ibid., p. 210–11.

100. Mabel Dodge Luhan, *Edge of Taos Desert* (New York, 1937), pp. 301–2. This memoir was published when Luhan was in her fifty-eighth year.

101. Jane Addams, *Twenty Years at Hull-House* (1910; reprint, New York, 1981), p. 59.

102. Ibid., p. 64.

103. Ibid., p. 72.

104. Lears, *No Place of Grace*, p. 174–76. James pointed out that he was prohibited by his "constitution" from experiencing mystical states directly and could "speak of them only at second hand." See also James, *Varieties of Religious Experience.*

105. Donald Meyer, *The Positive Thinkers: Religion as Pop Psychology from Mary Baker Eddy to Oral Roberts* (New York, 1980), p. 75.

106. James, *Varieties of Religious Experience*, pp. 89–91; also see Meyer, *Positive Thinkers*, pp. 83–88.

107. Meyer, *Positive Thinkers*, pp. 79–92.

108. Lears, *No Place of Grace*, p. 170.

109. Addams, *Twenty Years at Hull-House*, pp. 64–65.

110. Gillmore, "Confessions of an Alien," p. 171.

111. Ibid., p. 210.

112. Jessie Howard Taft in fact argued directly that the experience of alienation among women was structurally and institutionally based; see Taft, *The Woman Movement from the Point of View of Social Consciousness* (Chicago, 1915), pp. 53–54. In her *Democracy and Social Ethics* (New York, 1902), Jane Addams had been equally explicit; see esp. pp. 71–101. See also Rosalind Rosenberg, *Beyond Separate Spheres: Intellectual Roots of Modern Feminism* (New Haven, Conn., 1982), pp. 142–44.

113. Gillmore, "Confessions of an Alien," p. 170. She repeated the description more than a decade later in the *Nation*, noting that she had missed the "thrill of haphazard picturesque slum existence"; see Gillmore, "The Making of a Militant," in Elaine Showalter, ed., *These Modern Women: Autobiographical Essays from the Twenties* (New York, 1989), p. 35.

114. Addams, *Twenty Years at Hull-House*, p. 169.

115. Ibid., p. 176.

116. Randolph Bourne, "Trans-National America," in Bourne *The Radical Will: Randolph Bourne, Selected Writings, 1911–1918*, Olaf Hansen, ed. (New York, 1977), pp. 253–54; see also Sollors's discussion of Bourne in *Beyond Ethnicity*, pp. 184–86.

117. Ibid., p. 254.

118. Ibid., pp. 250 and 259.

119. Luhan, *Edge of Taos Desert*, p. 34.

120. Ibid., p. 62. Her usage here illustrates the appropriation of Emerson and James by popular psychology and mysticism.

121. Ibid., p. 60. She succeeded, this passage shows, in eliminating the tension between phenomenon and concept—but exactly opposite from the way she thought she

had. Rather than transcending intellection, she so completely objectified her surround that it existed only as a set of banal abstractions.

122. Ibid., pp. 221–22.

123. Lears, *No Place of Grace*, p. 52. They also commonly believed that prolonged exposure to tropical climates produced moral degeneracy. Even open-minded racial liberals like Josiah Royce, who was skeptical of racial essentialism, accepted that premise matter-of-factly. See Royce, *Race Questions, Provincialism and Other American Problems* (1908; reprint, Freeport, N.Y., 1967), pp. 18–19.

124. Lears, *No Place of Grace*, p. 274.

125. James, *Varieties of Religious Experience*, p. 80. James also understood Leo Tolstoy's conversion experience as a transcendence of overcivilization; he cautioned, though, that "not many of us can imitate Tolstoy, not having enough, perhaps, of the aboriginal human marrow in our bones" (pp. 157–58).

126. Lears, *No Place of Grace*, p. 159.

127. Ibid., pp. 129–31.

128. James, *Varieties of Religious Experience*, pp. 84–5.

129. William James, "The Moral Equivalent of War," in *Writings of William James*, p. 661.

130. Ibid., pp. 667–68.

131. James, *Will to Believe*, p. 301. See also James, *Varieties of Religious Experience*, p. 79.

132. James, "Moral Equivalent of War," p. 661.

133. Ibid., p. 668.

134. Ibid., p. 669.

135. Lears, *No Place of Grace*, p. 136.

136. Robert M. Crunden, *Ministers of Reform: The Progressives' Achievement in American Civilization, 1889–1920* (Urbana, Ill., 1984), p. 32.

137. Lears, *No Place of Grace*, p. 255. George Santayana made a similar claim; see his 1911 essay, "The American Philosophy," in *Santayana, The Genteel Tradition: Nine Essays by George Santayana*, Douglas L. Wilson, ed. (Cambridge, Mass., 1967), esp. p. 40.

138. Rosenberg, *Beyond Separate Spheres*, p. 42. Hall believed that the progress of civilization rested on ever-widening sex differentiation; therefore, coeducation or any practice which threatened to "virify women and feminize men . . . would be regressive" (G. Stanley Hall, *Adolescence* [New York, 1904], vol. 2, p. 569.

139. Lears, *No Place of Grace*, p. 249.

140. I recognize that, as Nancy F. Cott (*The Grounding of Modern Feminism* [New Haven, Conn., and London, 1987], pp. 3–10) notes, use of the term "feminism" to describe the strains of women's activism prominent much before the First World War is anachronistic and glosses significant shifts in foci and objectives. I use the term here not to refer to support for or opposition to concrete movements, but more generically as a shorthand reference to stances reinforcing or opposing women's subordinate status in society.

141. Aileen S. Kraditor, *The Ideas of the Woman Suffrage Movement, 1890–1920* (New York, 1971), esp. pp. 82–104. The tendency to appeal to such constructions of women's "nature" also appears commonly in contemporary feminist arguments by both scholars and activists. Micaela di Leonardo discusses this phenomenon critically in her "Morals, Mothers, and Militarism: Antimilitarism and Feminist Theory," *Feminist Studies* 11 (fall 1985): 599–617, and her "Habits of the Cumbered Heart: Ethnic Community

and Women's Culture as American Invented Traditions," in Jay O'Brien and William Roseberry, eds., *Golden Ages, Dark Ages: Imagining the Past in Anthropology and History* (Berkeley, Calif., 1991); see also Katha Pollitt, *Reasonable Creatures: Essays on Women and Feminism* (New York, 1994), pp. 42–62.

142. Jane Addams, "Utilization of Women in City Government" (1907), in *Jane Addams: A Centennial Reader* Emily Cooper Johnson, ed. (New York, 1960), p. 115.

143. Jane Addams, "The Larger Aspects of the Woman's Movement," *Annals of the American Academy of Political and Social Science* 56 (November 1914): 1–8.

144. Jane Addams, "Why Women Should Vote" in *A Centennial Reader* (New York, 1960). . . . She argued the negative consequences of disfranchisement in similar terms, noting that "many women today are failing to discharge their duties to their own households properly simply because they do not perceive that as society grows more complicated it is necessary that woman shall extend her sense of responsibility to many things outside of her own home if she would continue to preserve the home in its entirety" (p. 21).

145. See Louise Michele Newman, ed., *Men's Ideal/Women's Realities: Popular Science 1870–1915* (New York, 1985), especially essays by Alice Tweedy, Olivia R. Fernow, and Frances Gordon Smith. See also May Wright Sewall, ed., *The World's Congress of Representative Women, 1893* (Chicago and New York, 1894). One might argue that those who adopted that stance did so tactically, which is no doubt to a greater or lesser extent true for given individuals. The distinction between tactical and principled adoption of a position, however, is not a very neat one, even in the mind of the agent in question. In addition, willingness to concede a point tactically can imply that the agent had no strong opposition to the point in the first place. Finally, even if activists adopted the rhetoric of essential gender dichotomy in a purely tactical way, they did so because they believed that the presumptions of that rhetoric were hegemonic as "respectable" opinion among the constituencies they wanted to influence or enlist.

146. Charlotte Perkins Gilman, *Women and Economics: The Economic Factor between Men and Women as a Factor in Social Evolution* (1898; reprint, New York, 1966), p. 126.

147. Charlotte Perkins Gilman, *The Living of Charlotte Perkins Gilman: An Autobiography* (New York, 1935), p. 187; Gilman, *Herland* (1915; reprint, New York, 1979); Rosenberg, *Beyond Separate Spheres*, pp. 36–40; Hill, *Charlotte Perkins Gilman*, p. 230.

148. Anna Julia Cooper, *A Voice from the South* (1892; reprint, New York and Oxford, 1988), p. 60.

149. Ibid., p. 58. Cooper made a similar claim concerning the importance of "an elevated and trained womanhood" in the effort to "elevate the Negro" (p. 29).

150. Ibid., p. 73.

151. Ibid., p. 84.

152. Ibid., pp. 54–5.

153. Lester F. Ward, *The Psychic Factors of Civilization* (Boston, 1892), p. 179.

154. Ibid., pp. 193–94.

155. Ibid., p. 180.

156. Ibid., p. 189.

157. Hall, *Adolescence*, pp. 566–67. He contended, though, that differentiation is greatest among "highly civilized races," p. 569.

158. William I. Thomas, "On a Difference in the Metabolism of the Sexes," *American Journal of Sociology* 3 (July 1897): 37.

159. Ibid., p. 40. He already had pointed to women's "infantile somatic characters," p. 34.

160. Ibid., p. 50.

161. Ibid., p. 41.

162. Ibid., pp. 41–42.

163. Ibid., pp. 31–32. By 1907, interestingly, Thomas had forsaken biologism altogether and argued that apparent race and gender differences were artifacts of social injustice and bigoted observation; see Thomas, "The Mind of Women and the Lower Races," *American Journal of Sociology* 12 (January 1907): 435–69.

164. Edward A. Ross, "The Causes of Race Superiority," *Annals of the American Academy of Political and Social Science* 18 (July 1901): 72–74.

165. Ibid., p. 75.

166. Ibid., p. 83.

167. Ibid., p. 76. Ross's argument was a combination primer, jeremiad, and forecast of likelihood for success on behalf of Anglo-Saxon world supremacy under prevailing conditions of capitalist imperialism. Not surprisingly, therefore, he found the apotheosis of contemporary civilization in practices and institutions of predatory capitalism; see also Ward, *Psychic Factors of Civilization*, pp. 183–84. Ward saw the putative qualities of the businessman as the most highly evolved existing form of an "intuitive reason" originating in the natural world. Unlike Ross, though, his vision of a melioristic society led him to define that tendency as the highest articulation of prehuman forms which would be surpassed in the new order.

168. Hall, *Adolescence*, p. 561.

169. Ibid., p. 564. Just as Ross's description of primitives brings to mind Edward Banfield's characterizations of "lower class" and "backward" societies (*The Moral Basis of a Backward Society* [New York, 1958] and *The Unheavenly City* [New York, 1970]), Hall's characterization here seems uncannily like Carol Gilligan's argument concerning gender-based reasoning (*In a Different Voice* [Cambridge, Mass., 1982]).

170. Robert Ezra Park, "Education in Its Relation to the Conflict and Fusion of Cultures," in Park, *Race and Culture*, p. 280.

171. L. J. Jordanova, "Natural Facts: A Historical Perspective on Science and Sexuality," in Carol MacCormack and Marilyn Strathern, eds., *Nature, Culture and Gender* (Cambridge, 1980), p. 61; see also William Leiss, *The Domination of Nature* (Boston, 1973).

172. See, for example, Stephen Jay Gould, *Ontogeny and Phylogeny* (Cambridge, Mass., 1977), esp. pp. 126–35. George W. Stocking Jr., "Lamarckianism in American Social Science," in Stocking, *Race, Culture, and Evolution: Essays in the History of Anthropology* (Chicago, 1968), pp. 234–69. Mark Pittenger charts the centrality and ramifications of evolutionist thought in fin-de-siecle reform discourse; see his *American Socialists and Evolutionary Thought, 1870–1920* (Madison, Wis., 1993).

173. Gould, *Ontogeny and Phylogeny*, pp. 155–64. Gould also discusses the centrality of Jung's and Ferenczi's recapitulationist beliefs in their respective psychoanalytic theories.

174. Stocking, "Lamarckianism," in Stocking, *Race, Culture, and Evolution*, p. 265.

175. Ibid., p. 238.

176. Gilman, *Women and Economics*, pp. 331–32. For discussion of Gilman's particular mode of evolutionism see Maureen L. Egan, "Evolutionary Theory in the Social Philosophy of Charlotte Perkins Gilman," *Hypatia* 4 (spring 1989): 102–19.

177. Stocking, "Lamarckianism," p. 255; also see Dorothy Ross, *The Origins of American Social Science* (Cambridge and New York, 1991).

178. W. E. B. Du Bois, *Heredity and the Public Schools* (Washington, D.C., 1904),

p. 7. By the time of this address, however, he at least formally acknowledged the soundness of Weismann's critique.

179. W. E. B. Du Bois, *The Conservation of Races* (Washington, D.C., 1897), p. 6.

180. William I. Thomas, "The Scope and Method of Folk Psychology," *American Journal of Sociology* 1 (January 1896):438–39.

181. Ross, "Causes of Race Superiority," pp. 67–68. Du Bois's "The Relation of the Negroes to the Whites in the South," which appeared in the same *Annals* issue as Ross's article, was reprinted as the ninth chapter, "Of the Sons of Masters and Man," of *The Souls of Black Folk*.

182. Du Bois, *Conservation of Races*, pp. 6–7.

183. Anthony Appiah, "The Uncompleted Argument: Du Bois and the Illusion of Race," *Critical Inquiry* 12 (autumn 1985): 23–25.

184. Moses, *Golden Age of Black Nationalism*, p. 135.

185. Appiah, "Uncompleted Argument," p. 25. Appiah takes Du Bois's statement that racial differences "perhaps transcend scientific definition" as evidence that he contraposed scientific and sociohistorical conceptions. That interpretation overlooks the extent to which Du Bois understood himself to be engaged in a *scientific* project as a sociologist (see chapter 4); it imputes to Du Bois Appiah's equation of science and biology in this context. Du Bois's statement is more likely an expression of the cautious attitude of the practitioner who feels his technical arsenal—his "crude social measurements," as he put it in another context—to be inadequately developed for his task.

186. Thomas, "Folk Psychology," p. 439. Stocking, "Lamarckianism," pp. 244–47.

187. Du Bois, *Conservation of Races*, p. 9.

188. Ibid., p. 10; Thomas, "Folk Psychology," p. 440.

189. Du Bois, *Souls of Black Folk*, p. 164.

190. Ibid., pp. 11 and 179.

191. Ibid., pp. 163 and 179.

192. Ibid., p. 257.

193. Ibid., p. 198.

194. Ibid., p. 5.

195. W. E. B. Du Bois, *Efforts for Social Betterment among Negro Americans* (Atlanta, 1909), p. 133. Rampersad, *Art and Imagination*, pp. 62–63.

196. Du Bois, *Souls of Black Folk*, pp. 4–5.

197. Ibid., p. 4.

198. Ibid., p. 202.

199. Ibid., p. 5.

200. Ibid., pp. 11–12.

201. This challenges Thomas C. Holt's contention that the "two-ness" problem, which he characterizes as the effort to achieve "mature self-consciousness and an integrity or wholeness of self in an alienating environment . . . would become the dominant focus—political and cultural—of Du Bois's life and work" ("The Political Uses of Alienation: W. E. B. Du Bois on Politics, Race, and Culture, 1903–1940," *American Quarterly* 42 [June 1990]: 304). Jacqueline Stevens ("Beyond Tocqueville, Please!," *American Political Science Review* 89 [December 1995]: 987–90) rejects the argument that Du Bois's early views about race were embedded in the premises and categories of neo-Lamarckian discourse, adducing the authority of Paul Gilroy, David Levering Lewis, and Joel Williamson to support her assertion that Du Bois's ideas derived instead from Hegelian roots. In the first place, however, the sources she cites do not effectively do the work for which she enlists them. Neither Gilroy (*Black Atlantic*, p. 134) nor Williamson (*The Crucible*

of Race: Black-White Relations in the American South since Emancipation [New York and Oxford, 1984], pp. 402–13) provides more than suggestive, inferential support for the claim that Du Bois's double-consciousness formulation is distinctively Hegelian. Both rely crucially on extrapolating from the fact of Du Bois's academic engagement with Hegel to conclude that superficial textual similarities must reflect the latter's influence. Gilroy—whose acknowledged objective of establishing a black diasporic consciousness leads him to stress connections to ""European ways of linking race, nation, culture, and history" as an antidote to an "American intellectual ethnocentrism" (*Black Atlantic*, pp. 134 and 137)—rests his argument for Du Bois's definitive Hegelianism ultimately on Williamson (*Black Atlantic*, p. 134). Yet Williamson himself does not establish the claim on especially solid ground: "In what ways was Du Bois's solution Hegelian? It was not, in fact, purely Hegelian . . . Du Bois was eclectic. Habitually, he surveyed the field of contemporary knowledge, used what he wanted, and left the remainder to drift . . . It would be fruitless to search for a one-to-one appropriation of Hegelianism in Du Bois's essay" (*Crucible of Race*, pp. 402–3). Williamson decides that Du Bois's text is nonetheless "fundamentally Hegelian"—principally because he believes it "heavily laden with such favored Hegelian words as ideal, consciousness, strife, and self; spirit, soul, and genius; conflict and contradiction; Freedom . . . and, of course, folk" (*Crucible of Race*, p. 403). Williamson combines this observation with facts of Du Bois's biography to launch an interpretation that requires—like those proffered by Gilroy and Gooding-Williams ("Philosophy of History")—abstracting from the specific content of Du Bois's essay to construct conceptual parallels with Hegel at the level of metatheory; these are often quite general and remote, requiring for their force prior commitment to belief in specifically Hegelian influences.

Lewis is not much more helpful to Stevens's claim. While Lewis contends that Du Bois "borrowed more or less intact notions of distinct, hierarchical racial attributes" (*Biography of a Race*, p. 139) from Hegel, he also notes that the "vocabulary of Du Bois's generation resounded with the racialisms of Joseph-Arthur de Gobineau, Edouard Drumont, Francis Galton, Thomas Carlyle, and Bishop William Stubbs, with evolutionist buzzwords ranking 'superior' and 'inferior' races according to pseudo-anthropological findings." (p. 148). The key point, which I have argued in this chapter, is that Du Bois's formulation resonates with a particular discourse of racial hierarchy—rooted in the nature/culture dichotomy and the evolutionism prominent in the social sciences—that was hegemonic among his contemporaries. Whether or not Du Bois's participation in that discourse was mediated through frames drawn specifically from Hegel's texts is—apropos of my discussion above of Skinner's arguments regarding the problem of asserting lines of influence—both much more easily alleged than demonstrated and ultimately beside the point. At issue is not whether Du Bois derived his formulations via Hegel, Lamarck (a claim I do not make in any case), or elsewhere, but whether his formulations bear the stamp of the discursive field within which he generally operated and how taking account of his relation to that discursive context illuminates his thoguht.

What is troublesome and ironic about Stevens's objection is that, for all her intentions to break with establishmentarian conventions, in insisting on reducing the discussion of Du Bois's racial views to a matter of determining ahistorical lineages of influence, she reproduces perhaps the most barren and formalistic tendency in the study of the history of political thought.

202. W. E. B. Du Bois, *Dusk of Dawn: An Essay toward an Autobiography of a Race Concept* (1940; reprint, New York, 1968), p. 98.

203. Ibid., p. 99. Here Du Bois himself undermines Stevens's contention.

204. Ibid., p. 116. Compare this observation to Moses's and Appiah's frustration at Du Bois's apparent inconsistency.

205. Ibid.

206. Ibid., p. 153. Du Bois's movement toward a social constructionist view of race by no means happened all at once; as late as the mid-1920s, he was still capable of strikingly essentialist formulations of race temperament; see my discussion of *The Gift of Black Folk* in chapter 6. His discussion of the nature and meaning of race in *The Negro* (1915; reprint, New York, 1970), pp. 6–10, illustrates both his movement toward a social constructionist view and the persistence of his acceptance of the notion of race formation that characterized neo-Lamarckian social science.

Chapter 8

1. J. Saunders Redding, Introduction to W. E. B. Du Bois, *The Souls of Black Folk* (1903; reprint, New York, 1961), pp. vii–xi.

2. Nathan Hare, "W. E. Burghardt Du Bois: An Appreciation," in W. E. B. Du Bois, *The Souls of Black Folk* (1903; reprint, New York, 1969), pp. xiii–xxvii; Alvin Poussaint, "*The Souls of Black Folk*: A Critique," in Du Bois, *Souls of Black Folk* (1969 reprint), pp. xxviii–xlii

3. John Hope Franklin, Introduction to Franklin, ed., *Three Negro Classics: Up from Slavery, The Souls of Black Folk, The Autobiography of an Ex-Colored Man* (New York, 1965), pp. vii–xii.

4. Donald B. Gibson, Introduction to W. E. B. Du Bois, *The Souls of Black Folk* (1903; reprint, New York, 1989), pp. xv–xvi.

5. John Edgar Wedeman, Introduction to W. E. B. Du Bois, *The Souls of Black Folk* (1903; reprint, New York, 1990), pp. xii–xiv.

6. Henry Louis Gates Jr., Introduction to W. E. B. Du Bois, *The Souls of Black Folk* (1903; reprint, 1989), p. xviii f.

7. Anthony Appiah, Introduction to Appiah, ed., *Early African-American Classics* (New York, 1990), p. vii. The anthology includes the entire *Narrative of the Life of Frederick Douglass, an American Slave* and selections of over a hundred pages each from Harriet A. Jacobs's *Incidents in the Life of a Slave Girl: Written by Herself*, Booker T. Washington's *Up from Slavery*, and James Weldon Johnson's *The Autobiography of an Ex-Colored Man*, with the lone Du Bois essay as a "Prologue."

8. Gates, Introduction to Du Bois, *Souls of Black Folk* (1989 reprint), p. xvi.

9. Ibid., p. xiii.

10. Herbert Aptheker, Introduction to W. E. B. Du Bois, *The Souls of Black Folk* (1903; reprint, Millwood, N.Y., 1973), pp. 14–15. For the record, Aptheker does not refer to the double-consciousness idea in his essay.

11. Gates, Introduction to Du Bois, *Souls of Black Folk* (1989 reprint), p. xiv.

12. William H. Ferris, *The African Abroad*, 2 vols. (New Haven, Conn., 1913), vol. 1, p. 276.

13. Langston Hughes, "Tribute" in John Henrik Clarke et al., eds. *Black Titan: W. E. B. Du Bois* (Boston, 1970), p. 8.

14. Gates, Introduction to Du Bois, *Souls of Black Folk* (1989 reprint), pp. xiv; James Weldon Johnson, *Along This Way* (New York, 1933), pp. 203, 313.

15. Gates, Introduction to Du Bois, *Souls of Black Folk* (1989 reprint), pp. xvi–xvii.

16. Redding, Introduction to Du Bois, *Souls of Black Folk* (1961 reprint), p. ix. Redding went from this statement directly to the discussion of the Washington essay.

17. Appiah, Introduction to Appiah, ed., *Early African-American Classics*, p. xix. Appiah seems also not to notice Du Bois's heavy irony in invoking 1876—the symbol of the defeat of Reconstruction—in relation to Washington's ascent.

18. See, for example, Benjamin Brawley, *The Negro Genius: A New Appraisal of the Achievement of the American Negro in Literature and the Fine Arts* (New York, 1937), pp. 191–92; Roi Ottley and William J. Weatherby, eds. *The Negro in New York: An Informal Social History, 1626–1940* (1940; reprint, New York, 1967), p. 171; John Hope Franklin, *From Slavery to Freedom: A History of Negro Americans* (New York, 1966), pp. 393–95; Margaret Just Butcher, *The Negro in American Culture* (1956; reprint New York, 1971), p. 162; Rayford W. Logan, *The Betrayal of the Negro: From Rutherford B. Hayes to Woodrow Wilson* (New York, 1965), pp. 330, 341–42 (originally published in 1954 under the title *The Negro in American Life and Thought: The Nadir, 1877–1901*).

19. William T. Fontaine, "The Mind and Thought of the Negro of the United States as Revealed in Imaginative Literature, 1876–1940," *Southern University Bulletin* 28 (March 1942): 16–32; also see Fontaine, *Reflections on Segregation, Desegregation, Power and Morals* (Springfield, Ill., 1967), pp. 9–13.

20. Nellie Y. McKay, "The Souls of Black Women Folk in the Writings of W. E. B. Du Bois," in Henry Louis Gates Jr., ed., *Reading Black/Reading Feminist: A Critical Anthology* (New York, 1990), p. 230.

21. Arnold Rampersad, *The Art and Imagination of W. E. B. Du Bois* (Cambridge, Mass., 1976), p. 81.

22. The essays in Baker's *Long Black Song: Essays in Black American Literature and Culture* (Charlottesville, Va., 1972) exemplify his intellectual ties to the Black Aesthetic during the early 1970s, as do several of the essays reprinted in his *Afro-American Poetics: Revisions of Harlem and the Black Aesthetic* (Madison, Wis., 1988)

23. See, for example, Houston A. Baker Jr., *Blues, Ideology, and Afro-American Literature: A Vernacular Theory* (Chicago, 1984), pp. 17–22, 60–62, Baker, *Afro-American Poetics*, pp. 162–63; and Baker, "There Is No More Beautiful Way: Theory and the Poetics of Afro-American Women's Writing," in Baker and Patricia Redmond, eds., *Afro-American Literary Study in the 1990s* (Chicago, 1989), p. 125.

24. Baker, *Blues, Ideology*, p. 121

25. Houston A. Baker Jr. *Modernism and the Harlem Renaissance* (Chicago and London, 1987), pp. 17–18, 85–86.

26. Baker, *Blues, Ideology*, p. 62; Baker, *Afro-American Poetics*, pp. 7–8.

27. Baker, *Modernism*, pp. 31–32, 49–51.

28. Baker, *Afro-American Poetics*, pp. 88–89, 97; Baker, *Workings of the Spirit: The Poetics of Afro-American Women's Writings* (Chicago and London, 1991), pp. 75–77.

29. Baker, *Modernism*, p. 100. As he does repeatedly in this book, Baker then invokes images of his father's biography to buttress his claim. He even proffers his late father as a "metonym" for black history and dismisses criticism of the Harlem Renaissance as a failure on the grounds that "my father had not been a failure" (pp. xiv–xv). This sophistry is obviously ridiculous; it is also a cheap ploy, as it irrelevantly proposes that disagreement with Baker besmirches the legacy of his recently deceased father. His ploy stands in sharp contrast to the maudlin self-criticism and apology offered in the following year for his articles as a Black Aesthetic "mau mauer" in the early 1970s. The "you-can't-talk-about-my-daddy" canard certainly projects "bullet words rather than finer resonances of an Afro-American spirit" (*Afro-American Poetics*, p. 173). After all, that he had Houston Baker Sr.'s endorsement in doing so hardly justifies Booker T. Washington's role as rationalizer of disfranchisement and racial subordination.

30. See my discussion of this phenomenon in chapter 7. For recent statements of this view, see Joel Kotkin, *Tribes: How Race, Religion and Identity Determine Success in the New Global Economy* (New York, 1993), and Samuel P. Huntington, "The Clash of Civilizations?" *Foreign Affairs* 72 (summer 1993): 22–49. This cast of mind organizes a stream of literature on ethnicity that dates from Edward Banfield, *The Moral Basis of a Backward Society* (New York, 1958), and Daniel Patrick Moynihan and Nathan Glazer, *Beyond the Melting Pot: The Negroes, Puerto Ricans, Jews, Italians and Irish of New York City* (Cambridge, Mass., 1963). I have suggested this literature's conceptual overlap with nineteenth-century race theory in "The New Victorians," *Progressive* (February 1994): 20–22.

31. Baker, *Afro-American Poetics*, p. 6.

32. Ibid., pp. 7–8.

33. Ibid., pp. 89, 101. In this volume he also posits the existence of "black cultural compulsives" (p. 147).

34. Baker, "No More Beautiful Way," p. 150.

35. Baker, *Afro-American Poetics*, p. 109.

36. Baker, "No More Beautiful Way," pp. 149, 151; Also see his *Workings of the Spirit*, p. 12, and his *Blues, Ideology*, p. 56. See *Blues, Ideology*, pp. 48–49, for Baker's treatment of Frederick Douglass's ability to marry and form a patriarchal household as an unproblematically generic assertion of racial autonomy, one that "signifies . . . that the black man has *repossessed* himself in a manner that enables him to enter the kind of relationship disrupted, or foreclosed, by the economics of slavery."

37. Baker, *Modernism*, p. 71.

38. Baker, *Afro-American Poetics*, pp. 48, 7–8, 115; Baker, *Blues, Ideology*, pp. 39–55, 114–38, 196; and Baker, *Modernism*, pp. 41–47, 50, 17–24, 72–81.

39. Baker, *Blues, Ideology*, pp. 23–31, 60.

40. Baker, *Modernism*, pp. 21–22, 49–51, 67, 103–4.

41. Ibid., p. 8.

42. Baker, *Afro-American Poetics*, pp. 5–6; Baker, *Workings of the Spirit*, pp. 75–76.

43. Baker, "No More Beautiful Way," pp. 135–39; Baker, *Workings of the Spirit*, pp. 38–45.

44. Baker, *Modernism*, p. 33

45. Ibid., pp. 29–33, 62.

46. Ibid., p. 62.

47. James D. Anderson, *The Education of Blacks in the South, 1860–1935* (Chapel Hill, N.C., 1988), pp. 75–77. Anderson cites numerous laments by students who had gone to Hampton or Tuskegee with hopes of learning trades, only to be confronted with a regime of simple physical labor and rudimentary instruction in the three r's—and with virtually no time even for studying those.

48. Ibid., pp. 42, 44. Eric Foner similarly notes Washington's pernicious role in black education, arguing that the "divorce of schooling from ideals of equal citizenship would come only after the end of Reconstruction when, under the auspices of Armstrong's pupil Booker T. Washington and the South's white 'Redeemers', the Hampton philosophy gained ascendancy in Southern black education. Before then, most teachers favored equality before the law and black suffrage, and many promoted black political organization" (Foner, *Reconstruction: America's Unfinished Revolution, 1863–1877* [New York, 1988], p. 147).

49. Baker, *Workings of the Spirit*, p. 16.

50. Anderson, *Education of Blacks*, pp. 216–17.

51. Baker, *Modernism*, pp. 32–33.

52. Anderson, *Education of Blacks*, p. 73; Robert W. Rydell, *All the World's a Fair* (Chicago, 1984), pp. 74–75; Louis R. Harlan, *Booker T. Washington* 2 vols. (New York and London, 1972–83), vol. 1, pp. 227–28. For a flavor of the New South racial ideology see Henry Grady, *The New South: Writings and Speeches of Henry Grady*, (Savannah, Ga., 1971).

53. Baker, *Modernism*, p. 36.

54. Ibid., pp. 31–32

55. Ibid., pp. 100–101.

56. Anderson, *Education of Blacks*, pp. 63–67, 102–9, 261–62.

57. Baker, *Modernism*, p. 32.

58. Harlan, *Booker T. Washington*, vol. 1, p. 224–27. Even Washington noted black criticism of the speech; see Booker T. Washington, *Up from Slavery* (1901; reprint New York, 1986), pp. 229–30.

59. Anderson, *Education of Blacks*, pp. 103–4; Rydell, *All the World's a Fair*, pp. 84–85.

60. Baker, *Modernism*, pp. 104–6.

61. Ibid., p. 15. There is unintended irony in Baker's reference to "mass of black citizens." Both Washington's agenda and Baker's defense deny black Americans an automatic claim to autonomous participation as individuals in civic life.

62. See, for instance, Henning Eichberg, "The Nazi *Thingspiel*," *New German Critique* (spring 1977): 133–50; Rainer Stollmann, "Fascist Politics as a Total Work of Art," *New German Critique* (spring 1978): 41–60.

63. Baker, *Modernism*, p. 38.

64. Baker, *Blues, Ideology*, p. 28; Baker, *Afro-American Poetics*, pp. 96, 186–87.

65. See Adolph L. Reed Jr., "The 'Underclass' as Myth and Symbol: The Poverty of Discourse about Poverty," *Radical America* 24 (winter 1992): 21–40; Stephanie Coontz, *The Way We Never Were: American Families and the Nostalgia Trap* (New York, 1992).

66. Henry Louis Gates Jr., *Loose Canons: Notes on the Culture Wars* (New York, 1992), p. 39.

67. Henry Louis Gates Jr., "Criticism in the Jungle," in Gates, ed., *Black Literature and Literary Theory* (New York, 1984), p. 6

68. Henry Louis Gates Jr., *The Signifying Monkey* (New York, 1988), p. 239.

69. Gates, *Loose Canons*, p. 79. See also Gates, ed., *Black Literature*: "It is clear that black writers read and critique other black texts as an act of rhetorical self-definition. Our literary tradition exists because of these precisely chartable formal literary relationships, relationships of signifying" (p. 290).

70. Gates, *Signifying Monkey*, p. xxiv.

71. Ibid., pp. xxii–xxiii. See also Gates, *Loose Canons*, pp. 65–66.

72. Gates, *Signifying Monkey*, pp. 46–47.

73. Ibid., p. xxvii.

74. Ibid., p. xix

75. Diana Fuss, at least, shares Gates's view on this issue; see her discussion of his supposed "re-historicization" of race in *Essentially Speaking: Feminism, Nature and Difference* (New York and London, 1989), pp. 81–86. Fuss, interestingly, begins her chapter on race with a totally depoliticized, decontextualized discussion of Booker T. Washington (p. 73) and embraces double consciousness as a description of the fundamental condition of "the Afro-American subject" (p. 95).

76. For discussion of this shift see Reed, "New Victorians."

77. Henry Louis Gates Jr., "What's Love Got to Do with It?: Critical Theory, Integrity and the Black Idiom," *New Literary History* 18 (winter 1987): 356. In an essay originally published two years earlier, Gates notes the broader significance of race as a category: "Race has become a trope of ultimate, irreducible difference between cultures, linguistic groups, or practicioners of specific belief systems, who more often than not have fundamentally opposed economic interests" ("Writing, 'Race,' and the Difference It Makes," *Critical Inquiry* 12 [autumn 1985]: 5).

78. Recent expressions of this tendency in the respectable public forum are Kotkin, *Tribes*, and the indefatigable Thomas Sowell, *Race and Culture: A World View* (New York, 1994). It is a sign of this mode of thought's ascendance that the former is not broadly recognized as simply the sophistry of a malevolent dolt or the latter as that of an increasingly bilious, ultraright crank.

79. Gates, *Signifying Monkey*, p. xix.

80. Ibid., pp. xxiv–xxv.

81. Ibid., pp. 53–104.

82. Sometimes Gates reveals striking parallels to Matthew Arnold in his formulations. Compare Arnold's famous definition of culture as the "pursuit of our total perfection by means of getting to know . . . the best which has been thought and said in the world" (*Culture and Anarchy* [1869; reprint, Cambridge, 1978], p. 6) with Gates on constructing an Afro-American literary canon: "Our task will be to bring together the 'essential' texts of the canon, the 'crucially central' authors, those whom we feel to be indispensible to an understanding of the shape, and shaping, of the tradition" ("Canon-Formation, Literary History, and the Afro-American Tradition: From the Seen to the Told," in Baker and Redmond, eds., *Afro-American Literary Study* [Chicago, 1989], p. 38). Where Arnold unabashedly, in Victorian self-assurance, speaks of "perfection" and "best," Gates opts for this era's more value-neutral-sounding terminology—"essential," "crucially central"—which he further distances himself from with quotation marks. To be sure, he wishes to base his Afro-Americanist version of "the best which has been thought and said" on criteria ostensibly inflected toward more popular vernacular and folk expression. But as Barbara E. Johnson notes, though she is curiously untroubled by his move, Gates tries "to have it both ways, to have his Western theory and his vernacular theory too" (Johnson, "Response," in Baker and Redmond, eds., *Afro-American Literary Study*, p. 40). Kenneth W. Warren, less sanguine than Johnson about the issue, makes a similar observation in a review of Gates's *Signifying Monkey* in *Modern Philology* (November 1990): 224–26. Warren notes also that Gates's interpretation oscillates "between structural and/or cultural determination on the one hand and assertions of authorial autonomy on the other," and that Gates actually only genuflects toward vernacular discourse, focusing substantively on literary tradition instead.

83. Henry Louis Gates Jr., *Figures in Black: Words, Signs, and the "Racial" Self* (New York and Oxford, 1987), pp. 176–78; Gates, "Dis and Dat: Dialect and the Descent," in Dexter Fisher and Robert Stepto, eds., *Afro-American Literature: The Reconstruction of Instruction* (New York, 1979), p. 98.

84. Gates, ed., *Black Literature*, p. 286; Gates. *Signifying Monkey*, p. 6.

85. Gates, *Signifying Monkey*, p. xxiv.

86. Ibid.

87. Ibid.

88. For instance: "For reasons extremely difficult to reconstruct, the monkey became, through a displacement in African myths in the New World, a central character in this crucial scene of instruction" (ibid, p. 15), or, "While we lack archeological and

historical evidence to explain the valorized presence of the Monkey in Cuban mythology; in the textual evidence, on the other hand, we commonly encounter Esu with his companion, as depicted even in visual representations of Esu" (ibid, p. 20).

89. Ibid., p. 20.

90. Ibid., p. 42. This move is similar to Baker's pontifical announcement of the criteria of black authenticity.

91. Ibid., p. xxi

92. Ibid., pp. 4–5.

93. Ibid., p. 21.

94. Ibid., p. 105. This is perhaps an especially illustrative instance of his fallacy. Although the words contain the same letters, the latter combine to quite different effect, as should be obvious to anyone with elementary familiarity with spoken French. The initial vowel sounds—\ĕ\ in *singe*, \ĭ\ in *signe*—differ markedly. The order of juxtaposition of the *n* and *g* also has substantial consequences. The *gn* functions as a single consonant [ñ]; the *ng* is more a diphthong, producing a sound nearer a soft *j* (or \zh\). The words, moreover, stem from completely different Latin roots—*signe* from *signum*, *singe* from *simius*.

95. I am indebted to Corinne A. Kratz, in personal correspondance, for clarifying these problems with Gates's excursion into Kikongo and Kiswahili etymology.

96. Samuel M. Wilson, "Trickster Treats," *Natural History* (October 1991): 4. See also Paul Radin, *The Trickster* (London, 1956).

97. Lawrence W. Levine, *Black Culture and Black Consciousness: Afro-American Folk Thought from Slavery to Freedom* (New York, 1977); Eugene D. Genovese, *Roll, Jordan, Roll: The World the Slaves Made* (New York, 1976); Sterling Stuckey, *Slave Culture: Nationalist Theory and the Foundations of Black America* (New York and London, 1987).

98. See, for example, Henry Louis Gates Jr., "Preface to Blackness: Text and Pretext," in Fisher and Stepto, eds., *Afro-American Literature*, pp. 44–52; also his *Figures in Black*, pp. 3–28, 61–79; *Signifying Monkey*, pp. 66, 94, 113, 129, 167; "Canon-Formation," pp. 16–17; *Loose Canons*, pp. 54–78; "What's Love Got to Do with It?," pp. 347– 58; and "Writing 'Race' and the Difference It Makes," pp. 7–13.

99. Gates, "Preface to Blackness," p. 45.

100. Gates, "What's Love Got to Do with It?," p. 347.

101. Gates, "Preface to Blackness," pp. 54–68.

102. Gates, "Criticism in the Jungle," pp. 5–6.

103. See chapter 1 for my discussion of the vindicationist tendency and its critics. Criticism of this tendency has sometimes overlapped a standard black conservative complaint about the intellectually suffocating and infantilizing effects of a politicized race consciousness. Ellison in particular has been a target for appropriation by black conservatives, though it is hardly clear that his critique rests comfortably or unambiguously in that camp. The conservative articulation of the critique is represented more clearly by those like Hurston and George Schuyler, who tie it to disparagement of racial agitation in the political realm. See for example Zora Neale Hurston, *Dust Tracks in the Road* (Urbana, Ill., 1984), and "The 'Pet Negro' System," *American Mercury* 56 (May 1943): 593–600; George Schuyler, *Black and Conservative* (New Rochelle, N.Y., 1966). Schuyler's satirical novel *Black No More* (1931; reprint Amherst, Mass., 1989) also advances a version of this strain of criticism. (Wallace Thurman's satire of the Harlem Renaissance, *Infants of the Spring*, is another—but not conspicuously conservative—fictionalized attack on the limits of race consciousness in black intellectual life.) Gates, interestingly, has written

about both Hurston and Schuyler sympathetically, attempting to take full measure of their complexity and, arguably, sanitizing their political conservatism. See Gates, "A Fragmented Man: George Schuyler and the Claims of Race," *New York Times Book Review*, September 20, 1992; Gates, "A Negro Way of Saying," *New York Times Book Review*, April 21, 1985.

104. Gates, *Figures in Black*, p. 45.

105. Ibid., p. 44. See also Gates, "Preface to Blackness," pp. 58–68; Gates, *Loose Canons*, pp. 101–2.

106. Henry Louis Gates Jr., "African American Criticism," in Stephen Greenblat and Giles Gunn, eds., *Redrawing the Boundaries: The Transformation of English and American Literary Studies* (New York, 1992), p. 309.

107. Gates, "What's Love Got to Do with It?," pp. 346–47

108. Gates, *Signifying Monkey*, p. xi.

109. Gates, *Figures in Black*, pp. 56–57.

110. Gates, ed., "The Blackness of Blackness," in *Black Literaturey*, p. 3.

111. Gates, *Signifying Monkey*, p. xxii.

112. Gates, *Loose Canons*, pp. 65–66; Gates, ed., "Criticism in the Jungle," in *Black Literature*, p. 6; Gates, *Signifying Monkey*, pp. xxiv–xxv.

113. Gates, ed., *Black Literature*, p. 3.

114. Gates, "African American Criticism," p. 313.

115. Kenneth W. Warren, *Black and White Strangers: Race and American Literary Realism* (Chicago and London, 1993), p. 142. Warren also discusses the way that Gates relies on the image of professionalistic pluralism in interpretation "to establish some non-political notion of black unity" and points out the impossibility of that essentialist ideal. See his "Delimiting America: The Legacy of Du Bois," *American Literary History* 1 (spring 1989): 172–89.

116. Gates, *Figures in Black*, p. xxii.

117. Gates, "What's Love Got to Do with It?," pp. 352–53.

118. Gates, *Loose Canons*, p. 31; Gates, "Canon-Formation," pp. 37–38; His claim for the Norton anthology's legitimation as a black canon recalls Baraka's old notion of "unity without uniformity." He wants to "bring together a diverse array of ideological, methodological, and theoretical perspectives, so that we together might produce an anthology which most fully represents the various definitions of what it means to speak of the Afro-American literary tradition, and what it means to *teach* that tradition" (ibid., p. 38). Cf. Warren, "Delimiting America."

119. Gates, *Loose Canons*, p. 39.

120. Gates, "African American Criticism," p. 312.

121. Gates, "Canon-Formation," pp. 27–28.

122. Ibid., pp. 29–30. Gates mentions—with no sense of possible contradiction in the context of his argument here—that he takes the "passage from the seen to the told" formulation from Wlad Godzich's introduction to Paul de Man's *The Resistance to Theory*.

123. Gates, ed., "Criticism in the Jungle," in *Black Literature*, p. 4.

124. Ibid., p. 5. This passage is yet another instance of Gates's contention that this generation of Afro-Americanists has access to uniquely new intellectual vistas made available by their unprecedented technical sophistication.

125. Ibid., p. 6.

126. See, for example, Winthrop Jordan, *White over Black* (New York, 1968).

127. Gates, "What's Love Got to Do with It?," p. 357. Given Gates's subsequent

visibility as a "public intellectual" who pontificates on social affairs, are we to assume that Jackson has taken up theorizing about tropes in *Ulysses* and *Their Eyes Were Watching God?*

128. Ibid., p. 358.

129. Gates, *Signifying Monkey*, p. 45.

130. Theodore O. Mason Jr., "Between the Populist and the Scientist: Ideology and Power in Recent Afro-American Literary Criticism; Or, 'The Dozens' as Scholarship," *Callaloo* 11 (summer 1988): 612.

131. Ibid., p. 609.

132. Gates, *Figures in Black*, pp. 176–77.

133. Ibid., p. 178.

134. I am indebted to Joe Wood for the Egyptology comparison.

135. Gates, Introduction to Du Bois, *Souls of Black Folk* (1989 reprint), p. xiii.

136. Ibid., p. xvi.

137. Ibid., p. xvii.

138. David A. Hollinger, *In the American Province: Studies in the History and Historiography of Ideas* (Bloomington, Ind., 1985), p. 85.

139. Paul Lauter, *Canons and Contexts* (New York and Oxford, 1991), p. 148.

140. See, for instance, Jennifer Jordan, "Cultural Nationalism in the Sixties: Politics and Poetry," in Adolph L. Reed Jr., ed., *Race, Politics and Culture: Critical Essays on the Radicalism of the 1960s* (Westport, Conn., 1986), pp. 29–60.

141. Gates, *Figures in Black*, p. xxvii.

142. Gates, Introduction to Du Bois, *Souls of Black Folk* (1989 reprint), p. xiii.

143. Sam Haselby, "Muscular Humanism: Interview with Henry Louis Gates, Jr.," *Hungry Mind Review* (fall 1994): 23.

144. Compare, for example, the differences in both argument and tone between Gates's "Canon-Formation" and his "Good-Bye, Columbus? Notes on the Culture of Criticism," *American Literary History* 3 (winter 1991): 711–32, published slightly more than a year later.

145. Henry Louis Gates Jr., "A Pretty Good Society," *Time*, November 16, 1992, p. 86.

146. Gates, *Loose Canons*, p. xix.

147. Henry Louis Gates Jr., Introduction to Katharine Whittmore and Gerald Marzorati, eds., *Voices in Black and White* (New York, 1993), p. xiv.

148. Gates, "Pretty Good Society," p. 84.

149. Henry Louis Gates Jr., "The Fire Last Time: What James Baldwin Can and Can't Teach America," *New Republic*, June 1, 1992, pp. 37–43.

150. Ibid., pp. 41–42.

151. Ibid., p. 40–42.

152. Henry Louis Gates Jr., "Let Them Talk: Why Civil Liberties Pose No Threat to Civil Rights," *New Republic* (September 20 and 29, 1993, pp. 37–49.

153. Gates, "What's Love Got to Do with It?," p. 350.

154. Gates, "Let Them Talk," p. 48.

155. Karen J. Winkler, "Literary Scholars Mount a Counteroffensive against Bad Press, Conservative Critics," *Chronicle of Higher Education* January 15, 1992, p. A15. See also Fox Butterfield, "Afro-American Studies Get New Life at Harvard," *New York Times*, June 3, 1992; Gates, "Good-Bye Columbus?" p. 717–19.

156. Gates, "Good-Bye, Columbus?" p. 717.

157. Henry Louis Gates Jr., "Black Demagogues and Pseudo-Scholars," *New York*

Times, July 20, 1992; Gates, "Black Intellectuals, Jewish Tensions," *New York Times*, April 14, 1993. I have critized the notion of a distinctly virulent *black* anti-Semitism more extensively in "What Color is Anti-Semitism?" *Village Voice*, December 26, 1995, p. 26 and "Behind the Farrakhan Show," *The Progressive* (April 1994): 16–17.

158. Gates. "Let Them Talk," p. 48. He also draws on "the great political philosopher Sir Isaiah Berlin" in his paean to Bill Clinton, "Pretty Good Society," p. 86.

159. Gates. "Good-Bye, Columbus?" pp. 723–25.

160. Ibid., p. 727.

161. Ibid., p. 724.

162. Gates, "Pretty Good Society," p. 85. See also Gates's "The Black Leadership Myth," *New Yorker*, October 24, 1994, p. 7.

163. Gates, "Let Them Talk."

164. Henry Louis Gates Jr., "Two Nations . . . Both Black," *Forbes*, September 14, 1992, p. 138.

165. Henry Louis Gates Jr., "Two Nations . . . Both Black" (revised), in Robert Gooding-Williams, ed., *Reading Rodney King, Reading Urban Uprisings* (New York, 1993), p. 253.

166. Gates, "Two Nations," p. 138.

167. Ibid., p. 135; Haselby, "Muscular Humanism," p. 64.

168. Gates, "Two Nations," p. 138.

169. Haselby, "Muscular Humanism," p. 64.

170. Gates, "Two Nations," p. 135.

171. Ibid.

172. Gates, *Loose Canons*, p. 149.

173. Gates, "Two Nations," p. 134.

174. Gates, *Loose Canons*, p. 149.

175. Henry Louis Gates Jr., *Colored People: A Memoir* (New York, 1994), pp. xi–xv.

176. Ibid., p. xvi.

177. Ibid., p. 184.

178. Ibid., p. 216. I have examined this current nostalgia at greater length in "Romanticing Jim Crow: Black Nostalgia for a Segregated Past," *Village Voice*, April 16, 1996, p. 24–29

179. Haselby, "Muscular Humanism," p. 32.

180. Warren, "Delimiting America," pp. 184–86.

Chapter 9

1. Donald Green and Ian Shapiro, *Pathologies of Rational Choice Theory* (New Haven, Conn., London, 1994).

2. For a thoroughgoing critique of the essentializing formulations of the discourse of identity politics and its implications, see Micaela di Leonardo, "White Ethnicities, Identity Politics, and Baby Bear's Chair," *Social Text* (winter 1994): 165–91.

3. Trey Ellis, "The New Black Aesthetic," *Callaloo* 12 (winter 1989): 235.

4. Ibid.

5. Ibid., p. 236.

6. Ibid., p. 237. Ellis pats himself on the back for having hitchhiked across central Africa, which, he beleives, is "something only a second-generation middle-class person would ever volunteer to do" (pp. 241–42).

7. Ibid., p. 239.

8. Ibid.

9. Trey Ellis, "Response to NBA Critiques," *Callaloo* 12 (winter 1989): 250.

10. Ellis, "New Black Aesthetic," pp. 239–40.

11. Ellis, "Response," p. 250. The humility expressed in that statement rests uneasily against the previous paragraph, in which Ellis offers this assessment of his group's significance: "[T]his new movement is also fueled by naive exuberance and a for now unshakable belief that our youthful black power can perfect society and perfect the soul. A certain amount of disillusionment and cynicism will eventually set in as it always does when we discover that changing the world will take more than a couple of summers, but ingenuous arrogance has been the spark for all important movements, artistic and political, from Cubism to *Sandinismo* to the Beats."

12. Ellis, "New Black Aesthetic," p. 237.

13. Ibid., p. 237. Gates is more self-conscious in his praise of supposedly new black "mainstream" success. See Henry Louis Gates Jr., "Black Creativity: On the Cutting Edge," *Time*, October 10, 1994, pp. 74–75.

14. Ellis, "New Black Aesthetic," p. 237.

15. Martin Kilson, "The Black Bourgeoisie, Revisited" *Dissent* (winter 1984): 87.

16. Ibid., p. 89.

17. Ibid., pp. 90–91.

18. See, for instance, Shelby Steele, *The Content of Our Character* (New York, 1990); David L. Kirp, "No Angels, No Dreams," *San Francisco Examiner Image*, (October 7, 1990; and Deroy Murdock, " 'Oh, My God! It's a Black Man!' " *Chicago Tribune*, March 11, 1993.

19. See, for example, Signithia Fordham and John U. Ogbu, "Black Students' School Success: Coping with the Burden of 'Acting White.' " *Urban Review* 18 (1986): 176–206; Elijah Anderson, *Streetwise: Race, Class and Change in an Urban Community* (Chicago, 1992).

20. Lorene Cary, *Black Ice* (New York, 1991), p. 150.

21. Ibid., pp. 233–37.

22. Jacquelyn Mitchell, "Reflections of a Black Social Scientist: Some Struggles, Some Doubts, Some Hopes," *Harvard Educational Review* 52 (February 1982): 38–39. Mitchell refers to Du Bois directly as well.

23. Stephen L. Carter, "The Black Table, the Empty Seat, and the Tie," in Gerald Early, ed., *Lure and Loathing: Essays on Race, Identity, and the Ambivalence of Assimilation* (New York, 1993), p. 65.

24. Ibid., pp. 59, 64–65.

25. Ibid., p. 73.

26. Gerald Early, Introduction to Early, ed., *Lure and Loathing*, and the following other essays from that volume: Glenn C. Loury, "Free at Last?: A Personal Perspective on Race and Identity in America"; James McPherson, "Junior and John Doe"; Kristin Hunter Lattany, "Off-Timing: Stepping to the Different Drummer."

27. Ellis Cose, *The Rage of a Privileged Class* (New York, 1993), pp. 41, 65–66.

28. Richard Lacayo, "Between Two Worlds," *Time*, March 13, 1989, p. 58–59.

29. George E. Curry, "A Writer's Tortuous Flight from Home," *Chicago Tribune*, July 9, 1992.

30. Evan Thomas, "The Double Life of O. J. Simpson," *Newsweek*, August 29, 1994, p. 48.

31. Case, *Rage of a Privileged Class*, pp. 61–62.

32. See, for example, James Comer, *Maggie's American Dream: The Life and Times*

of a Black Family (New York, 1988); Sara Lawrence Lightfoot, *Balm in Gilead* (Cambridge, Mass., 1984); Paula Giddings, *When and Where I Enter: The Impact of Black Women on Race and Sex in America* (New York, 1984); Mamie Garvin Fields with Karen Fields, *Lemon Swamp and Other Places* (New York, 1983); Cynthia Neverdon-Morton, *Afro-American Women of the South and the Advancement of the Race, 1895–1925* (Knoxville, Tenn., 1989); Evelyn Brooks Higginbotham, *Righteous Discontent: The Women's Movement in the Black Baptist Church, 1880–1920* (Cambridge, Mass., 1993); and Willard B. Gatewood, *Aristocrats of Color: The Black Elite, 1880–1920* (Bloomington, Ind., 1990).

33. Leanita McClain, *A Foot in Each World* (Evanston, Ill., 1986).

34. Ibid., p. 7.

35. Ibid., p 12.

36. Ibid, p. 13.

37. Ibid., p. 14.

38. Ibid., pp. 14–15.

39. Ibid., p. 42.

40. Ibid., p. 159. She quotes a retired teacher's view that there "hasn't been a good class at Flower since 1969"—just after McClain graduated, coincidentally (p. 162).

41. Ibid., p. 162.

42. Ibid., pp. 162–63.

43. Ibid., p. 176.

References

Primary Sources by Du Bois

An ABC of Color. New York: International Publishers, 1963.
"Africa and the French Revolution," *Freedomways* 1 (summer 1961): 136–15.
Africa, Its Geography, People and Products. Girard, Kans.: Haldeman-Julius, 1930.
Africa, Its Place in Modern History. Girard, Kans.: Haldeman-Julius, 1930.
"African Roots of War," *Atlantic Monthly* 115 (May 1915): 707–14.
Against Racism: Unpublished Essays, Papers, Addresses, 1887–1961. Herbert Aptheker, ed. Amherst: University of Massachusetts Press, 1985.
"The American Negro and the Labor Movement" Reel 80 #894. *W. E. B. Du Bois Papers at the University of Massachusetts,* Amherst, Massachusetts.
"American Negroes and Africa's Rise to Freedom," (1961), in *The Seventh Son: The Thought and Writings of W. E. B. Du Bois,* vol 2. New York: Random House, 1970.
"As the Crow Flies," *Chicago Globe,* April 12, 1950.
"The Atlanta Conferences," *Voice of the Negro* 1 (March 1904): 85–90.
"Atlanta University," in *From Servitude to Service.* (multiauthor collection). Boston: American Unitarian Association, 1905.
Autobiography: A Soliloquy on Viewing My Life from the Last Decade of Its First Century. New York: International Publishers, 1968.
"Back to Africa," *Century* 105 (February 1923): 539–48.
"The Beginning of Slavery," *Voice of the Negro* 2 (February 1905): 104–6.
"Black Africa Tomorrow," *Foreign Affairs* 17 (October 1938): 100–110.

Black Folk Then and Now. New York: Henry Holt, 1939.

"The Black Man and Albert Schweitzer," in A. A. Roback, ed., *The Albert Schweitzer Jubilee Book.* Cambridge, Mass: Sci-Art, 1945.

"The Black Man Brings His Gifts," *Survey* 53 (March 1, 1925): 655–57.

Black Reconstruction. New York: Harcourt Brace, 1935.

The College-Bred Negro. Atlanta: Atlanta University Press, 1900.

The College-Bred Negro American. Atlanta: Atlanta University Press, 1910.

Color and Democracy: Colonies and Peace. New York: Harcourt Brace, 1945.

The Common School and the Negro American. Atlanta: Atlanta University Press, 1911.

"Conference of Encylopedia Africana," *Freedomways* 3 (winter 1963): 28–30.

The Conservation of Races. Washington, D.C.: American Negro Academy, 1897.

Contributions by W. E. B. Du Bois in Government Publications and Proceedings. Herbert Aptheker, ed. Millwood, N.Y.: Kraus-Thomson, 1980.

The Correspondence of W. E. B. Du Bois, 3 vols. Herbert Aptheker, ed. Amherst: University of Massachusetts Press, 1973–78.

Countee Cullen-Harold Jackman Collection, Collection No. 3, "Du Bois," Atlanta University, Atlanta, Georgia.

Creative Writings by W. E. B. Du Bois: A Pageant, Poems, Short Stories and Playlets. Herbert Aptheker, ed. Millwood, N.Y.: Kraus-Thomson, 1985.

"Credo," *Independent* 57 (October 6, 1904): 787.

"The Cultural Missions of Atlanta University," *Phylon* 3 (second quarter 1942): 105–15.

Dark Princess: A Romance. New York: Harcourt Brace, 1928.

Darkwater: Voices from within the Veil. 1920; reprint, New York: Schocken, 1969.

"Debit and Credit," *Voice of the Negro* 2 (January 1905): 677.

"The Dilemma of the Negro," *American Mercury* 3 (October 1924): 179–85.

"Does the Negro Need Separate Schools?" *Journal of Negro Education* 14 (July 1935): 328–35.

Dusk of Dawn: An Essay toward an Autobiography of a Race Concept. 1940; reprint, New York: Schocken, 1968.

"E. D. Morel," *Nation* 112 (May 25, 1921): 749.

Economic Cooperation among Negro Americans. Atlanta: Atlanta University Press, 1907.

"Editing the Crisis," *Crisis* 58 (March 1951): 147 ff.

"Education and Work," *Journal of Negro Education* 1 (April 1932): 60–74.

The Education of Black People: Ten Critiques, 1906–1960. Herbert Aptheker, ed. Amherst: University of Massachusetts Press, 1978.

Efforts for Social Betterment among Negro Americans. Atlanta: Atlanta University Press, 1909.

The Emerging Thought of W. E. B. Du Bois. Henry Lee Moon, ed. New York: Simon and Schuster, 1972.

"Eternal Africa," *Nation* 111 (September 25, 1920): 350–52.

"Federal Action Programs and Community Action in the South," *Social Forces* 19 (March 1941): 375–80.

"The Freedmen's Bureau," *Atlantic Monthly* 87 (March 1901): 354–65.

"The Freeing of India," *Crisis* 54 (October 1947): 301 ff.

"The Future and Function of the Private Negro College," *Crisis* 8 (August 1946): 234 ff.

"A Future for Pan-Africa: Freedom, Peace, Socialism," in *The Seventh Son: The Thought and Writings of W. E. B. Du Bois,* vol 2. New York: Random House, 1970.

"The Future of Wilberforce University," *Journal of Negro Education* 9 (October 1940): 553–70.

"Garrison and the Negro," *Independent* 59 (December 7, 1905): 1316–17.

"Georgia: Invisible Empire State," *Nation* 120 (January 21, 1925): 63–67.

"Ghana Calls—A Poem," *Freedomways* 2 (winter 1962): 71–74.

The Gift of Black Folk: The Negroes in the Making of America. 1924; reprint, New York: Washington Square, 1970.

"The Hampton Idea," *Voice of the Negro* 3 (September 1906): 632–36.

"The Hampton Strike," *Nation* 125 (November 2, 1927): 471–72.

The Health and Physique of the Negro American. Atlanta: Atlanta University Press, 1906.

Heredity and the Public Schools. Washington, D.C., 1904.

"His Last Message to the World," *Journal of Negro History* 49 (April 1964): 145.

The Horizon: A Journal of the Color Line (1907–10), in Countee Cullen-Harold Jackman Collection, Trevor-Arnett Library, Atlanta University, Collection No. 3, Du Bois.

"The Hosts of Black Labor," *Nation* 116 (May 9, 1923): 539–41.

'How United Are Negroes?,' (1956) in *The Seventh Son: The Thought and Writings of W. E. B. Du Bois,* vol 2. New York: Random House, 1970.

"I Bury My Wife," *Negro Digest* 8 (October 1950): 37–39.

In Battle for Peace: The Story of My 83rd Birthday. New York: Masses and Mainstream, 1952.

"Inter-racial Implications of the Ethiopian Crisis," *Foreign Affairs* 14 (October 1935): 82–92.

"Is Al Smith Afraid of the South?" *Nation* 127 (October 17, 1928): 392–94.

John Brown. 1909; reprint, New York: International Publishers, 1962.

"John Hope: Scholar and Gentleman," *Crisis* 55 (September 1948): 270–71.

"The Laboratory in Sociology at Atlanta," *Annals of the American Academy of Political and Social Science* 21 (May 1903): 160–63.

"Letter of Application for Admission to Membership in the Communist Party of the United States," *Political Affairs* 40 (December 1961): 9–10.

"Liberia and Rubber," *New Republic* 44 (November 18, 1925): 326–29.

"Liberia, the League, and the United States," *Foreign Affairs* 11 (July 1933): 682–95.

"Litany of Atlanta," *Independent* 61 (October 1906): 1173–75.

"Marrying of Black Folk," *Independent* 69 (October 13, 1910): 812–13.

"Marxism and the Negro Problem," *Crisis* 40 (May 1933).

The Moon Illustrated Weekly (1906), in Countee Cullen-Harold Jackman Collection, Trevor-Arnett Library, Atlanta University, Collection No. 3, Du Bois.

Morals and Manners among Negro Americans. Atlanta: Atlanta University Press, 1914.

"Moton of Hampton and Tuskegee," *Phylon* 1 (fourth quarter 1940): 344–51.

"My Evolving Program for Negro Freedom," in Rayford W. Logan, ed., *What the Negro Wants.* Chapel Hill: University of North Carolina Press, 1944.

The Negro. 1915; reprint, New York: Oxford University Press, 1970.

The Negro American Artisan. Atlanta: Atlanta University Press, 1912.

The Negro American Family. Atlanta: Atlanta University Press, 1908.

"The Negro and Crime," *Independent* 51 (May 18, 1899): 1355–57.

"The Negro and Socialism," in Helen L. Alfred, ed., *Toward a Socialist America: A Symposium of Essays.* New York: Peace Publications, 1958.

"The Negro and the Civil War," *Science and Society* 25 (December 1961): 347–52.

The Negro Artisan. Atlanta: Atlanta University Press, 1902.

The Negro Church. Atlanta: Atlanta University Press, 1903.

"The Negro Citizen," in Charles S. Johnson, ed., *The Negro in American Civilization.* New York: Henry Holt, 1930.

The Negro Common School. Atlanta: Atlanta University Press, 1901.

"The Negro Farmer, Negroes in the United States." *United States Department of Commerce and Labor, Bureau of the Census, Bulletin* 8 (1904): 6998.

The Negro in Business. Atlanta: Atlanta University Press, 1899.

"The Negro in Literature and Art," *Annals of the American Academy of Political and Social Science* 49 (September 1913): 233–37.

"The Negro Landholder of Georgia." *Bulletin of the United States Department of Labor* 6 (July 1901): 647–77.

"The Negro Mind Reaches Out," in Alain Locke, ed., *The New Negro: An Interpretation.* 1925; reprint, New York: Atheneum Press, 1968.

"A Negro Nation within the Nation," *Current History* 42 (June 1935): 265–70.

"The Negro People and the United States," *Freedomways* 1 (spring 1961): 11–19.

"A Negro Schoolmaster in the New South," *Atlantic Monthly* 83 (January 1899): 99–104.

"The Negro Scientist," *American Scholar* 8 (summer 1939): 309–20.

"The Negro since 1900: A Progress Report," *New York Times Magazine,* November 21, 1948, 54 ff.

"The Negro Soldier in Service Abroad during the First World War," *Journal of Negro Education* 12 (summer 1943): 324–34.

"The Negro Takes Stock," *New Republic* 37 (January 2, 1924): 143–45.

"Negroes and the Crisis of Capitalism in the United States," *Monthly Review* 4 (April 1953): 478–85.

"Negroes in College," *Nation* 122 (March 3, 1926): 228–30.

"The Negroes of Farmville, Virginia: A Social Study," *Bulletin of the United States Department of Labor* 3 (January 1898): 1–38.

"Of the Culture of White Folk," *Journal of Race Development* 7 (April 1917): 434–47.

"Of the Training of Black Men," *Atlantic Monthly* 90 (September 1902): 289–97.

"On Being Ashamed of Oneself: An Essay on Race Pride," *Crisis* 40 (September 1933): 199–200.

"On Being Black," *New Republic* 21 (February 18, 1920): 338–41.

A Pageant in Seven Decades, 1868–1938. Atlanta: Atlanta University, 1938.

"A Pageant in Seven Decades," in Philip S. Foner, ed., *W. E. B. Du Bois Speaks: Speeches and Addresses, 1899–1963,* vol. 2. Pathfinder Press, 1970.

Pamphlets and Leaflets. Herbert Aptheker, ed. White Plains, N.Y.: Kraus-Thomson, 1986.

"Pan Africa and the New Racial Philosophy," *Crisis* 49 (November 1933): 247.

"The Pan-African Movement," in George Padmore, ed., *Colonial and Coloured Unity: A Programme of Action. History of the Pan-African Congress.* Manchester, England: Pan-African Federation, 1945.

"The Passing of Jim Crow," *Independent* 91 (July 14, 1917): 53–54.

"Paul Robeson—Right," *Negro Digest* 8 (March 1950): 8 ff.

The Philadelphia Negro: A Social Study. 1899; reprint, New York: Schocken, 1967.

"The Position of the Negro in the American Social Order: Where Do We Go from Here?" *Journal of Negro Education* 8 (July 1939): 551–70.

"Possibilities of the Negro: The Advance Guard of the Race," *Booklovers* 2 (July 1903): 2–15.

Prayers for Dark People. Herbert Aptheker, ed. Amherst: University of Massachusetts Press, 1980.

"The Primitive Black Man," *Nation* 119 (December 17, 1924): 675–76.

"The Problem of Amusement," *Southern Workman* 27 (September 1897): 181–84.

"Prospect of a World without Race Conflict," *American Journal of Sociology* 49 (March 1944): 450–56.

"Pushkin," *Phylon* 1 (third quarter 1940): 265–69.

The Quest of the Silver Fleece: A Novel. Chicago: McClurg, 1911.

"Race Friction between Black and White," *American Journal of Sociology* 13 (May 1908): 834–38.

"Race Relations in the United States," *Annals of the American Academy of Political and Social Science* 140 (November 1928): 6–10.

"Race Relations in the United States: 1917–1947," *Phylon* 9 (third quarter 1948): 234–47.

"The Realities in Africa: European Profit or Negro Development?" *Foreign Affairs* 21 (July 1943): 721–32.

"Reconstruction and Its Benefits," *American Historical Review* 15 (July 1910): 781–99.

"Reconstruction: Seventy-Five Years After," *Phylon* 4 (third quarter 1943): 205–12.

"The Relation of the Negroes to the Whites in the South," *Annals of the American Academy of Political and Social Science* 18 (July 1901): 121–40.

"The Republicans and the Black Voter," *Nation* 110 (June 5, 1920): 757–58.

"The Saga of Nkrumah," *National Guardian* (July 30, 1956).

"A Second Journey to Pan-Africa," *New Republic* 29 (December 7, 1921): 39–42.

A Select Bibliography of the American Negro: For General Readers. Atlanta: Atlanta University Press, 1901.

A Select Bibliography of the Negro American. Atlanta: Atlanta University Press, 1905.

The Selected Writings of W. E. B. Du Bois. Walter Wilson, ed. New York: New American Library, 1970.

Selections from Phylon. Herbert Aptheker, ed. Millwood, N.Y.: Kraus-Thomson, 1980.

Selections from The Crisis. Millwood, N.Y.: Kraus-Thomson, 1983.

Selections from the Horizon. Herbert Aptheker, ed. White Plains, N.Y.: Kraus-Thomson, 1985.

The Seventh Son: The Thought and Writings of W. E. B. Du Bois. 2 vols. Julius Lester, ed. New York: Random House, 1970.

Shall the Negro Be Encouraged to Seek Cultural Equality? (a debate with Lothrop Stoddard). Chicago: Chicago Forum, 1929.

Social and Physical Condition of Negroes in Cities. Atlanta: Atlanta University Press, 1897.

"The Social Evolution of the Black South," *American Negro Monographs* 1, iv (March 1911).

"Social Planning for the Negro, Past and Present," *Journal of Negro Education* 5 (January 1936): 110–25.

Some Efforts of American Negroes for Their Own Social Betterment. Atlanta: Atlanta University Press, 1898.

Some Notes on Negro Crime, Particularly in Georgia. Atlanta: Atlanta University Press, 1904.

Some Notes on the Negroes in New York City. Atlanta: Atlanta University Press, 1903.

The Souls of Black Folk. Chicago: McClurg, 1903.

"The Souls of White Folk," *Independent* 69 (August 18, 1910): 339–42.

"The South and a Third Party," *New Republic* 33 (January 3, 1923): 138–41.

"Speech by Dr. William E. B. Du Bois, A.L.P. Candidate for U.S. Senator at A.L.P. Rally, Golden Gate Ballroom," *The Seventh Son: The Thought and Writings of W. E. B. Du Bois*, vol 2. New York: Random House, 1970.

"Strivings of the Negro People," *Atlantic Monthly* 80 (August 1897): 194–98.

"The Study of the Negro Problems," *Annals of the American Academy of Political and Social Science* 11 (January 1898): 1–23.

The Suppression of the African Slave-Trade to the United States of America, 1638–1870. 1896; reprint, Baton Rouge: Loui"siana State University Press, 1970.

"The Talented Tenth," in *The Negro Problem*. (multiauthor collection). 1903; reprint, New York: Arno; New York Times, 1969.

The Talented Tenth Memorial Address," *Boule Journal* 15 (October 1948): 3–13.

"Three Centuries of Discrimination," *Crisis* 54 (March 1947): 326 ff.

"The Tragedy of 'Jim Crow,' " *Crisis* 26 (August 1923): 170.

"The Training of Negroes for Social Power," *Outlook* 75 (October 17, 1903): 409–14.

"The Twelfth Census and the Negro Problem," *Southern Workman* 29 (May 1900): 305–9.

"The Value of Agitation," *Voice of the Negro* 4 (March 1907).

"Vardaman," *Voice of the Negro* 3 (March 1906): 189–194.

"A Voyage to Liberia," in Carlos H. Baker, ed., *The American Looks at the World*. New York: Harcourt Brace, 1944.

W. E. B. Du Bois Papers at the University of Massachusetts, Amherst, Mass.

W. E. B. Du Bois: A Reader. David Levering Lewis, ed. New York: Henry Holt, 1995.

W. E. B. Du Bois: A Reader. Meyer Weinberg, ed. New York: Harper and Row, 1970.

W. E. B. Du Bois on Sociology and the Black Community. Dan S. Green and Edwin D. Driver, eds. Chicago: University of Chicago Press, 1978.

W. E. B. Du Bois Speaks: Speeches and Addresses, 1899–1963. 2 vols. Philip S. Foner, ed. New York: Pathfinder Press, 1970.

W. E. B. Du Bois: The Crisis Writings. Daniel Walden, ed. Greenwich, Conn.: Fawcett, 1972.

"What Is Civilization?" *Forum* 73 (February 1925): 178–88.

What the Negro Has Done for the United States and Texas. Texas Centennial Commission, U.S. Department of Commerce, 1936.

The World and Africa: An Inquiry into the Part Which Africa Has Played in World History. 1947; reprint, New York: International Publishers, 1965.

"Worlds of Color," *Foreign Affairs* 3 (April 1925): 423–44.

Writings by W. E. B. Du Bois in Non-Periodical Literature Edited by Others. Herbert Aptheker, ed. Millwood, N.Y.: Kraus-Thomson, 1982.

Writings of W. E. B. Du Bois in Periodicals Edited by Others. Herbert Aptheker, ed. Millwood, N.Y.: Kraus-Thomson, 1982.

———, ed. *The Crisis: A Record of the Darker Races* 1–41 (November 1910–July 1934).

———, ed. *Phylon: The Atlanta University Review of Race and Culture* 1–5 (1940–1944).

Du Bois, W. E. B., and Booker T. Washington. *The Negro in the South: His Economic Progress in Relation to His Moral and Religious Development*. Philadelphia: Jacobs, 1907.

Secondary Sources

Aaron, Daniel. *Writers on the Left*. New York: Avon, 1961.

Adams, Henry. *The Education of Henry Adams*. Boston: Houghton Mifflin, 1918.

Addams, Jane. *Democracy and Social Ethics.* New York: Macmillan, 1902.
———. *Twenty Years at Hull-House.* 1910; reprint, New York: New American Library, 1981.
———. "The Larger Aspects of the Woman's Movement," *Annals of the American Academy of Political and Social Science* 56 (November 1914): 1–8.
———. "Americanization," *Publications of the American Sociological Society* 14 (1919): 206–14.
———. *Jane Addams: A Centennial Reader,* Emily Cooper Johnson, ed. New York: Macmillan, 1960.
———. "Utilization of Women in City Government" in *Jane Addams: A Centennial Reader,* Emily Cooper Johnson, ed. New York: Macmillan, 1960.
———. "Why Women Should Vote," in *Jane Addams: A Centennial Reader,* Emily Cooper Johnson, ed. New York: Macmillan, 1960.
Adorno, Theodor W. et al. *The Positivist Dispute in German Sociology.* London: Heinemann, 1976.
Amoda, Moyibi. *Black Politics and Black Vision.* Philadelphia: Westminster, 1972.
Anderson, Elijah. *Streetwise: Race, Class and Change in an Urban Community.* Chicago: University of Chicago Press, 1992.
Anderson, James D. "Philanthropic Control over Private Black Higher Education," in Robert F. Arnove, ed., *Philanthropy and Cultural Imperialism.* Bloomington, Ind.: University of Indiana, 1980.
———. *The Education of Blacks in the South, 1860–1935.* Chapel Hill: University of North Carolina Press, 1988.
Anderson, Jervis. *A. Philip Randolph: A Biographical Portrait.* New York: Harcourt Brace Jovanovich, 1973.
Appiah, Anthony. "The Uncompleted Argument: Du Bois and the Illusion of Race." *Critical Inquiry* 12 (autumn 1985): 21–37.
———. Introduction to Appiah, ed., *Early African-American Classics.* New York: Bantam, 1990.
Aptheker, Herbert. Introduction to W. E. B. Du Bois, *The Souls of Black Folk.* 1903; reprint, Millwood, N.Y.: Kraus-Thomson, 1973.
———. "W. E. B. Du Bois: The First Eighty Years," *Phylon* 9 (spring 1948): 58– 69.
———. "The Washington-Du Bois Conference of 1904," *Science and Society* 13 (fall 1949): 344–51.
———. "Du Bois on Douglass: 1895," *Journal of Negro History* 49 (October 1964): 264–68.
———. "Some Unpublished Writings of W. E. B. Du Bois," *Freedomways* 5 (winter 1965): 103–28.
———. "W. E. B. Du Bois: The Final Years," *Journal of Human Relations* 14 (first quarter 1966): 149–55.
Arendt, Hannah. *Between Past and Future.* New York: Penguin, 1961.
Arnold, Matthew. *Culture and Anarchy.* 1869; reprint, Cambridge: Cambridge University Press, 1978.
Arnove, Robert F., ed. *Philanthropy and Cultural Imperialism.* Bloomington: Indiana University Press, 1980.
Aronowitz, Stanley. *False Promises: The Shaping of American Working Class Consciousness.* New York: McGraw-Hill, 1973.
Ashcraft, Richard. "On the Problem of Methodology and the Nature of Political Theory," *Political Theory* 3 (February 1975): 5–25.

Awkward, Michael. *Inspiriting Influences: Tradition, Revision and Afro-American Women's Novels.* New York: Columbia University Press, 1989.

Bailey, Joseph A. "Perspective in the Teaching of Negro History," *Journal of Negro History* 20 (January 1935): 19–26.

Backer, Houston A., Jr. *Long Black Song: Essays in Black American Literature and Culture.* Charlottesville: University of Virginia Press, 1972.

———. *Blues, Ideology, and Afro-American Literature: A Vernacular Theory.* Chicago: University of Chicago Press, 1984.

———. *Modernism and the Harlem Renaissance.* Chicago and London: University of Chicago Press, 1987.

———. "In Dubious Battle," *New Literary History* 18 (winter 1987): 344–62.

———. *Afro-American Poetics: Revisions of Harlem and the Black Aesthetic.* Madison: University of Wisconsin Press, 1988.

———. "There Is No More Beautiful Way: Theory and the Poetics of Afro-American Women's Writing," in Houston A. Baker Jr. and Patricia Redmond, eds., *Afro-American Literary Study in the 1990s.* Chicago: University of Chicago Press, 1989.

———. *Workings of the Spirit: The Poetics of Afro-American Women's Writings.* Chicago and London: University of Chicago Press, 1991.

Baker, Houston A., Jr., and Patricia Redmond, eds. *Afro-American Literary Study in the 1990s.* Chicago: University of Chicago Press, 1989.

Baltzell, E. Digby. Introduction to W. E. B. Du Bois, *The Philadelphia Negro.* New York: Schocken, 1967.

Banfield, Edward. *The Moral Basis of a Backward Society.* New York: Free Press, 1958.

———. *The Unheavenly City.* New York: Little Brown, 1970.

Banfield, Edward C., and James Q. Wilson. *City Politics.* New York: Vintage, 1968.

Baron, Harold M. "The Web of Urban Racism," in Louis L. Knowles and Kenneth Prewitt, eds., *Institutional Racism in America.* New York: Prentice-Hall, 1969.

Bellamy, Edward. *Looking Backward.* 1888; reprint, New York: Penguin, 1982.

Benjamin, Walter. *Illuminations.* Boston: Beacon, 1968.

Benston, Kimberly. "I Yam What I Am: The Topos of (Un)naming in Afro-American Literature," in Henry Louis Gates Jr., ed., *Black Literature and Literary Theory.* New York and London: Oxford University Press, 1984.

Blair, Thomas L. *Retreat to the Ghetto.* London: Wildwood House, 1977.

Blauner, Robert. *Racial Oppression in America.* New York: Harper and Row, 1972.

Bledstein, Burton J. *The Culture of Professionalism: The Middle Class and the Development of Higher Education in America.* New York: Norton, 1976.

Bontemps, Arna, and Jack Conroy. *Anyplace but Here.* New York: Hill and Wang, 1966.

Boorstin, Daniel. *The Genius of American Politics.* Chicago: University of Chicago Press, 1953.

Boring, E. G. *A History of Experimental Psychology.* New York: Appleton-Century-Crofts, 1950.

Bourne, Randolph. *The Radical Will: Randolph Bourne, Selected Writings 1911–1918.* Olaf Hansen, ed. New York: Urizen, 1977.

———. "Trans-National America," in Bourne, *The Radical Will: Randolph Bourne, Selected Writings 1911–1918.* Olaf Hansen, ed. New York: Urizen, 1977.

Boxill, Bernard R. "Du Bois and Fanon on Culture," *Philosophical Forum* (winter-spring 1979): 326–38.

Bracey, John H., and August Meier, eds. *Black Nationalism in America*. Indianapolis: Bobbs-Merrill, 1970.

Braverman, Harry F. *Labor and Monopoly Capital: The Degradation of Work in the Twentieth Century*. New York: Monthly Review Press, 1974.

Brawley, Benjamin. *The Negro Genius: A New Appraisal of the Achievement of the American Negro in Literature and the Fine Arts*. New York: Dodd Mead, 1937.

Bridges, Charles Wesley, II. "The Curriculum Theory Context of Activity Analysis and the Educational Philosophies of Washington and Du Bois," Ph.D. dissertation, Ohio State University, Columbus, 1973.

Brisbane, Robert H., Jr. "His Excellency: The Provincial President of Africa," *Phylon* 10 (February 1949): 257–64.

———. "Some New Light on the Garvey Movement," *Journal of Negro History* 36 (January 1951): 53–62.

Broderick, Francis L. "The Academic Training of W. E. B. Du Bois," *Journal of Negro Education* 27 (winter 1958): 10–16.

———. "German Influence on the Scholarship of W. E. B. Du Bois," *Phylon* 19 (December 1958): 367–71.

———. *W. E. B. Du Bois: Negro Leader in a Time of Crisis*. Palo Alto, Calif.: Stanford University Press, 1959.

Brotz, Howard, ed. *Negro Social and Political Thought, 1850–1920: Representative Texts*. New York: Basic Books, 1966.

Bruce, Dickson D., Jr. "W. E. B. Du Bois and the Idea of Double Consciousness," *American Literature* 64 (June 1992): 299–309.

Bulmer, Martin. "W. E. B. Du Bois as a Social Investigator, *The Philadelphia Negro*, 1899," in Bulmer et al., eds., *The Social Survey in Historical Perspective, 1880–1940*. Cambridge: Cambridge University Press, 1991.

Burnham, James. *The Managerial Revolution*. Bloomington: Indiana University Press, 1941.

Bury, J. B. *The Idea of Progress*. New York: Macmillan, 1932.

Butcher, Margaret Just. *The Negro in American Culture*. 1956; reprint, New York: Knopf, 1971.

Butterfield, Fox. "Afro-American Studies Get New Life at Harvard," *New York Times*, June 3, 1992.

Butterfield, Herbert. *The Whig Interpretation of History*. 1931; reprint, New York: Norton, 1965.

Cain, William E. "From Liberalism to Communism: The Political Thought of W. E. B. Du Bois," in Amy Kaplan and Donald E. Pease, eds., *Cultures of United States Imperialism*. Durham, N.C.: Duke University Press, 1993.

Callahan, Raymond E. *Education and the Cult of Efficiency*. Chicago: University of Chicago Press, 1962.

Carby, Hazel. " 'On the Threshold of Woman's Era': Lynching, Empire, and Sexuality in Black Feminist Theory," *Critical Inquiry* 12 (autumn 1985): 262–77.

Carr, Edward Hallett. *What Is History?* New York: Random House, 1961.

Carter, Stephen L. "The Black Table, the Empty Seat, and the Tie," in Gerald Early, ed., *Lure and Loathing: Essays on Race, Identity and the Ambivalence of Assimilation*. New York: Penguin, 1993.

Cary, Lorene. *Black Ice*. New York: Knopf, 1991.

Cassirer, Ernst. *The Philosophy of the Enlightenment*. Boston: Beacon, 1955.

Cayton, Horace R., and St. Clair Drake. *Black Metropolis: A Study of Negro Life in a Northern City*. 2 vols. 1945; reprint, New York: Harper and Row, 1962.

Chaffee, Mary Law. "William E. B. Du Bois' Concept of the Racial Problem in the United States," *Journal of Negro History* 41 (July 1956): 241–58.

Chandler, Alfred D., Jr. *The Visible Hand: The Managerial Revolution in American Business*. Cambridge, Mass.: Belknap, 1977.

Clarke, John Henrik, Esther Jackson, Ernest Kaiser, and J. H. O'Dell, eds. *Black Titan: W. E. B. Du Bois*. Boston: Beacon, 1970.

Clecak, Peter. *Radical Paradoxes: Dilemmas of the American Left, 1945–1970*. New York: Harper and Row, 1973.

Cohen, Jean. "Max Weber and the Dynamics of Rationalized Domination," *Telos* 14 (winter 1972): 63–86.

Comer, James. *Maggie's American Dream: The Life and Times of a Black Family*. New York: New American Library, 1988.

Conn, Peter. *The Divided Mind: Ideology and Imagination in America 1898–1917*. Cambridge and New York: Cambridge University Press, 1983.

Connelly, Mark Thomas. *The Response to Prostitution in the Progressive Era*. Chapel Hill: University of North Carolina Press, 1980.

Connolly, William E. *The Terms of Political Discourse*. Princeton, N.J.: Princeton University Press, 1983.

Contee, Clarence. "Emergence of Du Bois as an African Nationalist," *Journal of Negro History* 54 (first quarter 1969): 48–63.

Cook, Samuel Du Bois. "Hacker's Liberal Democracy and Social Control: A Critique," *American Political Science Review* 51 (December 1957): 1027–39.

Coontz, Stephanie. *The Way We Never Were: American Families and the Nostalgia Trap*. New York: HarperCollins, 1992.

Cooper, Anna Julia. *A Voice From the South*. 1892; reprint, New York and Oxford: Oxford University Press, 1988.

Cose, Ellis. *The Rage of a Privileged Class*. New York: HarperCollins, 1993.

Cott, Nancy F. *The Grounding of Modern Feminism*. New Haven, Conn., and London: Yale University Press, 1987.

Cox, Oliver. *Caste, Class and Race*. 1948; reprint, New York: Monthly Review Press, 1959.
———. "Leadership among Negroes," in Alvin W. Gouldner, ed., *Studies in Leadership*. New York: Barnes and Noble, 1950.
———. "The Question of Pluralism," *Race* 12 (fourth quarter 1971): 385–400.

Croly, Herbert. *The Promise of American Life*. 1909; reprint, Indianapolis: Bobbs-Merrill, 1965.

Cronon, E. David. *Black Moses: The Story of Marcus Garvey and the Universal Negro Improvement Association*. Madison: University of Wisconsin Press, 1955.

Crummell, Alexander. *Destiny and Race: Selected Writings, 1840–1898*. Amherst: University of Massachusetts Press, 1992.

Crunden, Robert M. *Ministers of Reform: The Progressives' Achievement in American Civilization, 1889–1920*. Urbana: University of Illinois Press, 1984.

Cruse, Harold. *The Crisis of the Negro Intellectual: From Its Origins to the Present*. New York: Morrow, 1967.

Crutchfield, R. S., and D. Krech. *A Source Book in the History of Psychology*. Cambridge, Mass.: Harvard University Press, 1965.

Curry, George E. "A Writer's Tortuous Flight from Home," *Chicago Tribune*, July 9, 1992.

Curti, Merle, ed. *American Scholarship in the Twentieth Century*. Cambridge, Mass.: Harvard University Press, 1953.

Cywar, Alan Sigmund. "An Inquiry into American Thought and the Determinate Influence of Political Economic and Social Factors in the Early Twentieth Century: Bourne, Dewey, Du Bois, Nearing, Veblen, and Weyl," Ph.D. dissertation, University of Rochester, Rochester, N.Y., 1972.

Davis, Allison. *Leadership, Love and Aggression*. New York: Harcourt Brace, 1983.

Davis, John A., ed. *Africa from the Point of View of American Negro Scholars*. New York: American Society of African Culture, 1958.

Davis, William Allison. *Du Bois and the Problems of the Black Masses*. Atlanta: Atlanta University, 1974.

DeMarco, Joseph P. "The Rationale and Foundation of Du Bois' Theory of Economic Cooperation," *Phylon* 25 (March 1974): 5–15.

———. *The Social Thought of W. E. B. Du Bois*. Lanham, Md.: University Press of America, 1983.

di Leonardo, Micaela. "Morals, Mothers, and Militarism: Antimilitrarism and Feminist Theory," *Feminist Studies* 11 (fall 1985): 599–617.

———. "Habits of the Cumbered Heart: Ethnic Community and Women's Culture as American Invented Traditions," in Jay O'Brien and William Roseberry, eds., *Golden Ages, Dark Ages: Imagining the Past in Anthropology and History*. Berkeley: University of California Press, 1991.

———. "White Ethnicities, Identity Politics, and Baby Bear's Chair," *Social Text* (winter 1994): 165–91.

Diggins, John P. *The American Left in the Twentieth Century*. New York: Harcourt Brace Jovanovich, 1973.

———. *Up from Communism: Conservative Odysseys in American Intellectual History*. New York: Harper and Row, 1975.

Drake, St. Clair. "The Social and Economic Status of the Negro in the United States," in Talcott Parsons and Kenneth Clark, eds., *The Negro American*. Boston: Beacon, 1967.

———. "Anthropology and the Black Experience," *Black Scholar* 11 (September-October 1980): 2–31.

Draper, Theodore. *The Rediscovery of Black Nationalism*. New York: Viking, 1970.

Dreitzel, Hans-Peter. "Social Science and the Problem of Rationality," in Ira Katznelson et al., eds., *The Politics and Society Reader*. New York: McKay, 1974.

Dudziak, Mary Louise. "Cold War Civil Rights: The Relationship between Civil Rights and Foreign Affairs in the Truman Administration," Ph.D. dissertation, Yale University, New Haven, Conn., 1992.

Dunn, John. "The Identity of the History of Ideas," in Peter Laslett, W. G. Runciman, and Quentin Skinner, eds., *Philosophy, Politics and Society*. New York: Barnes and Noble, 1972.

———. *Western Political Theory in the Face of the Future*. New York: Cambridge University Press, 1979.

Eakins, David W. "The Origins of Corporate Liberal Policy Research, 1916–1922: The Political-Economic Expert and the Decline of Public Debate," in Jerry Israel, ed., *Building the Organizational Society*. New York: Free Press, 1972.

Early, Gerald, ed. *Lure and Loathing: Essays on Race, Identity and the Ambivalence of Assimilation*. New York: Penguin, 1993.

———. Introduction to Early, ed., *Lure and Loathing: Essays on Race, Identity and the Ambivalence of Assimilation*. New York: Penguin, 1993.

Egan, Maureen L. "Evolutionary Theory in the Social Philosophy of Charlotte Perkins Gilman," *Hypatia* 4 (spring 1989): 102–19.

Ehrenreich, Barbara, and John Ehrenreich. "The Professional Managerial Class," *Radical America* (March-April 1977): 175.

Eichberg, Henning. "The Nazi *Thingspiel*: Theater for the Masses in Fascism and Proletarian Culture," *New German Critique* (spring 1977): 133–50.

Eisenberg, Bernard. "Kelly Miller: The Negro Leader as a Marginal Man," *Journal of Negro History* 45 (July 1960): 182–97.

Ellis, Trey. "The New Black Aesthetic," *Callaloo* 12 (winter 1989): 233–43. With critiques and Ellis's response, "Response to NBA Critics": 244–51.

Ellison, Ralph. "*An American Dilemma*: A Review," in Ellison, *Shadow and Act*. New York: Vintage, 1972.

———. *Shadow and Act*. New York: Random House, 1972.

Ely, Richard T. *The Strength and Weaknesses of Socialism*. New York: Chautauqua Press, 1894.

Emerson, Ralph Waldo. *Young Emerson Speaks*. Arthur Cushman McGiffert, ed. Boston: Houghton Mifflin, 1938.

———. "Religion and Society," in Emerson, *Young Emerson Speaks*. Aurthur Cushman McGiffert, ed. Boston: Houghton Mifflin, 1938.

———. *The Portable Emerson*. Carl Bode, ed. New York: Penguin, 1981.

———. "Fate," in *The Portable Emerson*. Carl Bode, ed. New York: Penguin, 1981.

———. "The Transcendentalist," in *The Portable Emerson*. Carl Bode, ed. New York: Penguin, 1981.

Ewen, Stuart. *Captains of Consciousness: Advertising and the Social Roots of Consumer Culture*. New York: McGraw-Hill, 1976.

Ewen, Stuart, and Elizabeth Ewen. "Americanization and Consumption," *Telos* (fall 1978): 42–51.

Factor, Robert L. "Booker T. Washington and the Transformation of the Black Belt Negro: Disorganization and Change," in Jerry Israel, ed., *Building the Organizational Society. Essays on Associational Activities in Modern America*. New York: Free Press, 1972.

Fergerson, Gerard. "Race, Science, and Medicine in the Late Nineteenth Century: W. E. B. Du Bois and the Health and Physique of the Negro American," M.A. thesis, Yale University, New Haven, Conn., 1987.

Ferris, William H. *The African Abroad*. 2 vols. New Haven, Conn.: Turtle, Morehouse and Taylor, 1913.

Fields, Mamie Garvin, with Karen Fields. *Lemon Swamp and Other Places*. New York: Free Press, 1983.

Fine, Sidney. *Laissez-Faire and the General Welfare State*. Ann Arbor: University of Michigan Press, 1956.

Fleron, Frederic J., ed. *Technology and Communist Culture*. New York: Praeger, 1977.

Foner, Eric. "Reconstruction Revisited," *Reviews in American History* 10 (December 1982): 82–100.

———. *Reconstruction: America's Unfinished Revolution, 1863–1877*. New York: Harper and Row, 1988.

Fonlon, Bernard. "The Passing of a Great African," in John Henrik Clarke et al., eds., *Black Titan: W. E. B. Du Bois*. Boston: Beacon, 1970.

Fontaine, William T. "An Interpretation of Contemporary Negro Thought from the

Standpoint of the Sociology of Knowledge," *Journal of Negro History* 25 (January 1940): 6–13.

———. "The Mind and Thought of the Negro of the United States as Revealed in Imaginative Literature, 1876–1940," *Southern University Bulletin* 28 (March 1942): 5–50.

———. "'Social Determination' in the Writings of Negro Scholars," *American Journal of Sociology* 49 (January 1944): 302–15.

———. *Reflections on Segregation, Desegregation, Power and Morals.* Springfield, Ill.: Thomas, 1967.

Forcey, Charles. *The Crossroads of Liberalism: Croly, Weyl, Lippmann, and the Progressive Era, 1900–1925.* New York: Oxford University Press, 1961.

Fordham, Signithia, and John Ogbu. "Black Students' School Success: Coping with the 'Burden of "Acting White," '" *Urban Review* 18 (1986): 176–206.

Fox, Daniel M. *The Discovery of Abundance: Simon N. Patten and the Transformation of Social Theory.* Ithaca, N.Y.: Cornell University Press, 1967.

Frankfurt Institute for Social Research. *Aspects of Sociology.* Boston: Beacon, 1972.

Franklin, John Hope. Introduction to Franklin, ed., *Three Negro Classics: Up from Slavery, The Souls of Black Folk, The Autobiography of an Ex-Colored Man.* New York: Avon, 1965.

———. *From Slavery to Freedom: A History of Negro Americans.* New York: Random House, 1966.

Franklin, John Hope, and August Meier, eds. *Black Leaders of the Twentieth Century.* Urbana, Chicago, and London: University of Illinois Press, 1982.

Frazier, E. Franklin. *Black Bourgeoisie: The Rise of a New Middle Class.* New York: Free Press, 1957.

———. *On Race Relations.* Chicago: University of Chicago Press, 1968.

———. "Durham: Capital of the Black Middle Class," in Alain Locke, ed., *The New Negro: An Interpretation.* 1925; reprint, New York: Antheum, 1968.

———. "The Failure of the Negro Intellectual," in Frazier, *On Race Relations.* Chicago: University of Chicago Press, 1968.

Frederickson, George M. *The Black Image in the White Mind: The Debate of Afro-American Character and Destiny, 1817–1914.* Middletown, Conn.: Wesleyan University Press, 1987.

Freedman, Martin Neil. "The Rhetorical Adaptation of Social Movement Leaders: Booker T. Washington and W. E. B. Du Bois," Ph.D. dissertation, Purdue University, Lafayette, Ind., 1975.

Fuller, Hoyt W. "The New Black Literature: Protest or Affirmation," in Addison Gayle, ed., *The Black Aesthetic.* Garden City, N.Y.: Doubleday, 1971.

Fullinwider, S. P. *The Mind and Mood of Black America.* Homewood, Ill.: Dorsey, 1969.

Fuss, Diana. *Essentially Speaking: Feminism, Nature and Difference.* New York and London: Routledge, 1989.

Gadamer, Hans-Georg. *Truth and Method.* New York: Seabury, 1975.

Gaines, Kevin. "Black Americans' Racial Uplift Ideology as 'Civilizing Mission': Pauline E. Hopkins on Race and Imperialism," in Amy Kaplan and Donald E. Pease, eds., *Cultures of United States Imperialism* (Durham, N.C.: Duke University Press, 1993).

Gardner, Bettye J. "The Teaching of Afro-American History in Schools and Colleges," in Darlene Clark Hine, ed., *The State of Afro-American History: Past, Present and Future.* Baton Rouge: Louisiana State University Press, 1986.

Garrow, David. *Bearing the Cross: Martin Luther King, Jr. and the Southern Christian Leadership Conference.* New York: Morrow, 1986.

Gates, Henry Louis, Jr. "Dis and Dat: Dialect and the Descent," in Dexter Fisher and Robert Stepto, eds., *Afro-American Literature: The Reconstruction of Instruction.* New York: Modern Language Association, 1979.

———. "Preface to Blackness: Text and Pretext," in Dexter Fisher and Robert Stepto, eds., *Afro-American Literature: The Reconstruction of Instruction.* New York: Modern Language Association, 1l979.

———. "The Blackness of Blackness: A Critique of the Sign and the Signifying Monkey," in Henry Louis Gates, Jr., ed., *Black Literature and Literary Theory.* New York and London: Oxford University Press, 1984.

———. "Criticism in the Jungle," in Henry Louis Gates, Jr., *Black Literature and Literary Theory.* New York and London: Oxford University Press, 1984.

———. "A Negro Way of Saying," *New York Times Book Review,* April 21, 1985.

———. "Writing, 'Race,' and the Difference It Makes," *Critical Inquiry* 12 (autumn 1985): 1–20.

———. *Figures in Black: Words, Signs and the "Racial" Self.* New York and Oxford: Oxford University Press, 1987.

———. "What's Love Got to Do with It?: Critical Theory, Integrity and the Black Idiom," *New Literary History* 18 (winter 1987): 344–62.

———. *The Signifying Monkey: A Theory of Afro-American Literary Criticism.* New York and Oxford: Oxford University Press, 1988.

———. "Canon-Formation, Literary History, and the Afro-American Tradition: From the Seen to the Told," in Houston Baker and Patricia Redmond, eds., *Afro-American Literary Study in the 1990s.* Chicago: University of Chicago Press, 1989.

———. Introduction to W. E. B. Du Bois, *The Souls of Black Folk.* 1903; reprint, New York: Bantam, 1989.

———. "Good-Bye, Columbus? Notes on the Culture of Criticism," *American Literary History* 3 (winter 1991): 711–32.

———. "African American Criticism," in Stephen Greenblat and Giles Gunn, eds., *Redrawing the Boundaries: The Transformation of English and American Literary Studies.* New York: Modern Language Association, 1992.

———. "Black Demagogues and Pseudo-Scholars," *New York Times* July 20, 1992.

———. "The Fire Last Time: What James Baldwin Can and Can't Teach America," *New Republic,* June 1, 1992, pp. 37–43.

———. "A Fragmented Man: George Schuyler and the Claims of Race," *New York Times Book Review,* September 20, 1992.

———. "A Pretty Good Society," *Time,* November 16, 1992, p. 86.

———. *Loose Canons: Notes on the Culture Wars.* New York: Oxford University Press, 1992.

———. "Two Nations . . . Both Black," *Forbes,* September 14, 1992, pp. 132–38.

———. Introduction to Katherine Whittmore and Gerald Marzorati, eds., *Voices in Black and White.* New York: Franklin Square, 1993.

———. "Black Intellectuals, Jewish Tensions," *New York Times,* April 14, 1993.

———. "Let Them Talk: Why Civil Liberties Pose No Threat to Civil Rights," *New Republic,* September 20 and 29, 1993, pp. 37–49.

———. "Two Nations . . . Both Black" (revised), in Robert Gooding-Williams, ed., *Reading Rodney King, Reading Urban Uprisings.* New York: Routledge, 1993.

———. *Colored People: A Memoir.* New York: Knopf, 1994.

————. "Black Creativity: On the Cutting Edge," *Time*, October 10, 1994, pp. 74–75.

————. "The Black Leadership Myth," *New Yorker*, October 24, 1994.

————, ed. *Black Literature and Literary Theory*. New York and London: Oxford University Press, 1984.

————. *Reading Black/Reading Feminist: A Critical Anthology*. New York: Meridian, 1990.

Gatewood, Willard B. *Aristocrats of Color: The Black Elite, 1880–1920*. Bloomington: Indiana University Press, 1990.

Gayle, Addison, Jr., ed. *The Black Aesthetic*. Garden City, N.Y.: Doubleday, 1971.

Genovese, Eugene D. *Roll, Jordan, Roll: The World the Slaves Made*. New York: Random House, 1976.

George, Francois. "Forgetting Lenin," *Telos* (winter 1973–74): 53–88.

Gibson, Donald B. Introduction to W. E. B. Du Bois, *The Souls of Black Folk*. 1903; reprint, New York: Penguin. 1989.

Gibson, Lovie Nancy. "Du Bois' Propaganda Literature: An Outgrowth of His Sociological Studies," Ph.D. dissertation, State University of New York-Buffalo, 1977.

Giddings, Paula. *When and Where I Enter: The Impact of Black Women on Race and Sex in America*. New York: Morrow, 1984.

Gilbert, James. *Designing the Industrial State: The Intellectual Pursuit of Collectivism in America, 1880–1940*. Chicago: Quadrangle Books, 1972.

Gilligan, Carol. *In a Different Voice*. Cambridge, Mass.: Harvard University Press, 1982.

Gillmore, Inez Haynes. "Confessions of an Alien," *Harper's Bazaar* 48 (April 1912): 170–71.

————. "The Making of a Militant," in Elaine Showalter, ed., *These Modern Women: Autobiographical Essays from the Twenties*. New York: Feminist Press, 1989.

Gilman, Charlotte Perkins. *Women and Economics: The Economic Factor between Men and Women as a Factor in Social Evolution*. 1898; reprint, New York: Harper and Row, 1966.

————. "The Waste of Private Housekeeping," *Annals of the American Academy of Political and Social Science* 48 (July 1913): 91–96.

————. *Herland*. 1915; reprint, New York: Pantheon, 1979.

————. *The Living of Charlotte Perkins Gilman: An Autobiography*. New York: Ayer, 1935.

Gilroy, Paul. *The Black Atlantic: Modernity and Double Consciousness*. Cambridge, Mass.: Harvard, 1993.

Gipson, Carolyn Renee. "Intellectual Dilemmas in the Novels of W. E. B. Du Bois," Ph.D. dissertation, University of Michigan, Ann Arbor, 1971.

Golden, L. Hanga, and Ov Milikian. "William E. B. Du Bois: Scientist and Public Figure," *Journal of Human Relations* 14 (first quarter 1966): 156–68.

Goldmann, Lucien. *The Philosophy of the Enlightenment: The Christian Burgess and the Enlightenment*. Cambridge, Mass.: MIT Press, 1973.

Gooding-Williams, Robert. "Philosophy of History and Social Critique in *The Souls of Black Folk*," *Social Science Information* 26 (first quarter 1987): 99–114.

Gould, Stephen Jay. *Ontogeny and Phylogeny*. Cambridge, Mass.: Harvard University Press, 1977.

————. *The Mismeasure of Man*. New York: Norton, 1981.

Gouldner, Alvin W. *The Coming Crisis of Western Sociology*. New York: Avon, 1970.

————. *The Dialectic of Ideology and Technology: The Origins, Grammar, and Future of Ideology*. New York: Seabury, 1976.

————. *The Future of Intellectuals and the Rise of the New Class.* New York: Seabury, 1979.

————. *The Two Marxisms: Contradictions and Anomalies in the Development of Theory.* New York: Seabury, 1980.

Grady, Henry. *The New South: Writings and Speeches of Henry Grady.* Savannah, Ga.: Beehive, 1971.

Graham, George J., Jr., and George W. Carey, eds. *The Post-Behavioral Era: Perspectives on Political Science.* New York: McKay, 1972.

Graham, Loren R. *Science and Philosophy in the Soviet Union.* New York: Random House, 1974.

Graham, Shirley. *His Day Is Marching On: A Memoir of W. E. B. Du Bois.* Chicago: Johnson, 1976.

Green, Dan S. and Edwin D. Driver. "W. E. B. Du Bois: A Case in the Sociology of Sociological Negation," *Phylon* 37 (December 1976): 308–33.

————. Introduction to Green and Driver, eds., *W. E. B. Du Bois on Sociology and the Black Community.* Chicago: University of Chicago Press, 1978.

Green, David. *Shaping Political Consciousness: The Language of Politics in America from McKinley to Reagan.* Ithaca, N.Y.: Cornell University Press, 1987.

Green, Donald and Ian Shapiro. *Pathologies of Rational Choice Theory.* New Haven, Conn., and London: Yale University Press, 1994.

Gronlund, Laurence. *The Cooperative Commonwealth in Its Outlines: An Exposition of Modern Socialism.* Boston: Lee and Shepard, 1884

Gruber, Carol S. *Mars and Minerva: World War I and the Uses of the Higher Learning in America.* Baton Rouge: Louisiana State University Press, 1975.

Gunnell, John, G. "Social Science and Political Reality: The Problem of Explanation," *Social Research* 35 (spring 1968): 159–201.

————. "Deduction, Explanation and Social Scientific Inquiry," *American Political Science Review* 63 (December 1969): 1233–62. With reply and riposte by Arthur S. Goldberg and A. James Gregor and rejoinder by Gunnell.

————. "The Idea of the Conceptual Framework: A Philosophical Critique," *Journal of Comparative Administration* 1 (August 1969), 140–76.

————. "Interpretation and the History of Political Theory: Apology and Epistemology," *American Political Science Review* 76 (June 1982): 317–27.

Guzman, Jessie P. "W. E. B. Du Bois—The Historian," *Journal of Negro Education* 30 (fall 1961): 377–85.

Haber, Samuel. *Efficiency and Uplift: Scientific Management in the Progressive Era.* Chicago: University of Chicago Press, 1964.

Habermas, Jurgen. "Technology and Science as 'Ideology,'" in Jurgen Habermas, *Toward a Rational Society: Student Protest, Science and Politics.* Boston: Beacon, 1970.

————. *Toward a Rational Society: Student Protest, Science and Politics.* Boston: Beacon, 1970.

————. *Knowledge and Human Interests.* Boston: Beacon, 1975.

————. *Legitimation Crisis.* Boston: Beacon, 1975.

Hall, G. Stanley. *Adolescence.* New York: Appleton, 1904.

Hamilton, Virginia. *W. E. B. Du Bois: A Biography.* New York: Crowell, 1972.

Harding, Vincent. "W. E. B. Du Bois and the Black Messianic Vision," in John Henrik Clarke et al., eds., *Black Titan: W. E. B. Du Bois.* Boston: Beacon, 1970.

————. *There Is a River: The Black Struggle for Freedom in America.* New York: Random House, 1981.

Hare, Nathan. "W. E. Burghardt Du Bois: An Appreciation," in W. E. B. Du Bois, *The Souls of Black Folk*, 1903; reprint, New York: New American Library, 1969.

Harlan, Louis R. *Booker T. Washington*. 2 vols. New York: Oxford University Press, 1972–83.

Harris, Abram. *The Negro as Capitalist*. 1936; reprint, New York: Negro Universities Press, 1969.

Harris, Abram, and Sterling Spero. *The Black Worker*. 1931; reprint, New York: Atheneum, 1968.

Harris, Leonard, ed. *Philosophy Born of Struggle: Anthology of Afro-American Philosophy from 1917*. Dubuque, Iowa: Kendall-Hunt, 1983.

Hartz, Louis. *The Liberal Tradition in America: An Interpretation of American Political Thought since the Revolution*. New York: Harcourt Brace, 1955.

Haselby, Sam. "Muscular Humanism: Interview with Henry Louis Gates, Jr.," *Hungry Mind Review*, (fall 1994): 22–23.

Haskell, Thomas L. *The Emergence of Professional Social Science*. Urbana: University of Illinois Press, 1977.

Hawkins, Richmond Laurin. *Positivism in the United States (1853–1861)*. Cambridge, Mass.: Harvard University Press, 1938.

Hawthorn, Geoffrey. *Enlightenment and Despair: A History of Sociology*. London: Cambridge University Press, 1976.

Hays, Samuel P. *The Response to Industrialism, 1885–1914*. Chicago: University of Chicago Press, 1957.

———. *Conservation and the Gospel of Efficiency*. Cambridge, Mass.: Harvard University Press, 1959.

———. "The Politics of Reform in Municipal Government in the Progressive Era," *Pacific Northwest Quarterly* 55 (October 1964): 157–69.

Henderson, Lenneal J., Jr. "W. E. B. Du Bois," *Black Scholar* 1 (January-February 1970): 48–57.

Henderson, Vivian W. *Race, Economics, and Public Policy: With Reflections on W. E. B. Du Bois*. Atlanta: Atlanta University, 1974.

Herbst, Julian. *The German Historical School in American Scholarship: A Study in the Transfer of Culture*. Ithaca, N.Y.: Cornell University Press, 1965.

Herrnstein, Richard, and Charles Murray. *The Bell Curve: Intelligence and Class Structure in American Life*. New York: Free Press, 1994.

Higbee, Mark David. "W. E. B. Du Bois, F. B. Ransom, the Madam Walker Company, and Black Business Leadership in the 1930s," *Indiana Magazine of History* 89 (June 1993): 101–24.

Higginbotham, Evelyn Brooks. *Righteous Discontent: The Women's Movement in the Black Baptist Church, 1880–1920*. Cambridge, Mass.: Harvard University Press, 1993.

Higham, John. "The Schism in American Scholarship," *American Historical Review* 72 (October 1966): 1–21.

———. *Send These to Me: Jews and Other Immigrants in Urban America*. New York: Atheneum, 1975.

———. Introduction to Higham and Conkin, eds., *New Directions in American Intellectual History*. Baltimore: Johns Hopkins University Press, 1979.

———. *Strangers in the Land: Patterns of American Nativism, 1860–1925*. New York: Atheneum, 1981.

———. *History: Professional Scholarship in America*. Baltimore and London: Johns Hopkins University Press, 1983.

Higham, John, and Paul K. Conkin, eds. *New Directions in American Intellectual History.* Baltimore: Johns Hopkins University Press, 1979.

Hill, Mary A. *Charlotte Perkins Gilman: The Making of a Radical Feminist, 1860–1896.* Philadelphia: Temple University Press, 1980.

Hirschfeld, Charles. "Nationalist Progressivism and World War I," *Mid-America* 45 (July 1963): 139—56.

Hobsbawm, E. J. *Revolutionaries.* New York: Pantheon, 1973.

Hofstadter, Richard. *The Age of Reform.* New York: Random House, 1955.

———. *Social Darwinism in American Thought.* Boston: Beacon, 1955.

———. "The Revolution in Higher Education," in Arthur M. Schlesinger Jr. and Morton White, eds., *Paths of American Thought.* Boston: Houghton Mifflin, 1963.

Hollinger, David A. "Historians and the Discourse of Intellectuals" in John Higham and Paul K. Conkin, eds., *New Directions in American Intellectual History.* Baltimore: Johns Hopkins University Press, 1979.

———. *In the American Province: Studies in the History and Historiography of Ideas.* Bloomington: Indiana University Press, 1985.

Holloway, Jonathan Scott. "Confronting the Veil: New Deal African-American Intellectuals and the Evolution of a Radical Voice," Ph.D. dissertation, Yale University, New Haven, Conn., 1995.

Holmes, Eugene C. "W. E. B. Du Bois: Philosopher," in John Henrik Clarke et al., eds., *Black Titan: W. E. B. Du Bois.* Boston: Beacon, 1970.

Holt, Thomas C. "The Lonely Warrior: Ida Wells-Barnett and the Struggle for Black Leadership," in John Hope Franklin and August Meier, eds., *Black Leaders of the Twentieth Century.* Urbana, Ill.: Chicago and London: University of Illinois Press, 1982.

———. "The Political Uses of Alienation: W. E. B. Du Bois on Politics, Race, and Culture, 1903–1940," *American Quarterly* 42 (June 1990): 301–23.

Hopkins, Charles. "Pan-Africanism: A Theoretical Examination of Contemporary Afro-American Involvement," M.A. thesis, University of North Carolina, Chapel Hill, N.C., 1974.

Horkheimer, Max, and Theodor W. Adorno. *The Dialectic of Enlightenment.* New York: Herder and Herder, 1972.

Horne, Gerald. *Black and Red: W. E. B. Du Bois and the Afro-American Response to the Cold War, 1944–1963.* Albany: SUNY Press, 1986.

Horsman, Reginald. *Race and Manifest Destiny: The Origins of American Racial Anglo-Saxonism.* Cambridge, Mass.: Harvard University Press, 1981.

Huggins, Nathan I. *Harlem Renaissance.* New York: Oxford University Press, 1971.

Huggins, Nathan I., Martin Kilson, and Daniel Fox. *Key Issues in the Afro-American Experience.* 2 vols. New York: Harcourt Brace Jovanovich, 1971.

Hughes, Langston. *The Big Sea.* New York: Hill and Wang, 1940.

———. *I Wonder as I Wander.* New York: Hill and Wang, 1956.

———. "Tribute," in John Henrik Clarke et al., eds., *Black Titan: W. E. B. Du Bois.* Boston: Beacon, 1970.

Huntington, Samuel P. "The Clash of Civilizations?," *Foreign Affairs* 72 (summer 1993): 22–49.

Hunton, W. Alphaeus. "W. E. B. Du Bois: The Meaning of His Life," in John Henrik Clarke et al., eds., *Black Titan: W. E. B. Du Bois.* Boston: Beacon, 1970.

Hurston, Zora Neale. "The 'Pet Negro' System," *American Mercury* 56 (May 1943): 593–600.

———. *Dust Tracks in the Road.* Urbana: University of Illinois Press, 1984.

Hwa Yol Jung, ed. *Existential Phenomenology and Political Theory: Reader.* Chicago: Gateway, 1972.

Inge, W. R. *The Idea of Progress.* Oxford: Oxford University Press, 1920.

Isaacs, Harold R. "The American Negro and Africa: Some Notes," *Phylon* 20 (fall 1959): 219–33.

———. *The New World of Negro Americans.* New York: John Day, 1963.

———. *Idols of the Tribe.* New York: Harper and Row, 1975.

Israel, Jerry, ed. *Building the Organizational Society: Essays on Associational Activities in Modern America.* New York: Free Press, 1972.

Jackson, Walter A. *Gunnar Myrdal and America's Conscience: Social Engineering and Racial Liberalism, 1938–1987.* Chapel Hill: University of North Carolina Press, 1990.

Jacoby, Russell. "The Politics of Objectivity: Notes on the U.S. Left," *Telos* (winter 1977–78): 74–88.

———. "What Is Conformist Marxism?" *Telos* (fall 1980): 19–44.

James, William. *The Principles of Psychology.* 1890; reprint, Cambridge, Mass.: Harvard University Press, 1983.

———. *Human Immortality.* 1891; reprint, New York: Dover, 1956.

———. *The Will to Believe.* 1897; reprint, New York: Dover, 1956.

———. *The Varieties of Religious Experience.* 1902; reprint, New York: Macmillan, 1961.

———. *Pragmatism.* Cleveland and New York: Meridian, 1955.

———. *Essays in Radical Empiricism and A Pluralistic Universe.* New York: Dutton, 1971.

———. "Does Consciousness Exist?," in James, *The Writings of William James.* John J. McDermott ed. Chicago: University of Chicago Press, 1977.

———. "The Moral Equivalent of War," in James, *The Writings of William James.* John J. McDermott ed. Chicago: University of Chicago Press, 1977.

———. *The Writings of William James.* John J. McDermott, ed. Chicago: University of Chicago Press, 1977.

Jaynes, Gerald D. "Urban Policy and Economic Reform," *Review of Black Political Economy* 13 (summer-fall 1984): 103–15.

Johnson, Adolph, Jr. "A History and Interpretation of the William Edward Burghardt Du Bois-Booker Taliaferro Washington Higher Educational Controversy," Ph.D. dissertation, University of Southern California, Los Angeles, Calif., 1976.

Johnson, Arthur L. "The Social Theories of W. E. B. Du Bois," M.A. thesis, Atlanta University, 1949.

Johnson, Barbara. "Metaphor, Metonymy and Voice in *Their Eyes Were Watching God,*" in Henry Louis Gates, Jr. ed., *Black Literature and Literary Theory.* New York and London: Oxford University Press, 1984.

———. "Response," in Houston Baker and Patricia Redmond, eds., *Afro-American Literary Study in the 1990s.* Chicago: University of Chicago Press, 1989.

Johnson, Charles S. "The New Frontage on American Life," in Alain Locke, ed. *The New Negro: An Interpretation.* 1925; reprint, New York: Atheneum, 1968.

———. "After Garvey: What?" *Opportunity* 1 (August 1923): 231–33.

Johnson, James Weldon. *Black Manhattan.* 1930; reprint, New York: Atheneum, 1968.

———. *Along This Way.* New York: Viking, 1933.

Jones, Greta. *Social Darwinism and English Thought: The Interaction between Biological and Social Theory.* Atlantic Highlands, N.J.: Humanities Press, 1980.

Jones, LeRoi, and Larry Neal, eds. *Black Fire: An Anthology of Afro-American Writing.* New York: Morrow, 1968.

Jones, Mack H., and Alex Willingham. "The White Custodians of the Black Experience: A Reply to Rudwick and Meier," *Social Science Quarterly* 51 (June 1970): 31–36.

Jordan, Jennifer. "Cultural Nationalism in the Sixties: Politics and Poetry," in Adolph L. Reed Jr., ed., *Race, Politics and Culture: Critical Essays on the Radicalism of the 1960s.* Westport, Conn.: Greenwood, 1986.

Jordan, Winthrop. *White over Black.* Chapel Hill: University of North Carolina Press, 1968.

Jordanova, L. J. "Natural Facts: A Historical Perspective on Science and Sexuality," in Carol MacCormack and Marilyn Strathern, eds., *Nature, Culture and Gender.* Cambridge: Cambridge University Press, 1980.

Joyce, Joyce A. "The Black Canon: Reconstructing Black American Literary Criticism," *New Literary History* 18 (winter 1987): 335–44.

———. " 'Who the Cap Fit': Unconsciousness and Unconscionableness in the Criticism of Houston A. Baker, Jr. and Henry Louis Gates, Jr.," *New Literary History* 18 (winter 1987): 371–84.

Kakar, Sudhir. *Frederick Taylor: A Study in Personality in Innovation.* Cambridge, Mass.: MIT Press, 1971.

Kallen, Horace M. *Culture and Democracy in the United States.* New York: Boni and Livewright, 1924.

———. *Cultural Pluralism and the American Idea.* Philadelphia: University of Pennsylvannia Press, 1956.

Kaplan, Sidney. "Social Engineers as Saviors: Effects of World War I on Some American Liberals," *Journal of the History of Ideas* 17 (June 1956): 347–69.

Karenga, Maulana. "Society, Culture, and the Problem of Self-Consciousness: A Kawaida Analysis," in Leonard Harris, ed., *Philosophy Born of Struggle: Anthology of Afro-American Philosophy from 1917.* Dubuque, Iowa: Kendall-Hunt, 1983.

Keane, John. "On the 'New' History: Quentin Skinner's Proposal for a New History of Political Ideology," *Telos* (spring 1981): 174–83.

Kent, George E. "Patterns of the Harlem Renaissance," in Arna Bontemps, ed., *The Harlem Renaissance Remembered.* New York: Dodd Mead, 1972.

Kettler, David. "The Vocation of Radical Intellectuals," in Ira Katznelson et al., eds., *The Politics and Society Reader.* New York: McKay, 1974.

Key, R. Charles. "Society and Sociology: The Dynamics of Black Sociological Negation," *Phylon* 39 (March 1978): 35–48.

Kilson, Martin. "The Black Bourgeoisie, Revisited," *Dissent* (winter 1984): 70–78.

Kilson, Martin, and Adelaide Hill, eds. *Apropos of Africa: Afro-American Leaders and the Romance of Africa.* Garden City, N.Y.: Doubleday, 1971.

Kimbrough, Marvin Gordon. "W. E. B. Du Bois as Editor of *The Crisis*," Ph.D. dissertation, University of Texas, Austin, 1974.

Kipnis, Ira. *The American Socialist Movement, 1897–1912.* New York: Columbia University Press, 1952.

Kirp, David L. "No Angels, No Dreams," *San Francisco Examiner Image*, October 7, 1990, pp. 23–29.

Kloppenberg, James T. *Uncertain Victory: Social Democracy and Progressivism in European and American Thought, 1870–1920.* New York and London: Oxford University Press, 1986.

Kolko, Gabriel. *The Triumph of Conservatism: A Reinterpretation of American History, 1900–1916.* New York: Harper and Row, 1963.

Konrad, George, and Ivan Szelenyi. *The Intellectuals on the Road to Class Power: A Sociological Study of the Role of the Intelligentsia in Socialism*. New York: Harcourt Brace Jovanovich, 1979.

Korsch, Karl. *Marxism and Philosophy*. New York: Monthly Review Press, 1970.

Kosik, Karel. *Dialectics of the Concrete*. Boston: Reidel, 1976.

Kotkin, Joel. *Tribes: How Race, Religion and Identity Determine Success in the New Global Economy*. New York: Random House, 1993.

Kraditor, Aileen S. *The Ideas of the Woman Suffrage Movement, 1890–1920*. New York: Doubleday, 1971.

———. *The Radical Persuasion, 1890–1917: Aspects of the Intellectual History and the Historiography of Three American Radical Organizations*. Baton Rouge: Louisiana State University Press, 1981.

Kuklick, Bruce. *The Rise of American Philosophy: Cambridge, Massachusetts, 1860–1930*. New Haven, Conn., and London: Yale Univesity Press, 1977.

Lacayo, Richard. "Between Two Worlds," *Time*, March 13, 1989, pp. 58–59.

Lacy, Leslie Alexander. *Cheer the Lonesome Traveler: The Life of W. E. B. Du Bois*. New York: Dial, 1970.

Ladner, Joyce, ed. *The Death of White Sociology*. New York: Random House, 1973.

Lasch, Christopher. *The American Liberals and the Russian Revolution*. New York: Columbia University Press, 1962.

———. *The New Radicalism in America, 1889–1963: The Intellectual as a Social Type*. New York: Random House, 1965.

———. *Haven in a Heartless World: The Family Besieged*. New York: Basic, 1977.

Lash, John S. "Thought, Research, Action: Dr. Du Bois and History," *Phylon* 18 (April 1957): 184–85.

Lattany, Kristin Hunter. "Off-Timing: Stepping to the Different Drummer," in Gerald Early, ed., *Lure and Loathing: Essays on Race, Identity and the Ambivalence of Assimilation*. New York: Penguin, 1993.

Lauter, Paul. *Canons and Contexts*. New York and Oxford: Oxford University Press, 1991.

Lears, T. J. Jackson. *No Place of Grace: Antimodernism and the Transformation of American Culture, 1890–1920*. New York: Pantheon, 1981.

Leiss, William. *The Domination of Nature*. Boston: Beacon, 1973.

Lenin, V. I. *What Is to Be Done?: Burning Questions of Our Movement*. New York: International Publishers, 1943.

———. *Selected Works*. 3 vols. New York: International Publishers, 1967.

Lerner, Daniel, and Harold Lasswell. *The Policy Sciences*. Stanford, Calif.: Stanford University Press, 1965.

Lester, Julius. Introduction to W. E. B. Du Bois, *The Seventh Son: The Thought and Writings of W. E. B. Du Bois*, Julius Lester, ed. New York. Random House, 1970.

Levine, Lawrence W. *Black Culture and Black Consciousness: Afro-American Folk Thought from Slavery to Freedom*. New York: Oxford University Press, 1977.

Levy, David. *Herbert Croly of the* New Republic. Princeton, N.J.: Princeton University Press, 1985.

Lewis, David Levering. "Parallels and Divergences: Assimilationist Strategies of Afro-American and Jewish Elites from 1910 to the Early 1930s," *Journal of American History* 71 (December 1984): 543–64.

———. *W. E. B. Du Bois: Biography of a Race, 1868–1919*. New York: Henry Holt, 1993.

Lewis, J. David, and Richard L. Smith. *American Sociology and Pragmatism: Mead, Chicago Sociology, and Symbolic Interaction.* Chicago: University of Chicago Press, 1980.

Lewis, R. W. B. *The American Adam: Innocence, Tragedy, and Tradition in the Nineteenth Century.* Chicago: University of Chicago Press, 1955.

Lightfoot, Sara Lawrence. *Balm in Gilead.* Cambridge, Mass.: Harvard University Press, 1984.

Lindsay, Louis. "The Pluralist Persuasion in American Democratic Thought," *Social and Economic Studies* 22 (December 1973): 479–513.

Lipow, Arthur. *Authoritarian Socialism in America: Edward Bellamy and the Nationalist Movement.* Berkeley: University of California Press, 1982.

Lloyd, Henry Demarest. *Wealth against Commonwealth.* New York: Harper, 1894.

Locke, Alain, ed. *The New Negro: An Interpretation.* 1925; reprint, New York: Atheneum, 1968.

Loewenberg, B. J. *American History in American Thought.* New York: Simon and Schuster, 1972.

Logan, Rayford W. *The Betrayal of the Negro: From Rutherford B. Hayes to Woodrow Wilson.* New York: Macmillan, 1965. Originally published in 1954 as *The Negro in American Life and Thought: The Nadir, 1877–1901.*

Logan, Rayford W., ed. *W. E. B. Du Bois: A Profile.* New York: Hill and Wang, 1971.

Loury, Glenn. "Free at Last: A Personal Perspective on Race and Identity in America," in Gerald Early, ed., *Lure and Loathing: Essays on Race, Identity and the Ambivalence of Assimilation.* New York: Penguin, 1993.

Lovejoy, Arthur D. *The Great Chain of Being.* Cambridge, Mass.: Harvard University Press, 1936.

Luhan, Mabel Dodge. *Edge of Taos Desert.* New York: Harcourt Brace, 1937.

Lustig, R. Jeffrey. *Corporate Liberalism: The Origins of Modern American Political Theory, 1890–1920.* Berkeley: University of California Press, 1982.

Luxemburg, Rosa. "Organizational Question of Social Democracy" in Luxemburg, *Rosa Luxemburg Speaks.* Mary Alice Waters, ed. New York: Pathfinder Press, 1970.

———. *Rosa Luxemburg Speaks,* ed. Mary-Alice Waters. New York: Pathfinder Press, 1970.

Lynd, Robert. *Knowledge for What?* Princeton, N.J.: Princeton University Press, 1939.

MacCormack, Carol, and Marilyn Strathern, eds. *Nature, Culture and Gender.* Cambridge: Cambridge University Press, 1980.

Macpherson, C. B. *The Political Theory of Possessive Individualism: Hobbes to Locke.* New York: Oxford University Press, 1962.

Manning, Kenneth. *Black Apollo of Science.* New York: Oxford University Press, 1983.

Marable, Manning. *Black American Politics: From the Washington Marches to Jesse Jackson.* London: Verso, 1985.

———. "The Black Faith of W. E. B. Du Bois: Structural and Political Dimensions of Black Religion," *Southern Quarterly* 23 (spring 1985): 15–33.

———. *W. E. B. Du Bois: Black Radical Democrat.* Boston: Twayne, 1986.

———. "The Contradictory Contours of Black Political Culture," in Mike Davis et al., eds., *Toward a Rainbow Socialism: Essays on Race, Ethnicity, Class and Gender. The Year Left 2.* London: Verso, 1987.

Marcuse, Herbert. *Negations: Essays on Critical Theory.* Boston: Beacon, 1968.

Martin, Waldo E. *The Mind of Frederick Douglass.* Chapel Hill: University of North Carolina Press, 1984.

Mason, Theodore O., Jr. "Between the Populist and the Scientist: Ideology and Power in Recent Afro-American Literary Criticism; or, 'The Dozens' as Scholarship," *Callaloo* 11 (summer 1988): 606–15.

McClain, Leanita. *A Foot in Each World.* Evanston, Ill.: Northwestern University Press, 1986.

McGuire, Robert Grayson, III. "Continuity in Black Political Protest: The Thought of Booker T. Washington, W. E. B. Du Bois, Marcus Garvey, Malcolm X, Joseph Casely Hayford, Joseph B. Danquah, and Kwame Nkrumah," Ph.D. dissertation, Columbia University, New York, 1974.

McKay, Claude. *A Long Way from Home.* 1937; reprint, New York: Arno; New York Times, 1969.

McKay, Nellie Y. "The Souls of Black Women Folk in the Writings of W. E. B. Du Bois," in Henry Louis Gates Jr., ed., *Reading Black/Reading Feminist: A Critical Anthology.* New York: Meridian, 1990.

McPherson, James M. *Battle Cry of Freedom: The Civil War Era.* New York: Oxford University Press, 1988.

McPherson, James. "Junior and John Doe," in Gerald Early, ed., *Lure and Loathing: Essays on Race, Identity and the Ambivalence of Assimilation.* New York: Penguin, 1993.

Meier, August. *Negro Thought in America, 1880–1915: Racial Ideologies in the Age of Booker T. Washington.* Ann Arbor: University of Michigan Press, 1963.

———. Introduction to Booker T. Washington et al., *The Negro Problem.* 1903; reprint, New York: Arno, 1969.

Meier, August, and Francis L. Broderick. *Negro Protest Thought on the Twentieth Century.* Indianapolis: Bobbs Merrill, 1965.

Meier August, and David Levering Lewis. "History of the Negro Upper Class in Atlanta, Georgia, 1890–1958," *Journal of Negro Education* 28 (spring 1959): 128–39.

Meier, August, and Elliott M. Rudwick. *From Plantation to Ghetto: An Interpretive History of American Negroes.* New York: Hill and Wang, 1966.

Meier, August, Elliott M. Rudwick, and Francis L. Broderick, eds. *Black Protest Thought in the Twentieth Century.* Indianapolis: Bobbs-Merrill, 1971.

Meyer, Donald. *The Positive Thinkers: Religion as Pop Psychology from Mary Baker Eddy to Oral Roberts.* New York: Pantheon, 1980.

Mielke, David Nathaniel. "W. E. B. Du Bois: An Educational Critique," Ph.D. dissertation, University of Tennessee, Knoxville, 1977.

Miller, Eugene. "Positivism, Historicism and Political Inquiry," *American Political Science Review* 66 (September 1972): 796–817.

Miller, Kelly. "Howard: The National Negro University," in Alain Locke, ed., *The New Negro: An Interpretation.* 1925; reprint, New York: Atheneum, 1968.

———. "Radicals and Conservatives" and Other Essays on the Negro in America. New York: Schocken, 1968. Originally published in 1908 as *Race Adjustment.*

———. *Out of the House of Bondage.* 1914; reprint, New York: Schocken, 1971.

Mills, C. Wright. "The Professional Ideology of Social Pathologists," *American Journal of Sociology* 49 (1943): 165–80.

———. *White Collar.* New York: Oxford University Press, 1951.

———. *Power, Politics and People: The Collected Essays of C. Wright Mills.* Irving Louis Horowitz, ed. New York: Oxford University Press, 1963.

———. *Sociology and Pragmatism.* New York: Oxford University Press, 1964.

Mitchell, Jacquelyn. "Reflections of a Black Social Scientist: Some Struggles, Some Doubts, Some Hopes," *Harvard Educational Review* 52 (February 1982): 27–44.

Mitchell, Michele. "Adjusting the Race: Gender, Sexuality and the Question of African-American Destiny, 1877–1930," Ph.D. dissertation, Northwestern University, Evanston, Ill., 1997.

Moon, Henry Lee. Introduction to W. E. B. Du Bois, *The Emerging Thought of W. E. B. Du Bois*. Henry Lee Moon, ed. New York: Simon and Schuster, 1972.

Moore, Jack B. *W. E. B. Du Bois*. Boston: Twayne, 1981.

Moore, Richard B. "Africa Conscious Harlem," *Freedomways* 3 (summer 1963): 315–34.

Morgan, Edmund. *American Slavery, American Freedom*. New York: Norton, 1975.

Moses, Wilson J. *The Golden Age of Black Nationalism, 1850–1925*. New York: Oxford University Press, 1988.

———. *Alexander Crummell: A Study of Civilization and Discontent*. New York and London: Oxford University Press, 1989.

———. "W. E. B. Du Bois's 'The Conservation of Races' and Its Context: Idealism, Conservatism and Hero Worship," *Massachusetts Review* (summer 1993): 275–94.

Moss, Alfred O., Jr. *The American Negro Academy—Voice of the Talented Tenth*. Baton Rouge: Louisiana State University Press, 1980.

Moss, Richard Lawrence. "Ethnographic Perspectives and Literary Strategies in the Early Writings of W. E. B. Du Bois," Ph.D. dissertation, State University of New York-Buffalo, 1975.

Mosse, George. *Toward the Final Solution: A History of European Racism*. New York: Fertig, 1978.

Moton, Robert R. "Hampton-Tuskegee: Missioners of the Mass," in Alain Locke, ed., *The New Negro: An Interpretation*. 1925; reprint, New York: Antheum, 1968.

Murdock, Deroy. "Oh, My God! It's a Black Man!" *Chicago Tribune*, March 11, 1993.

Myers, Gerald E. *William James: His Life and Thought*. New Haven, Conn., and London: Yale University Press, 1986.

Myrdal, Gunnar. *An American Dilemma: The Negro Problem and Modern Democracy*. 2 vols. 1944; reprint, New York: Harper and Row, 1962.

Namasaka, Boaz Nalika. "William E. B. Du Bois and Thorstein Veblen: Intellectual Activists of Progressivism, A Comparative Study, 1900–1930," Ph.D. dissertation, Claremont Graduate School and University Center, Claremont, Calif., 1971.

National Advisory Commission on Civil Disorders. *Report*. New York: Bantam, 1968.

Neal, Larry, "And Shine Swam On," in LeRoi Jones and Larry Neal, eds., *Black Fire: An Anthology of Afro-American Writing*. New York: Morrow, 1968.

Nelson, Truman. "W. E. B. Du Bois as a Prophet," in John Henrik Clarke et al., eds., *Black Titan: W. E. B. Du Bois*. Boston: Beacon, 1970.

Neverdon-Morton, Cynthia. *Afro-American Women of the South and the Advancement of the Race, 1895–1925*. Knoxville: University of Tennessee Press, 1989.

Newman, Louise Michele, ed. *Men's Ideal/Women's Realities: Popular Science, 1870–1915*. New York: Pergamon, 1985.

Newsome, Elaine Mitchell. "W. E. B. Du Bois' 'Figure in the Carpet': A Cyclical Pattern in the Belletristic Prose," Ph.D. dissertation, University of North Carolina, Chapel Hill, 1971.

Nisbet, Robert. *History of the Idea of Progress*. New York: Basic Books, 1979.

Noble, David F. *America by Design: Science, Technology and the Rise of Corporate Capitalism*. New York: Knopf, 1977.

Novick, Peter. *That Noble Dream: The "Objectivity Question" and the American Historical Profession*. Cambridge and New York: Cambridge University Press, 1988.

Oakes, James. *Slavery and Freedom: An Interpretation of the Old South.* New York: Knopf, 1990.

O'Neal, John. "Black Arts Notebook," in Addison Gayle, ed., *The Black Aesthetic.* Garden City, New York: Doubleday, 1971.

Ortun, William A. *The Liberal Tradition: A Study of the Social and Spiritual Conditions of Freedom.* New Haven, Conn.: Yale University Press, 1945; reprint, Port Washington, N.Y.: Kennikat, 1969.

Ottley, Roi. *New World A-Coming.* 1943; reprint, New York: Arno; New York Times, 1969.

Ottley, Roi, and William J. Weatherby, eds. *The Negro in New York: An Informal History, 1626–1940.* 1940; reprint, New York: Praeger, 1967.

Outlaw, Lucius. "African-American Philosophy: Social and Political Case Studies," *Social Science Information* 26 (first quarter 1987): 75–97.

Ovington, Mary White. "The National Association for the Advancement of Colored People," *Journal of Negro History* 9 (April 1924): 107–16.

Parekh, Bhiku, and R. M. Berki. "The History of Political Ideas: A Critique of Q. Skinner's Methodology," *Journal of the History of Ideas* 34 (April-June 1973): 163–84.

Park, Robert E. "The Conflict and Fusion of Cultures with Special Reference to the Negro," *Journal of Negro History* 4 (April 1919): 111–33.

———. "Our Racial Frontiers: A Frame of Reference," *Survey* 56 (1926).

———. "The Nature of Race Relations," in Edgar T. Thompson, ed., *Race Relations and the Race Problem.* Durham, N.C.: Duke University Press, 1939.

———. "Education in Its Relation to the Conflict and Fusion of Cultures," in Park, *Race and Culture: Essays in the Sociology of Contemporary Man.* New York: Free Press, 1950.

———. *Race and Culture: Essays in the Sociology of Contemporary Man.* New York: Free Press, 1950.

Parsons, Talcott, and Kenneth B. Clark, eds. *The Negro American.* Boston: Beacon, 1967.

Partington, Paul G. *"The Moon Illustrated Weekly*—The Precursor of *The Crisis," Journal of Negro History* 48 (July 1963): 206–16.

Patten, Simon H. *The New Basis of Civilization.* 1907; reprint, Cambridge, Mass.: Harvard University Press, 1968.

———."The Standardization of Family Life," *Annals of the American Academy of Political and Social Science* 48 (July 1913): 81–90.

Patterson, Orlando. "The Moral Crisis of the Black American," *Public Interest* (summer 1973): 43–69.

———. "Toward a Study of Black America," *Dissent* (fall 1989): 476–86.

Pattison, Mrs. Frank A. "Scientific Management in Home Making," *Annals of the American Academy of Political and Social Science* 48 (July 1913): 96–103.

Payne, James Chris, II. "A Content Analysis of Speeches and Written Documents of Six Black Spokesmen: Frederick Douglass, Booker T. Washington, Marcus Garvey, W. E. B. Du Bois, Martin Luther King, Jr. and Malcolm X," Ph.D. dissertation, Florida State University, Tallahassee, 1973.

Pinkney, Alphonso. *Red, Black and Green: Black Nationalism in the United States.* New York: Cambridge University Press, 1976.

Pittenger, Mark. *American Socialists and Evolutionary Thought, 1870–1920.* Madison: University of Wisconsin Press, 1993.

Pocock, J. G. A. "The History of Political Thought: A Methodological Enquiry," in P. Laslett and W. G. Runciman, eds., *Philosophy, Politics and Society*. Oxford: Basil Blackwell, 1962.

———. *Politics, Language, and Time: Essays on Political Thought and History*. New York: Atheneum, 1971.

Pollard, Sidney. *The Idea of Progress: History and Society*. Baltimore: Penguin, 1968.

Pollitt, Katha. *Reasonable Creatures: Essays on Women and Feminism*. New York: Knopf, 1994.

Postman, Leo. *Psychology in the Making*. New York: Knopf, 1962.

Poussaint, Alvin. "*The Souls of Black Folk*: A Critique," in W. E. B. Du Bois, *The Souls of Black Folk*, 1903; reprint, New York: New American Library, 1969.

Prothro, James W. *The Dollar Decade: Business Ideas in the 1920's*. Baton Rouge: Louisiana State University Press, 1954.

Quandt, Jean B. *From the Small Town to the Great Community: The Social Thought of Progressive Intellectuals*. New Brunswick, N.J.: Rutgers University Press, 1970.

Radin, Paul. *The Trickster*. London: Routledge, 1956.

Rampersad, Arnold. *The Art and Imagination of W. E. B. Du Bois*. Cambridge, Mass.: Harvard University Press, 1976.

———. "Biography and Afro-American Culture," in Houston Baker and Patricia Redmond, eds., *Afro-American Literary Study in the 1990s*. Chicago: University of Chicago Press, 1989.

Raucher, Alan R. *Public Relations and Business, 1900–1929*. Baltimore: Johns Hopkins University Press, 1968.

Reddick, L. D. "A New Interpretation for Negro History," *Journal of Negro History* 22 (January 1937): 17–28.

Redding, J. Saunders. Introduction to W. E. B. Du Bois, *The Souls of Black Folk*. 1903; reprint, New York: Fawcett, 1961.

———. "Portrait of W. E. B. Du Bois," *American Scholar* 18 (January 1949): 93–96.

———. "*The Souls of Black Folk*: Du Bois' Masterpiece Lives On," in John Henrik Clarke et al., eds., *Black Titan: W. E. B. Du Bois*. Boston: Beacon, 1970.

Redkey, Edwin. *Black Exodus: Black Nationalist and Back-to-Africa Movements, 1890–1910*. New Haven, Conn.: Yale University Press, 1969.

Reed, Adolph L., Jr. "The Political Philosophy of Pan-Africanism: A Study of the Writings of Du Bois, Garvey, Nkrumah and Padmore and Their Legacy," M.A. thesis, Atlanta University, 1975.

———. Review of *Prophesy Deliverance! An Afro-American Revolutionary Christianity*, by Cornel West. *Telos* (summer 1984): 211–18.

———. *The Jesse Jackson Phenomenon: The Crisis of Purpose in Afro-American Politics*. New Haven, Conn., and London: Yale University Press, 1986.

———. "Pan-Africanism as Black Liberalism: Du Bois and Garvey." In W. Ofuatey-Kodjoe, ed., *Pan-Africanism: New Directions in Strategy*. Lanham, Md.: University Press of America, 1986.

———. "The 'Underclass' as Myth and Symbol: The Poverty of Discourse about Poverty," *Radical America* 24 (winter 1992): 21–40.

———. "The New Victorians." *Progressive* (February 1994): 20–22.

———. "Behind the Farrakhan Show," *Progressive* (April 1994): 16–17.

———. "Looking Backward," *Nation*, November 28, 1994, pp. 654–62.

———. "What Color Is Anti-Semitism?" *Village Voice*, December 26, 1995, p. 26.

————. "Romancing Jim Crow: Black Nostalgia for a Segregated Past," *Village Voice*, April 16, 1996, pp. 24–29.

————. *Stirrings in the Jug: Black American Politics in the Post-Segregation Era*. Minneapolis: University of Minnesota Press, forthcoming 1998.

————, ed. *Race, Politics, and Culture: Critical Essays on the Radicalism of the 1960s*. Westport, Conn.: Greenwood, 1986.

Reid, Herbert G. "Morris Cohen's Case for Liberalism," *Review of Politics* 33 (October 1971): 489–512.

Ricci, David M. *The Tragedy of Political Science: Politics, Scholarship and Democracy*. New Haven, Conn., and London: Yale University Press, 1984.

Robeson, Paul. *Here I Stand*. Boston: Beacon, 1958.

Robinson, Dean E. "To Forge a Nation, to Forge an Identity: Black Nationalism in the United States, 1957–1974," Ph.D. dissertation, Yale University, New Haven, Conn., 1995.

Rodgers, Daniel T. *The Work Ethic in Industrial America, 1850–1920*. Chicago: University of Chicago Press, 1978.

————. *Contested Truths: Keywords in American Politics since Independence*. New York: Basic Books, 1987.

Rogers, Ben F. "William E. B. Du Bois, Marcus Garvey and Pan-Africa," *Journal of Negro History* 15 (January 1955): 154–65.

Rosenberg, Rosalind. *Beyond Separate Spheres: Intellectual Roots of Modern Feminism*. New York and London: Yale University Press, 1982.

Ross, Dorothy. *The Origins of American Social Science*. Cambridge and New York: Cambridge University Press, 1991.

Ross, Edward A. "The Causes of Race Superiority," *Annals of the American Academy of Political and Social Science* 18 (July 1901): 67–89.

Royce, Josiah. *Race Questions, Provincialism and Other American Problems*. 1908; reprint, Freeport, N.Y.: Books for Libraries, 1967.

Rudwick, Elliott M. "The Niagara Movement," *Journal of Negro History* 42 (July 1957): 177–200.

————. "W. E. B. Du Bois: In the Role of *Crisis* Editor," *Journal of Negro History* 18 (July 1958): 214–40.

————. "Du Bois versus Garvey: Race Propagandists at War," *Journal of Negro Education* 28 (fall 1959): 421–29.

————. *W. E. B. Du Bois: A Study in Minority Group Leadership*. Philadelphia: University of Pennsylvania Press, 1960.

————. *W. E. B. Du Bois: Propagandist of the Negro Protest*. New York: Atheneum, 1968.

————. "Notes on a Forgotten Black Sociologist: W. E. B. Du Bois and the Sociological Profession," *American Sociologist* 4 (November 1969): 303–36.

————. "W. E. B. Du Bois as Sociologist," in James E. Blackwell and Morris Janowitz, eds., *Black Sociologists: Historical and Contemporary Perspectives*. Chicago: University of Chicago Press, 1974.

Rydell, Robert. *All the World's a Fair*. Chicago: University of Chicago Press, 1984.

Santayana, George. "The American Philosophy," in Santayana, ed., *The Genteel Tradition: Nine Essays by George Santayana*. Cambridge, Mass.: Harvard University Press, 1967.

————. *The Genteel Tradition: Nine Essays by George Santayana*, Douglas L. Wilson, ed. Cambridge, Mass.: Harvard University Press, 1967.

Schlesinger, Arthur M., Jr. *The Age of Jackson*. Boston: Little Brown, 1945.

———. *The Vital Center*. Boston: Houghton Mifflin, 1949.

Schlesinger, Arthur M., Sr. "A Critical Period in American Religion, 1875–1900," in John M. Mulder and John F. Wilson, eds., *Religion in American History: Interpretive Essays*. Englewood Cliffs, N.J.: Prentice Hall, 1978.

Schochet, Gordon J. "Quentin Skinner's Method," *Political Theory* 2 (August 1974): 261–76.

Schrieke, Bertram F. O. *Alien Americans: A Study of Race Relations*. New York: Viking, 1936.

Schutz, Alfred. *On Phenomenology and Social Relations*. Chicago: University of Chicago Press, 1970.

Schuyler, George. *Black No More*. 1931; reprint, Amherst: University of Massachusetts Press, 1989.

———. *Black and Conservative*. New Rochelle, N.Y.: Arlington House, 1966.

Scott, Emmett. *Negro Migration during the War*. 1920; reprint, New York: Arno Press; New York Times, 1969.

Seeley, John R. *Americanization of the Unconscious*. New York: International Science Press, 1967.

Seidelman, Raymond, with the assistance of Edward J. Harpham. *Disenchanted Realists: Political Science and the American Crisis, 1884–1984*. Albany: SUNY Press, 1985.

Sewall, May Wright. *The World's Congress of Representative Women, 1893*. Chicago and New York: Rand-McNally, 1894.

Shapiro, Ian. "Realism in the Study of the History of Ideas," *History of Political Thought* 3 (November 1982): 535–78.

———. *The Evolution of Rights in Liberal Theory*. New York and Cambridge: Cambridge University Press, 1986.

———. *Political Criticism*. Berkeley: University of California Press, 1990.

———. Review of *Meaning and Context: Quentin Skinner and His Critics*, by James Tully, ed. 10 *Canadian Philosophical Reviews* (July 1990): 291.

Sharpe, R. A. "Ideology and Ontology," *Philosophy of the Social Sciences* 4 (first quarter 1974): 55–64.

Shepperson, George. "Pan-Africanism and 'Pan-Africanism': Some Historical Notes," *Phylon* 22 (winter 1962): 346–58.

Shils, Edward. *The Intellectuals and the Powers and Other Essays*. Chicago: University of Chicago Press, 1972.

Showalter, Elaine, ed. *These Modern Women: Autobiographical Essays from the Twenties*. New York: Feminist Press, 1989.

Shryock, Richard. "The Academic Profession in the United States," *American Association of University Professors Bulletin* 38 (spring 1952): 32–70.

Skinner, Quentin. "The Limits of Historical Explanations," *Philosophy* 41 (July 1966): 199–215.

———. "Meaning and Understanding in the History of Ideas," *History and Theory* 8 (first quarter 1969): 3–53.

———. "Conventions and the Understanding of Speech Acts," *Philosophical Quarterly* 20 (April 1970): 118–38.

———. " 'Social Meaning' and the Explanation of Social Action," in Peter Laslett, W. G. Runciman, and Quentin Skinner, eds., *Philosophy, Politics and Society*, pp. 136–57. New York: Barnes and Noble, 1972.

———. "Some Problems in the Analysis of Political Thought and Action," *Political Theory* 2 (August 1974): 277–303.

———. "Language and Social Change," in James Tully, ed., *Meaning and Context: Quentin Skinner and His Critics.* Princeton, N.J.: Princeton University Press, 1988.

Sklar, Martin J. "Woodrow Wilson and the Political Economy of Modern United States Liberalism," *Studies on the Left*, vol. 1, no. 3 (1960): 17–47.

———. *The Corporate Reconstruction of American Capitalism, 1890–1916: The Market, the Law and Politics.* Cambridge: Cambridge University Press, 1988.

Skowronek, Stephen. *Building a New American State: The Expansion of National Administrative Capacities, 1877–1920.* Cambridge and New York: Cambridge University Press, 1982.

Slaughter, Thomas F., Jr. "Epidermalizing the World: A Basic Mode of Being Black," in Leonard Harris, ed., *Philosophy Born of Struggle: Anthology of Afro-American Philosophy from 1917.* Dubuque, Iowa: Kendall-Hunt, 1983.

Smith, Henry Nash, ed. *Popular Culture and Industrialism, 1865–1900.* New York: New York University Press, 1979.

Smith, Rogers M. "Constitutional Interpretation and Political Theory: American Legal Realism's Continuing Search for Standards," *Polity* 15 (summer 1983): 492–514.

———. *Liberalism and American Constitutional Law.* Cambridge, Mass.: Harvard University Press, 1985.

———."The 'American Creed' and American Identity: The Limits of Liberal Citizenship in the United States," *Western Political Quarterly* 41 (June 1988): 225–51.

———. "Beyond Tocqueville, Myrdal, and Hartz: The Multiple Traditions in America," *American Political Science Review* 87 (September 1993): 549–66.

Sollors, Werner. *Beyond Ethnicity: Consent and Descent in American Literature.* New York: Oxford University Press, 1986.

———. "A Critique of Pure Pluralism," in Sacvan Bercovitch, ed., *Reconstructing American Literary History.* Cambridge, Mass.: Harvard University Press, 1986.

Southern, David W. *Gunnar Myrdal and Black-White Relations: The Use and Abuse of An American Dilemma, 1949–1969.* Baton Rouge and London: Louisiana State University Press, 1987.

Sowell, Thomas. *Race and Culture: A World View.* New York: Basic Books, 1994.

Spring, Joel H. *Education and the Rise of the Corporate State.* Boston: Beacon, 1972.

Stack, Carol B. *All Our Kin: Strategies for Survival in a Black Community.* New York: Harper and Row, 1974.

Stanfield, John H. *Philanthropy and Jim Crow in American Social Science.* Westport, Conn.: Greenwood, 1985.

Staples, Robert. *Introduction to Black Sociology.* New York: McGraw-Hill, 1976.

Starobin, Joseph R. *American Communism in Crisis, 1943–1957.* Berkeley: University of California Press, 1972.

Steele, Shelby. *The Content of Our Character.* New York: St. Martin's, 1990.

Stein, Judith. " 'Of Mr. Booker T. Washington and Others': The Political Economy of Racism in the United States," *Science and Society* 38 (winter 1974–75): 422–63.

———. *The World of Marcus Garvey: Race and Class in Modern Society.* Baton Rouge: Louisiana State University Press, 1986.

———. "Defining the Race, 1890–1930," in Werner Sollors, ed., *The Invention of Ethnicity.* New York and Oxford: Oxford University Press, 1989.

Steinberg, Stephen. *Turning Back: The Retreat From Racial Justice in American Thought and Policy.* Boston: Beacon, 1995.

Stevens, Jacqueline. "Beyond Tocqueville, Please!," *American Political Science Review* 89 (September 1995): 987–90.

Stocking, George W., Jr. "Larmarckianism in American Social Science," in *Race, Culture and Evolution: Essays in the History of Anthropology*. Chicago: University of Chicago Press, 1982.

———. "On the Limits of 'Presentism' and 'Historicism' in the Historiography of the Behavioral Sciences," in Stocking, *Race, Culture and Evolution: Essays in the History of Anthropology*. Chicago: University of Chicago, 1982.

———. *Race, Culture, and Evolution: Essays in the History of Anthropology*. Chicago: University of Chicago Press, 1982.

Stollmann, Rainer. "Fascist Politics as a Total Work of Art: Tendencies of the Aesthetization of Political Life in National Socialism," *New German Critique* (spring 1978): 41–60.

Stonequist, Everett V. "Race Mixture and the Mulatto," in Edgar T. Thompson, ed., *Race Relations and the Race Problem: A Definition and an Analysis*. Durham, N.C.: Duke University Press, 1939.

Storing, Herbert, ed. Introduction to *What Country Have I?: Political Writing of Black Americans*. New York: St. Martin's, 1970.

———. *What Country Have I?: Political Writing of Black Americans*. New York: St. Martin's, 1970.

Stuckey, Sterling. *The Intellectual Origins of Black Nationalism*. Boston: Beacon, 1972.

———. *Slave Culture: Nationalist Theory and the Foundations of Black America*. New York and London: Oxford University Press, 1987.

Sundquist, Eric. *To Wake the Nations: Race in the Making of American Literature*. Cambridge, Mass.: Harvard University Press, 1993.

Swidler, Ann. "The Concept of Rationality in Max Weber," *Sociological Inquiry* 43 (first quarter 1973): 34–42.

Taft, Jessie Howard. *The Woman Movement from the Point of View of Social Consciousness*. Chicago: University of Chicago Press, 1915.

Talmon, J. L. *The Origins of Totalitarian Democracy*. London: Secker and Warburg, 1955.

Tarlton, Charles D. "Historicity, Meaning and Revisionism in the Study of Political Thought," *History and Theory* 12 (third quarter 1973): 307–28.

Taylor, Frederick Winslow. *The Principles of Scientific Management*. New York: Norton, 1967.

Thomas, Evan. "The Double Life of O. J. Simpson," *Newsweek*, August 29, 1994.

Thomas, John L. *Alternative America: Henry George, Edward Bellamy, Henry Demarest Lloyd and the Adversary Tradition*. Cambridge, Mass.: Harvard University Press, 1983.

Thomas, William I. "The Scope and Method of Folk Psychology," *American Journal of Sociology* 1 (January 1896): 434–45.

———. "On a Difference in the Metabolism of the Sexes," *American Journal of Sociology* 3 (July 1897): 31–63.

———. "The Mind of Women and the Lower Races," *American Journal of Sociology* 12 (January 1907): 435–69.

Thompson, Vincent Bakpetu. *Africa and Unity: The Evolution of Pan-Africanism*. London: Longmans, 1969.

Thorpe, Earl E. *The Mind of the Negro: An Intellectual History of Afro-Americans*. Baton Rouge, La.: Ortlieb, 1961.

————. *The Central Theme of Black History.* Durham, N.C.: Seeman, 1969.

Thurman, Wallace. *Infants of the Spring.* 1932; reprint, Carbondale, Ill.: Southern Illinois University Press, 1979.

Todd, Lewis P. *Wartime Relations of the Federal Government and the Public Schools, 1917–1918.* New York: Bureau of Publications, Teachers College, Columbia University, 1945.

Toll, William S. *The Resurgence of Race: Black Social Theory from Reconstruction to the Pan-African Conferences.* Philadelphia: Temple University Press, 1979.

Trachtenberg, Alan. *The Incorporation of America: Culture and Society in the Gilded Age.* New York: Hill and Wang, 1982.

Traub, Rainer. "Lenin and Taylor: The Fate of 'Scientific Management' in the (Early) Soviet Union," *Telos* (fall 1978): 82–92.

Tully, James, ed. *Meaning and Context: Quentin Skinner and His Critics.* Princeton, N.J.: Princeton University Press, 1988.

Tuttle, William M., Jr. "W. E. B. Du Bois' Confrontation with White Liberalism during the Progressive Era: A *Phylon* Document," *Phylon* 35 (September 1974): 241–58.

Urban, Michael. *The Ideology of Administration: American and Soviet Cases.* Albany: SUNY Press, 1982.

Valentine, Charles A. "Deficit, Difference and Bicultural Models of Afro-American Behavior," *Harvard Educational Review* 41 (May 1971): 137–57.

Van Tassel, David D. and Michael G. Hall, eds. *Science and Society in the United States.* Homewood, Ill.: Dorsey, 1966.

Veblen, Thorstein. *The Engineers and the Price System.* New York: Harcourt Brace and World, 1963.

Veysey, Laurence R. *The Emerqence of the American University.* Chicago: University of Chicago Press, 1965.

————. "Intellectual History and the New Social History," in John Higham and Paul K. Conkin, eds., *New Directions in American Intellectual History.* Baltimore: Johns Hopkins University Press, 1979.

Vidich, Arthur J., and Stanford M. Lyman. *American Sociology: Wordly Rejections of Religion and Their Directions.* New Haven, Conn., and London: Yale University Press, 1985.

Vincent, Theodore G. *Black Power and the Garvey Movement.* San Francisco: Ramparts, 1972.

————, ed. *Voices of a Black Nation: Political Journalism in the Harlem Renaissance.* San Francisco: Ramparts, 1973.

Volkomer, Walter E. *The Liberal Tradition in American Thought.* New York: Capricorn, 1970.

Walden, Daniel. "The Contemporary Opposition to the Political Ideals of Booker T. Washington," *Journal of Negro History* 45 (April 1960): 103–15.

————. "W. E. B. Du Bois's Essential Years: The Link from Douglass to the Present," *Journal of Human Relations* 14 (first quarter 1966): 115–27.

Walden, Daniel, and Kenneth Wylie. "W. E. B. Du Bois: Pan-Africanism's Intellectual Father," *Journal of Human Relations* 14 (first quarter 1966): 28–41.

Walker, Pat, ed. *Between Labor and Capital.* Boston: South End, 1979.

Walton, Hanes. "Black Political Thought: The Problem of Characterization," *Journal of Black Studies* 1 (December 1970): 213–18.

Walzer, Michael. *What It Means to Be an American: Essays on the American Experience.* New York: Marsilio, 1992.

Ward, Lester F. *The Psychic Factors of Civilization*. Boston: Ginn, 1892.

———. *Pure Sociology: A Treatise on the Origin and Spontaneous Development of Society*. New York: Macmillan, 1907.

Warren, Kenneth. "Delimiting America: The Legacy of Du Bois," *American Literary History* 1 (spring 1989): 172–89.

———. Review of Signifying Monkey, by Henry Louis Gates, Jr. 88 *Modern Philology* (November 1990): 224–26.

———. *Black and White Strangers: Race and American Literary Realism*. Chicago and London: University of Chicago Press, 1993.

Washington, Booker T. *Up from Slavery*. 1901; reprint, New York: Penguin, 1986.

———. "The Economic Development of the Negro Race since Its Emancipation," in Du Bois and Washington, *The Negro in the South: His Economic Progress in Relation to His Moral and Religious Development*. Philadelphia: Jacobs, 1907.

Washington, Booker T. et al. *The Negro Problem*. 1903; reprint, New York: Arno, 1969.

Weinstein, James. *The Corporate Ideal in the Liberal State, 1900–1918*. Boston: Beacon, 1968.

———. *The Decline of Socialism in America, 1912–1925*. New York: Random House, 1969.

Wellmer, Albrecht. *Critical Theory of Society*. New York: Seabury, 1971.

Wesley, Charles H. "W. E. B. Du Bois: The Historian," in John Henrik Clarke et al., eds., *Black Titan: W. E. B. Du Bois*. Boston: Beacon, 1970.

West, Cornel. *Prophesy Deliverance! An Afro-American Revolutionary Christianity*. Philadelphia: Orbis, 1982.

———. *The American Evasion of Philosophy: A Genealogy of Pragmatism*. Madison: University of Wisconsin Press, 1989.

White, Morton G. *Social Thought in America: The Revolt against Formalism*. New York: Viking, 1949.

———. *Pragmatism and the American Mind*. New York: Oxford University Press, 1973.

Wideman, John Edgar. Introduction to W. E. B. Du Bois, *The Souls of Black Folk*. 1903; reprint, New York: Vintage, 1990.

William Du Bois: Scholar, Humanitarian, Freedom Fighter. Moscow: Novosti Press Agency Publishing House, 1971.

Wiebe, Robert H. *Businessmen and Reform*. Cambridge, Mass.: Harvard University Press, 1962.

———. *The Search for Order, 1877–1920*. New York: Hill and Wang, 1967.

Wiener, P. P. "Some Problems and Methods in the History of Ideas," *Journal of the History of Ideas* 22 (October-December 1961): 531–48.

Williams, Robert C. "W. E. B. Du Bois: Afro-American Philosopher of Social Reality," in Leonard Harris, ed., *Philosophy Born of Struggle: Anthology of Afro-American Philosophy from 1917*. Dubuque, Iowa: Kendall-Hunt, 1983.

Williamson, Joel. *The Crucible of Race: Black-White Relations in the American South since Emancipation*. New York and Oxford: Oxford University Press, 1984.

Willingham, Alex. "Black Political Thought in the United States: A Characterization," Ph.D. dissertation, University of North Carolina, Chapel Hill, 1974.

———. "Ideology and Politics: Their Status in Afro-American Social Theory," in Adolph L. Reed, Jr., ed., *Race, Politics, and Culture: Critical Essays on the Radicalism of the 1960s*. Westport, Conn.: Greenwood, 1986.

Wilson, James Q., and Richard Herrnstein. *Crime and Human Nature*. New York: Simon and Schuster, 1985.

Wilson, Samuel M. "Trickster Treats," *Natural History* (October 1991): 4f.

Winkler, Karen J. "Literary Scholars Mount a Counteroffensive gainst Bad Press, Conservative Critics," *Chronicle of Higher Education*, January 15, 1992.

Wolff, Robert Paul. *The Poverty of Liberalism*. Boston: Beacon, 1968.

Wolin, Sheldon. *Politics and Vision: Continuity and Innovation in Western Political Thought*. Boston: Little Brown, 1960.

————. "Paradigms and Political Theories," in Preston King and Bhiku Parekh, eds., *Politics and Experience*. New York: Cambridge University Press, 1968.

————. "Political Theory as a Vocation," *American Political Science Review* 63 (December 1969): 1062–82.

Woodward, C. Vann. *Origins of the New South: 1877–1913*. Baton Rouge: Louisiana State University Press, 1951.

————. *The Strange Career of Jim Crow*. New York: Oxford University Press, 1966.

Young, Harding. "Negro Participation in American Business," *Journal of Negro Education* 32 (fall 1963): 390–401.

Index

Adams, Henry, 109, 112, 224n.96
Addams, Jane, 83, 109–15
American Communism, 87
Anderson, James, 135–36, 209n.63, 233n.47
Antimodernism, 25
Appadurai, Arjun, 158
Appiah, Anthony, 121, 127–29, 200n.83,
    229n.185
Aptheker, Herbert, 128
Armstrong, General Samuel Chapman, 135
Arnold, Matthew 141, 148, 151
Aronowitz, Stanley, 197n.9

Baker, Houston A. Jr., 93, 130, 131–38, 139, 141,
    154, 159, 163, 167, 175, 232–34nn.29, 36,
    235n.82
  "Black Aesthetic" ideology, 131, 137
  Blues, Ideology and Afro-American Literature,
    133
  on black vernacular expression, 132–33, 139,
    141
    Cullen, Countee, 133
    Chestnutt, Charles, 133
    Day, Morris, 133
    Dunbar, Paul Laurance, 133
    Hughes, Langston, 133
    Run-DMC, 133
  canonical interpretations' deemphasis of politics,
    130–31, 133, 141
  double consciousness, 93
  essentialism, 130–34, 136–39, 141
  literary studies, 163

middle-class sensibilities and appeal, 159, 175
Modernism and the Harlem Renaissance, 133–34
on politics, 154, 167
rehabilitation of Booker T. Washington, 131–38
  interpretation of the Atlanta Compromise,
    134–37
  on *Up From Slavery*, 134
Baldwin, James, 145, 156
Banfield, Edward C., 228n.169
Baraka, (Imamu) Amiri, 148–49, 155
Baron, Harold M., 93
Bellamy, Edward, 24, 107
Berlin, Isaiah, 157
Black Aesthetic Movement, 96, 131, 144–48, 153,
    162
Black Power, 92, 94, 97, 153
Blauner, Robert, 92, 219n.8
Bolshevism, 21–22, 86
Boulé, 67–68
Bourne, Randolph, 98, 111–12
Boxill, Bernard R., 202n.9
Braverman, Harry F., 199n.53
Broderick, Francis L., 5, 48, 76, 98, 207n.19
Brotz, Howard, 212n.3
Brown v. Board of Education, 182
Bukharin, Nikolai, 20
Burnet, Charles, 175

Canonical interpretations, 99–107, 128–34, 141,
    147–55, 161–64
  See also Baker, Houston A. Jr.; Double
    consciousness; Gates, Henry Louis Jr.;

276

Gardner, Bettye J., 94
Gates, Henry Louis Jr., 96, 127–30, 138–62, 164–
    65, 220–21n.32, 234–37nn.69, 82, 88, 94,
    122
  on "black anti-Semitism," 157
  on the black middle class, 158–60
  on black vernacular expression, 138–39, 141,
    151
  canonical interpretations' deemphasis of politics,
    128–30, 147–55, 161–62, 164–65, 234–
    35nn.69, 82, 88
  Colored People, 160–61
  commonality with Black Arts nationalism, 144–
    54
  double consciousness, 127, 160, 220–21n.32
  essentialism of, 138–47, 152–54, 160–61, 164–
    65, 236–37n.94, 122
  on the Nation of Islam, 161
  nostalgia for Jim Crow, 160
  political centrism, 154–62, 167
  as public intellectual, 154–62
    Forbes, 154, 158–59
    New Republic, 156
    Newsweek, 154
    New York Times, 154–55
    New Yorker, 154–55
    Time, 155
  racial vindicationism, 145
  The Signifying Monkey, 140–44, 146–48, 152
    Esu, 142, 152
    Yoruba, 142
  on *The Souls of Black Folk*, 128, 130, 148, 151–
    53, 155
  Washington-Du Bois controversy, 128
Genovese, Eugene D., 144
Gibson, Donald B., 127
Giddings, Paula, 240n.32
Gilbert, James, 18–24, 47, 84, 87, 194–95n.54,
    202n.17, 204n.33 (collectivism)
Gillmore, Inez Haynes, 108, 110, 112–13, 122–23,
    225n.113
Gilman, Charlotte Perkins, 109, 114–16, 120,
    197n.26, 199n.55
Gilroy, Paul, 220n.27, 229n.201
Gooding-Williams, Robert, 98, 192n.44,
    221n.43
Gould, Stephen Jay, 119, 154, 198n.228
Gouldner, Alvin W., 18, 21, 193–94n.15, 203n.19
Gramm, Phil, 173
Gramsci, Antonio, 94
Great Depression, 74, 88
Green, Dan S., 5, 188n.9, 203n.27
Green, Donald, 164, 239n.1
Gronlund, Laurence, 24
Gruber, Carol S., 16, 193n.10
Gunnell, John G., 192n.48

Hall, G. Stanley, 113, 116
Harding, Vincent, 72, 133
Hare, Nathan, 127–28
Harlan, Louis, 136, 208n.39, 234n.58
Harlem Renaissance, 3, 58, 93
Hartz, Louis, 188n.14
Haskell, Thomas L., 193n.10
Hegelianism, 21, 94, 98. *See also* Du Bois, Wil-
    liam Edward Burghardt
Henderson, Stephen, 133
Herder, Johann Gottfried Von, 98–99
Hernnstein, Richard, 198n.42
Higginbotham, Evelyn Brooks, 240
Higham, John, 189n.16, 193n.10, 213–14nn.40,
    43
Hofstadter, Richard, 192, 196
Hollinger, David A., 153, 191n.38, 214n.42
Holloway, Jonathan Scott, 190n.24
Holmes, Eugene C., 5, 83, 202n.9
Holt, Thomas C., 208n.53, 229n.201
Hopkins, Charles, 215n.65
Horne, Gerald, 53, 83, 205n.2, 211n.87, 216n.86,
    218n.110
Howe, Irving, 154
Hughes, Langston, 128, 133
Hull House, 110
Hume, David, 151
Huntington, Samuel P., 232n.30
Hurston, Zora Neale, 141, 236n.103

Isaacs, Harold R., 92, 219n.3

Jackson, Jesse, 151
James, William, 48, 98, 100–107, 110, 112,
    222n.45, 225n.120
Jaynes, Gerald D., 189n.18
Jefferson, Thomas, 151
Jim Crow. *See* Segregation
Johnson, Barbara E., 235n.82
Johnson, Charles S., 56
Johnson, James Weldon, 128
Jones, Kellie, 165–66
Jones, Lisa, 165–66
Jones, Mack H., 190n.23
Jordan, Jennifer, 238n.140
Jordanova, L. J., 119

Kakar, Sudhir, 199n.53
Kallen, Horace, 77, 78, 98, 213n.40
Karenga, (Maulana) Ron, 148–49
Kautskyan Social Democracy, 20
Kelley, Edmund, 20
Kikongo, 143
Kilson, Martin, 168–69, 173
King, Martin L. Jr., 68
Kirp, David L., 240n.18